CONNECTED TO PLACE

CONNECTED TO PLACE

Regenerating Nature, Communities, and Local Economies Through Systems Change

Matt Biggar

COMSTOCK PUBLISHING ASSOCIATES

AN IMPRINT OF CORNELL UNIVERSITY PRESS   ITHACA AND LONDON

First published 2025 by Cornell University Press

Library of Congress Cataloging-in-Publication Data

Names: Biggar, Matt, 1970- author
Title: Connected to place : regenerating nature, communities, and local
  economies through systems change / Matt Biggar.
Description: Ithaca : Comstock Publishing Associates, an imprint of Cornell
  University Press, 2025. | Includes bibliographical references and index.
Identifiers: LCCN 2025004268 (print) | LCCN 2025004269 (ebook) | ISBN
  9781501784026 hardcover | ISBN 9781501783999 paperback | ISBN
  9781501784019 epub | ISBN 9781501784002 pdf
Subjects: LCSH: Community development—United States | Social
  systems—Growth | Quality of life—United States | Social change—United
  States | Social problems—United States | Place attachment—United
  States | Common good | Social ecology—United States | Human
  ecology—United States | Sustainable development—United States
Classification: LCC HN90.C6 B54 2025 (print) | LCC HN90.C6 (ebook) | DDC
  307.1/40973—dc23/eng/20250609
LC record available at https://lccn.loc.gov/2025004268
LC ebook record available at https://lccn.loc.gov/2025004269

To Lisa, Kat, and Jack,
May you live deeply connected to place with happiness,
meaning, and hope.

In memory of Richard D. Biggar (1939–2023), a wonderful
father and lover of books and nature

Place Acknowledgment

I recognize the place where I live and work as the unceded ancestral homeland of the Ramaytush Ohlone, who called this place Yelamu (now known as San Francisco). The Ohlone and other First Peoples across the greater region understand and respect the web of life and have lived deeply connected to place and in balance with nature for millennia.

Starting with the arrival of the Spanish in 1769, land was forcibly taken from the First Peoples, severing the long-standing, mutually beneficial relationship between the land and its people. The ensuing colonization led to genocide, forced relocation and labor, and attempted erasure of Indigenous culture. Yet First Peoples have endured, and their example provides a way for us to restore harmony with nature and each other.

Over 18,500 Ohlone, Miwok, Yokuts, and Patwin peoples live, work, carry on cultural traditions, and uphold sacred relations with the land throughout the San Francisco Bay Area. Their sense of hope is expressed in the Chochenyo Ohlone saying—*ewweh tuuxi huyyuwis*, brighter days are ahead for us—and is rooted in an enduring commitment to *wahrep*, Mother Earth. May we live with full awareness of the history of the places where we live and work together with all people toward a brighter future for our places and the land on which we depend.

Contents

Place Acknowledgment   vi

Preface   ix

Introduction   1

Part 1 **SYSTEMS, PLACE, AND HOW WE LIVE IN THE
        TWENTY-FIRST CENTURY**   **17**

    1. Changing How We Live   19

    2. Place-Based Systems, Well-Being, and Regeneration   33

    3. The Path to Place-Based Systems Change   48

Part 2 **FROM CORPORATE CAPITALIST TO
        PLACE-BASED SYSTEMS**   **61**

    4. Housing   63

    5. Local Business and Work   82

    6. Transportation   101

    7. Community Spaces   121

    8. Nature Spaces   136

    9. Food   151

    10. Building Energy   170

    11. Consumer Goods   191

Part 3 **CATALYZING PLACE-BASED SYSTEMS CHANGE**   **209**

    12. Strategic Collaboration   211

    13. Systems-Oriented Government   227

    14. Place-Based Education   247

    15. Personal Change   263

Acknowledgments   273

Notes   275

Index   303

Preface

My goal in writing this book is to demystify systems change and provide a practical and inspiring guide to making our places and thus our world better. I've researched and worked on place-based initiatives and collaboratives for over a decade. I've learned what can move systems in a regenerative direction, why much of this change needs to happen at regional and local levels, and how it can be done. In this book, I share these learnings and lay out a theory-to-action road map for changing systems.

I have enjoyed the privilege of working with planners, advocates, local government officials and staff, philanthropists, community leaders, researchers, and educators. They work for regional and local collaboratives, city and county governments, regional agencies, consulting firms, foundations, small and large nonprofits, universities, school districts, and other entities that support the public good. This book is for those working in these types of settings and all who are interested in contributing to the health of their place and addressing our biggest societal problems.

We know systems change is necessary to meaningfully address climate change, growing inequality, and our other entrenched crises. We also recognize that human behavior lies at the heart of the climate crisis and our biggest problems. However, the path to systems and human behavior change has been unclear and elusive.

Over time, I've learned how changing complex systems to shape how we live can be approached strategically. My dissertation research involved behavioral science and examined how conditions influence personal transportation behavior. Since then, I've researched and worked on efforts to change how we live in systems ranging from transportation to food to nature and community spaces. As a consultant and former educator, I have been involved in strategic plan development and implementation throughout my career. I approach systems and behavior change from a strategy lens and share this in this book.

Systems change can easily be disconnected from what people are actually trying to do in communities, cities, counties, and regions. To embrace a systemic approach, it's important that we understand the why, what, and how of systems change. Like others interested in making systems change happen, I've read much literature on the topic.

Systems literature provides ways to contemplate systems change but lacks practical application to place-based societal change. Leverage points, popularized by

Donella Meadows, are ways to intervene in systems and change them. In *Thinking in Systems*, Meadows explains several leverage points, including paradigms and transcending them, reinforcing and balancing feedback loops, and stock-and-flow structures. While the leverage points are helpful in thinking about the nature of systems, their multitude and abstract nature don't lend themselves easily to organizations and individuals seeking to make change.

Other books offer helpful guidance. Paul Hawken's *Regeneration* (and his preceding book, *Drawdown*) lays out a comprehensive approach to addressing the climate crisis with solutions specific to food, building energy, and other systems. In *The Future We Choose*, UN Paris Agreement architects Christiana Figueres and Tom Rivett-Carnac depict a vision and pathways for government, corporations, and individuals to avert a worsening of the climate crisis. The Club of Rome's *Earth for All: A Survival Guide for Humanity* explores systems and lays out global solutions to our environmental and social crises. In *Strong Towns*, Charles Marohn brings focus to the local level, describing tactical approaches to building stronger communities and local economies. Transition Towns leader Rob Hopkins's *From What Is to What If* illustrates strategies for creating self-sustaining, interdependent communities that promote environmental and social good.

These books and others add greatly to our knowledge about complex social change. However, this body of literature falls short in helping readers like you implement or be a part of systems change that alters how people live. Human behavior is often lightly touched on, and the link among systems, local action, strategy, and human behavior is even less so.

I've found systems-change approaches to be ineffective for three main reasons. First, systems-change principles and goals can be vague and difficult to turn into action. Discussions of systems change typically involve one or more of the following: relationships, power dynamics, policy, using data, and getting to the root causes of problems. These elements are important but lack direction in specifying outcomes or what changed systems will look like. Second, efforts at changing systems rarely go deep enough into the underlying forces that hold current systems and related human behavior and problems in place. As discussed throughout this book, understanding corporate capitalism's hold on society is foundational to embarking on systems change. And third, systems-change practices are often framed around a singular problem like homelessness or teen pregnancy. Instead of seeing how larger systems lend themselves to multiple problems, we tend to rely on tackling one issue at a time.

To address these challenges in designing and implementing systems change, this book provides a fundamental, actionable, and holistic guide to systems change. It starts with an understanding of what is holding our status quo systems and human behavior in place—power, culture, land use, and silos influenced by corporate capitalism.

The systems-change framework discussed in this book builds on these understandings in offering systems-oriented strategies that can be applied to any place-based initiative as a launching point, guide, or lens for evaluation. The framework is intentionally simple and easy to remember. I've used it in multiple collaborative projects. Individuals quickly grasp the four featured systems-change levers—shifting power, resetting culture, transforming land use, and leveraging other systems—and apply them to their strategy for making place-based change. The levers are applicable to long-term and short-term planning as well as big and small steps.

The pathway depicted in this book is holistic, covering eight systems that collectively shape much human behavior and underlie our social and environmental crises. While no book can cover everything, the featured systems are highly interrelated, heavily impact lifestyles and daily life choices, and account for most of our greenhouse gas emissions.

In this book, I also address the reality that awareness of or concern about climate change and other crises have not been enough to motivate systems and behavior change. I learned about the gap between knowledge and action in my research on personal transportation behavior. I've witnessed this dynamic repeatedly in practice, as we remain stuck in status quo systems and behavior patterns, even when we know they are doing much harm.

No matter how we come at systems change, the desired outcomes must be viable. This does not mean they are easy or quick to achieve. Rather, it must lead to something that people want.

The place-based systems presented in this book are an alternative to dominant corporate capitalist systems. They tap into people's intrinsic motivation to be connected to place, community, and nature. Reorienting our lives around the places where we live has the potential for broad appeal. I've found that a shared love of place is one thing that can bring people together around systemic change and open them up to changes in how they live.

Whether you're a dreamer, a realist, or somewhere in between, I hope this book will help you work effectively toward the meaningful change you seek. Planners, government leaders and staff, advocates, funders, educators, and others invested in social change can use this book to align what they do with systems and behavior change and increase their impact.

There is no easy path to changing systems and human behavior. They are complex, and resistance can be intense. I've written this book because I believe we have no choice but to change systems that, in turn, change how we live.

CONNECTED TO PLACE

Introduction

> **You never change things by fighting the existing reality. To change something, build a new model that makes the existing model obsolete.**
>
> —Buckminster Fuller

Within one decade, the city of Paris underwent a massive transformation of its streets and transportation system. From 2015 to 2024, Paris closed more than one hundred streets to motor vehicles. These streets have become spaces where people can safely and joyfully walk, bike, roll, and gather as a community. In addition, close to fifty thousand parking spots were removed to make room for over eight hundred miles of bike lanes, bike parking, and a robust bike share system. By a ratio of almost 3 to 1, more people were biking than driving in the city center by 2024.[1] Sidewalks have been widened to encourage more walking. Paris is showing cities around the world how to end car dependence and promote well-being and health through active transportation.

The positive impact on the environment and people's lives in Paris has been substantial. Parisians now breathe 40 percent less polluted air.[2] Paris is taking the climate crisis head-on by dramatically reducing transportation-related greenhouse gas emissions (GHGE). Spending less time behind windshields, people are becoming more connected to each other and their neighborhoods. Their personal health benefits from the physical exercise and the clearing of one's mind that occurs when individuals walk or bike. In addition to the environmental, social, and personal benefits, studies show that more people walking and biking increases shopping at local businesses.[3] Paris has made pedestrian infrastructure near shopping centers and retail districts a priority. The benefits extend to children and youth who can more safely walk and bike to school with cars banned from most streets surrounding schools.

An explicit aim of Paris's government is to have "fifteen-minute communities" across the city, in which individuals have all the amenities they need within a fifteen-minute walk or bike ride from their homes. These neighborhood features include places to shop, eat, and work, as well as spaces for connecting to community and nature that boost personal well-being. Sidewalk trees and urban gardens have been planted. Near where many Parisians live, the roads along the Seine River have been converted into places for strolling, relaxation, and activities. The production of local food on rooftops and in other underutilized urban spaces is another part of Paris's metamorphosis into a fifteen-minute city.

Paris's changes have been dramatic, but the French capital is not alone in reinventing itself as a healthy, community-centered, and environmentally friendly place to live. Regions, cities, and communities worldwide are making bold moves to address the climate crisis, restore community bonds, and reinvigorate local economies.

In this book, we'll unpack the why, what, and how of these positive developments using a system lens. Pushback on these reforms varies from place to place, but change everywhere faces resistance from the status quo. A systems-change approach is needed to overcome these barriers. The systems-change framework detailed in this book can be applied to regional and local initiatives and is aimed at changing how people live, as reflected in the Paris example. Changing systems to change human behavior is the pathway to creating the world we desperately need and want.

How We Live and Its Link to Our Crises and Alienation

Human behavior is inextricably linked to our growing environmental and social crises. It's easy to shy away from the link. When we say, "People won't change," we look away from our individual and collective behavior and look instead to international agreements, institutions, and technology to solve our problems. We no longer have time to avoid the reality of the consequences of our aggregate human behavior. Despite much effort on many fronts, we've made little progress in taking on our biggest societal challenges. The inconvenient truth is not that climate change and other crises are happening but that we must change human behavior to mitigate them.

Looking at what's changed over the past fifty years, there are clear links between environmental degradation and human activity. The human population has doubled during this time, but our consumption of the earth's resources and related pollution has grown even more rapidly. The extraction of materials for human consumption has tripled.[4] Energy consumption has grown fourfold.[5] Our growing crises are sending a strong signal that we cannot continue to use energy and materials at these rates.

Changed ways of living over the past fifty years help explain our rapid consumption of the earth's resources. The growth of car dependency provides one proxy for how lifestyles have changed. From 1970 to 2024, the number of cars grew over sevenfold, from 200 million[6] to almost 1.5 billion worldwide.[7] On top of this growth in car ownership, vehicle miles traveled per car rose during many of the past fifty years.[8] The average weight of vehicles has also increased. The average car sold in the United States in 2022 was one thousand pounds heavier than the average car sold in 1980.[9] The number, use, and weight of energy- and material-intensive automobiles reflect the growing impact of human living on the planet upon which we depend.

In addition to cars, the average footprint of homes, consumer goods, and food has also expanded. Even as household size declined in the United States, the average home size increased from 1,660 square feet in 1973 to 2,631 square feet in 2017.[10] Larger homes have provided room for a proliferation of consumer goods and increased demand for building energy. Plastics, a major component of consumer goods and packaging, have increased twenty-fold over the past fifty years.[11] Human diets have also become more resource-intensive and polluting, with meat intake growing over threefold.[12] The rising use of resources to support these changes in human living is a primary contributor to the climate and biodiversity loss crises.

Knowing where people spend their time helps us better understand the connection between human behavior and the depth of our environmental and social crises. The average American now spends only 8 percent of their life outdoors, compared with an estimated 87 percent in buildings and 5 percent in cars.[13] The average American spends over seven hours a day online.[14] A study in the United Kingdom estimated that the average person will spend thirty-four years of their life looking at television screens, computers, and mobile devices.[15] Spending most time inside and on screens translates into more time consuming energy and goods and little time for community and nature connection.

Although nature and community remain essential to our well-being, so much time indoors, on devices, and in cars has alienated us from both in daily life. Alienation underlies our crises. Separation from nature and people with different lived experiences makes it more likely that people see "other" people and species as less than themselves. These views have been ingrained in cultures, often subconsciously influencing personal views and behavior. People are unlikely to change their attitudes and the treatment of others and nature when daily experiences involve little of either.

With fewer nature experiences in everyday life, we forget how we are a part of nature and depend on it. It becomes easy to lose sight of nature as the source of our food and other resource needs. Disconnection from nature can lead to ignoring how extraction and consumption of materials and energy are degrading the environment. This separation has led to a default situation where we exploit nature rather than live in balance with it.

Alienation occurs along racial and economic lines and adds to our inequality crisis. Wealthier, often white households have increasingly separated themselves from families and individuals with less means by residing in wealthy enclaves that are the result and legacy of racially restrictive covenants and redlining.[16] With typically large homes and yards, people in these neighborhoods feel less need for public space and other types of infrastructure that benefit society and bring diverse people together. Hardship, inequities, and systemic racism become invisible to those who don't experience them. Separation makes it easier for those benefiting from current systems to ignore the welfare of those oppressed by them.

Human behavior has led directly to our crises through overall and inequitable resource use. It's also fed the alienation that underlies and exacerbates our social and environmental problems. We must change how we live. Bringing place back into the center of people's lives is an integral part of motivating and making this change.

Living Connected to Place for Well-Being and Regeneration

Place-based ways of living are an antidote to alienation. Experiencing community and nature in daily life is central to what it means to live connected to place. By community, I mean fellowship with others built on sharing and living together in a place. Nature is present below, above, and around us every time we step outside. Though it is diminished in many places where people live, we can revitalize it.

Living connected to place provides an alternative to energy- and resource-intensive lifestyles, helping mitigate the climate and biodiversity loss crises. Place-based living also directly counters social breakdown and inequality by building community bonds and strengthening local economies.

A place-based orientation to living dismantles divisions the only way we truly can: by building in-person relationships and tight-knit communities. So much today divides us. Views on elections, guns, vaccinations, climate change, and other topics can make us seem worlds apart. Yet a shared love of and engagement with the places where we live can help us overcome differences. We can narrow the great chasms in our country when we spend time in our communities, work together to make them better, and get to know one another. Living connected to place enriches lives through deeper everyday connections with community, other people, and nature.

Connection with nature in daily life reminds us of who we are and promotes well-being. Nature is the foundation of life and our human existence. It's reflected in our economies and cultures and impacts our health and ability to thrive. Psychology Professor Peter H. Kahn Jr. uses a pill metaphor to capture the health benefits of nature in people's lives: "What if there was a pill that could reduce depression, anxiety, stress, obesity, diabetes, and ADHD symptoms, as well as improve mental health and life satisfaction, eyesight, birth outcomes, pain control, sleep, and social connectedness? What if that pill had virtually no side effects, and was comparatively inexpensive? We have something like that now. Though it's not a pill. It's called nature."[17] Regular contact with nature boosts physical and mental health and keeps people connected to what sustains them.

Meaning and happiness in life also depend on high-quality relationships and in-person connections within communities.[18] Humans are social creatures, and personal well-being depends on intimate connection with others.[19] When people step away from their screens, cars, and private spaces and engage with their place, they enter a world of real-life connections and experience more contentment.

Virtual relationships do not offer the same benefits. Frequent online interactions and regular use of social media are linked to anxiety, depression, and neuroticism.[20] Time spent on social media can displace nurturing in-person relationships. Virtual interactions can be beneficial, such as the lifeline they offer LGBTQ+ youth living in noninclusive local communities. We can keep the helpful parts of online community while prioritizing rich, authentic social connections in the places where people live, so fundamental to happiness.

The need for daily connection to nature and community runs deep in our "hunter-gatherer" DNA. We were hunter-gatherers for over 99 percent of human history. Our ancestors had an intimate knowledge of local ecology, flora, fauna, and weather—all that constitutes nature in the places where they lived. Humans evolved to rely on each other in localized communities in which each person and family played an important role. People were rooted in interdependence with local nature and each other, and this orientation fostered sustainable ways of using natural resources. Understanding of local nature, community, and culture forms the basis of Indigenous knowledge passed on from generation to generation in First Peoples communities around the world. Living connected to place taps into this knowledge and brings us back into healthy, interdependent ways of living.

Strengthening our connection to place invites us to firmly embed ourselves in our physical surroundings and nearby human community. This engagement with place can pervade daily life through walking, biking, and using public transit; being stewards of local nature; eating food and using energy from local and regional sources; supporting local businesses; and, as much as possible, living, working, and recreating locally. It's true that everyday life actions can feel mostly like chores and routines, but they can also enhance the connections that make people feel alive and well. We need strong bonds with the places we inhabit.

Rooted in place, people not only enhance their personal well-being; they also start a virtuous cycle of regenerating community and nature. The more invested people become in their communities, the more likely they are to take care of their place and contribute to civic life. Likewise, connecting with nature motivates people to be good stewards and live in a balanced way with it. We protect what we love and love only what we know. We align with the fundamental forces of life and connectedness, knowing that our well-being is deeply intertwined with the health of our communities and nature.

When most or all our energy, food, and consumer goods are produced near where we live, we will do a better job of living within natural limits. We will no longer be exporting the harms of human consumption to vulnerable communities and other places. The impacts of consumer choices are more difficult to hide with nearby sourcing and production of goods and services.

Living connected to place also regenerates local economies. Buying local and regional energy, food, consumer goods, and services keeps money in the cities and regions where it is generated. Corporations siphon less money to their headquarters when people become less dependent on their global products and services.

Regenerating local economies is an important way to reduce inequality and build community resilience. Resources can be more equitably distributed when not controlled by large economic interests. Diversification of local business and industry makes communities more resilient; they won't be devastated when a corporation's operations pick up and leave.

Global exchange of information and services is needed but should be deployed selectively in support of strong local economies. Through these exchanges, communities can avoid parochialism and support each other in transitioning to place-based living and rejuvenating strong local economies. Regions and cities can become more self-reliant without being cut off from the wider world.

Connection to place is not a vision for some people. Place-based systems that support living connected to place provide more ownership and fair wage opportunities in the economy than a corporate-dominated system. These systems and related ways of living also bring down living costs that burden many families and individuals. As we'll explore in part 2, this starts with providing affordable housing for everyone near where they work and efficient, less costly nonauto modes to get to and from work.

As a vision for better living, place-based connection can build a broad-based movement for social change. It gets at the root of our crises and regenerates nature, community, and local economies. When people anchor their lives in a place, connect to all it has to offer, and help their community grow and thrive, they go from being part of the problem to becoming part of the solution.

If living connected to place has such appeal and is critical to addressing our biggest problems, why aren't we living in these ways? An examination of the role of corporations in people's lives helps explain why.

Corporate Capitalism's Hold on How We Live

We are living in an age of corporate capitalism. The marketplace is dominated by large, often multinational corporations that control production and profits in the economy.

Disconnectedness with place is intertwined with the prominent role of corporations in today's world. Retail corporations and their online portals have become more familiar than local businesses. We recognize corporate logos more than we know native flora and fauna in our places. Corporate global supply chains foster the alienation we experience from the natural resources and labor that produce many of the products we buy and the food and energy we use. The harm from exploiting labor and nature to maximize corporate profits remains hidden from many consumers (though it is all too obvious to others). As referenced earlier, the products of corporations, from cars to digital devices, further feed into living disconnected from place.

Corporations have bred much of the alienation through their firm grip on how we live today. They have a vested interest in people consuming more, driving more, using digital devices, and being more connected to these things than to their places, community, and nature. Much corporate revenue is based on people living in these ways.

Corporate control of the housing, work, and transportation systems has played a strong role in making it hard for people to live connected to place. Housing is in short supply and unaffordable to many near where they work, shop, or recreate. Corporate developers, banks, and real estate stakeholders are reluctant to build housing that does not maximize profits. In addition, the interests of Big Auto, Big Oil, and now Big Tech (with electric and autonomous vehicles) have been served by developing communities and housing around the automobile. It's hard to connect with nearby community and nature when we must drive nearly everywhere we need to go. Furthermore, the corporate takeover of retail, food, and other industries has eroded local work opportunities. Local businesses have struggled to compete with corporations' lower costs made possible by the extraction of cheap labor and nature around the globe. Opportunities to own businesses and shop locally have consequently diminished.

Corporate capitalism's tentacles touch nearly every part of people's lives. Food, energy, and consumer goods have become largely corporate-controlled. In these systems, people's choices are heavily influenced by pervasive corporate advertising and limited to what corporations provide across complex supply and distribution chains. The systems are designed to encourage consumerism and waste so that more food, consumer goods, and energy are sold from one fiscal quarter to the next. This dynamic has made it hard to transition to a clean energy economy. Rising demand for energy often outstrips the growth in renewable energy, leading to more fossil fuel burning for electricity. Despite the decades-long push to reduce GHGE, the United States extracted more crude oil than any other nation in history and became the world's leading exporter of liquefied natural gas in 2023.[21] Collective human consumption and GHGE have grown exponentially over the past fifty years with the rise of corporate dominance in the economy.

In the past quarter century, Big Tech corporations and the digital society they have fostered have put the corporate control of systems and how we live into overdrive. Social media, smartphones, and the computerization of everyday tasks have pushed much of our lives into the digital realm. In moderation, these can be positive forces in lives and communities. Video conferencing, for example, is a helpful alternative to unnecessary carbon-intensive business travel. It helps loved ones connect when they cannot be together in person. In their current form, however, Big Tech and its products play an outsized role in everyday choices and lives. Corporations like Meta envision a "metaverse" in which humanity is wholly immersed in virtual spaces. Big Tech is pulling people away from the places where they live and the people and nature with whom they share those places.

Growing Interest in Alternatives to Corporate Capitalism

Our mounting crises are forcing us to rethink how society is structured, including our dependence on corporate capitalism. When the COVID-19 pandemic spread through international travel and interrupted the global supply chain, it called into question the wisdom of our global capitalist economy. Essential medical supplies being sourced, assembled, and shipped worldwide were in short supply. The lack of N95 masks, ventilators, syringes, and other supplies compromised the response to the pandemic in the United States. The Russian invasion of Ukraine in 2022 exposed more vulnerabilities in the global corporate economic system. The war disrupted the worldwide market for energy, food, and other products, creating shortages and high prices for consumers.

Climate change is also shaking the foundation of corporate capitalism. Hurricanes, floods, wildfires, and other extreme weather events increasing in frequency and intensity are disrupting supply chains.[22] In December 2021, a typhoon caused historic flooding in Malaysia, severely damaging a major port hub for shipping semiconductors from Taiwan. This climate-related weather event led to a global semiconductor shortage. Rising sea levels will inundate ports and coastal infrastructure, further interfering with global markets and the sourcing of goods by corporations.

In addition, increasing calls for justice and equity are fueling a backlash against corporate capitalism. Most of the benefits of corporate capitalism go to a small number of wealthy individuals, while those providing labor in the complex supply and distribution chains receive little. Rising frustration with extreme inequality is leading to calls for transformative change.

Place-based ways of living are gathering interest as an important way to reduce our dependence on corporate capitalism. In his article "The Localist Revolution," political and cultural commentator David Brooks explains the growing movement toward living more connected to place. He describes power, knowledge, and attention as shifting to the local level: "Under localism, the crucial power center is at the tip of the shovel, where the actual work is being done. Expertise is not in the think tanks but among those who have local knowledge, those with a feel for how things work in a specific place and an awareness of who gets stuff done. Success is not measured by how big you can scale, but by how deeply you can connect."[23] The aptly named revolution Brooks describes implies living in ways much more influenced by place than corporate capitalism.

The experience of sheltering in place during the COVID-19 pandemic accelerated this shift. Urban homesteading—growing food and making items at home—expanded. More people engaged in activities such as raising backyard chickens, gardening, making jellies and jams, and baking sourdough bread.[24] The relative safety of gathering outdoors rekindled interest in public space and brought more people outside to be with each other and enjoy nature. Collectively, these changes helped us envision new ways that place can shape our lives and different possibilities for how we can shape our places.

Changing how we live is about much more than good intentions. Thought leader Maya MacGuineas works on and writes about the intersection of the economy, technology, and capitalism. In her *Atlantic* article "Capitalism's Addiction Problem," she reflects on the increasing amount of time we are spending on digital devices, stating that "we're dismayed with how we're spending our days but feel powerless to abandon our new bad habits."[25] Whether smartphones, cars, or the push toward larger homes and more stuff, corporate capitalism and the products it sells us have us stuck in patterns of living that we know are problematic but don't feel able to change. To live differently, we need place-based systems that change the conditions influencing everyday life choices and lifestyles.

Place-Based Systems

Freeing ourselves from corporate capitalism and living more connected to place become possible when we have supportive systems around us. Renowned systems thinker Donella Meadows defines systems as "a set of things . . . interconnected in such a way that they produce their own pattern of behavior over time."[26]

The systems featured in this book create the physical, economic, social, and cultural conditions that shape human choices and habits.

Place-based systems are those anchored in the communities, culture, and natural resources of a particular place. They support people living in interdependent ways with each other and nature. By utilizing local and regional resources to provide what a population needs, people better understand natural resource limits and are motivated to conserve and protect nature. Place-based systems encourage people to spend time and energy in their local context, which facilitates the rebuilding of local economies, the strengthening of community life, and the restoration of nature. In contrast to corporate capitalist-based systems, place-based systems facilitate sustainable, equitable ways of living.

Place-based systems correspond to the major dimensions of daily life:

- **Housing** is available and affordable in mixed-income, mixed-use communities.
- **Local businesses** provide meaningful work and shopping for people where they live.
- Active, community-oriented, and pollution-free **transportation modes** are easily accessed and safe.
- **Community spaces** are safe, car-free, and vibrant.
- **Nature spaces** are abundant, accessible, and nearby.
- Regional, healthy, and seasonal **food** is available and affordable.
- **Building energy** is regionally harvested from renewable sources, and conservation and efficiency are default choices.
- **Consumer goods** are regionally made, shared, repaired, and recirculated with minimal waste.

These systems operate synergistically at varying geographic scales to influence how people are housed, work, play, get around, use energy, eat, and consume goods. They add up to mixed-use neighborhoods and self-reliant regions that enable people to live, work, shop, and recreate locally. With sufficient affordable housing, communities are mixed-income and more people benefit from the opportunities and amenities within them. These place-based systems provide a road map for reorienting society around the places where people live and improving the well-being of the environment, communities, and people.

The Paris transformation can be viewed through the lens of place-based systems. The transportation system has become less car-dependent and more oriented around active forms of transportation that connect people to community and nature in daily life. Nature and community spaces have expanded to make it easier and more enjoyable to live connected to place. Growing more local food is augmenting the place-based food system.

We can meet and overcome the challenges of the twenty-first century with place-based systems. When housing, work, and transportation systems support traveling less distance in daily life and instead immerse people in nearby surroundings, we reduce GHGE, conserve natural resources, and strengthen the social fabric. Nature can be restored, and social interaction can flourish through nearby community and nature space systems. Regional and local orientation to building energy, food, and consumer goods systems requires us to confront ecological limits and thus reduce material and energy consumption while building stronger local economies and reducing inequality. Paradoxically, our most significant global problems can be solved effectively in our local context.

* * *

The need to regenerate nature, community, and local economies provides both the "why" and the desired outcome of place-based systems change. The relationship among corporate capitalism, how people live, and our crises helps us understand why systems change needs to be focused on human behavior and diminishing the influence of corporations on it. The promise of living connected to place to promote people's well-being and regeneration provides a direction for systems change. Yet place-based systems that support living connected to place are just an idea unless we understand and can apply the "what" and "how" of systems change.

Systems-Change Levers and Catalysts (The "What" and "How" of Systems Change)

Place-based social movements to change how people live are not new. The Transition Movement is helping cities, neighborhoods, and communities to become more resilient and just through vibrant, localized ways of living. Approximately twenty-five national hubs support more than one thousand Transition groups across the globe.[27] The Slow Cities Movement includes chapters in 301 small cities and towns across thirty-three countries and territories.[28] This movement prioritizes eating local food, shopping in locally owned stores, reducing waste, and connecting people to the sources of their water, food, and consumer goods. These movements are supporting people to live connected to place.

These models, respectively supported by the Transition Network and Cittaslow, offer guidance through principles, ingredients, and requirements. For example, the Transition Network outlines seven essential ingredients for community transition: healthy groups, vision, community involvement, networks and partnerships, practical projects, connecting with the larger movement, and reflection and celebration.[29] Although these elements help define an approach to transformative change at the local level, they are not grounded in a systems-change approach.

Determining how to deploy systems change starts with understanding what is holding current systems and their associated problems in place. Applying behavioral science and analyzing corporate capitalism's hold on our systems provides that basis. Across the systems featured in this book, we will see how corporate capitalist interests have used power, land use, and culture to create the conditions that shape how we live. Learning from corporate capitalism, we can turn these factors into systems-change levers.

Systems-change levers answer the "what" of systems change; in other words, what exactly do we change about systems to produce a different pattern of human behavior? To change these systems, we need to shift power, transform land use, and reset culture. A fourth lever—leverage systems together—breaks down silos and creates reinforcing feedback loops, making it possible to create broader and deeper change. These four levers harness the insights of behavioral science by changing the physical, economic, cultural, and social conditions that organize everyday life and lifestyle choices.

The changes in Paris involve all four levers. Power has been built among advocates and like-minded residents. Their power has influenced the leaders of the city and overcome resistance to the removal of car infrastructure where the auto industry and its affiliates hold much power. Land use has been transformed, including the expansion of public space, streets flexed to nonauto uses, bike parking, and rooftops and other land being adapted to food production. The cultural embrace of cycling has been significant, with many people riding bikes who had not previously done so in the city. The culture has been reset through mechanisms such as highly visible public bike-share stations all over the city that normalize cycling. An approach of leveraging the transportation and community spaces systems together has led to streets that now prioritize biking and walking and serve as places for communities to gather.

Knowing "what" to change is necessary but insufficient to enact systems change. We also need guidance in the "how." The examples of systems change in this book reflect four key catalysts that make systems change happen: strategic collaboration among organizations, systems-oriented government, place-based education, and personal change. In Paris, the city administration under Mayor Ann Hidalgo played a particularly catalytic role in place-based systems change. Well-run collaboratives can put pressure on the government and other institutions to change and directly create change by bringing organizations together to strategically enact initiatives. The catalytic power of education and personal change can directly impact communities while also readying people's hearts and minds for systems change.

Each lever and catalyst has a limited impact on its own. Systems change happens when they align. Power, land use, and culture across multiple systems can head in the same direction when collaboration, government, education, and individuals pull these levers together. From this momentum, transformation unfolds. Lives of placelessness become centered by connection to place. Regional and local self-reliance replaces external economic dependence. Communities become less vulnerable and more resilient. Nature degradation stops and reverses into restoration. Exclusive enclaves become inclusive communities. People feel inspired to move forward with these changes because of their profound impact on their well-being, building more collective will for further change.

The systems-change framework in this book weaves together the "why," "what," and "how" of place-based systems change. Figure I.1 reflects the relationships and flow among well-being and regeneration (the "why"), the catalysts (the "how"), the levers (the "what"), place-based systems, and how we live. The vision of well-being and regeneration pushes and motivates collaboration among organizations and the other catalysts to spark systems change. The catalysts focus on applying the systems-change levers in their work to be most impactful. Place-based systems emerge and support people in living connected to place. As more people live in these ways, their well-being, nature, communities, and local economies improve. Positive momentum builds, encouraging the catalysts to continue pulling the levers of systems change. In this book, we'll explore these critical mechanisms of place-based systems change and see how this self-reinforcing cycle can create the world we need and want.

As the "why" explains the need for place-based systems change, we'll start there in part 1. Chapter 1 dives into the relationship between how we live and the well-being of the environment, communities, and individuals and explores

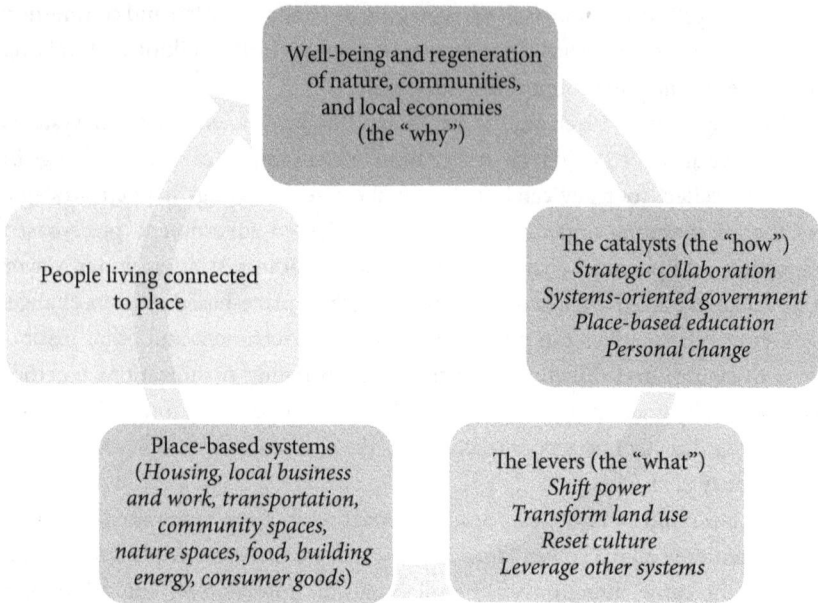

FIGURE I.1. Systems-change framework: The how, what, and why

the relationship between systems and human behavior. Chapter 2 presents the place-based systems and their role in regenerating nature, community, and local economies and advancing the well-being of all people. Chapter 3 explains how systems-change levers can be applied to each system and thus become systems-change strategies that stakeholders can employ in change efforts.

Part 2 details the "what" of systems change by showing how the levers can and are applied to create place-based systems. The systems include housing (chap. 4), local business and work (chap. 5), transportation (chap. 6), community spaces (chap. 7), nature spaces (chap. 8), food (chap. 9), building energy (chap. 10), and consumer goods (chap. 11). These eight systems together influence many aspects of how people live and are strongly linked to the overall quality of nature, communities, and people's lives.

Finally, the "how" of place-based systems change is presented in part 3 with chapters on strategic collaboration (chap. 12), systems-oriented government (chap. 13), place-based education (chap. 14), and personal change (chap. 15). By the end of part 3, you will be armed with the know-how to implement place-based systems change in new and existing efforts.

This book deals with more than systems change. It is a blueprint for the generational change needed to avert a climate catastrophe and build a more just, sustainable world. By 2050, the world will be dramatically different. If we don't free ourselves from the grip of corporate capitalism, we'll find ourselves in a Mad Max world. But with place-based systems, it is within our power to create a world where people and nature thrive together.

We have the resources to transition to place-based systems. Governments and institutions can provide funding and support for systemic change in regions, cities, and communities. Funds for climate resilience and economic development can be directed to develop place-based systems using systems-change levers and catalysts. Funding should go to projects that employ residents, grow local businesses, add affordable infill housing, promote active transportation, expand nature and community spaces, increase energy efficiency, reduce material waste, and source and produce local and regional food, energy, and consumer goods. We can write a new and better chapter for the twenty-first century if we seize the opportunity to change systems and reorient our society and our lives around the places where we live.

Part 1
SYSTEMS, PLACE, AND HOW WE LIVE IN THE TWENTY-FIRST CENTURY

When a flower doesn't bloom, you fix the environment in which it grows, not the flower.

—Alexander Den Heijer

Part 1 shows why systems change that alters how people live is critical to solving our biggest problems and improving the quality of life for all people. As we'll see, reorienting systems around the places where people live makes systems change concrete and supports human behavior change. The links between living connecting to place, regeneration, and well-being appeal to a broad cross-section of stakeholders in these critical societal shifts.

In chapter 1, we'll explore the argument for focusing systems change on altering people's lifestyles and daily life choices and why systems must be overhauled to make that possible.

Chapter 2 illustrates the promise of place-based systems in regenerating nature, community, and local economies and advancing the well-being of all people. The transition from the "why" of systems change to the "what" of systems change occurs in chapter 3. This final chapter of part 1 presents the systems-change levers as the guide to what we need to change about systems.

CHANGING HOW WE LIVE

It is fortunate that the lifestyle we must somehow forge for ourselves may be enjoyable to live in.

—Raymond DeYoung, University of Michigan

In 1994, I began teaching high school economics in Palo Alto, California. After the trial and error of learning how to manage a classroom full of teenagers, I overhauled the curriculum to feature a sustainable economics theme that challenged students to think critically about our economic system. At the time, more people were becoming aware of climate change and growing inequality, along with the threats they posed to people and society. Yet few people connected those things to our systems and ways of life.

The Sustainable Economics course took students on a journey of examining such topics as consumerism, externalities, disparities among local economics, and economic globalization. In the Economic Vote Project, students researched a corporation and presented their argument for or against buying products or services from their chosen corporation. Getting students to analyze consumer choices elevated their consciousness and knowledge about the impact of what they chose to consume.

From time to time, my former students reached out and shared with me how the curriculum had influenced them. Some even chose jobs that fit with a sustainable economy. These stories touched me and gave me hope. At the same time, I had a nagging feeling that any efforts they may have made to create positive change were likely hindered or even thwarted by the dominant economic system and culture. I also worried that as they grew into adults and faced the everyday realities of living in our society, they would yield to the status quo and give up on being part of the change.

Part of this worry grew out of my own experience. After I moved on to school and district leadership positions, I strayed from my focus of trying in my own small way to help society become more sustainable, equitable, and healthy. Yes, I supported environmental education and empowering students to act on social and environmental issues. But this effort represented only a small portion of my work and responsibilities. When I wasn't working, my wife and I spent most of our time raising two kids and maintaining our home. Just as I had speculated would be the case for my former students, it seemed that day-to-day obligations were distracting me from my larger aspirations.

Finally, in 2011, as the climate crisis was worsening with record-breaking extreme weather, I decided to refocus my energy on working toward social and environmental good. I returned to graduate school to pursue my PhD and study how humanity might live more sustainably. I conducted three studies on personal transportation behavior, the United States' largest source of individual carbon emissions. Hoping to contribute to research on environmentally responsible behavior, I wanted to understand why some people use sustainable transportation modes regularly.

It turned out that most of my original hypotheses were wrong. Those who biked, walked, and took public transit didn't do it because they were more concerned about the environment and climate change than other people. It also had less to do with personal considerations around finances, time, and other practical matters than I expected.

The main reason people chose alternatives to cars to get around was the intersection of personal well-being and a transportation system that supported people using those other modes. Study participants who regularly traveled without a car felt connected to their local surroundings and enjoyed interacting with others in the bike lane, on the sidewalk, or on the train. One participant talked about walking by the same beautiful grove of trees daily; others shared about walking through their parklike neighborhood; and another discussed seeing the same group of people on the train every day. A bike commuter described the excitement of seeing a coyote on her way to work. Many shared how they learned from and received support from others as they reduced their car dependence and used other modes instead. The local infrastructure, whether commuter train service or a network of protected bike lanes, made it possible to travel in these ways and benefit from the experience. The nature and community connections, along with the health benefits, kept them coming back for more.

In other words, people used sustainable transportation because it was available to them, other people validated or supported that choice, the behavior was culturally valued, and it made their lives better. In this chapter, we'll explore why we need to change how we live and the role of well-being and supportive systems in making that happen.

The Siren Song of Techno-Salvation

According to the Intergovernmental Panel on Climate Change, unprecedented and far-reaching societal change is needed to limit planetary warming to 1.5 degrees Celsius and avert climate catastrophe.[1] This assessment, shared by scientists and economists around the world, typically leads to calls for federal government policy, international agreements, corporate investments, and technological solutions. The idea is that a planetary crisis like climate change can only be solved on a grand scale. We need these big solutions, but they are insufficient for the required scope of change.

Our society has become oriented toward techno-salvation, or relying on technology as the answer to our problems. The overwhelming response to the climate crisis has been to advance renewable energy and electrification technologies. In 2023, solar- and wind-generated electricity production hit a new record but still accounted for only 13.4 percent of global electricity.[2] There were forty million electric vehicles (EVs) on the roads in 2023.[3] Despite growth in sales each year, this number of EVs made up just over one-quarter of 1 percent of the global car stock. We need all motorized vehicles to be zero emission and all energy to be renewable, but to make this possible, we must also reduce our energy consumption.

The challenge of achieving 100 percent renewable energy is compounded by growing demand, making the goal a moving target. Global energy consumption increases every year, aside from economic recessions, and is expected to do so until 2050.[4] With the growth of energy-intensive data centers and technologies to power artificial intelligence and cryptocurrency, this projection of future energy use may be far underestimated. The number of cars and miles driven also continues to expand. Researchers Raymond DeYoung and Thomas Princen explain that reliance on technology has failed to reduce energy use, such as in how gains from fuel-efficient engines are quickly outstripped by heavier vehicles driven farther and faster.[5] Modern ways of living, with our ever-growing appetite for energy, make it challenging to transition to a green energy economy. We cannot manufacture our way out of the climate crisis.

The climate crisis is far from the only reason to reduce the demand for cars and energy.

Extracting the natural resources needed to produce EVs, wind turbines, solar panels, batteries, and supportive infrastructure has led to ecological and human rights abuses in developing countries.[6] For example, the town of Kasulo in the Congo was torn up after a mining strip for cobalt, used in EV batteries, was discovered.[7] The Russian invasion of Ukraine in 2022 was targeted in the eastern region, where there are large untapped reserves of lithium. This metal is a critical component of EV batteries. In 2025, the President of the United States was trying to extort Ukraine into ceding rights to lithium and other minerals in exchange for any further support in protecting the country from Russia.

In the United States, Lithium Americas is building a lithium mine in Nevada. The area known as Thacker Pass is located on land rich with cultural artifacts, traditional foods, and medicinal plants sacred to the Paiute and Shoshone. Tribal leaders tried to stop the construction of the mine, knowing the land and water degradation it would cause, but were unsuccessful. The mine was approved for construction by the federal government and received a $2.26 billion federal loan to build processing facilities at the site.

A goal that would give us a shot at limiting climate change to 1.5 degrees Celsius and reducing other harms would be to halve our energy use and replace the remaining half with all renewable sources. We need a consumption-based approach as much as a production-based approach to heal the planet effectively. We must change how we live.

Researchers and experts in both social and natural sciences have been calling for drastic changes in our unsustainable and inequitable behavior patterns for decades.[8] The need for human behavior change is particularly relevant to wealthy countries like the United States. The average per-person consumption rates of resources in affluent countries are thirty times higher than in poor countries.[9] Journalist Hiroko Tabuchi shares research that illustrates the disproportionate amount of greenhouse gas emissions (GHGE) generated by the wealthy: "A typical two-person, very wealthy household—one with more than $1 million in investments in addition to a home and personal property—produces roughly 129 tons of planet-warming carbon dioxide per year, or about ten times the global average. . . . Overall, emissions from the world's wealthiest 0.5 percent produce . . . almost 15 percent of the world's lifestyle-related carbon emissions. . . . In comparison, the world's poorest 50 percent have been estimated to be responsible for only about 10 percent of lifestyle emissions."[10]

These disparities in emissions also exist among communities in the United States. For example, in San Francisco and Oakland, the carbon footprint in some neighborhoods is five times greater than in other neighborhoods in the same city.[11] University of California, Berkeley, researchers Daniel Kammen and Chris Jones, who determined this finding, add that people in the high-emission neighborhoods have high incomes, high vehicle ownership, and large homes. Across our country and the globe, affluent lifestyles—often disconnected from place—drive much of the climate crisis.

We cannot sustain current consumption levels and have a healthy planet. The average American's carbon footprint is 14.4 tons of GHGE annually, three times the global average.[12] To avert a climate disaster, researchers estimate that average personal emissions must be reduced to two tons annually by 2050.[13]

A review of the carbon footprints of households, using consumption-based emissions accounting, reveals where human behavior needs to change. Over the last few decades, consumption-based emissions analyses have consistently found transportation, home energy, food, and consumer goods as the most signifi- cant sources of consumer-related emissions.[14] Shifting to living, working, shop- ping, and recreating in local communities, as well as regional sourcing of food, energy, and goods, can significantly alter these patterns and substantially reduce emissions.

In *The Future We Choose: Surviving the Climate Crisis*, Christiana Figueres and Tom Rivett-Carnac, the United Nations (UN) architects of the historic 2015 Paris Agreement on Climate, offer two possible scenarios for the future.[15] The one in which we survive the climate crisis centers on a local orientation to living. This hopeful scenario features homes and buildings that sustain their own energy and water use through efficiency and by producing electricity; food grown in community and rooftop gardens across urban landscapes and supplemented by nearby local farms; products and housing manufactured locally with 3D print- ers; people opting for local life over long commutes; and folks engaging with their community and sharing resources with neighbors. It is striking that their description of the world we must create focuses more on satisfying daily life needs in the places where people live than on international or national policy.

Figueres, Rivett-Carnac, and many others who have written about local living don't dive deeply into what motivates and supports people to change how they live. As I'll explain shortly, the urgency of addressing the climate crisis is not suf- ficient motivation for people to change their behavior. First, behavioral science shows that people must see that change will lead to better living, not just in the future but as soon as they start engaging in new behaviors. Second, good inten- tions are never enough. We need a vision and systems that motivate and support living in climate-friendly ways.

Where do we start in overcoming resistance to change? We counter the dom- inant narratives that keep people living in unsustainable, inequitable ways by offering a vision of personal well-being. Our shared tendency is to hang on to old visions of the "good life" (such as suburbia and consumerism), especially to the extent that privilege allows us to benefit from them. These visions were intro- duced by the industries and corporations that benefit from them, and they play a central role in our twenty-first-century crises (as discussed in the introduction). In this new vision of the good life, people will be able to make choices that protect and sustain natural resources while taking better care of themselves, one another, and their communities.

Storytelling about how the world we need to create may be more pleasant to live in is essential because it gives people something to move toward. Philosopher Ivan Illich explains, "You must tell a more powerful tale, one so persuasive that it sweeps away the old myths and becomes the preferred story, one so inclusive that it gathers all the bits of our past and present into a coherent whole, one that even shines some light into our future so that we can take the next step."[16]

The tale can illustrate what we will gain rather than lose. The appeal of a societal reset is already intuitive to people with less to lose from change, those for whom the current systems are not working. Regardless of people's perspectives and situations, living connected to place offers an improved quality of life that can motivate needed behavior change.

Better Lives, Not Sacrifice

Although the COVID-19 pandemic had a devastating impact, it also opened our eyes to the great potential of changing human behavior and seeing the effects of those changes. With people sheltered in place across the world's cities, we traveled much less in cars and planes, and air pollution took a noticeable dive. Appreciation for clear skies was widely shared. Carbon emissions fell 7 percent in 2020, the most significant one-year drop in history.[17] During this time, birdsong resurged throughout our most populous cities. Without visitors and cars, bobcats, coyotes, and bears freely roamed Yosemite Valley. Nature benefited during the shelter-in-place phase of the pandemic, as did we in terms of clean air. The link between behavior and impact on the environment became abundantly clear.

This behavior change, however, was felt mainly as a sacrifice. So much time in residences disconnected from community and loved ones; the shuttering of local organizations, including schools and businesses; and the general loss of freedom of movement were a hefty price to pay for the benefits to air and nature. There was little tolerance in the United States and other countries for prolonged sheltering in place. Given that our crises, especially climate, require long-term changes in ways of living, the pandemic experience made it clear that sacrifice was not an appealing path.

Adopting climate-friendly lifestyles is often perceived as giving something up, which is one reason we have been slow to change our lifestyles despite the growing crisis. More and more Americans are personally experiencing the effects of climate change and are becoming increasingly concerned about it.[18] Still, lifestyles and everyday human behavior have changed little. Concern about climate change may be enough motivation for signing a petition, voting for political candidates who share the concerns, and making socially and environmentally responsible choices at times, but these are insufficient for the more profound shifts necessary in our lives. In daily decisions, people tend to choose what is comfortable, familiar, and "normal." We must tap into other motivations for climate action in everyday life.

Behavioral science provides insights into how we can motivate individual change at scale.

People are more likely to engage in behavior that benefits the environment when it enhances their quality of life, as opposed to a purely altruistic approach implying self-sacrifice.[19] People prefer environmentally responsible choices when they are not disadvantaged by them and are more willing to engage in sustainable behavior when it feels satisfying.[20] We have a better chance of creating lasting change in behavior if it enhances personal well-being.

Fortunately, living connected to place simultaneously enhances personal, community, and environmental well-being. Positive feelings from being part of a community can be generated by participating in reusing goods through community swaps. A sense of appreciation for the craftsmanship of local manufacturers or makers a person knows can lead her to treasure material goods and consume fewer of them. A desire to spend time outside and in one's community or look after personal health may lead one to bike, walk, or take public transit rather than drive. An interest in personal health or animal welfare may be the reason one chooses a more plant-based diet, reducing consumption of meat, dairy, and processed foods. It may be an appreciation for fresh, seasonal food that encourages people to buy local produce or grow it themselves. These types of motivations can be powerful forces for change in people's lives. Some may feel additional satisfaction from behavior change, knowing that they have become part of the solution to societal problems. Changing how people live will require a blend of altruistic and self-interested motivations. Living connected to place allows people to significantly reduce GHGE while simply enjoying life more. It is our best path to healing people and the planet.

Indigenous wisdom and scientific knowledge both point to the interconnectedness of all life and matter on our planet. This fundamental truth of "oneness" explains why our well-being as individuals is inextricable from that of our communities and the environment. Research on personal well-being, explored in the next section, clarifies these connections. These factors help dispel dominant societal narratives about what makes people happy and show how living connected to place can be the good life.

Personal Well-Being

Americans are presented with a mind-boggling variety of goods, services, technological advances, and opportunities. Yet these things have not, on the whole, made people healthier or happier. In fact, we seem to be headed in the wrong direction. The *Gallup-Sharecare Well-Being Index* measures subjective well-being. In 2018, the index was falling for the second year in a row. It revealed growing stress, worry, and anger among Americans, matching or topping previous highs in all three categories.[21] This research was conducted during a time of strong economic growth and before the COVID-19 pandemic, which made life worse for most people. Despite enormous comparative wealth, the United States tied with Iran, Albania, and Sri Lanka as the fourth-most stressed country of 143 countries included in the study.

Life expectancy in the United States dropped from seventy-nine years in 2019 to seventy-six years in 2021, the largest drop over two years since the 1920s.[22] Despite the world's highest per capita health care spending,[23] the United States is ranked forty-eighth globally in life expectancy in 2024—well behind most developed countries.[24]

A sense of lost control and hopelessness from the massive economic shifts of the past half century has taken a toll on communities across America. This impact is pointedly reflected in the rise of deaths of despair: premature deaths related to drug overdoses, alcohol abuse, and suicide.[25] Suicide rates in the United States increased by 35 percent across most age groups between 2000 and 2020.[26] Deaths of despair have risen, particularly among white men aged forty-five to fifty-four without a college degree and whose joblessness has been on the rise and wages have been falling. This demographic has also become vulnerable to strong-handed leaders like Donald Trump, whose strain of populism pits people against each other with racial undertones. The resulting political polarization can keep people in a state of anger that is harmful to their well-being.

Americans are living shorter lives and experiencing less happiness in the twenty-first century. Alienation from nature, community, and each other may explain why. Research on the downturn in personal well-being has shown how it stems from an overall erosion in social well-being.[27] Trusting relationships with others have been in decline.[28] This social alienation arises from many factors, including increasing economic inequality, growing residential segregation, and diminishing community life.

Researchers have found that Americans' decreasing happiness relates to an increasing amount of time people spend on electronic devices.[29] Less happiness among teens has been linked to time spent on digital media rather than interacting with each other in person or doing things in the offline, physical realm.[30] Social media use was found to add to, not alleviate, the mental health trauma from the social isolation imposed by the COVID-19 pandemic and to be linked to depression.[31] The drop in personal well-being correlates with growing alienation from the real, physical world.

In thinking about what actually makes people happy and healthy, as opposed to what we've been told will achieve that, it's helpful to consider the research on well-being. The *Gallup-Sharecare Well-Being Index*, the *New Economic Foundation's Five Ways to Well-Being*,[32] and the *Blue Zones Habits for a Happier, Healthier Life*[33] provide some evidence-based answers (see table 1.1).

- According to the *Gallup-Sharecare Index*, well-being depends on supportive personal and family relationships, connection to community, financial and economic security, physical health and wellness, and a sense of purpose.
- The UK government commissioned the *Five Ways to Well-Being* to help develop a vision for well-being beneficial to society and individuals. The five ways are everyday actions of connecting with people, giving through acts of kindness and volunteering, being active, being present through quality attention, and continuing to learn.
- The *Blue Zones Habits for a Happier, Healthier Life* include socializing in person for five to six hours a day, getting out every day and being involved in one's community, using money more for security and less for things, acting to promote physical health and relieve stress, and knowing and nurturing one's purpose.

What do these three conceptualizations of personal well-being have in common? Social connections, community connections, financial security, physical health, mental capital, and a sense of purpose in one's life.

Social and community connections formed and deepened over time add meaning to our lives. This network includes relationships with family, friends, and colleagues, as well as relations among neighbors, local store owners, and all who share a place. Caring, in-person relationships and participation in community life support happiness. They make life worth living.

Purpose also gives meaning to life and promotes overall well-being. Working toward fulfilling one's purpose helps meet the high-level human need for self-actualization. A person can find purpose in work and family life and also through making communities better and taking care of the local environment.

A fundamental level of financial security and comfort is essential to meeting basic human needs such as housing and food. Living without reliable access to these necessities is profoundly stressful. It's interesting to note, however, that additional material wealth beyond what is needed to fulfill these basic needs does not lead to happiness. Studies have confirmed no relationship between gross domestic product per capita (wealth generated per person) and happiness.[34] Research in the United States found that emotional well-being, an essential component of happiness, does not increase after a certain threshold of annual household income ($95,000 in 2018).[35] Above a baseline income level, the adage that money can't buy happiness rings true.

Mental capital refers to a person's cognitive and emotional health and resilience in the face of stress. Physical health is supported by exercise, activity, plant-based diets, not overeating, and sleep.

In addition, connection with nature is increasingly recognized as an essential part of personal well-being. Abundant research shows that it enhances physical, mental, and emotional health. The 2020 World Happiness Report was the first of its kind to examine the impact of the natural environment on well-being and happiness. The authors noted that exposure to nature reduces stress, increases positive emotions, and strengthens cognitive functioning and self-regulation.[36] Intuitively, we know that connecting with nature, community, and each other promotes personal well-being, and a growing body of research confirms these linkages.

TABLE 1.1 Well-being factors

WELL-BEING FACTOR	GALLUP-SHARECARE WELL-BEING INDEX	NEW ECONOMIC FOUNDATION'S FIVE WAYS TO WELL-BEING	BLUE ZONES HABITS FOR A HAPPIER, HEALTHIER LIFE
Social connections	Supportive personal relationships	Connect with people	Eat meals with family and friends; make new friends; 5 or 6 hours a day socializing
Community connections	Connection to one's community	Give—acts of kindness and volunteering	Get out every day; belong to a group (hobbies, religion, etc.); get involved in your community; volunteer; donate
Nature connections			Get out every day
Physical health	Physical health and wellness	Be active	Eat less overall, more beans and veggies, less meat and dairy; moderate drinking; move throughout the day; sleep 7.5 hours a night
Mental capital		Take notice—be present with quality attention; keep learning	Downshift with stress-relieving habits
Purpose	Sense of purpose		Know and nurture your purpose
Financial security	Financial and economic security		Use money for security and less for things

The *Habits for a Happier, Healthier Life* are based on fifteen years of examining what makes people healthy and happy in places known as Blue Zones (see chap. 2). For boosting happiness, the lead researcher Dan Buettner recommends the practical strategies of having a front porch and spending time on it; having at least three close friends and spending time with them; observing nature; spending money to build financial security rather than buying things; and volunteering.[37] These recommendations collectively increase time connecting to nature, community, and each other.

Living connected to place aligns well with these important well-being factors. Social, community, and nature connections form the core of living connected to place. Being outside and active, such as walking and biking, boosts mental and physical health. Opportunities to make a difference locally and participate with others add purpose to people's lives. Financial security increases with the cost-saving effects of living connected to place, which can include driving less, using less building energy, and buying fewer new consumer goods. Furthermore, thriving local economies provide ownership and fair wage opportunities to more people.

Living with Hope

Happiness and meaning in life may be elusive without some sense of hope. With societal crises worsening, we can feel overwhelmed and even flattened by despair. Anne Lamott describes our planet as beset by conflict, climate change, and other hazards. Joanna Macy and Chris Johnstone acknowledge that we are experiencing multiple tragedies in our world. Rebecca Solnit describes the twenty-first century as akin to a nightmare with extreme inequality and the rapid, destructive arrival of climate change. As these authors collectively suggest, we are losing confidence in effectively addressing our complex problems. In a world filled with crises, it's understandable that we would feel hopeless and that our well-being would suffer.

Yet the central message of the works of Lamott, Macy and Johnstone, and Solnit is one of hope. The titles of their books, respectively, are *Almost Everything: Hope Noted*; *Active Hope: How to Face the Mess We're in with Unexpected Resilience and Creative Power*; and *Hope in the Dark: Untold Histories, Wild Possibilities*. Lamott reflects on how giving to others provides her with a sense of hope: "By showing up with hope to help others, I'm guaranteed that hope is present. Then my own hope increases. By creating hope for others, I end up awash in the stuff. We create goodness in the world and that gives us hope."[38] Solnit connects hope to a call to action despite uncertain outcomes. Macy and Johnstone describe hope as based not on optimism or weighing chances for success but rather on taking action toward making the world we want to see.

Living connected to place can give people hope in the era of climate change. If daily life choices make people, communities, and the environment better, a sense of hope can be experienced every day. When this hope spreads, as Lamott notes, the potential for others to act also spreads. We know it will take a lot to reduce the threat of climate change and other twenty-first-century crises. Place-based living allows everyone to be part of the solution and, in doing so, adds meaning to lives while sowing seeds of hope.

Place-based living provides a path to regenerating nature, community, and local economies. Living connected to place reduces environmental harm by lowering GHGE, infringing less on wildlife habitat, and cutting waste and pollution. Relationships built in person and around local projects strengthen community bonds and resilience. Shopping at local businesses and seeking nearby experiences boosts the local economy.

Living connected to place requires more than personal commitment. Even with the best intentions, it's unlikely that people will live in place-based ways without external support. Context matters, and systems create the context for how people live.

Behavior, Context, and Systems

Over fifty individuals and organizations collaborated to write the national bestseller and official book of Earth Day 1990, *50 Simple Things You Can Do to Save the Earth*. Now well-known environmental crises are explained in the book, albeit in nascent terminologies such as *greenhouse effect* and *vanishing wildlife*. The fifty actions will be familiar to today's readers, too. Some are commonly practiced in many places, including recycling and bringing reusable bags to the grocery store. Other actions, and ones that generate the most emissions and pollution, haven't been widely adopted. Rather than driving less, we're driving more; meat-based diets remain more common than plant-based diets; and our consumption of goods and packaged food generates more and more plastic waste. How we get around, what we eat, and our consumption choices are arguably more complex than recycling and reusing shopping bags.

Another important difference, and one that's often overlooked, is that the context of people's lives does not widely support the most critical environmentally friendly behaviors. Human behavior depends heavily on context.[39] People's intentions, plus psychological nudges (such as emphasizing what people may lose with a less desirable behavior), may help people start to change their behavior. Supportive conditions, however, are generally needed for change to last and become a part of one's lifestyle.

Given the threat of climate change, we might have hoped to see total transformation across every sector of society in recent decades. Instead, corporate capitalist forces have attempted to shift responsibility for climate change to individuals while people remain stuck in systems that make it difficult to change their lives and reduce emissions.[40] Focusing on personal carbon footprints is a prime example. Weighing in on how Big Oil coined the term *carbon footprint*, Rebecca Solnit makes the connection between systems and personal choices: "Personal virtue is made more or less possible by the systems that surround us. If you have solar panels on your roof, it's because there's a market and manufacturers for solar and installers and maybe an arrangement with your power company to compensate you for energy you're putting into the grid. . . . I do some of my errands by bicycle because the San Francisco Bicycle Coalition worked for decades to put bicycle paths across the city and otherwise make it safer to get about on two wheels. I can take public transit because there is public transit."[41]

The essence of what Solnit experiences is transportation and energy systems that provide a supportive context for her to use clean energy, ride a bike, and take public transit. Humanity can live in climate- and planet-friendly ways, but people need support from their contexts.

My research identified four types of contexts that influence human behavior.

Physical context includes the infrastructure and services that relate to a specific behavior. With the transportation system, these include mass transit routes and types, street design, parking availability, bike paths, and sidewalks. These elements vary from one location to the next and influence how people get around. If it takes an hour to get to a destination by bus but only half an hour by car, and there's plenty of parking when a person gets there, he will almost certainly drive. But if a clean, uncrowded streetcar delivers a person quickly to her destination, and parking is scarce there, she'll likely take the streetcar rather than deal with the hassles of traffic and parking.

Cultural context involves what is popular and accepted in society. For example, reusing shopping bags and travel coffee mugs has become widely accepted in numerous communities. Riding bikes to most places is considered normal in cities like Copenhagen and Amsterdam.

Social context overlaps with culture but centers on social influence within one's immediate context. These conditions include social norms: the rules and standards that result from the attitudes and expectations of people close to themselves toward a specified behavior or are based on observations of their behavior. If colleagues are enthusiastic about transit and often take it to work, chances are good that others in that workplace will, too.

Economic context also plays a large role in how people live, particularly in how it intersects with the physical, cultural, and social context. The price of housing and goods and services relative to one's income influence where one lives, how one gets around, and how much and what one consumes. Many families and individuals are priced out of living in cities and neighborhoods that have limited affordable housing supplies, an economic context based on land use decisions and patterns (physical context). Consumerism (cultural context) has led to prioritizing an abundance of cheap goods and the low prices create an economic context for buying more.

Physical, cultural, social, and economic contexts form a rich web of influence around human habits and ways of living. Systems shape the context for human behavior. Living connected to place is possible at scale within supportive systems. Individuals, for example, are more likely to recycle if all packaging is truly recyclable and recycled and consumers aren't asked to sort recyclables or drop them off at a distant collection site. It's easier to eat sustainably when a person has access to farmer's markets, easy and delicious plant-based recipes, and public health initiatives like Meatless Mondays. Integrating sustainable behaviors like these into everyday life requires a context of supportive systems, which will be the subject of chapter 2.

PLACE-BASED SYSTEMS, WELL-BEING, AND REGENERATION

> **The future cannot be predicted, but it can be imagined and made real with love. Systems cannot be controlled, but they can be designed and redesigned.**
>
> —Donella Meadows

In the fourth season of the television series *The Good Place*, the main characters learn that in recent years, no one who has died has made it to the Good Place. They think there must be a flaw in the tracking system. Why is no one earning enough points to get into the Good Place? They find a human who seems to be perfectly selfless, and still, he does not get into the Good Place when he dies.

Upon investigation, they learn that nearly every choice humans make in modern society has negative consequences. A simple tomato is produced using greenhouse gas–emitting energy and toxic pesticides, shipped thousands of miles, and processed by workers in poor conditions with low wages. No one can earn points when nearly every choice leads to harm.

This predicament is not far from the truth, particularly regarding the climate crisis. No matter how carefully one tries to live, personal choices within corporate capitalist systems ripple across the globe, doing damage often hidden from the end consumer. People can never be "good enough" by themselves through their choices. We need an overhaul of the context in which people live.

In this chapter, I lay out the place-based systems that support living connected to place and lead to the regeneration of nature, community, and local economies. Within these systems, lifestyles benefit personal, community, and environmental well-being at the same time. When living connected to place, a person may be able to get into the *The Good Place* after all.

Place-Based Systems: Mixed-Use Neighborhoods to Self-Reliant Regions

When place-based systems shape how people live, regions, counties, cities, and communities promote well-being and become climate-friendly, resilient, and thriving. The influence of corporate capitalism fades as people gravitate to place-based ways of living that are not just viable but attractive and life-enriching as well. By reducing alienation, place-based systems get at the root cause of our twenty-first-century crises, increase people's life satisfaction, and put society on the path to regeneration.

In contrast to corporate capitalist systems, place-based systems add up to mixed-income, mixed-use neighborhoods and self-reliant, or self-sufficient, regions (see table 2.1). Housing is available and affordable near work, shopping, and recreation. Through the design of community spaces and the availability of nearby nature spaces, people connect more readily to their community and the natural world. Transportation infrastructure makes it easy to get around without a car. Building energy, food, and consumer goods are regionally produced and conserved. Place-based systems make all this possible.

To break down disparities and ensure that all people have access to healthy, thriving communities, place-based systems, by design, help make places inclusive and welcoming to people of all races, ethnicities, incomes, and backgrounds. It starts with a housing system that enables all people to live in the city where they work. In addition, trust broken between local institutions and Black, Indigenous, and people of color (BIPOC) communities must be rebuilt. We see this in terms of policing, of course, and how communities have been devastated in order to build infrastructure like freeways or power plants. Repairing these relationships through community-led planning for place-based systems is critical to dismantling systemic racism and inequities in communities.

Each place-based system has a geographic scope that allows for the sourcing, production, and distribution of what people need in their daily lives. Many systems or system components fit within mixed-used neighborhoods and can primarily be directed and supported at the city or county level. Some elements of these systems, like public transportation, require regional coordination to be effective. Other systems require more regional focus to ensure adequate supply for a population.

Food, energy, and consumer goods place-based systems generally fit best at the regional level. Self-reliant regions produce the food (chap. 9), building energy (chap. 10), and consumer goods (chap. 11) that a population needs within regional boundaries. The composition of regions varies but often includes a grouping of counties in a metropolitan area like the sixteen-county Chicago

TABLE 2.1 From corporate capitalist to place-based systems

EVERYDAY LIFE SYSTEM	CORPORATE CAPITALIST	PLACE-BASED
Housing	Housing is segregated from other land use and by income. Affordability and supply are limited in many regions.	Housing is available and affordable in mixed-income, mixed-use communities.
Local business and work	Corporations provide jobs, such as in chain stores and warehouses, that provide little meaning or satisfaction. Many people struggle to get by on jobs with low wages.	Local businesses provide meaningful work and shopping for people where they live.
Transportation	Automobiles are the dominant mode. Other modes are often unreliable or dangerous.	Active, community-oriented, and pollution-free modes are easily accessed and safe.
Community spaces	Community spaces are limited, unsafe, and dominated by cars.	Community spaces are safe, car-free, and vibrant.
Nature spaces	Concrete and cement cover nature where people live. Nature spaces are polluted in BIPOC communities.	Nature spaces are abundant, accessible, nearby, and safe.
Food	Food is generally processed, high in sugar and fat, and nutrient-deficient. Meat-based diets predominate. Most foods are globally sourced. Much food is wasted.	Regional, healthy, and seasonal food is available and affordable. Food waste is minimal.
Building energy	Building energy is generated from fossil fuels and large-scale renewables. Electricity is transmitted over long distances. Energy waste is commonplace.	Building energy is regionally harvested from renewable sources, and conservation and efficiency are default choices.
Consumer goods	Consumer goods are made globally, sold in big-box stores and online corporate marketplaces, and are disposable.	Consumer goods are regionally made, shared, repaired, and recirculated with minimal waste.

metro area. In states with small populations or land size, the region may be the state or group of states, such as New England. Each region can encompass components of place-based systems that cannot be fully executed at the county and city levels.

Applying the concept of watersheds to regional systems, foodsheds, energysheds, fibersheds, and makingsheds can emerge. These regional sheds provide opportunities for local businesses, careers, and jobs in various sectors. The sheds also facilitate thriving regional economies where wealth is not exported to corporate headquarters and is more equitably shared. Each person, in turn, becomes more connected to what gives him life and comfort and feels more compelled to protect the nature and community that provides it. As we will see in part 2, self-reliant regions are much more possible than we have been led to believe.

Livable, vibrant mixed-use neighborhoods bring together many place-based systems: mixed-income communities with affordable housing (chap. 4), local business and work (chap. 5), biking and pedestrian infrastructure and access to public transit (chap. 6), abundant community spaces (chap. 7), and nearby nature spaces (chap. 8). Elements of some of the regional systems can also be found at this more local level, such as microgrids in the building energy system (chap. 10). These neighborhoods have small environmental footprints and promote resilience and equity through community bonds and local economies.

Mixed-use neighborhoods and self-reliant regions foster a sense of belonging and positive interdependence. Mixed-income housing sends a message that everyone belongs. Local business and work become intertwined with the well-being of a place and its residents. People biking, walking, and enjoying nearby public spaces feel more a part of their community. The closer food, energy, and other needs are sourced, the more people identify with their place and what it has to offer. The sense of belonging and interdependence adds happiness, meaning, and hope to people's lives, motivating further change in systems and living.

There must be clear links between place-based systems and addressing our biggest problems like climate change to solicit investment in them.

Climate Solutions

Mitigating the climate crisis requires getting greenhouse gas emissions (GHGE) to zero by 2050 and keeping the emissions at zero. Corporate capitalism that depends on the ever-expanding consumption of resources and energy makes that unachievable. In contrast, place-based systems require that we rely on and protect the resources and energy available in our regions and localities. They provide the most robust path for addressing overconsumption and getting to and staying at zero GHGE.

Direct emissions from transportation and building energy decrease significantly through place-based systems. People use personal vehicles much less in place-based transportation systems. Robust regional public transit systems play an essential role. In 2021, C40 Cities, a global network of almost one hundred mayors of large cities taking climate action, set a goal of doubling global public transit use by 2030 as a crucial step toward meeting the 1.5 degrees Celsius target.[1] Accessible, attractive community and nature spaces encourage people to get outside where they use less energy. A regional energy system reduces electricity lost in transmission and capitalizes on local renewable sources.

Indirect emissions from food and consumer goods can move toward zero when shifting their sourcing, production, and disposal to regions and localities. Regional consumer goods and food systems depend on minimal transportation. Local goods produced in regions with clean power further reduce emissions. Researchers estimate that shifting lifestyles away from the mass consumption of imported goods to ones oriented around local services, including entertainment and social activities, will generate two to three times fewer emissions.[2] Thriving places help us loosen our addiction to stuff and prioritize what really matters for happiness: experiences rooted in community, nature, and social connections.

We need place-based systems across regions, counties, and cities to drive emission-reducing changes in human behavior. Climate actions are integrated into people's lives and become the default choice in place-based systems.

Local Resilience

Place-based systems support economic, climate, and community resilience. Thriving local economies and community bonds that result from these systems provide a foundation for local resilience.

Mixed-use neighborhoods, derived from intersecting place-based systems, support strong local economies. When local businesses and organizations predominate, and you don't need a car to work or shop, corporate capitalism loses its power over communities. The dollars flow out less, stay in the community, and start a virtuous cycle of local investment and spending.

A fabric of local businesses avoids overreliance on one or a few industries, as has happened in American cities and towns built around a corporation or industry. When the industry experiences a downturn, the whole city or town dependent on it suffers. If the corporation leaves, the place can be devastated. This hardship has happened to communities across the Rust Belt and other regions of the United States. In contrast, a place-based work system includes a diversity of businesses and increases the economic resilience of the place.

Place-based systems also protect against external threats. When a public health crisis like COVID-19 hits, self-reliant regions with food, energy, and essential goods sourcing can manage and even close themselves off until the danger subsides. Global supply chain breakdowns, increasing with climate change events, cause less harm when regional economic self-reliance increases. Regions and communities with place-based systems foster resilience to survive and even thrive in the face of threats.

When people work, shop, and play in their neighborhoods, they build stronger bonds with each other, promoting community resilience. These bonds include diverse local businesses that know residents and their needs. Community-based nonprofits and groups, from community health clinics to food banks to community gardens, also support community resilience. Networks of these organizations create a community of care that helps individuals and the community get through challenges.

The small rural town of Orland, Maine, demonstrates how a community of care promotes resilience. Journalist Marguerite Holloway describes the town's resource center, founded in 1970, for low-income and homeless families: "[Originally] a crafts-making operation for the local community and a gift shop—and then a child-care center, a shelter program, an auto repair garage, a sawmill, a shingle mill, a garden and a greenhouse, a GED (General Education Development) program, a food co-op that has become a food bank, and a home-construction unit."[3] More recently, the center added a wood bank to provide residents in need with firewood for home heating, making use of wood from trees killed by extreme weather and pests. Orland's center is essentially a mixed-use neighborhood that advances equity and resilience centered on an ethic of caring for one another.

Alignment of Places of Well-Being with Place-Based Systems

The positive impacts of place-based systems in mitigating the climate crisis and promoting local resilience motivate institutions, organizations, and individuals to work toward their creation. Support will be limited, however, unless the case can be made for how place-based systems directly benefit people's lives and their well-being.

Whether organized at the neighborhood, city, county, or regional level, place-based systems support a high quality of life. Places found to have high levels of well-being among their populations share many of the attributes of place-based systems. Using data from the annual *Gallup-Sharecare Well-Being Index*, Dan Buettner of National Geographic and researchers identified the world's and America's happiest places (connected to the *Blue Zones Habits for a Happier, Healthier Life*, mentioned in chap. 1). Buettner describes the impact of these places on their residents: "The places where they live . . . give them an invisible lift, constantly nudging them into behaviors that favor long-term well-being."[4] These Blue Zones of happiness demonstrate the positive relationship between place-based systems and how people live.

Costa Rica, Denmark, and Singapore rank among the highest on the combined measures of how people rate their lives, daily happiness, and physical well-being.[5] Each of these countries has between five and six million people, which is comparable in population to a US metropolitan region.

In Copenhagen, the biggest population center in Denmark, a robust biking infrastructure and culture support people in biking nearly everywhere. Social and cohousing communities enable people of different income levels to live near amenities. Residents in cohousing are known to cook for one another in social gatherings.

Despite a poor record of human rights abuses, Singapore exhibits high social cohesion and interaction among its three major ethnic groups (Malay, Indian, and Chinese). Typically, generations of a family live with or near each other. With the second-highest population density among countries worldwide, Singaporeans live near work, places to shop, and recreation. Amidst this density, Singapore has an impressive array of nature spaces for daily connection to nature.[6]

People in Costa Rica have much less financially than those in many other countries, yet they are found to be some of the happiest people in the world. Costa Ricans generally have easy access to nearby nature and community spaces. Social interaction in daily life is prioritized in the culture.

In the happiest cities in America, Buettner found specific conditions that supported people in living well.[7] These cities had ample sidewalks and safe streets; nearby nature, including parks, open space, and trees; opportunities for civic engagement; a clean environment; and availability of healthy food.

In Boulder, Colorado, the city with the highest level of well-being in America, people have easy access to recreation and nature. The streets are built for people, not just cars. There is a large pedestrian mall in the center of town. People often choose biking over driving cars, as reflected in bike-to-work rates seventeen times higher than the national average. There are no billboards, which reduces the presence of corporate advertising. The city supports sustainable local food production and equitable access to healthy food. With community gardens, agriculture in nearby open spaces, farmers' markets, and programs for food assistance, all residents have access to local, healthy, and seasonal food.

In Boulder, Singapore, and Copenhagen, as well as cities and towns in Costa Rica, conditions support well-being and make it easier to live locally. Residents regularly interact with their neighbors and so come to trust them. People are outside walking in their communities and experiencing nature. They have high rates of healthy behaviors and low rates of smoking, drug abuse, and obesity. They are engaged with and confident in their local government with few exceptions.

The place-based systems align well with the characteristics of Blue Zones and the research-based well-being factors discussed in chapter 1 (see table 2.2). This alignment is not a coincidence. These systems lead to conditions that support the primary ingredients of personal well-being: physical health, mental capital, social connections, community connections, and nature connections. Affordable housing near amenities builds community and social connections. Access

TABLE 2.2 Place-based systems and personal well-being

PLACE-BASED SYSTEM	CHARACTERISTICS OF BLUE ZONES	WELL-BEING FACTORS (CHAP. 1)
Housing	Mixed-use neighborhoods; community assets valued	Community, social, and nature connections; financial security (less money spent on transportation)
Work	Local business and work opportunities	Community connections; financial security (keep money in the local economy)
Transportation	Sidewalks and safe streets; biking infrastructure; less car dependence	Physical health and mental capital; community and nature connections; financial security (less money spent on transportation)
Community spaces	Community gathering spaces; trust in neighbors and local institutions	Community and social connections; physical health (time outside)
Nature spaces	Nearby nature (parks, open spaces, trees, etc.)	Nature connections; mental capital and physical health (time outside)
Food	Access to local, healthy food (farmers markets, local farms, gardens, grocery stores, etc.)	Physical health; community and nature connections
Building energy	Time outside and on the front porch	Financial security (less energy needed inside)
Consumer goods	Emphasis on experiences and interaction (less stuff)	Financial security (spend less on stuff)

to local, healthy, and seasonal food promotes health and connection to nature. Regular time outdoors in community and nature spaces, combined with healthy, active modes of everyday transportation, promotes physical fitness and improves mental capital (i.e., cognitive and emotional health). Community and nature connections are also enhanced through shopping at local businesses and farmers' markets, consumer goods made and recirculated in local regions, harvesting local renewable energy, and local work opportunities.

Importantly, the place-based systems also support financial security. This essential well-being factor is facilitated in multiple ways by place-based systems. Local businesses provide more ownership opportunities and fair wages in comparison to corporations squeezing labor costs to continually grow profits. More money stays in the local economy and goes to people's wallets in the community. Walking, biking, and using transit is far more affordable than owning, maintaining, insuring, and fueling a car. Time outside in community and nature spaces leads to less money spent on household energy (heating, cooling, lighting, etc.). Sharing and treasuring consumer goods and minimizing waste means less money spent on stuff.

Place-based systems can meaningfully address the inequality crisis, increasing financial security for more people. In corporate capitalist systems, the privileged and affluent often have large homes, multiple cars, plentiful electronics and digital devices, and access to a seemingly unlimited amount of globally produced consumer goods. Place-based systems emphasizing connections and experiences help break the attachment to material items. In this way, they help reduce the drive for more and more money that has widened economic inequality. With place-based systems also supporting regional and local career and work opportunities, wealth can be distributed more fairly than in the global economy controlled by corporations and elites. With place-based systems, we make it possible for more people to live secure and satisfying lives.

Transformation and Regeneration

Place-based systems that combine into mixed-use neighborhoods and self-reliant regions lead to the societal transformation we need for regeneration. In contrast to what happens in the global economy, the impacts of individual and collective choices cannot be easily hidden or placed on those with less power and resources. The more a person comes to depend on his locality for his needs, the more likely he is to carefully steward resources, minimize pollution, and take care of other people.

Place-based systems transform lives and communities with far-reaching benefits to people and nature. They embody interconnection, mutual care, and respect for all life and diminish alienation bred by corporate capitalism. Thriving local economies, livable communities, prioritization of in-person relationships, and a culture based on experiences more than consumerism emerge from a confluence of place-based systems. Place-based systems show us that transformation is possible.

Self-Reliant Regions

With well-managed resources and a conservation ethic, regional self-reliance can challenge the global economy narrative. Regional economies can thrive as money is circulated and multiplied locally. When faced with the challenge of producing what we need within our regions, innovation flourishes and leads to productive land use, less harmful means of sourcing inputs, and circular economies with little waste. Self-reliant regions unify people across them by building local wealth, resilience, and cultural connection to their place.

Place-based innovation can arise in many ways at the regional level. Changes in feeding elephants at the Reteti Elephant Sanctuary in Kenya provide a surprising and interesting example.[8] Before the COVID-19 pandemic and resulting disruption to trade, the elephant calves drank imported human infant formula. During the pandemic, the elephant caretakers found another source for feeding the calves: goat milk from nearby pastoralists. This solution increased regional economic activity and strengthened ties between villagers and elephant caretakers. The goat milk was nutritious for the elephants and cheaper than the infant formula.

For regional self-reliance to reach its full potential, it must be understood as interdependence in which we rely on nature and community and help regenerate both. This reciprocity is much more possible at the regional scale than at the global scale of corporate capitalism. People can see and experience what sustains them in their localities and be motivated to take care of it. The Movement Generation Justice and Ecology Project based in Oakland, California, illuminates what an economy can be using this more local perspective: "Economy means management [*nomy*] of home [*eco*]. How we organize our relationships in a place, ideally, to take care of the place and each other. . . . The purpose of our economy could be turning land, life, and labor into . . . a balanced web of stable relationships."[9] This place-based and relationship-based understanding of the economy would serve us well and can be manifested through place-based systems.

Regional self-reliance develops and strengthens a sense of place. Local culture and character strengthen as the types of food, consumer goods, and energy sources reflect what's available in the region. Connection to nature grows with increased proximity to the natural resources that sustain us. People deepen their familiarity, knowledge, and relationships with the producers of their food, energy, and consumer goods.

The Regenerative Communities Network supports twenty-six bioregional network initiatives across eight countries.[10] Much like place-based systems, it aims to transform people's relationships with the places where they live and regenerate biological and social systems. The network seeks to create conditions for all life to thrive within self-reliant regional systems.

Costa Rica Regenerativa is one of these network initiatives and has five primary projects underway. Its regenerative agriculture and food security project replenishes depleted soils and provides long-term local food sources. The food is grown organically in community and family gardens. Local chicken and egg production are included. Another food-related program is the holistic livestock management hub, which supports regenerative ranching that restores soil and improves ecosystems. A project aim is also to facilitate opportunities for jobs and small businesses and thus help build local business and work systems. The initiative gets into the housing system with its regenerative real estate development project, which encourages environmentally responsible development that enhances rather than depletes nature and community. The initiative supports a sixteen-month program for young people to earn a certificate in regenerative entrepreneurship in which they develop a project to revitalize local nature and community. Through building place-based systems for food, work, local business, housing, community spaces, and nature spaces, Costa Rica Regenerativa is regenerating nature, community, and local economies.

Mixed-Use Neighborhoods

Place-based systems change at the neighborhood level includes urban revitalization and suburban retrofits. Urban revitalization can learn from the suburbs by adding amenities, such as nature spaces, that improve people's quality of life. Likewise, suburbs can be retrofitted to have some urban feel by adding housing and mixed uses to neighborhoods near existing main streets and downtowns. This urbanization-suburbanization blend can help spread mixed-use neighborhoods that support well-being and regeneration.

In Buffalo, New York, the nonprofit PUSH (People United for Sustainable Housing) supported a twenty-five-acre Green Development Zone on the city's low-income west side. Guided by residents' needs and energy audits, affordable housing was built or retrofitted to be energy-efficient and save money with lower utility bills. Many of the new houses included local solar power. Vacant lots transformed into community gardens and parks. Housing was mainly built by neighborhood residents. Among other local workforce projects, youth help grow and distribute organic produce from urban farms. Combining workforce development, affordable housing, community-based renewable energy, building energy retrofits, and urban agriculture created a mixed-use neighborhood that weaved together multiple place-based systems.

In Toronto, Canada, Riverdale is a streetcar-dependent (not car-dependent) suburb developed in the 1960s. A subway now connects to it, keeping it transit-oriented. It has a variety of housing types and prices. The neighborhood centers around a large park and several small parklets spread throughout it. Narrow, tree-lined streets slow down car traffic, making for pleasant, safe biking and walking. Children can easily walk to their neighborhood schools. Nearby commercial streets provide multiple grocery stores and places to shop. Parking lots are small, freeing up land for other uses. Cafés and other community gathering spaces are located on residential streets. Place-based transportation, housing, local business and work, nature spaces, and community spaces systems make it easy for River-dale residents to live connected to place.

In *Retrofitting Suburbia* and a follow-up book with thirty-two case studies, Ellen Dunham-Jones and June Williamson explain and document how single-use, suburban landforms are being transformed. They show how shopping malls, office parks, parking lots, and other past developments have been retrofitted into mixed-use neighborhoods. Their examples give us hope that change is possible and that suburbs can go from being drivers of environmental and social crises to part of the solution.

Amanda Holson Hurley, author of *Radical Suburbs*, also sees promise in and documents a changing suburbia that reflects a convergence of place-based systems. She sees the urbanization of suburbs as an emerging landform, which includes pedestrian downtowns, light-rail lines, and denser forms of housing. Hurley notes the growing preference for this type of land use in the suburbs, especially among younger generations.

Bold plans for changing suburbs are being approved and implemented. In 2021, Mesa, Arizona, retrofitted its downtown. The Grove on Main project added 240 apartments, twelve townhomes, ground-floor retail, and landscaped open space.[11] The development was built around a light-rail line. If such change can happen in this auto-centric, large suburb outside Phoenix, it can happen anywhere.

Between San Francisco and San Jose, the suburban town of Burlingame has laid out similar changes in its general plan, including a town square on a for-mer parking lot and a mixed-use neighborhood in a former industrial section of town. The rezoning allows industrial warehouses to be converted to six-story apartment buildings to house potentially thousands of residents. These building conversions add much-needed affordable housing in a suburb with high hous-ing prices that have forced lower-wage workers to live elsewhere and commute long distances. Light industrial and indoor recreational businesses will remain, and others, including restaurants, will be added, allowing people to work close to where they live. Within a ten-minute walk, the regional subway and commuter train from San Francisco to San Jose can be accessed. An existing main street is within walking and biking distance. Open space and streetscape improvements are also being planned to enhance the livability and walkability of the future mixed-use neighborhood.

Building a mixed-use neighborhood from the ground up further demon-strates the potential of place-based systems in promoting a high quality of life and collective well-being.

With the rise of online shopping, shopping malls have been in decline. In their place, mixed-use neighborhoods are being built. In 2024, Cupertino, California, approved a fifty-acre housing, office, retail, and parkland development on the land where a large shopping mall existed. The development will serve as Cupertino's new downtown neighborhood. Resident input helped guide the planning. Dining, entertainment, and community events will anchor community life, including farmers' markets and music performances. Six miles of trails and bike paths will encourage active transportation. Time outdoors will be supported by forty acres of open space, including a twenty-nine-acre green roof, the largest in the world. Playgrounds, recreational lawns, and fields will support youth activities. Shopping malls and other large land-use conversions like this show how mixed-use neighborhoods that reduce car dependency and promote place-based living can emerge in the suburbs.

The 175-acre EcoVillage in Ithaca, New York, started in 1991 to meet residents' needs for shelter, food, energy, livelihood, and social connection. Located two miles from downtown Ithaca, the EcoVillage consists of three cohousing neighborhoods that house 220 residents in 100 highly energy-efficient homes. Over half of the village buildings' electricity comes from rooftop and ground-mounted solar arrays in the village. Consumer goods sharing is supported by reusing electronics, clothes, toys, and furniture. EcoVillage's ten-acre fruit and vegetable farm and five-acre berry farm provide produce for residents and others in the surrounding area. A ten-acre teaching farm supports agriculture workforce development. Almost half of the residents work in the village through farming, an on-site B&B, and remote work. The remaining half work in nearby Ithaca in professional services, as small business owners, and in other types of work. The ecological footprint of EcoVillage residents is 70 percent less than the average American.[12] Local living enabled by many place-based systems is regenerating nature, community, and the local economy.

Social and personal benefits are highly evident at the EcoVillage, with residents reporting that they enjoy a high quality of life. There is an abundance of nearby nature and community spaces. Shared spaces include children's play areas, laundry facilities, offices, dining rooms, and community kitchens in three common houses. Organic farming and wildlife habitat occupy 90 percent of the land. Two swimming and skating ponds, community gardens, hiking trails, and play spaces keep people active and connected.

Children play, interact with, and learn from adults and other children across the village. There are no cars to contend with when playing outside. Nature, playgrounds, and indoor recreation are always available.

EcoVillage Ithaca may sound like a commune, making it seem impractical and ideologically misaligned with many Americans. Residents volunteer two to three hours a week in the village, and sharing is central to living there. However, there is a balance with private living. The cohousing design includes private homes with kitchens. Shared dinners are optional. Many people's livelihoods are based nearby but outside the village. Residents have cars but keep them parked on the village perimeter.

The EcoVillage concept has become popular. There are more than ten thousand Ecovillages worldwide.[13] Many produce their own food and renewable energy. Many of the villages, like the one in Ithaca, are on the outskirts of a town or in rural locations. Ecovillage-like neighborhoods are starting to spread to cities.

In Utrecht, Netherlands, Merwede is a seventeen-block district that is being redeveloped and will house twelve thousand residents in six thousand homes.[14] Thirty-five percent of the new homes will be social or affordable housing, and an additional 25 percent will be priced in the middle of the market. It will be largely car-free with bike and pedestrian infrastructure and nearby amenities including shopping and schools, and it will be located only a kilometer from pedestrian-friendly downtown Utrecht. The canal-side setting and plan for abundant, car-free green space will support daily opportunities for nature connection. Sports fields, a town square, and a promenade along the canal will encourage community and social connections. In addition to all of these place-based systems, Merwede will source hyperlocal energy for heating and cooling via the canal from an underground heat and cold storage facility. Developments like Merwede exemplify mixed-use neighborhoods that incorporate many place-based systems.

* * *

There is great demand and need for walkable, livable places in urban centers and suburban cities and towns. Seventy percent of Americans want to live in these types of neighborhoods, but not nearly enough of these neighborhoods exist.[15] Consequently, property values are high in these neighborhoods, locking out most people. As Daniel Herriges of Strong Towns puts it, "It's precisely because 98% of the North American built environment is so blah that the 2% of places that are really well-designed environments quickly get bid up by the rich and become inaccessible to the rest of us."[16] Urban revitalization and suburban retrofits into mixed-use neighborhoods must be deployed at scale across the United States and the world. Leveraging place-based systems and combined with self-reliant regions, they have the potential to radically alter our lives for the better, benefiting both people and the planet.

Still, in modern society, the pull away from meaningful connection to place in our lives is unrelenting. It will not be easy to reduce the role of digital devices, automobiles, consumerism, high energy use, meat-based diets, and a global food supply in everyday life. There will be fierce resistance from vested economic interests that profit from corporate capitalist systems that shape human behavior.

In addition, people will have internal resistance because habits, identity, abilities, and a sense of personal control are interwoven with these systems.

We need a guide to systems change that can be applied across contexts and overcome status quo resistance. In chapter 3, I detail the systems-change approach that is being used to move from corporate capitalism to place as the dominant influence on the systems that shape our lives.

THE PATH TO PLACE-BASED
SYSTEMS CHANGE

**If we are not acting to change the system, we are complicit, casting
our silent vote to maintain the status quo.**

—Soul Fire Farm on the unceded land of the Stockbridge-Munsee Band of the
Mohican Nation (now Petersburg, New York)

Systems change is difficult work. It's hard to know where to start. Common guidance is to determine a leverage point and take a small step to make use of it. This approach helps a group get out of the planning and thinking stage and into action. It is, however, essential to choose initial and future steps that directly address what holds the current systems and our associated problems in place.

Current systems primarily result from the grip of corporate capitalism on power, land use, and culture. These three factors help maintain the status quo of corporate dominance in society and make it hard to change systems.

At the same time, these factors illuminate the pathway to systems change. If corporate capitalism has used power, land use, and culture to shape society and people's lives, then we can use those same factors to change systems. In this chapter, we'll explore how regions, counties, cities, and communities can effectively approach systems change using the levers of shifting power, transforming land use, and resetting culture. In addition, a fourth lever of leveraging other systems will be introduced as a means to break down silos and use change in one system to boost change in another system.

The systems-change levers provide a flexible approach that is not dependent on a particular time or context. As we'll explore throughout part 2, they can be applied to all of the systems that shape how people live in places across the globe. The levers answer the "what" of systems change; in other words, what do we need to alter to change systems? To begin understanding how these levers work, we'll first examine how corporate capitalism has effectively used them.

What Holds Corporate Capitalist Systems in Place

Despite growing interest in place-based living, it remains mainly in the margins. We're largely locked into high energy use, driving cars, mass consumerism, digital living, and dependence on the global economy. People may set out to live in ways that benefit their communities and the environment, then change course when they encounter barriers.[1] In many American regions, counties, and cities, it's hard to eat a local and plant-based diet, take daily trips without a car, use local and renewable energy, or shop at local businesses.

We need to understand what's getting in the way of breaking these harmful patterns. Who has the power to influence political decisions? Who has power in the marketplace? What are the dominant land uses and what behaviors do they support? What are the dominant cultural narratives, attitudes, and behaviors? Probing these questions, it becomes clear that corporate capitalism pulls the strings of the systems that guide our lives today.

Power

Powerful corporate interests have configured systems to their benefit. Global industries and multinational corporations exercise their sheer economic power to maintain the status quo that allows them to grow profits. The largest global sectors include automobile, fossil fuels, real estate and tourism, as well as the banking and insurance industries that generate much of their revenue from the former.[2] Collectively, these industries accounted for $35.5 trillion (T) in revenue in 2024, or 32 percent of global gross domestic product. Many of our systems have been built by these clusters of corporate power (see table 3.1).

The technology industry has grown rapidly, edging its way into the most prominent global industries. By August 2023, the so-called Magnificent Seven

TABLE 3.1 Systems and corporate power influence

SYSTEM	CORPORATE POWER
Housing	Big Real Estate
Work	Corporate employers, Big Retail, and Big Tech
Transportation	Big Auto, Big Oil, and Big Tech
Public spaces (community + nature)	Big Auto and Big Tech
Food	Big Ag
Building energy	Big Oil and Gas and Big Utilities
Consumer goods	Big Retail (and advertising), Big Plastic

of Big Tech—Apple, Microsoft, Google parent Alphabet, Amazon, Nvidia, Tesla, and Meta Platforms—accounted for over \$12T in combined stock market value, representing 27 percent of the S&P 500.[3] Amazon and Walmart (Big Retail) have become consumer marketplaces that sell just about everything through big-box stores and online platforms. Their revenue now surpasses all other corporations except for a few international oil corporations.[4] Over the past couple of decades, Big Tech and Big Retail have led a dramatic shift from locally oriented economies to a global economy favoring their economic interests. Likewise, Big Ag corporations have created a global food economy to maximize their profits.

Large corporations exert their power on the government to secure many advantages. Corporate interests, directly and indirectly through trade associations, invest heavily in lobbying and other means of political influence. The wealthy elite who control these industries buy politicians through donations. Campaign dollars in the US from the top one-tenth percent of donors grew from 10 percent of the total in 1982 to 46 percent by 2018, with four hundred mega-donors accounting for 22 percent of political donations.[5] As political scientists Jacob Hacker and Paul Pierson document and share in their book *Let Them Eat Tweets*, "America's corporate and financial elites . . . have become much bigger, much richer, much better organized—and hence much more powerful."[6] They have done this, in part, using "dark money," which is virtually unrestricted funds that flow to nonprofits not required to disclose donors. This phenomenon has surged since the 2010 *Citizens United vs. FEC* Supreme Court ruling.

We know that "big money" dominates politics. Corporations, developers, and other corporate-like entities pressure elected officials to support their interests over those of local communities. People may want change, but a big business with deep pockets will likely have more influence.

Local leaders may have the best of intentions to improve the well-being of the communities they serve, but they are bombarded by shiny new ideas from corporate interests. Advanced technologies are often central to these so-called solutions that purport to improve local conditions. In reality, these technologies do little more than boost the profits of corporations based in other locations or corporate startups seeking to scale across geographies.

"Smart cities" have been touted as the cities of the future in which technology and data drive nearly everything in the city, from government services to transportation. Renowned urbanist and architect Jan Gehl sees through the veil of smart cities, particularly around how autonomous cars are presented as the solution to urban problems: "As far as I can see, no problems would be solved, except the problems of the automobile industry—how they can sell another five billion units. . . . Whenever you hear the word 'smart,' beware, because that is somebody who wants to sell as many millions as possible of some new gimmick.

And he is not necessarily giving you a better quality of life."[7] Autonomous ride-share vehicles emerged in cities like San Francisco in 2023, furthering car dependency and adding to car traffic, which discourages people from biking, walking, or using public transit (especially when buses or light rail get stuck in traffic). If Big Auto, Big Tech, and their affiliates (such as consulting and financial services firms) continue to have the ear of politicians, we will have smart cities that benefit corporations far more than those who live there.

Corporations and elites have used their power and influence to win favorable policies, deregulation, subsidies, and public funding. With government support, multinational corporations have built a playing field highly advantageous to their interests, in which markets for their products continually expand and global supply chains keep their costs low and profits high.

Land Use

Suburban sprawl provides the clearest example of how corporate capitalist interests dictate land use. Big retail stores, from Walmart to Dollar General, take up a lot of space with their large stores and parking lots. They're rarely located close to where people live and encourage mass purchasing, making it hard to shop without a car, which adds to the demand for streets, freeways, and parking lots. Big Real Estate, with the support of Big Banks, develops residential subdivisions and tracts away from city and town centers. Big Auto and Big Oil have long embraced and facilitated the separation of shopping, housing, offices, and other amenities such that people must travel across large networks of roads and highways designated for motor vehicles. With Big Tech now involved in the electric vehicle industry, there is further corporate reliance on suburban sprawl for selling products.

Corporations have had such an impact on land use that changing how people live seems daunting, at the least. Automobile dependence remains as long as we lack viable transportation options and must travel considerable distances among places to live, shop, work, and recreate. Even the most ardent advocates may say car-dependent travel is an immutable reality. Increasingly larger homes support Big Retail and Big Tech. They provide more space for living indoors and accumulating consumer goods and digital services. Land dedicated to manufacturing and distribution centers for material goods worldwide facilitates consumerism and the global economy. All these land uses cater to corporate capitalist interests.

In addition, Big Ag drives an unsustainable food system that uses vast tracts of land. Worldwide, agriculture accounts for 44 percent of habitable land use.[8] Between land used for animal feed crops and grazing, 80 percent of agricultural land is used for livestock.[9] Meat-packers, fast-food chains, and other corporations grow profits from selling all this meat. Their operations consume land that could be conserved or used for more land-efficient food production and other purposes. Like other corporate capitalist land uses, meat-based production holds in place a food system that benefits corporate interests rather than local economies or people.

Culture

The emphasis on convenience in American culture supports corporate interests through consumerism and the everyday use of automobiles and digital technologies. Columbia University professor Tim Wu calls it the "tyranny of convenience": "In the developed nations of the 21st century, convenience—that is, more efficient and easier ways of doing personal tasks—has emerged as perhaps the most powerful force shaping our individual lives and our economies."[10] The sense of escalating time pressure and increased pace has led to a vigilant pursuit of convenience in everyday life. Saving time becomes paramount to personal decisions. People have come to expect one-click shopping, same-day delivery, and access to everything they need with little effort.

Convenience is often prioritized over other values and needs. Fast food emphasizes convenience, low prices, and addictive flavoring over food quality, dining experience, and health. The convenience of driving a car from one's driveway is valued over community and social connections, financial security, physical health, and mental capital. Cars negatively impact these well-being factors by keeping people behind windshields and disconnected from one another, costing lots of money to own and maintain, promoting a sedentary lifestyle, and causing anger when stuck in traffic or feeling delayed by another road user's behavior.

As Wu and others argue, when convenience is the dominant force in people's lives, it precludes other experiences—like walking and exploring, tending a garden, repairing something—that emphasize the quality of experience over its speed. Our culture's overvaluing of convenience, supported by corporate capitalism, makes living connected to nature, community, and each other challenging.

The main benefit of convenience, saving time and energy, is not equitably shared. Someone who is financially struggling might spend hours waiting in line for benefits at a government office. That same person may benefit from fast food's convenience (and low prices), but that comes at the cost of their health and local food businesses. Transportation systems also generally disadvantage lower-income people who cannot afford to live in communities where they work. For some, that may lead to another inconvenience of taking an infrequent, inefficient bus to work. Those without public transportation options endure long-distance commutes by car. Transportation constitutes their highest household expense.

Two other cultural priorities—comfort and cleanliness—support corporate capitalist interests. Professor Elizabeth Shove's research on everyday practices in modern life demonstrates how much they are guided by comfort and cleanliness in addition to convenience.[11] With comfort, Shove illustrates that our society has developed a narrow range of comfort. This value particularly applies to the indoors, where people spend most of their time. Accepted indoor temperatures vary little from place to place, regardless of how hot or cold it is outside and how much air-conditioning or heating is needed. This cultural value supports excessive energy use to the benefit of Big Utilities, Big Oil and Gas, and other corporations in the energy industry. Similarly, cleanliness has become much more than just removing dirt and germs. Frequent cleaning with an abundance of consumer goods is normalized. Big Retail provides a nearly infinite supply of bath, laundry, and house cleaning products. Most of these cleaners come in disposable plastic packaging, adding to our massive amount of plastic waste and the profits of Big Plastic.

In addition to cultural norms of convenience, comfort, and cleanliness, corporations have effectively peddled consumerism by defining happiness as accumulating material items. Their marketing and advertising have blurred the line between human wants and needs. All types of electronics, household cleaning products, a car for every driver in a household, and frequent new clothing are some of the things that corporations have convinced people they need.

Consumer culture has made people think that satisfying their wants is the path to happiness. However, after they get what they want, happiness tends to return to a baseline level. This repeated experience is known as being on the "hedonic treadmill," continually seeking happiness without ever really increasing it.[12] The treadmill keeps people buying corporate products.

Digital society has become a formidable force in contemporary culture that is based on capturing people's attention. Increasing people's time spent on social media, browsing the internet, and shopping online leads to increased advertising revenue for corporate technology platforms. Facebook alone is used by about one-third of humanity.[13] Watching digital entertainment adds another significant stream of revenue.

Our reliance on digital technology may be more appropriately described as addiction. The neurotransmitter dopamine—which supports craving, desire, habit, and addiction—is triggered when a person gets a new text message, social media reaction, or just about any electronic communication. Maya MacGuineas explained in *The Atlantic* how this addiction has been designed into the devices and platforms by the technology companies that profit from it.[14] MacGuineas details how people hand over private data, often without knowledge, to these corporations. Big Tech studies what individuals search for, look at, and respond to online. They use this data to manipulate people into clicking on ads and buying products. Corporations like Amazon have also enlisted people to influence their followers on social media to purchase consumer goods. These mechanisms all serve to get people buying and using corporate products.

Systems-Change Levers

To build an alternative model of place-based systems, we must use the right levers. The prior analysis of how corporate capitalism has come to dominate systems shows the way: exerting economic and political power, directing land use, and shaping the cultural narrative. These three levers have done great harm in service of corporate capitalism, but they can be used to build regenerative place-based systems. People and organizations can work together and with government in regions, counties, cities, and communities to shift power, transform land use, and reset culture. Schools and individuals can contribute to the change.

Each lever utilizes different mechanisms:

- Shifting power involves a compelling vision, collaboration, policy change, and resource flows. A vision of well-being and regeneration, presented in chapters 1 and 2, can bring diverse stakeholders together into place-based coalitions that build collective power and become a force for change. Policies and resources from different levels of government can reduce corporations' economic and political power while boosting that of communities, regional and local businesses, and other local stakeholders.
- Transforming land use requires effective regional and local planning, supportive policies, and infrastructure investments. Shifting to a place-based transportation system, for example, involves policies and investments directed at protected bike lane networks, wide sidewalks, and dedicated transit lanes.
- Resetting culture revolves around changing mindsets and daily life practices and employs policies and other means to encourage beneficial behaviors. Grassroots movement building, campaigns, programs, services supportive of desired behaviors, subsidies, taxes, and other means can help move culture in support of place-based living.

In addition:

- Leveraging other systems breaks down silos and changes multiple systems simultaneously, leading to lasting societal transformation.

The four systems-change levers—shift power, transform land use, reset culture, and leverage other systems—are highly interrelated. The levers can be applied to any system that shapes how people live, including ones connected to but beyond the scope of this book, such as the travel system. Taxing airfare at increasingly higher rates per flight in a calendar year, for example, is a policy that helps reset travel culture to be less centered on flying to destinations. This mechanism also shifts economic power to entities that support more local travel, such as regional rail. It can transform land use, with space used for big airports and related facilities converted to regional transit hubs, local farms, or other land use that supports living connected to place. With space reallocated to local farms, the food system becomes more place-based by leveraging change in the travel system. One system can be used to change another.

In part 2, we'll explore examples of systems-change levers by their dominant trait (power, land use, culture, other systems) while recognizing their interrelatedness. It's essential to get all four levers working synergistically to change systems to the degree necessary to alter how people live and our societal trajectory. To emphasize the application of the levers to real change efforts, we refer to them as systems-change strategies in part 2.

Shift Power

Collective power is necessary to counter corporate capitalist actors' formidable, concentrated power. A vision of shared well-being can get that rolling by offering a "big tent" for all those concerned about and working on various environmental, social, and economic issues. Such a vision helps diverse organizations and people find common ground, leading to strategic collaboration that builds power. Even for those not involved in change efforts, a vision of well-being can help them see that they have a stake in the change. They may then resist change less or not at all. Regenerating nature, community, and local economies appeals to many people when tied to a vision that addresses their needs.

Power grows in our places when we bring forth collective intelligence and wisdom. This dynamic emerges when we work together locally in inclusive communities. Many problems can be solved when the community defines them, uses local knowledge to develop solutions, and builds capacity to put the solutions into action. People can come together in localities to strengthen community bonds and support local economies, shifting power away from corporations and toward people and their places.

Power shifts from corporate interests to local stakeholders and people through various mechanisms at different levels. Enforcement of antitrust and related federal and state policies checks concentrated corporate power. Local businesses, farms, and other entities build market and political power to counter consolidated corporate power through cooperative arrangements. Anchor institutions in cities and regions shift power to local and regional companies by purchasing local goods, food, energy, and supplies. Communities and municipalities can develop and own services like community solar and bike share, taking power away from Big Utilities and Big Auto. These are some of the many power shifts explored in part 2.

THE UNIVERSAL POWER-SHIFT POLICY: CAMPAIGN FINANCE AND CONFLICT-OF-INTEREST REGULATION

Reducing corporate power and making room for place-based power will be tough without significant reform to campaign finance and lobbying laws and enforcement. Changing every system could be made easier by diminishing the role of corporate money in politics. As such, this policy mechanism will be discussed here and not repeated in each part 2 chapter.

Many politicians have become dependent on financing their campaigns through contributions from wealthy donors. Strong conflict-of-interest and campaign finance regulations are needed to reduce the influence of moneyed interests. Such laws enable political leaders to prioritize improving the quality of life for residents above the interest of their largest donors.

Ken Schwartz was the mayor of San Luis Obispo in the 1970s and led the city to adopt the first local campaign finance and conflict-of-interest regulations in California. These policies helped him and other leaders focus on community enhancements and the local economy. Today, San Luis Obispo has a thriving local business district, ample community and nature spaces including a large central plaza and street trees everywhere, and a robust cycling and pedestrian infrastructure. It is ranked as one of the happiest places to live in the United States.[15]

Real estate developers are major campaign contributors, and they steer elected officials away from measures requiring more affordable housing that is less profitable to developers. In 2022, Los Angeles became the first jurisdiction in the country to limit developer campaign contributions. These types of restrictions limit the influence of corporate power on government.

Every state, county, and city needs stringent regulations and enforcement that break the corporate capitalist hold on political power and create systems that enhance well-being and build shared, place-based prosperity. The corporate interests that have shaped systems through their political and economic influence will continue to do so if politicians remain in their pockets.

Transform Land Use

We must change our relationship with land to regenerate nature, communities, and local economies. Policies and infrastructure investments can help reshape land use patterns toward mixed-use neighborhoods and self-reliant regions encompassing place-based systems. Urban growth boundaries protect greenbelts around cities and provide space for regional agriculture, regional energy generation, and accessible open spaces. Increasing funding for transit, biking, and walking infrastructure—combined with policies that convert streets into dedicated lanes for these modes—builds the foundation of an effective, place-based transportation system. Public space used for cars can be converted to other uses, from urban farms to promenades. These and other place-based approaches to land use, such as regional and local manufacturing, need policy and infrastructure investments to come to fruition.

Research on the potential for local agricultural productivity (shared in detail in chap. 9) shows that surrounding regions can provide sufficient food for all inhabitants of almost every US metropolitan area. With a pivot toward renewable energy and consuming less, the same regional potential could exist for energy and consumer goods. Transforming land in these ways can lead to innovative practices and thriving regional systems.

We need to change zoning and related regulations to live locally and create a more equitable society. Ending the segregation of households by income and the separation of people from where they work, shop, and play is critical. This shift involves committing sufficient space to housing for all those who work in a neighborhood or city.

Land use can also transform to favor nature-based solutions. Trees and wetlands, for example, can support wastewater management and climate resilience. We don't need newer technologies backed by profit-seeking corporations that purport to address the same issues. No technology will ever have as much societal value as intact ecosystems. Policies and funding can help restore nature and all its benefits in our places.

Reset Culture

Resetting culture starts with dispelling some of the false narratives of corporate capitalism concerning economic globalization. When I taught high school economics nearly three decades ago, the concept of comparative advantage was highlighted in textbooks. The idea is that every nation has unique natural resources or products for export and must import whatever else its population needs. It seems logical, but this supposed truism benefits wealthy nations and corporations far more than others. The reality is that developing nations provide cheap natural resources and labor for corporations mostly based in the Global North. The logic of specialization and global trade obscures the inevitable reality of winners and losers in the global economy.

Comparative advantage and other corporate capitalist doctrines are being questioned and challenged, elevating interest in place-based systems. For example, social ecologist Eduardo Gudynas makes the case for why Latin America needs to move away from international trade: "Bolivia is increasingly exporting food crops, while a large part of its population lives in poverty and is starving. In Colombia, agriculture is dominated by the flower sector. The flowers are mainly exported to the United States. The country itself has to import an increasing proportion of its food. Open-pit mining has also been booming in Latin America and the resulting environmental damage is significant. Even Uruguay, an agricultural country, isn't able to escape the large-scale mining operations."[16] The "logic" of comparative advantage dictates that Latin America produces crops and extracts minerals for global corporations while failing to feed all of its residents and damaging local nature in ways that further harm those who live there. By revealing what is taking place, Gudynas and many others are helping shift mindsets toward making economies more regionally self-sufficient.

At the local level, we can reset culture toward valuing stronger everyday relationships with place, community, and nature and among people of different lived experiences. A YIMBY ("yes in my backyard") attitude toward housing welcomes people of all income levels and races into every community. We can encourage, incentivize, and reward buying local, using active transportation, and harvesting local and renewable energy. Waste reduction, energy conservation, and plant-based diets can become culturally valued when people and organizations work toward regional and local self-reliance. In these ways and more, a new mindset and way of living can emerge to lead the way out of our societal crises.

Media and film can change how we see systems and everyday activities. In her documentary *Motherload*, Liz Canning reflects on biking with her kids for exercise and daily transport: "I was alive and evolving. I think of climate change this way as a cry for help from the forgotten part of our world, refusing to be ignored any longer. If we are listening, we'll see the opportunity here to rethink the culture. If we are listening, we'll take the step towards connection and balance."[17] Canning has helped form a network of moms who bike and are each making their communities better places to live. They all share the joy of biking. Every time they bike, they connect to their community and local nature and reshape culture through their example. Biking, walking, using transit, and otherwise moving in communities outside the envelope of cars is all about connection and balance, hearing and responding to the planet's cry for help.

For cultural change to succeed, it must challenge the dominance of convenience, comfort, and cleanliness in modern life and bring forth new values and priorities like those found in *Motherload*. Localism movements surface the importance of slowing down, connecting with nature, participating in community, and building strong, healthy relationships with each other. Slowing down applies to busy professionals as well as people who have to work multiple jobs. It needs to be possible to make a living on just one job, so every person has time to rest, connect, and tend to their well-being. These cultural and economic shifts will take time, but they leverage wisdom that predates corporate capitalism.

Engaging whole communities in the change process can lead to a virtuous cycle of supportive social conditions that facilitate systems change. The more a person sees others live in ways that are connected to place, the more likely she is to do the same. People can help each other learn to live in these ways. When a person feels supported by others or assists others, the hormone oxytocin is released, and this generates positive feelings. This chemical booster helps people wean off dopamine-inducing digital technology and shift their state of mind to break from the grip of consumerism and automobile dependency.

Resetting culture can also reframe the constructs used to support corporate capitalist systems. Automobile and airline companies, for example, have long worked to associate personal freedom with being able to drive and fly. An alternative view associates freedom with biking, walking, or taking transit and not having to maintain, fuel, and insure a private automobile, let alone sit in traffic. Likewise, exploring within one's region can meet the need for "getting away" in a way that doesn't involve the exhaustion of waiting in airport security lines, traveling across multiple time zones, and experiencing jet lag. A new perspective on values like freedom supports systems change.

Leverage Other Systems

Systems change will be most effective when it happens across systems in mutually reinforcing ways. More housing near where people work and shop, for example, reduces the need for cars and thus helps change the transportation system. While this book features eight distinct systems that influence how people live, they should not be understood as separate systems. Instead, our change efforts must break down silos and link systems together. Rather than focus narrowly, our goal can be to work across as many systems as possible.

* * *

Given the relationship between context and behavior (introduced in chap. 1), we need to pull levers in each system and across systems to realize a world where place has more influence than corporate capitalism. Shifting power is essential for loosening corporate capitalism's grip on systems and generating new place-based sources of power. Transforming land use changes the physical context for human behavior. Resetting culture changes the cultural context. The synergy among the levers leads to a more supportive social context as more and more people adopt new behaviors. In addition, less expensive ways of living are inherent to place-based systems and provide supportive economic context for changing behavior.

The physical, cultural, social, and economic conditions created through place-based systems change make it possible and even rewarding to change our ways of living. People prioritize experiences in their place when they can access nearby abundant nature, engaging community spaces, and amenities like local restaurants and entertainment venues. An individual is likelier to buy secondhand clothes from a local store if his friends also shop there, talk positively about it, or even shop there with him. A person can eat fresh, regionally grown food when it is available in local grocery stores and farmers' markets. These are among the conditions needed to live connected to place.

Part 2

FROM CORPORATE CAPITALIST TO PLACE-BASED SYSTEMS

A place becomes home when it sustains you, when it feeds you in body as well as spirit.

—Robin Wall Kimmerer, "Putting Down Roots" in *Braiding Sweetgrass*

In part 2, we'll look closely at the context that shapes people's lives and how we can change it so people can live connected to place. The "what" of systems change is explored by showing the relationship of systems-change levers to the creation of conditions that enable living connected to place. The chapters are arranged in a sequence that relates to each system's centrality in people's lives from both a human needs and a geographic perspective.

The first three chapters in this part discuss the fundamentals of daily life and financial security—a place to live (chap. 4: "Housing"), working and shopping (chap. 5: "Local Business and Work"), and getting around (chap. 6: "Transportation"). These three systems are highly interrelated and influence the remaining systems. Next, we explore the important psychological needs of connecting to local community (chap. 7: "Community Spaces") and nearby nature (chap. 8: "Nature

Spaces"). These first five systems, as explained in chapter 2, can be primarily organized at city and county levels.

The final three systems require regional organization. Additionally, although these systems address critical human needs like the preceding systems, they can also easily generate "wants" and waste in modern society. Systems that meet the physiological needs of nourishment (chap. 9: "Food") and comfort (chap. 10: "Building Energy") produce excess well beyond those needs in corporate capitalist systems. Part 2 concludes with a system that fulfills mostly "wants" but is a valued part of modern life (chap. 11: "Consumer Goods") and fits into place-based systems in moderation.

Each chapter in part 2 offers a brief examination of how the system impacts people's lives and collective well-being. We then look at how corporate capitalism has shaped conditions around the specified area of people's lives before presenting a place-based alternative. The latter half of each chapter demonstrates how systems-change levers can be flexed into strategies to develop the featured place-based system. Each chapter provides examples of people building place-based systems, fostering know-how and hope for a better present and future.

HOUSING

The pathway to housing should be fair and equitable for everyone, and access to affordable housing is the infrastructure people in our communities need to elevate families into the working class and the middle class. It is the foundation that helps people support their families and contribute to their economies.

—Raphael Warnock, US Senator from the state of Georgia

In 2004, my family and I moved into San Francisco's Castro neighborhood. We were fortunate to buy a home there where we still reside today. We were attracted to the community's abundant amenities—parks, schools, transit access, and local businesses—and the socioeconomic diversity of its residents. Most of the buildings on our block are multifamily residential, including a five-unit neighboring property.

Until 2016, the units in the next-door building were rent-controlled. That year, the longtime landlord passed away, and his family sold the property for $2.55 million to an investment group. A little over a year later, another investor purchased it for $3.75 million, bought out three of the five tenants, and sold their units. California's Ellis Act allows new property owners to convert rental units to condos or tenancies-in-common and sell them.

Caught in the middle of this were our retired neighbors, Jeanine and Gale, who had lived in the building since 1980. They were wonderful neighbors, quick to engage in a sidewalk conversation and always looking out for others. They tried everything they could to stay in their apartment but were eventually forced out in 2024. Gale reflected on being faced with eviction well into her seventies: "You spend your whole life working in a city. Why should you just be pushed out and forced to make a whole new life somewhere else? We just want to live out the rest of our days here."[1] It was a major blow. The Castro had been welcoming and invigorating to them as an interracial lesbian couple, so their sense of home had been more than just the apartment. It extended into the neighborhood and the city. But despite being connected to this place most of their lives, like many others devalued in the current housing system, those ties and all their associated benefits were severed in one fell swoop. Unfortunately, Jeanine and Gale's story is far from atypical.

* * *

Everyone should be able to live close to where they work and stay there once they retire. However, the current housing system makes this challenging for many people, and it's become more difficult over time.

Average rents went up more than 30 percent between 2020 and 2024 in the United States.[2] Spending more than one-third of income on housing is generally considered a significant cost burden on individuals and families. In 2024, almost a third of renters in California were considered "severely cost-burdened," meaning they spent more than half of their income on rent.[3] Being forced to move from a rent-controlled apartment to a higher-priced rental likely landed Jeanine and Gale in this category.

Also, from 2020 to 2024, average home prices in the United States rose 47 percent.[4] As rent became less affordable, the prospect of buying a home for many Americans became even worse.

Whether renting or owning, housing prices have generally been highest in job centers.

When low- and middle-income workers are unable to live close to where they work, they endure further economic and personal hardship. Dependent on car travel, personal transportation costs skyrocket, and quality of life diminishes with so much time on the road away from community, family, and friends.

Long commutes and driving everywhere, due to limited housing availability and affordability where needed, harm collective well-being. Harvard University researchers found that commuting time is the most critical factor in whether people escape poverty; it is more significant than crime, school, and family-related factors.[5] Communities and the environment suffer too. Lengthy commutes and automobile dependency deter local living, connection to local community, and reduction in transportation-related emissions.

This chapter looks at what underlies the housing availability and affordability crisis faced in communities across the country and shows a path forward to turn the tide on this complex problem. We'll first identify how the levers of power, land use, and culture hold the current housing system in place. The chapter then focuses on an alternate, place-based housing system of mixed-use, mixed-income communities that prioritize housing availability and affordability and how we can get there. By strategically applying the same levers that maintain the status quo and leveraging other systems, we can reshape and sustain communities where all people can live close to where they work (and stay there once retired) with daily life amenities nearby as a foundation to living connected to place and a good life.

Systems-Change Strategies for Making Housing Available and Affordable

- Shift power to nonprofit, cooperative, and community housing ownership
- Shift power to networks of local developers
- Shift power to more state oversight and enforcement
- Transform land use with urban growth boundaries and mixed-use zoning
- Transform space for cars into housing and mixed-use communities
- Transform downtowns into mixed-use communities
- Transform land use with mixed-income zoning and development incentives
- Transform land use with workforce housing
- Reset culture through YIMBYism ("yes in my backyard")
- Leverage other systems

Holding the Status Quo Housing System in Place

Powerful real estate entities have a vested interest in the status quo housing system. In addition, zoning, parking minimums, and bureaucratic hurdles make it hard to build housing where it is most needed. Homeowner resistance can thwart nearly any new housing development, especially those that provide affordable housing units. Together, these factors stand in the way of making housing available and affordable systematically.

Power: Big Real Estate

Housing in the United States and other places around the world is treated as a commodity more than a place to live. The system revolves around real estate investments, not housing people.

Keeping housing scarce benefits those involved in the buying, selling, and renting of existing buildings and properties by driving up prices and thus increasing profits. Additionally, developers avoid building affordable housing units with lower-potential profit margins. The housing system benefits those seeking to profit from it while leaving housing unavailable and unaffordable to many.

Big Real Estate is a primary beneficiary of the status quo housing system. The term *Big Real Estate* is not common parlance, but it should be. Powerful public and private businesses, including brokerage firms, developers, investment trusts, and banks dominate the residential real estate market within regions and across the country. Big Real Estate stakeholders have amassed significant wealth from land holdings and the financing arrangements that support the industry.

Since World War II, builders, real estate brokers, and landlords have become increasingly corporate and consolidated. The five largest realtor firms—Realogy Holdings, Keller Williams Realty, RE/MAX, HomeServices of America, and Compass—accounted for more than 42.4 percent of home sales volume in 2020.[6] Corporate-structured ownership of rental units in the United States now exceeds the number owned by individual landlords.[7] More than two-thirds of rental properties in Los Angeles, for example, are owned by corporate investment vehicles and trusts with extensive holdings.[8] Those who largely control the housing market are often far removed from communities and people's actual housing needs.

Likewise, large corporate developers and their investors end up with the lion's share of construction projects in almost every US location. They use their market power to wield political influence. Government incentives or subsidies directed at urban zone redevelopment or the building of suburban neighborhoods, for example, go almost exclusively to large corporate developers. With their economic and political power, Wall Street and corporate investors direct where most residential development occurs across the country.

Strong Towns is a national advocacy organization dedicated to restoring local economies and communities and shifting power away from large corporate interests. Its investigations help reveal the layers of Big Real Estate's firm grip on housing development across the country, including the financing of projects. According to Strong Towns' Daniel Herriges, big banks prefer "cookie-cutter" conforming loans that finance large housing developments, which are the domain of big corporate developers.[9] Mid- and small-size local firms are often denied such loans. The inflexibility of the dominant banks limits local developer projects.

Housing availability and affordability in the right places remain elusive when the housing system is driven by Big Real Estate with little connection to the places or communities from which they extract profits. Meanwhile, smaller local developers who know their communities best struggle to compete when the field is stacked against them.

Land Use: Zoning, Parking Minimums, Codes, and Fees

The housing system has been built around single-family zoning to the advantage of big developers and investors. More than 70 percent of many US metropolitan areas are exclusively zoned for single-family homes.[10] In essence, apartments and other multifamily housing types, let alone retail or commercial uses, are banned from most communities.

Single-family zoning, on top of a history of legal racial segregation and discrimination in housing, has led to the proliferation of affluent, mostly White suburban communities and enclaves within cities. These single-family residential communities were designed to exclude people of color and households with limited income. A 2020 University of California, Berkeley, study of the San Francisco Bay Area found that "home values in [heavily single-family zoned] cities are $100,000 higher, incomes are $34,000 higher, and these areas are nearly 20 percent whiter than the rest of the [region's] cities."[11] Residential zoning restrictions help maintain an unequal housing system that prevents mixed-income, mixed-race communities from emerging.

Single-family zoning is a subset of single-use zoning in which only one kind of use is permitted within a designated neighborhood or zone. Even if an area is zoned residentially for single- and multifamily residential units, retail, commercial, or recreational may be excluded. A range of housing may be available in such neighborhoods. However, the distance to other daily life amenities furthers car dependence, adds transportation costs to household budgets, and inhibits living connected to place.

Parking minimums are intended to limit demand for street parking space, but they hinder the availability and affordability of apartment and multifamily buildings. The cost of each parking space is typically tens of thousands of dollars and is passed on to households through higher rents or purchase prices.[12] In addition, parking areas take up space that could be used for additional housing units.

Building codes and fees imposed on new development can discourage the building of apartment and multifamily buildings. The United States has stringent life safety and electrical codes not found in other countries. One fire alarm per bedroom and two stairwells per corridor are requirements that add cost and impede the development of small buildings. Impact fees for infrastructure upgrades are also levied on new developments, disincentivizing housing production. Riaz Capital, a midsize local real estate development firm in the San Francisco Bay Area, for example, was required to pay $5.3 million in fees, or about 8 percent of the total cost of a project in Berkeley, California.[13] These costs and fees are hard to absorb in the small- and midsize developments needed to make housing more available and affordable.

Culture: Homeowner Resistance

Ending single-family zoning and parking minimums and reducing costs associated with building affordable housing are logical ways to break down residential segregation and make housing more available and affordable. Yet these changes have been very difficult to make. One reason is local homeowner resistance.

Concerns from existing homeowners often take center stage when new housing projects are proposed. This is particularly true in affluent suburbs where proposed apartment buildings and other affordable housing projects are frequently met with fierce opposition from residents.

The status quo resistance infects local government, which then stymies housing production. In the wealthy suburban town of Lafayette, California, a proposal to build 315 apartments near a regional subway station surfaced around 2012. Lafayette has a population of twenty-five thousand that is 85 percent white. Residents mobilized against the proposed development and organized under a highly vocal nonprofit called Save Lafayette. The proposal was delayed for years and reduced to forty-four single-family homes, and yet it was still defeated. (See chap. 13 for a later, hopeful turn in this story that reflects the power of systems change.) This story has played out across many wealthy US communities, doubling down on residential segregation and keeping low- and middle-income earners often far from work and reliable transit service.

In late summer 2022, journalist Lisa Prevost documented homeowner resistance across suburbs in Fairfield County, Connecticut. Over two thousand residents had signed a petition to stop nineteen affordable housing units from being built in the downtown section of the town of Fairfield. In New Canaan, homeowners fought a proposed downtown apartment complex that included thirty-one rent-restricted units for households with moderate incomes. Arnold Karp, the local developer proposing that project, shared, "I already have a list of 20-plus people who work in town who would love to live here in a building that they could afford. My view is people who work in town deserve to be able to live in town."[14] This pattern across the United States makes life more difficult for millions of families and individuals who want to live closer to their workplace and in mixed-use, mixed-income communities.

Homeowner resistance is a cultural barrier to affordable, available housing with deep under-pinnings. Local control is a value touted by those impeding change in their communities. Yet local government exercising its power in these ways is far from democratic, leaving out the voices of those who work in cities and towns but cannot afford to live there.

We need an alternative place-based housing system composed of mixed-income and mixed-use communities that provide housing in locations beneficial to all people and the environment.

A Vision of Mixed-Use, Mixed-Income Communities

A fair, just housing system provides housing for all those working in restaurants, grocery stores, retail, public safety, schools, and other essential jobs in the communities where they serve. Commenting on the 45 percent of Montgomery County, Maryland, employees not living in the county, including most younger firefighters, retired firefighter Richard Hoye wondered, "Why should somebody risk their lives in a county where they can't afford to live?"[15] Hoye's question gets to the heart of the matter. If their work is essential, then stable and nearby housing should be too.

Mixed-use communities provide housing, work opportunities, and amenities, advancing equity and sustainability while facilitating easier living. Less travel to work and for other daily life needs saves money and time and reduces stress. A bonus that can add motivation for individuals is that fewer cars in mixed-use communities reduce greenhouse gas emissions and improve local walkability and livability.

Opportunities to connect with a place and community expand when you live, work, and spend much time there, often through simple interactions. You may converse with a neighbor, wave to a friend, or notice the changing foliage on trees when you can get to work or school without a car. Conversations with colleagues include more of what's happening in your community when you all live there. These connections motivate collective efforts to take care of a place.

Mixed-income communities with a range of affordable housing are necessary for more people to live in the county, city, or neighborhood where they work. Apartment buildings with affordable rent are a cornerstone for ensuring low-income families and individuals have housing. Townhomes, bungalow courts (several small houses around a central garden), and multiunit housing provide other forms of housing and can be built into existing neighborhoods. These housing types can be affordable to middle-income earners and were abundant until the postwar boom of suburban development and single-family residential zoning. Thus, these types of dwellings are often referred to as the "missing middle."

Living together in diverse, inclusive communities is the most fundamental, direct, and impactful way to dismantle racism and remove the barriers to opportunity inflicted on Black, Indigenous, and people of color and low-income households. Researchers found that children from lower-income families in Seattle who moved to more affluent neighborhoods using federal housing vouchers made an additional $210,000 over their lifetime.[16] Those who are able to live in mixed-income communities, compared to high-poverty communities, benefit from increased access to decent-paying jobs, social networks that can lead to job opportunities and careers, quality health care and schools, resources and activities for children, and other amenities that support financial security and overall well-being.

Existing mixed-income, mixed-race cities also often rank among the best places to live in the United States. Mountain View, California, is a city of over eighty thousand in the San Francisco Bay Area, with racial, ethnic, and economic diversity reflective of the larger region and state. The city ranks among the top suburbs to live in California, including for those raising families and young professionals.[17] Oak Park, Illinois, a Chicago suburb of over fifty thousand is known for its ethnic and economic diversity. It ranks among the top places to live in Illinois, with excellent schools, access to good jobs, and easy connections to community life and nature for its residents.[18] Values of inclusion and opportunity for all anchor these communities.

Columbia, Maryland, a city of over one hundred thousand residents, is an example of a successful mixed-income, mixed-use city. The city has been racially and ethnically diverse by design since it opened in 1967 and ranks among the top cities in the United States for raising a family, having a good quality of life, and buying a house.[19] As a planned community, the original goals were to build a self-sustaining community where residents both live and work, respect the land, provide for the growth of people, and make a profit. Ten villages make up the city, with nine having a village center of gathering places, shopping, and services and the tenth one being a downtown district in the city's center. Today, the evolution of Columbia is guided by principles of diversity and inclusion, environmental stewardship, livability, and economic opportunity.

Despite all their benefits, mixed-income, mixed-use communities are far from the norm. Mixed-income communities have even been in decline. From 1980 to 2013, Americans living in affluent areas grew almost fourfold, while Americans living in poor areas grew nearly threefold, resulting in a significant decline in neighborhoods with more average or median income.[20] A 2018 study of census data found that only seven million Americans (out of approximately 330 million people in the United States) live in neighborhoods with high levels of racial, ethnic, and income diversity.[21] Likewise, nearly every metropolitan area in the United States has been divided into separate uses, often characterized by commercial, retail urban centers surrounded by residential suburbs.

Changing the makeup of communities to provide housing for all is difficult, long-term work. Systems-change levers must be applied to close the large gap between the status quo and housing in mixed-income, mixed-use communities.

Systems-Change Strategies for a Place-Based Housing System

Despite resistance from status quo interests, change toward a more equitable and sustainable housing system is happening. With the convergence of the climate and inequality crises, land use patterns are being upended to create more mixed-income, mixed-use neighborhoods. In the process, we're learning how to shift power to local stakeholders, change zoning and build housing where it is most needed, and reset culture through YIMBYism. By utilizing these systems-change strategies, housing can be made available and affordable across the country.

Shift Power to Nonprofit, Cooperative, and Community Housing Ownership

When we view housing more as a human need and less as a commodity for wealthy investors and corporations, different types of housing ownership and arrangements become more central to the system. European countries have long traditions of treating housing as a right and providing it for their residents. Social housing that is government-supported, mixed-income, and rent-restricted is common. In some countries, nonprofit organizations develop and own affordable housing. For example, in Denmark, nonprofits own about 20 percent of the housing stock.[22]

Local nonprofit acquisitions of multifamily buildings protect people who are vulnerable to displacement. In San Francisco, the nonprofit Mission Economic Development Agency has bought more than twenty-five rent-controlled buildings that house mostly working-class Latino residents. Nonprofit ownership like this prevents speculators from coming in, evicting tenants, and flipping properties.

Housing cooperatives and community land trusts also increase access to housing. The San Jerardo Cooperative in Salinas, California, has provided affordable housing for approximately four hundred people since it was founded forty years ago, creating a foundation of financial security for farmworkers and their families who are housed there. Utilizing grants, donations, and government funds, community land trusts buy properties and make them permanent affordable housing (or protected for another purpose like cultural space). Residents take ownership of the property and govern the trust. Approximately 250 of these trusts existed in 2022, and the number continues to grow.[23] Cooperative and community land trusts help put the community in control of real estate.

To bring more nonprofit, cooperative, and community housing ownership online, these entities need support to purchase multifamily buildings or parcels when they go on the market. Subsidizing nonprofits, cooperatives, and community land trusts in buying buildings and lots is a form of reparations for systematically underserved communities. Municipal-owned land that is undeveloped or has vacant buildings can be prioritized for these housing types. Additionally, city staff can be charged with supporting these ownership transfers. Shifting power in the system away from Big Real Estate and toward local, community ownership is an important step in providing affordable housing for people to live in the communities where they work.

Shift Power to Networks of Local Developers

Power also needs to shift to local developers who are well suited to build additional housing within existing neighborhoods. Developers who work where they live are likely to be invested in the long-term interest of the local community and residents. They have the local knowledge to enrich neighborhood character while adding housing to diversify the community.

Networks of local developers built American neighborhoods into the mid-twentieth century until the postwar suburban boom of cookie-cutter neighborhoods. In a series of articles in 2021, Daniel Herriges of Strong Towns laid out how a "swarm" of local developers can address the housing shortage and affordability crisis by building small apartment buildings, duplexes, additional dwellings on existing properties, and other forms of housing without adding to suburban sprawl.[24] This constitutes an incremental development approach where housing grows across multiple small projects instead of a few big ones generally only built by large national corporations.

The "swarm" needs support. Local regulations and fees need to be simplified and reduced to make it more profitable for local developers to build multifamily housing. Hope may lie in groups like the Incremental Development Alliance (IDA), as Herriges explains, that work with city planning staff to identify and address the specific problems local regulations create for small developers. Loosening or getting rid of parking minimums, building height limits, setback requirements, and building footprint restrictions as a percentage of a land parcel are regulatory changes that will make it easier for local developers to construct incremental housing.

In South Bend, Indiana, changes in such regulations led to small developers working on more than one hundred properties in low-income, disinvested neighborhoods in 2021.[25] Collectively, they have become the largest developer in the city. The city holds workshops to support residents in becoming part of the ecosystem of contractors, architects, engineers, and others involved in the development. This initiative, known as Build South Bend, has been recognized as a model for communities across the United States.

Local developers need access to funding. Local banks and investors, by their nature, know their communities well. They can be a critical funding conduit for developers working on incremental projects who cannot get loans or reasonable terms from big banks. Government and nonprofits can fill the gap for what banks can't cover. Tax incentives and other grants and subsidies that often benefit big developers can and should be redirected to support small developers.

Local developers embody living connected to place, which, in concert with their connection to each other, can support their success. Referencing the IDA's small-developer workshops, Herriges explains,

> One recipe for success as a small developer is to pick an area—smaller than a neighborhood, maybe just a few blocks—where you intend to commit for the long haul, and then come to know that area intimately. Live there, if you can. Frequent its businesses. Get to know every neighbor, every property. Do multiple projects there: You'll find opportunities once you're a known, trusted quantity to your neighbors, and you'll bring them along with you. . . . Incremental developers, because of their deep connection to a place, are able to identify underappreciated opportunities and undervalued property. They can prove the market where the conventional wisdom is that there isn't one.[26]

Local developers can build community while making a good living. They support one another through a network across a jurisdiction and help each other find opportunities. They can also reduce their individual costs when acting together. In South Bend, for example, local developers buy materials as a collective and share expensive equipment.

In a place-based housing system, who builds the housing matters. Where the housing is built is also critical. Building in the right locations to create mixed-income, mixed-use communities requires simplifying regulations, financial incentives, access to financing, and other support for local developers.

Shift Power to More State Oversight and Enforcement

It seems antithetical for place-based systems to require more state control. State oversight and enforcement, however, are needed to overcome homeowner resistance and local government bureaucratic barriers that get in the way of building more housing. Without state action, status quo pushback to adding affordable housing or mixed uses to established neighborhoods has typically prevailed. Most of the land use changes to develop mixed-income, mixed-use communities described in this chapter have come about because of pressure from state governments.

California, as referenced earlier, has one of the worst housing shortages and affordability crises in the country. For decades, the state's formula for adding housing to regions and cities was largely ignored. With YIMBY pressure, described later in this chapter, the state has passed a number of laws to mandate housing increases in every county and city in the state where they are needed. Local governments are finally complying. Though many obstacles still exist, more housing is being built and in the development pipeline.

Transform Land Use with Urban Growth Boundaries and Mixed-Use Zoning

Urban growth boundaries deter suburban sprawl and favor housing development through urban revitalization. Generally voter-approved, urban growth boundaries prevent development on natural and agricultural lands, or the greenbelt, around metropolitan areas. The boundaries incentivize urban revitalization: redevelopment within an existing urban setting, also known as infill development, that creates or enhances a mixed-use neighborhood without gentrification. The tighter these boundaries are drawn, the more potential for livable neighborhoods, making it possible for more people to live connected to place.

Zoning reform also provides a strong impetus for transforming land use to provide more housing. With remote work and online shopping playing a role in their decline, empty strip malls, office parks, and parking lots provide ample land to build more housing. Local governments are rezoning such spaces for mixed-use and providing incentives and subsidies for their development. As described in chapter 2, the former Valco Mall in the suburb of Cupertino, California, is being converted into a sizeable mixed-use community. Rezoning was required to make this happen. The new community will include almost twenty-seven hundred residential units, with almost one-third of them affordable for lower-income households.

Form-based codes are another way to achieve mixed-use zoning. Rather than prescribed uses, these types of codes dictate the design and appearance of buildings and land parcels. Form-based codes standardize elements such as building height, lot coverage, sidewalks, and street trees. They can be used to preserve neighborhood character without standing in the way of mixed-use development.

Transform Space for Cars into Housing and Mixed-Use Communities

The most transformative housing systems change replaces harmful land uses with those that regenerate nature, community, and local economies. A priority should be taking down freeways built to separate communities of color from wealthier white communities. The reclaimed space can be used for housing, parks, and other community-desired amenities.

Funding from government is needed for these large projects and to make reparations for the more than 475,000 households displaced by the 41,000 miles added to the interstate highway system, mainly in the 1950s and '60s.[27] The US Department of Transportation's Reconnecting Communities Initiative, included in the 2022 Infrastructure Act, funded $1 billion for freeway demolition to restore communities and housing historically eliminated by freeways. One of the first projects planned was removing part of the I-375 that cuts through Detroit. When it opened in 1964, this section of highway displaced 130,000 people and hundreds of small businesses in two Black neighborhoods.[28] Though put on hold by the Trump administration, the plan is to replace it with a multimodal street with ample walkways and green space and the potential for adding housing. To make true reparations, that housing must be built.

The New York city of Rochester's Inner Loop freeway was taken down in the 2010s. In its place, a complete street was built with wide sidewalks and bike lanes to move through the neighborhood and access nearby downtown. Mixed-use redevelopment has been taking place on six recovered acres around the street. Five hundred houses were completed by early 2023, with 60 percent of them affordable to low-income households.[29] The community is being revitalized and reconnected to the rest of the city.

Space for parking cars is also being replaced with housing developments. A large parking lot on a community college campus in San Francisco is being converted into much-needed housing. The Balboa Reservoir Project will provide 1,100 housing units, half of which will be affordable, a community center, a childcare center, four acres of green space, and $10 million to improve nearby transit.[30] One hundred and fifty of the housing units are for community college staff, helping to counteract job-housing imbalances. The land is located near transit stops for city and regional transit and on a street with many retail stores, reducing car dependence and enhancing community connections and the quality of life for residents.

Getting rid of parking minimums for new developments helps prevent the cars-over-housing problem from starting in the first place. London and other British cities have eliminated parking minimum requirements for new developments. These cities have instead instituted parking maximums, reversing long-held regulations that supported dependency on cars. Paris and São Paulo have instituted similar changes, with Paris eliminating any parking requirement for developments within five hundred meters, or a little over a quarter-mile, of a public transit stop. In 2017, Hartford, Connecticut, and Buffalo, New York, were the first cities to abolish parking requirements. Since then, more than three thousand cities in the United States have reduced or eliminated parking minimums in at least one area of their jurisdiction.[31] Twenty percent of these restrictions have been citywide. In all of these locations, less parking provides more space for housing units.

Removing parking requirements for new developments also creates more opportunities for local developers to build housing by reducing the cost of development. The midsize city of Norman, Oklahoma, changed off-street parking from required to recommended and saw an uptick in housing development constructed by local developers.[32]

Transform Downtowns into Mixed-Use Communities

Many downtown offices were empty during the heart of the COVID-19 pandemic and, with the subsequent growth in hybrid work, are now underutilized. At the end of 2022, almost one billion square feet of office real estate across the United States was vacant.[33] Many real estate experts initially weighed in to say converting office space to housing was too expensive or impossible.

It doesn't take much investigation, however, to prove the skeptics wrong. In the 1990s, New York City and Philadelphia showed how to turn commercial neighborhoods into mixed-use ones with housing. With a tax abatement program that encouraged converting old offices into housing, 13 percent of Lower Manhattan's office real estate became residential space between 1995 and 2006.[34] Through a similar program, Philadelphia converted 180 buildings, which resulted in a 55 percent increase in the number of people living downtown.[35]

Cities with lingering high office vacancy rates can do the same. A 2023 postpandemic study of office-to-housing conversions in San Francisco found that 40 percent of office buildings downtown are good conversion candidates, providing eleven thousand new homes.[36] The projects are physically possible but need economic incentives or subsidies to make them financially feasible. To do so, the city could lower development-related fees, which are among the highest in the country, and make these projects exempt from some requirements and extensive reviews that add significant costs.

Less dense downtowns with smaller buildings can also add housing by building on vacant lots and replacing abandoned buildings. In 2022, a downtown housing boom started in Berkeley, California, nestled among retail and commercial spaces and a transit corridor. Ten apartment buildings with five to fourteen stories each were being constructed, with many more being planned. Many of the new buildings include ground-floor retail and public plazas on their grounds, enhancing the livability of this mixed-use downtown neighborhood.

A twelve-acre Squamish First Nation reserve in downtown Vancouver, British Columbia, exemplifies even more transformative change in boosting the housing supply and providing opportunities for those with limited incomes to live in a robust mixed-use neighborhood. The project will include six thousand apartment units for roughly nine thousand people in eleven tall towers.[37] Existing and future transit stops are nearby. Thousands of secure bike parking spaces and bike-share services will be available, enabling car-free or car-light living and reducing transportation costs for residents. With less parking needed, this significant addition of housing to this downtown area has become more possible. Over half the site will be a nature-filled public space, and other ground-floor amenities will include restaurants, a fitness center, a grocery store, and daycare.

This substantial housing and community development in Vancouver is also righting past wrongs. It is located on the site of the former *Senákw* Village, where Squamish ancestors lived. As a form of reconciliation, the revenue from the development will benefit the people of this First Nation.

Declining hotel use in downtown areas presents another opportunity for increasing the housing supply. When the COVID-19 pandemic–induced decline in tourism met the growing crisis of people living unhoused in cities nationwide, urban hotels and motels were converted to homeless shelters. This raised awareness about how housing for tourists could be utilized to provide shelter for the unhoused and help communities meet housing needs. We should be providing homes for residents before tourists.

Transform Land Use with Mixed-Income Zoning and Development Incentives

We also need to have housing for a range of income levels in every community. Building affordable housing in affluent neighborhoods and mixed-income housing in poorer neighborhoods without gentrification requires zoning changes as a starting point.

States are curbing single-family zoning that has been in place for decades. In 2019, Oregon essentially banned single-family zoning by requiring all towns with more than one thousand people to allow duplexes and all cities with more than twenty-five thousand people to allow townhouses, triplexes, and fourplexes. In 2021, Massachusetts required many of its cities and towns to have at least one district within a half mile of transit stations that accommodates multifamily housing as a condition of receiving state funding for transportation infrastructure and projects. California has chipped away at single-family (and single-use) zoning. A 2021 state law allowed property owners to split a single-family lot into duplexes or fourplexes. A 2022 law legalized mixed-income, multifamily housing in all commercial areas. States from Connecticut and Maine to Utah and Washington have passed similar laws.

Zoning changes are not a panacea to the housing affordability crisis. Early reports on California's zoning reform showed little new development underway.[38] Ending single-family zoning is more of a precondition. Development incentives are also needed to add housing.

Public housing neighborhoods have been transformed into mixed-income communities in metropolitan areas with funding from the Choice Neighborhoods and other US Department of Housing and Urban Development initiatives. The East Lake community of Atlanta, Georgia, was highly distressed until mixed-income development replaced public housing. In addition to the mixed-income housing, a new charter school, early learning centers, a health and fitness community center, and new commercial and retail spaces were added to the neighborhood. Crime decreased dramatically, employment soared, and student outcomes skyrocketed as the neighborhood population grew by 50 percent.[39]

While resistance is persistent, exclusionary walls are also starting to come down around affluent neighborhoods. Under California's statewide reform, two affluent suburban California cities, Saratoga and Danville, stood out for receiving many applications for new duplexes and fourplexes on existing single-family home lots.[40] The tide is slowly turning away from exclusive neighborhoods and toward mixed-income ones, particularly in providing "missing middle" housing.

Affordable housing units can be added to properties in affluent neighborhoods as Accessory Dwelling Units (ADUs). Zoning reform has increased interest and planning for ADUs that can be freestanding small buildings in a backyard, in-law units added to existing structures, or space converted within an existing home to an additional housing unit. Backyard ADU solutions include what are being termed *granny flats* for seniors. These housing units allow multigenerational families to reduce housing costs. These dwellings also make it easier for adult children to help care for their aging parents and for grandparents to help with childcare. Planners sometimes refer to ADUs as "gentle density," which is more amenable than large new structures to communities resistant to change.

Transform Land Use with Workforce Housing

Nothing makes living connected to place more possible for those who can't work remotely than to have housing near where they work. Major employers working with cities can play a major role in making this a reality. In 2021, the University of California at San Francisco, for example, agreed to build more than twelve hundred new housing units for students, staff, and faculty as part of its planned expansion of a hospital campus.

About seventy-five thousand acres of school district land in California could be developed into over two million housing units for the education workforce.[41] Supported by voter-approved bonds, the Jefferson Union High School District in Daly City, California, built 122 apartment homes on school district property that became available to teachers and staff in fall 2022. In the high-priced Bay Area housing market, these units are rented out at 50 percent of the market rate. The development includes a community lounge, fitness center, and landscaped courtyard with seating, barbecues, and a children's playground. A new California law passed around the same time allowed school districts to build educator housing on district property without applying for zoning changes. More projects like the one in Daly City are in the works.

More middle- and low-income Americans can live near where they work when employers, with government and voter support, directly provide housing. Workforce housing can create a strong sense of belonging to a place and thus strengthen the community fabric.

Reset Culture through YIMBYism

A cultural reset around where and how much housing is created opens opportunities for infill development that local developers can build. The rise of the YIMBY movement in opposing NIMBY groups is leading to cultural change supportive of more infill housing and mixed-income communities. YIMBY groups are influencing state and local governments to change zoning and regulations and approve new housing with affordable units to stem the tide of displacement. Part of YIMBY's "yes" is that people should be able to live close to where they work.

The YIMBY movement has expanded by articulating the benefits of infill and affordable housing while addressing existing homeowner fears. Studies show, for example, that adding affordable housing into suburban or middle-class neighborhoods does not increase crime.[42] The research also demonstrates that low-income people who live in mixed-income communities have better life outcomes and are less likely to need government assistance. Ending wealthy residential enclaves and building more diverse neighborhoods, rather than causing continued harm in disinvested communities, ultimately enrich the lives of all people.

One of YIMBYism's tenets is that building more housing is more effective than other measures like rent control in creating housing and affordable rent. According to Chris Batson of Riaz Capital, "Allowing for the easy creation of abundant housing is the best way, in my opinion, to allow for rents to fall naturally. The City of Oakland has produced roughly ten thousand new units in the last fifteen years, and its rents have stabilized at 2016 rates despite 80 percent or greater occupancy in its buildings."[43] In multiple jurisdictions, increasing the supply of housing has counteracted rising rents.[44] The YIMBY movement is helping spur new affordable housing development.

The YIMBY movement has gained strength by bridging with other interest groups. Broader coalitions, for example, are being forged in support of building and land use conversions in downtowns. In 2024, an unlikely alliance of YIMBYs and historic preservationists supported a California state bill to streamline and speed up converting downtown buildings to residential use while preserving their historic exteriors.

The YIMBY movement has grown across California communities. As of 2024, over eighty thousand Californians were participating in a local YIMBY group.[45] California YIMBY, the statewide umbrella organization, has been instrumental in getting the state to curtail exclusionary zoning and pass other legislation that addresses the state's significant housing shortage.

Leverage Other Systems

The housing system is highly interrelated with the work and transportation systems, the respective subjects of chapters 5 and 6. The positive implication is that making any of these systems more place-based can have a ripple effect on the other systems, collectively leading to places where people can live affordably, work, and get around actively. For example, local workforce training is one strategy to make the work system more place-based (see chap. 5), and this includes training local developers, architects, and engineers who can design and build local housing.

Place-based transportation systems (chap. 6) can spur place-based housing systems by reducing car dependence and, consequently, space needed for cars. As discussed earlier, auto infrastructures such as freeways can and are being converted into housing and livable neighborhoods. Parking lots, garages and spots, and car-oriented streets occupy a lot of space in cities that could be used for housing and vibrant, mixed-use neighborhoods. In a country with eight parking spots per car[46] and up to 30 percent of land in cities used for parking,[47] space exists for housing many more people if we can reduce our car dependence.

Mixed-use communities, as a centerpiece of a place-based housing system, depend on the quality of other systems. The safety and features of parks, plazas, gardens, and other public spaces dictate their appeal and use. The quality of nearby stores and services matter. Limiting car use and speed in a neighborhood encourages walking and biking. Thriving mixed-use neighborhoods require well-designed and implemented place-based systems for local businesses and retail (chap. 5), transportation (chap. 6), community spaces (chap. 7), and nature spaces (chap. 8), as we will learn about in future chapters.

Many people want to live in communities with these types of place-based systems that enhance the quality of life. The challenge has been that the demand for these neighborhood amenities tends to increase surrounding property values, adding further to the housing affordability crisis. To avoid worsening inequality and limiting opportunities for many people to live connected to place, place-based housing systems must be developed in tandem with these other systems.

LOCAL BUSINESS AND WORK

Without that local ownership, without that community ownership in the neighborhood, you're at the mercy of these corporations.

—Tony Kelly, Bayview Community Cooperative, San Francisco

The neighborhood where my family and I live is an urban village. Nearly everything we need is within walking distance. With such local vibrancy, strolls down the street lead to saying hello to familiar faces and conversations with neighbors or local merchants we have known for years. What makes our neighborhood thrive is a collection of local restaurants, cafés, retail stores, and service providers.

We frequent the neighborhood market, Buffalo Whole Food and Grain Company, which is one block from our home. The store sells reasonably priced fresh produce, primarily sourced from the region, and an impressive amount of other grocery items in a small space. Several times over the years, I have suggested a product, and within days, they have it in stock. The owners and employees at that market greet customers with a smile and get to know them, making their work more enjoyable and rewarding in return.

A couple mornings a week, I make it to a Pilates class at CORE MVMT, a locally owned, independent studio a few blocks from our home. I benefit from the exercise to start my day and experience a strong sense of community, knowing the teachers and fellow students on a first-name basis. The owner, Lisa Thomure, opened the business shortly before the COVID-19 pandemic. The city's strict regulations shut down the studio for months, and it seemed it would not survive. Yet, thanks to the relationships Lisa and her teaching team had already built with many residents, the community rallied to support the business. Many of us purchased class series passes in advance and made donations. The studio came back strong and has a loyal following.

Between Buffalo Whole Food and CORE MVMT lies a retail store that has been in operation since 1936. Cliff's Variety Store is a full-service hardware store that also carries cookware, garden supplies, toys, crafts, and assorted gifts. It offers services like knife sharpening and rekeying. The store's longtime employees are highly knowledgeable and eager to help customers.

Then there's Spike's Coffees and Teas, a neighborhood fixture for decades and a daily gathering spot for local retirees. We get a pound of their organic coffee with a free cup of coffee and a kind greeting from the staff almost every week. Rolo is a local clothing store that's been around since 1977 and has survived and thrived despite the onslaught of corporate clothing retail chains. Castro Tarts is a café run by the same family for years who provide delicious Vietnamese and American breakfast and lunch food, indoor and sidewalk tables for dining, and quick service.

Together, these and dozens of other local businesses make a livable, walkable neighborhood that fulfills many daily life needs and adds to residents' quality of life. In addition, they provide meaningful ownership and work opportunities for many people.

* * *

Local business districts like those in our neighborhood once dominated the center of small towns and urban neighborhoods, but they are now far from the norm. The growing market dominance of Big Retail, notably Walmart, Dollar stores, and Amazon, has led to the loss of thousands of local grocery, hardware, book, and other retail stores. Walmart is the United States' largest employer, with 1.6 million employees of the megacorporation's 2.1 million worldwide employees in 2024.[1] Amazon is the second-largest employer, with 1.1 million people of its 1.5 million workforce in the United States.[2]

Many fear Big Retail's continued growth will eliminate most local retail. Amazon has become almost synonymous with online shopping. In 2024, a record 83 percent of US households shopped on Amazon.[3] On the brick-and-mortar side, Dollar stores run by Dollar General, Dollar Tree, and Family Dollar (owned by Dollar Tree) grew from twenty thousand locations in 2011 to thirty-five thousand by 2023.[4] In 2022, one in three stores that opened in the United States was a Dollar store.[5] One of their target locations for growth has been impoverished, rural communities, taking customers away from local general and other stores. Like Amazon and Walmart, they use low prices, massive inventories of seemingly infinite goods, and their ubiquitous presence to lure consumers away from local businesses.

Owning and finding jobs in independent, local stores have consequently become increasingly difficult. The number of small, local retailers has been in decline for a few decades, including a loss of sixty-five thousand of them between 2007 and 2017.[6] By 2014, the percentage of retail jobs stood at 47.2 percent in large chains compared to 35.6 percent in small retail businesses, a complete reversal since 1980.[7] Cliff's Variety Store co-owner Terry Bennett puts it bluntly, "Get rid of Amazon. It's killing businesses like ours."[8] If these trends continue, will Amazon, Walmart, and Dollar be all we experience in the retail marketplace?

Big Retail corporations suggest that they offer superior employment opportunities and perpetuate the myth that they pay higher wages than small businesses. When small businesses were thriving into the 1970s, wages for most Americans were rising. Since then, wages for most workers have stagnated concurrently with corporate retail's growth. Average income is higher mainly because upper management is paid so much, while those lower in the corporate hierarchy receive low pay.

Less local retail translates to a lot less for communities and people: lower wages and fewer ownership opportunities, little opportunity to shop and work close to where you live, and less vibrancy and economic activity in our neighborhoods.

In this chapter, we'll focus on retail as one aspect of the business and work system. We'll explore how corporations have come to increasingly corner the retail economic market with far-reaching impacts. Dispelling the claims of Big Retail, we'll envision a different reality of thriving local stores across various communities. Armed with an understanding of Big Retail's systemic tactics, the chapter will then highlight systems-change strategies that can make thriving local stores the cornerstone of our cities and neighborhoods again.

Systems-Change Strategies for Revitalizing Local Business and Work

- Shift power through corporate retail power restrictions
- Shift power through reducing cost burdens and providing targeted resources
- Shift power through local purchasing by anchor institutions
- Shift power to fair online marketplaces
- Shift power to worker cooperatives
- Shift power to small business networks
- Transform land use with big-box store and warehouse bans or restrictions
- Transform land use with local business districts in mixed-use communities
- Transform land use by adding local stores to residential neighborhoods
- Reset culture through "buy local" campaigns
- Leverage other systems

Holding the System of Corporate Retail in Place

Big Retail has a firm grip on power and land use underlying its market control, stacking the odds against owning and working in local stores. Knowing the cultural value of local business, Big Retail also co-opts the term *local* and uses it to expand its market share.

Power: Big Retail and Unfair Business Practices

The massive shifts in retail ownership and employment do not result from fair competition between corporations and local businesses. The Institute for Local Self-Reliance (ILSR) has led the way in exposing the anticompetitive behavior that Big Retail uses to undercut local businesses. Its research has shown how Walmart, for example, uses its market power to drive down wholesale prices that smaller, independent competitors cannot access.[9] This monopolistic practice—predatory buying—gives megacorporations a significant advantage in the marketplace.

Amazon has come to exemplify how unfair business practices facilitate corporate market dominance. Its avoidance of taxes for years (see chap. 13) gave the company a significant leg up over local businesses, allowing it to cut retail prices and grow market share. Furthermore, Amazon engages in predatory pricing, which refers to selling items below cost to drive smaller companies out of a particular market. They then raise prices once the competition is diminished.

Furthermore, Amazon's "marketplace" prioritizes its products and further disadvantages small businesses. The retail giant uses proprietary data on third-party sellers, such as small retailers, and imposes high fees on them. Small businesses provide, on average, 30 percent of their sales revenue to Amazon, which added up to $121 billion in revenue for Amazon in 2021.[10] A change in Amazon's algorithms can drive sales down for a third-party seller overnight. In the current e-commerce system, independent businesses have little choice but to sell on Amazon's dominant marketplace with almost no power to set terms.

Big Retail has been able to exert its power on government to prevent a crackdown on its business maneuvering to secure advantages. While regulatory laws to prevent predatory practices exist, enforcement has been minimal in recent decades as corporate influence has deepened.

Big Retail also uses its power to pressure counties and cities to offer subsidies or tax breaks for locating big-box stores, offices, or warehouses in them. Jurisdictions purportedly do this in anticipation of higher tax revenue from workers and sales receipts over time. However, costs for roads, police, and other public services needed for these facilities are often high. Furthermore, the presence of Big Retail has been found to decrease the value of nearby downtown and commercial buildings, leading to less municipal tax revenue.[11] Consequently, Big Retail tends to drain rather than increase local public funds. In addition, corporate teams of litigators often aggressively dispute property valuations and win lower taxes.[12] Big Retail's power to secure these concessions has supported its growth and facilitated the decline of local retail.

Power Stacked Against Small Business

At the same time, government at all levels has become less favorable to local businesses—even programs designed to help small businesses often don't. Half of the Paycheck Protection Program, the small business lifeline during COVID-19, went to just 5 percent of recipients: six hundred large companies, including dozens of national chains.[13] Local government can add to the challenges. Bureaucratic hurdles can prevent independent retail businesses from opening for months and add costs. Government has become less and less attentive to the needs of small business.

A disproportionate cost burden for local stores is swipe fees that range from 2 to 4 percent for every purchase, costing more than utilities or rent in some cases. The duopoly Visa and Mastercard controls over 70 percent of the credit card market.[14] Visa and Mastercard impose swipe fees on US merchants seven times higher than their regulated fees in Europe.[15] Visa and Mastercard's ability to set fees with little real negotiation is another hardship for small businesses.

Increasing rents add to the challenges facing local enterprises that lack the economic power to counter corporate and other prominent real estate–holding landlords. Columbia University professor Tim Wu has written extensively about the consolidation of the American economy since the 1990s and how American capitalism has turned against small business. In a *New York Times* opinion piece, Wu shared the story of the once-thriving Chelsea Convenience Hardware store in the Manhattan neighborhood of New York City that closed in November 2019.[16] The store had been losing customers to Amazon and other e-commerce platforms. The nail on the coffin occurred when the store was subjected to a near-doubling of rent. As Wu explains, rents have risen considerably in coastal cities with concentrations of wealth and contributed to the closure of small businesses.

Land Use: Big-Box Retail, Warehouses, and Use-Based Zoning

With government support, Big Retail is largely responsible for the cookie-cutter, homogeneous design of strip malls across the United States. Whether Target,

Walmart, Dollar, Costco, Home Depot, or another big-box store, the stores and their parking lots take up considerable land. With the shift to online shopping, big-box stores are in decline but still dominate much of the brick-and-mortar retail landscape.

As e-commerce has proliferated, Big Retail has expanded its land use footprint through warehouses and data centers that facilitate online delivery. In addition to other facilities, Amazon has over 110 large warehouses—or fulfillment centers, as the corporation euphemistically calls them—in the United States alone, with dozens more planned to enable even faster deliveries.[17] Each fulfillment center ranges from six hundred thousand to one million square feet, or up to twenty-three acres.

The conditions in warehouses seem like something that existed before workplace protections were put in place. Work is monotonous as employees pick hundreds of items off shelves every hour for shipping. With the emphasis on speed, warehouse workers are often injured and have been fired for being sick or injured.[18] Conditions inside a New Breed Logistics' warehouse in Memphis, for example, were described as follows: "Hundreds of workers, many of them women, lifted and dragged boxes that could weigh up to 45 pounds. To save money, there was no air-conditioning, even in the middle of southern summers, causing temperatures to rise past 100 degrees. Employees at the warehouse were disciplined using a 'point system,' in which they could be fired once they racked up 10 points. Asking for a break to go to the doctor could earn you a point, as could taking too long on a break."[19] At a fundamental level, such work is not only dangerous; it also feeds a sense of alienation. Employees handle packages without knowledge of the products inside, and they are disconnected from the customers who will receive them. The monotony, hazards, and loss of meaning in this work will likely continue to increase with the growth of online Big Retail.

A third component of land use that favors Big Retail at the expense of local stores is use-based zoning, discussed in chapter 4. Driving a car to shop becomes the default transportation option when stores are separated from residential neighborhoods. Local stores typically can't afford large parking lots; thus car-dependent, single-use zoned communities favor shopping at big-box stores.

Culture: Co-Opting *Local*

Corporations know that people value local businesses and try to co-opt the term *local*. In 2023, Amazon was a top sponsor of San Francisco's Small Business Week. Other sponsors included Wells Fargo and Bank of America. Events included an Amazon Small Business Panel and a workshop titled "How to Start Selling in Amazon's Store." The event website hailed Amazon as a "small business champion." To suggest that this week supported small businesses seemed like a sad joke, and this wasn't lost on local store owners. Eileen McCormick, the manager of a local bookstore commented, "It's in incredibly poor taste. It's insulting. It's ridiculous."[20] Local retailers are fed up with Amazon and its thin veil of caring about local businesses.

American Express supports Small Business Saturdays to promote local shops and districts. It's been popular with local businesses, and American Express distributes some money back to small businesses, including $2.3 million in 2022. Yet this represents a tiny fraction of the swipe fees that local companies pay to American Express. Proper support for local businesses would translate into much-reduced swipe fees year-round.

The corporate capitalism retail system is failing us. Wage inequality and the loss of local community, stores, and work are some of the casualties. To help communities and more people within them thrive, we must reshape the system around local businesses and stores and away from corporations.

A Vision of Local Business, Work, and Shopping

Living connected to place becomes more feasible when residents can easily access local stores and when those businesses, in turn, provide livelihoods for people where they live. Like stable housing, economic opportunity through work is foundational to financial security and personal well-being. Local economies can be significant job creators and sustainers, providing financial security for families and individuals. Local stores offer opportunities for employees to be owners, managers, and otherwise empowered to influence conditions in their workplace.

Independent businesses spur local economic growth. Studies have shown how money spent on local stores rather than national or international chain stores provides substantially more value to the local economy[21] and more tax revenue for local government.[22] A study on bookstores in Austin, Texas, found that spending money at an independent bookstore versus a chain store kept three times as much money circulating locally.[23] This multiplier effect leads to more jobs, income, and tax revenue in the local economy.

Local retail associations like Oklahoma's Independent Shopkeepers Association support and track data on independent businesses. The association's 2023 State of Retail Study showed that local retail stores pay higher-than-average retail wages and make higher sales per square foot than mall department stores.[24] In an age when corporate retail has considerable power, local businesses, when valued, find ways to do well for their communities and employees.

The perception that bigger is better for efficiently delivering goods and services is often untrue. Stacy Mitchell of the aforementioned ILSR shared that West

Virginia and North Dakota were far ahead of other states in giving out doses of the COVID-19 vaccine early in the rollout in 2021.[25] Both states relied almost exclusively on independent, locally owned pharmacies rather than national retailers like CVS and Walgreens. Mitchell further cites studies that show independent pharmacies have lower prices for prescription drugs and provide shorter wait times and faster delivery than large pharmacy corporations.

Local stores provide opportunities for meaningful work anchored in direct relationships with customers. When a business primarily serves a neighborhood or town, the owners and employees get to know their customers' preferences and needs. Independent businesses, like Buffalo Whole Food in my neighborhood, adjust inventory to the local customer base and provide better care and services like local pharmacies. These dynamics make owning or working in a local store engaging and rewarding.

Independent stores build community. Local bookstores, for example, often serve as community spaces where neighbors see one another and learn together through book talks and other events. In his retrospective article on the closing of the Chelsea Convenience Hardware store, Professor Tim Wu described the contributions of the store to the community: "Chelsea Convenience is a social hub; it seems as if someone from the neighborhood is always hanging out, chatting about something. 'People come in here,' Mr. Feygin [the owner] says, turning up his palms in a gesture of blasé wonderment. 'They want to talk about their life, my life.'"[26] Customers, employees, and owners add to local economic life together and become a community within the larger neighborhood. Mutual appreciation defines the relationships. The closing of Chelsea Convenience in Manhattan left a big hole in the neighborhood.

Thriving neighborhoods filled with local enterprises were once commonplace in the United States. Community bonds were strong in these places. Greenwood was once such a neighborhood in Tulsa, Oklahoma, and its story must be remembered for many reasons.

Greenwood's origin in the early twentieth century was steeped in racism, and its destruction showed the worst of the United States. Much of the thirty-five-block Greenwood neighborhood was burned down in the Tulsa Race Massacre of 1921. What happened to Greenwood is horrific and left a deep scar on our nation's history. For its brief existence, though, it proved to be a model of flourishing local business, perhaps more self-sufficient than any community in US history. Part of the reparations for such past harm and its legacy should be the rebuilding of thriving local business districts.

Greenwood, also known as "Black Wall Street," was developed by Black Americans who had been excluded from other neighborhoods in Tulsa. Together, they built a hyperlocal economy and vibrant culture. Residents could shop down the street for groceries and other items, be entertained in theaters and pool halls, get services like haircuts, and eat out at a host of restaurants and cafés. Star Williams, a descendant of a resident family, reflected on how his grandfather experienced the neighborhood: "My grandfather often talked about how you could enjoy a full life in Greenwood, that everything you needed or wanted was in Greenwood. You never had to go anywhere."[27] More than two hundred diverse jobs existed in Greenwood, including at many local stores.[28] Greenwood shows how strong local economies and communities can be built around local enterprise, adding to livability and meaningful place-based work opportunities.

Local businesses can have a transformative impact on collective well-being. In addition to the personal, community, and economic benefits of local work outlined above, transportation-related greenhouse gas emissions decline with short commutes and more goods and services available locally.

Systems-Change Strategies for a Place-Based Business and Work System

Systems of local business and work are being rebuilt in many places with support from government and residents. From the federal to the local level, power can be shifted away from corporations to independent businesses and worker cooperatives. Power is being built locally and nationally through small business networks. Land use is being transformed to limit the big-box footprint and better support local stores in mixed-use communities where small businesses can thrive. Awareness around the importance of buying locally is growing, spurred by "buy local" campaigns. These systems-change strategies, in concert with leveraging other systems, are helping build local ecosystems of business and work.

Shift Power Through Corporate Retail Power Restrictions

Turning the system around and making it more place-based starts with shifting power to local independent businesses. Government at all levels plays an essential role in implementing policies that reduce the disproportionate power of corporate retail.

Efforts at the federal level to rein in the size and power of corporations are critically needed for local independent businesses to compete fairly. After four decades of ignoring corporate consolidation across the economy, federal enforcement of antimerger and antitrust laws started to return under the Biden administration in 2020. The Federal Trade Commission and the Department of Justice revitalized antimerger guidelines, making it more difficult for large corporations to further grow in power and consolidate industries. In 2020, Congress also led an investigation of competition in digital markets through the House Judiciary Committee. The fifteen-month investigation concluded with an assessment that Amazon "has monopoly power over many small- and medium-sized businesses." The committee called for breaking up Amazon into separate business lines and enacting measures to ensure fairer treatment of sellers on its online marketplace. Notably, both Republicans and Democrats expressed support for these measures.

Curbs on corporate power can also occur at state and local levels. In North Dakota and West Virginia, where small pharmacies beat out the corporate ones in delivering COVID-19 vaccines, only pharmacists are allowed to own pharmacies. Consequently, local pharmacies predominate, and only a few grandfathered corporate chain pharmacy stores exist.

Shift Power Through Reducing Cost Burdens and Providing Targeted Resources

In addition to curbing the power of corporations, government can change policies and direct resources to create economic conditions supportive of locally owned stores.

At the federal and state levels, universal health care should be viewed, in addition to its many other benefits, as an important means to shift economic power to small businesses. Local stores are at a competitive disadvantage in recruiting employees when they cannot offer health insurance like larger enterprises. If they provide benefits, they typically must increase prices to absorb significant health insurance costs, risking a decline in customers. Universal health care would take this significant expense from all businesses and help independent stores stay afloat.

Similarly, the push for universal community-based broadband benefits small businesses by reducing costs and ensuring reliable internet access. Laws like the American Rescue Plan Act (ARPA), passed in 2021, supported its development.

Swipe fees, another cost burden for local store owners, can be reduced with supportive policy. A federally proposed law, the Credit Card Competition Act, is designed to create more competition among financial transaction providers and minimize credit card fee rates. The bipartisan bill was unsuccessful in 2023. With mounting pressure from local retail stores nationwide, it may eventually pass.

The federal government can use some of its immense resources to directly support small businesses. The government does not have a good track record on this, but in 2021, things started to change. ARPA provided $350 billion in relief from the impact of the COVID-19 pandemic to state and local governments. The ILSR called ARPA "small business's big moment" and showed how those funds could collectively shift the business and work system.[29] Its list of recommendations closely matched the specific strategies for changing the system to be more place-based, as detailed in the remaining sections of this chapter.

Local government can tilt tax policy benefits toward independent businesses. Tax breaks or financial incentives to lure corporations to locate offices, facilities, or stores in specific jurisdictions should be redirected to create and sustain local stores. Full cost-accounting of new development like required in Vermont is another promising measure. As discussed earlier, local jurisdictions almost always lose out on tax revenue when it comes to large corporations. Laws like those in Vermont deter deals from being made for corporate big-box stores and other developments. Vermont has more small businesses and fewer big-box stores per capita than any other state.[30]

Shift Power Through Local Purchasing by Anchor Institutions

For local businesses overall, power can also be shifted through preferences by anchor institutions. These local entities are major employers and service providers with considerable purchasing power.

Local government serves as an anchor institution in many places. Government procurement policies can set thresholds for contracts going to locally owned enterprises. The city of San Francisco, for example, runs a Local Business Enterprise program. Under it, certified local businesses are given a competitive advantage over nonlocal businesses in the process of obtaining contracts with the city. Such procurement policies can apply to buying from local retail businesses.

Local anchor institutions can work together to aggregate their purchasing power in support of local enterprises. In *From What Is to What If*, transition movement leader Rob Hopkins describes how this approach was utilized in the city of Preston in Northern England.[31] In the 2010s, seven anchor institutions including the police department, two universities, the city government, and a large housing association developed and implemented local procurement policies. This resulted in over twelve thousand new local jobs. Working together, anchor institutions can build the market power of local businesses while spurring the development of more.

Shift Power to Fair Online Marketplaces

Understanding that brick-and-mortar stores need a visible online presence to compete in the twenty-first century, local businesses can benefit from an "if you can't beat them, join them" approach.

Faced with decreasing business from large online retailers, independent bookstores have banded together through sites such as bookshop.org. Once one selects a book on these sites, a list of local bookstores that have the book appears. An online order can then be placed from a store for pickup or shipping. Alternatively, a person can order directly from bookshop.org, which shares proceeds with its networks of independent bookstores. After an order is placed, the customer receives this message: "Thank you for your part in supporting local bookstores, a vital and essential part of our culture." Bookshop.org provides an online marketplace that benefits independent bookstores and reminds customers of their important mission every time an order is made.

To further support local enterprise, independent manufacturers and makers that sell locally need fair online platforms. For many, the sole choice has become selling through Amazon, which imposes an average 30 percent fee on their sales. Local or regional online platforms tailored to customers in their locations would instead help keep wealth local. In the meantime, any alternative to Amazon that can get the attention of customers or retailers is a step in the right direction.

The aptly named Faire is an online business-to-business marketplace that facilitates connecting independent brands with retailers to buy their products. Its founding vision is to help small businesses compete on a more level playing field with Amazon, Walmart, and other megaretail corporations. As of 2024, over one hundred thousand independent businesses were selling everything from home decorations to food and drink items to pet products to the seven hundred thousand retailers buying on the platform.[32] Faire's commission and payment processing fees for sellers average around 17 percent.[33] Though still high, it's a lot better for small businesses than Amazon and shows that small businesses can be provided a fairer fee for the use of online platforms.

Federal and state laws that curb the power of technology companies, like the American Innovation and Choice Online Act introduced in 2021, are also needed to level the online playing field for local businesses. The bill prohibits Amazon, Google, and other Big Tech corporations from self-preferencing—favoring their own goods and services, such as at the top of search results. Additionally, the bill would require Amazon to offer small businesses and Prime customers package delivery service provider choices. This would potentially save businesses on the platform considerable money in terms of being able to use UPS, the postal service, FedEx, or another carrier competing with Amazon.

Shift Power to Worker Cooperatives

Economic power is shifted deeper and more widely into a place when it flows to workers. Worker-owned cooperatives have been around for decades and started going through a renaissance in the 2020s. The employee ownership business model builds wealth for worker-owners while empowering them to participate in decision-making and oversight of their business.

Critical elements of financial security are often missing from many low- and middle-wage jobs in the corporate capitalist work system. Employee-owned firms put workers first and typically support or provide childcare, health care, paid leave, and transportation access-commuter benefits. Sharing ownership also spreads the risks and responsibilities of small businesses and motivates everyone involved to make it work.

Rainbow Grocery is a worker-owned cooperative (co-op) that has been around since 1975 in San Francisco. The store is known for providing a wide selection of organic and locally sourced products. There are more than 250 worker-owners, some of whom have been there for over forty years. The store also serves as a hub supporting the community and other local organizations with resources and information.

Grocery co-ops have been expanding to communities historically deprived of grocery stores and fresh produce. In Oakland, California, the Mandela Worker-Owned Cooperative provides fresh, local products sourced from Black and Brown farmers and food makers. The co-op pays livable wages that can support families. It supports community residents through healthy cooking classes and offering 50 percent off fruits and vegetables for those who qualify for food assistance.

The nonprofit Project Equity supports businesses transitioning to worker co-op structures. Project Equity helps companies finance the transition to co-ops through its Employee Ownership Catalyst fund. Assisting businesses through the intricacies of becoming a co-op, nonprofit support organizations like Project Equity play an invaluable role.

The promise of worker co-ops in strengthening local economies and supporting livable wages and meaningful livelihoods spurred the California state government to pass the California Employee Ownership Act in 2022. The law established an Employee Ownership Program to align state agencies in support of the growth of co-ops. The program also facilitates outreach and technical assistance grant programs. Subsidies and other funding mechanisms for businesses trying to become co-ops were included in this legislation.

With so many baby boomers retiring, local businesses are experiencing ownership turnover. This presents a significant opportunity for local worker cooperatives to grow in number. It is a great way to avoid closing a business and express value for the employees who made the business happen. In addition, selling a business to its employees boosts retirement savings for the prior owners and leaves a legacy of meaningful local work opportunities.

Shift Power to Small Business Networks

Small business networks help locally owned stores in attracting customers and lobbying for policy change. Local nonprofits or associations often play a role as the glue that holds these networks together. Some networks encompass local businesses within geographic settings, while others focus on types like worker cooperatives.

The Wellspring Cooperative supports almost a dozen community-based, worker-owned companies in inner-city Springfield, Massachusetts. A key network strategy is getting local anchor institutions to purchase products from the network's co-ops.

The Castro/Upper Market Community Benefit District (CBD) is a business improvement district, and it is an important reason why Castro residents like me can shop locally for almost anything. The district is one of eighteen San Francisco CBDs authorized to assess local properties within targeted commercial districts and mixed-use neighborhoods for quality-of-life improvements. Led by local stores, the Castro/Upper Market CBD meets monthly to discuss and respond to neighborhood issues and allocate funding. Funds have been directed to daily sidewalk cleaning, beautification projects, streetscape improvements, a business attraction campaign, safety patrols, and support of community events. In one major project, the CBD partnered with the city to widen sidewalks and crosswalks, add street trees, and otherwise enhance the streetscape. The changes led to increased pedestrian traffic and customers for local businesses.

It's important to note that cities have reputations for being unfriendly to small business, and San Francisco is no exception. The bureaucratic hurdles to starting and operating a business can be overwhelming and frustrating. Fees, taxes, and a vast array of requirements can sink a company. The fact that so many local businesses have persisted in the Castro and other San Francisco neighborhoods is a testament to the community benefit districts that support their enterprises.

To counter the immense power of corporations and level the playing field, national networks of small businesses and independent stores are also needed. More than two hundred thousand independent businesses nationwide have joined Small Business Rising. This coalition consists of thirty small business groups that include the American Booksellers Association, the Main Street Alliance, and place-based business associations. Their campaign calls for breaking up and regulating tech monopolies like Amazon that corner online markets and making rules that create fairer competition. Small business coalitions were a force behind the resurgence of federal antitrust and antimerger regulatory enforcement, as described earlier.

Transform Land Use with Big-Box Store and Warehouse Bans or Restrictions

Communities are also rising up against corporate chain expansion that has decimated local stores and work. More than seventy-five cities and towns rejected chain Dollar stores from 2019 to 2022.[34] Other local jurisdictions have passed permanent bans or limits on Dollar stores to protect local grocery and retail businesses.

The town of Salisbury, North Carolina, reversed course on approving a Dollar General Store in 2022. The town's planning board initially voted 4 to 3 to rezone a parcel to accommodate the store. After the community spoke up in opposition, the board unanimously opposed it. Some residents said they saw no need for the chain store with other Dollar stores in the county and nearby hardware, drug, and grocery stores. The decision was based on safety concerns around increased car traffic and inconsistencies with the city's vision of having local stores accessible to pedestrians and near transit stops.

The state of Maine took on Big Retail by confronting its continual pressure to lower property taxes for its big-box stores. In 2022, a new law in the state restricted the workarounds that Walmart and other corporate retailers were using to lower their property taxes. Removing these unfair advantages levels the playing field for local store owners who don't have the resources to fight and win tax appeals. Taking action like the Maine legislature makes Big Retail think twice about adding more stores.

Communities have also thwarted additional land holdings by Amazon. Unions and other groups successfully pressured Arvada, Colorado, and Oceanside, California, to reject proposals and abandon plans for Amazon facilities. These communities are showing others that they can successfully stand up against Amazon. Stopping the growth of the footprint of Amazon, Dollar General, and other Big Retail is protecting land that can be saved for other uses more beneficial to local communities.

Transform Land Use with Local Business Districts in Mixed-Use Communities

Cities can boost shopping at local stores by helping make main streets and public markets safe, attractive, and inviting spaces for people. These investments in local business districts help entice consumers to stores.

The National Main Street Center (Main Street) recommends that local governments support revitalization and innovation on main streets by developing a clear strategy. Elements include streamlining adaptations of existing buildings to new and flexible uses and providing pop-up spaces for emerging enterprises. Main Street has put its money behind these approaches, directing over $107 billion to cities for reinvestment in main streets and business districts between 1980 and 2023.[35] This funding resulted in 335,675 rehabilitated buildings, 782,059 net jobs gained, and 175,323 net new businesses.[36] Strategic investments in local business districts have a big payoff.

Public markets, in which vendors are organized in public spaces, make up another type of district for local businesses. Local vendors predominate in these vibrant spaces. Cities are committing to their expansion and increasing access for residents. London has 280 public markets, supported by a Market Board created in 2017 to ensure these markets continue flourishing. Pittsburgh, Seattle, and Toronto leaders participated in the Market Cities Initiative to expand infrastructure, policies, and investments for public markets in their cities. Barcelona aims to ensure that every resident is within a ten-minute walk of a public market.

Ensuring these business districts are in mixed-use neighborhoods where people can live, work, recreate, and shop locally further boosts local stores and jobs. Relationships between customers and businesses can be strong and lasting when they coexist in the same neighborhood. It becomes a mutually reinforcing cycle of local economic activity and connection, as workers at different businesses live nearby and frequent one another's businesses.

Transform Land Use by Adding Local Stores to Residential Neighborhoods

Architect Sam Kraft laments the loss of corner stores in the urban neighborhoods of Seattle, many of which have been zoned for single-family residences. He highlights one exception in the Ravenna neighborhood where he lived: Seven Coffee Roasters Market and Café. It has been a community fixture for over one hundred years. Kraft describes what Seven Coffee Roasters and the other few remaining corner stores bring to a neighborhood: "They are beloved local places that connect to us—to Seattle's past; to each other; to the food, drink, art, culture, and life of a specific neighborhood. They create more activity on the sidewalk, reducing crime and cars and increasing walking, biking, skipping, scootering and maybe even laughing."[37]

Bringing back corner stores can get urban and suburban neighborhoods back on the path to vibrancy and community while increasing local work opportunities. Imagine every neighborhood with stores that are owned locally and woven into the community fabric.

In an increasing number of jurisdictions, property owners can add Accessory Commercial Units (ACUs). With ACUs, homeowners or renters, with their landlords' permission, can turn their garage, basement, backyard, or some other place on their property into a storefront.

Local journalist Christina Campodocino profiled ACU entrepreneurs in San Francisco.[38] Roy Tahtinen converted his garage into an art gallery that show-cases his photos. It was inexpensive for Tahitinen to create this local business space, investing a few hundred dollars in lights. Dan Streetman started a coffee roasting business in his garage. He directly sells the beans three days a week to locals, offers a subscription-based coffee delivery service, and supplies local corner stores and groceries. In 2021, his business grossed about $200,000 in sales.

Reset Culture Through "Buy Local" Campaigns

The linchpin for local economies that provide good-paying jobs and careers for residents in local stores is the commitment of the local population to buying local.

In a culture dominated by corporate narratives, raising awareness about opportunities to shop locally is critical to building sufficient demand for local businesses. Local government, nonprofits, and business associations play an essential role in administering "buy local" campaigns. These efforts help independent businesses compete with the marketing budgets and online platforms of large corporations.

Many resources are available to support "buy local" campaigns from associations such as the Business for Local Living Economies and the American Independent Business Alliance. These groups provide examples of tools to promote local shopping, such as coupon books, apps, advertisements, local reward programs, and local gift cards. These tools encourage and incentivize local shopping and help reset shopping culture.

StayLocal started in 2001 in New Orleans. The organization frames local shopping as a call to action to support the local economy and community. StayLocal educates consumers on the benefits of staying local and conducts an active marketing campaign for their member businesses. In addition, the organization connects businesses to cost- and time-saving resources, including discounted advertising and member-to-member discounts. In these ways and more, StayLocal shifts power by facilitating a network of local businesses and resets culture with its marketing campaign.

Living Local 413 is a regional effort in Western Massachusetts for eating, shopping, and living locally. Its programs include media campaigns, a business talk podcast, and a college experiential learning program in which students from a local university gain experience in locally owned businesses. Like StayLocal, its "buy local" campaign is embedded in larger services provided to independent businesses.

"Buy local" campaigns have an impact. A teen-led campaign in Miner County, South Dakota, encouraged residents to increase their spending at local businesses. Money spent locally increased by $15 million the following year.[39] In 2013, a data analysis in San Francisco found that 10 percent of spending redirected from Big Retail to local stores would generate $192 million in economic activity and almost thirteen hundred new jobs.[40] To work, "buy local" campaigns must become a central strategy of local government and business entities, sidelining groups that promote corporate interests and creating a tipping point for "buy local" enthusiasm.

Leverage Other Systems

The system of business and work connects to all the other systems featured in this book. Jobs and careers exist in each system and extend well beyond the local retail store focus of this chapter. In the energy system, for example, local public power consists mostly of municipally owned utilities. These entities employ almost one hundred thousand people in hometown jobs.[41] The most impactful lever for changing the overall work system is to leverage other place-based systems.

In *The Great Pivot*, Justine Burt shared her research on the jobs needed to build a sustainable future. Many of the highlighted opportunities are locally oriented, reflecting that our best path to sustainability is through place-based systems that provide local work.

Burt categorizes work into five sustainability categories: advanced energy communities, low-carbon mobility systems, a circular economy, reduced food waste, and a healthy natural world. These correlate respectively with building energy (chap. 10), transportation (chap. 6), consumer goods (chap. 11), food (chap. 9), and nature spaces (chap. 9) place-based systems. Within these categories, Burt specifies "30 great pivot projects" that can collectively create millions of local and regional jobs in the United States alone. For example, a regional recycling industry can evolve in lieu of exporting recyclables to other countries. Supportive jobs include waste prevention coordinators and regional recycling market development managers. The aggregation of recyclables within a region can spur the growth of businesses that turn recyclables into products, adding more local employment opportunities.

Workforce development specific to the different place-based systems helps leverage the other systems to increase the local workforce. In support of Paris-culteurs, Paris's urban farming initiative (see chap. 9), the Breuil School trains people to be urban farmers. In Detroit, the Get Down Farm teaches local youth to work in urban agriculture. GRID Alternatives (see chap. 10) has provided almost fifty thousand people with solar installation training and hands-on experience installing systems in low-income communities.[42] This win-win approach in delivering renewable energy to low-income households and hands-on workforce development provides local solar installation companies with trained employees.

As discussed in this chapter and chapter 4, local careers and jobs are not local if people can't live near where they work. Therefore, the place-based housing system (chap. 5) that makes housing available and affordable in all communities is essential to a place-based work system. Strategies like removing parking minimums to boost the housing supply, as discussed in this chapter, can also benefit the local work system by not burdening small businesses with having to provide on-site parking.

The place-based housing system can boost local work directly too. The construction of new housing can provide local jobs when there is a commitment to local hiring. The University of California, San Francisco, project, introduced in this chapter, to build twelve hundred housing units for faculty, staff, and students provides an example. The project is committed to hiring residents for at least 30 percent of the construction workforce needs and the eventual new jobs the expansion creates.

Walkable, bikeable mixed-use neighborhoods help local economies, businesses, and work thrive. In a 2023 report, Smart Growth American reported that walkable urbanism in the largest thirty-five metro areas accounted for 19.1 percent of real US gross domestic product while using only 1.2 percent of land and housing 6.8 percent of the population.[43] A body of research summarized by Transport for London found that improving conditions for walking and biking boosts nearby retail by up to 30 percent.[44] The research also revealed that owners tend to overestimate how many customers come to their store by car. Surfacing these findings, especially in concert with building trust, can potentially help quell opposition to lost parking spaces. Walkable, bikeable neighborhoods also benefit businesses with increased staff retention and productivity and reduced health care costs when they can get to work actively.[45] These neighborhood features can be great for local businesses and work and are essential elements of place-based transportation systems, featured in chapter 6.

TRANSPORTATION

When you see that these [streets] can be used for other things, walking with your children, jogging, biking, people start to think differently about how this space can be used, how much space the cars use up.

—Sergio Montero, Assistant Professor of Urban and Regional Development, Universidad de los Andes, Bogotá, Colombia

I grew up just north of Los Angeles. It was the 1970s and '80s. Southern California had become the land of the automobile. The car was woven into the cultural fabric, from the Autopia ride at Disneyland, where kids like me experienced the excitement of driving for the first time, to drive-in restaurants and theaters. Freeways and roads were filled with cars. Finding refuge from the loud hum of engines or smog-filled skies was increasingly difficult.

On my sixteenth birthday, I got my driver's license, by then a common rite of passage in the United States. Shortly afterward, I was gifted a used car. Prior to that, my older brother had been driving me to school in our grandparents' old car each day. Now we could each drive independently wherever we felt we needed to go. Each of us having our own car and our parents each having a car was unquestioned.

It wasn't until I was in college that I began thinking more about the dominance of automobiles in our transportation system. At the University of California, Berkeley, I rediscovered the joy of biking. It brought back positive feelings from biking to elementary and middle school. I experienced public transportation near where I lived for the first time through the Bay Area Rapid Transit (BART) subway system. BART made it easy to get into San Francisco for the occasional trip.

Once adulthood and parenthood kicked in, I resorted to mostly driving the car. I was aware of and concerned about automobile pollution, but thinking a car was always needed was automatic. Not until 2011 did I kick the car habit, when traveling by commuter train and bike became my default. The dependable Caltrain service between my new workplace and home and being able to store my bike on the train made it possible. I soon became hooked.

* * *

People who drive little or not at all remain outliers in the United States. Driving a car and mostly alone remains the norm. The amount of time people spend in personal vehicles has tripled since the 1970s.[1] The average American spends almost an hour driving a car each day and travels, on average, over thirty miles daily.[2] In most communities, transportation alternatives are limited, devalued, or both. Making a change is not easy within a system designed to keep us in our cars.

Automobile dependency places the heaviest financial burden and the greatest loss of time on those who can afford it least. The housing affordability crisis in work centers (see chap. 4) has forced low-income workers to endure long commutes and spend much of their income on transportation. With the costs of owning and maintaining cars, transportation is Americans' second-largest household expense.[3] For those who can't afford cars, the transportation system often leaves them with low-quality options such as bus service that is infrequent and slow. A survey of low- and moderate-income workers in San Mateo County, California, found that one in five respondents had quit or lost a job because of difficulty getting to work.[4] The auto-oriented system leaves many people and entire communities transportation-disadvantaged with limited access to nonauto modes and high transportation costs.

Automobile dependency has contributed to a cycle of environmental, social, and public health harm reflected in our crises. Many people are unaware of the entirety of these impacts.

The environmental impact is enormous when considering life-cycle emissions and all that goes into automobiles and their infrastructure. As of 2024, there were nearly three hundred thousand cars in the United States alone.[5] In addition to emissions from driving, the manufacturing and servicing of so many autos emit a significant amount of pollutants and use considerable resources. Other environmental harms from motorized vehicles result from pavement use for roads and parking lots and vehicle runoff of auto fluids and tire particles.

Our social and public health crises are intertwined with automobile dependency. Public health suffers from pollution, crashes, and sedentary transportation. Social isolation and community breakdown grow when people stay in cars. Inequality worsens with the expense of car ownership for low-income families.

A revolution in the automobile industry toward electrification and automation is underway. It is far less revolutionary than we have been led to believe. Electric vehicles (EVs) are important in addressing the climate crisis. The other detrimental effects of cars, however, will remain and even worsen if the number of automobiles or the miles traveled within them continue to increase.

Open-pit mining of lithium, cobalt, nickel, and other elements needed for electric car batteries should give us further pause on an all-in EV strategy. The invasion of Ukraine and significant environmental damage in mostly Global South communities are linked to extracting these minerals (see chap. 1). The search for these EV battery inputs has spread across the globe, exposing more places to the harm. In Nevada, Lithium America's mine (introduced in chap. 1) will degrade almost five thousand acres of habitat and use over three thousand gallons of water a minute and up to fifty-eight hundred tons of sulfuric acid a day, causing great concern to nearby farmers and ranchers.[6] The local Paiute and Shoshone people will bear the brunt of polluted water and other impacts. Hundreds, if not thousands, of such mines will be needed to support the EV revolution. Continuing to extract and burn fossil fuels for transportation is not the answer, but decreasing the number of cars on the road will reduce harm to nature from mining.

Even the climate crisis will not be easily mitigated by EVs. Despite ambitious policy goals for increasing EV adoptions, slow turnover and embodied emissions in vehicle production make it hard to reduce emissions as rapidly as needed. Even with the most optimistic projections, most road vehicles will still be gas-powered in 2050.[7] The fastest and surest way to cut transportation emissions is for people to drive less. It's time we break the hold cars have on our communities and lives.

Many people don't want to drive so much but feel stuck. As discussed in chapter 2, most Americans prefer to live in communities where they can easily walk and access transit.[8] Additionally, more Americans are increasingly concerned about climate change as it bears down in catastrophic ways on their communities.[9] And we know that auto emissions are a significant cause of the crisis.

In this chapter, we'll first dive into what is holding our system of car dependency in place. A different system that prioritizes active (walking, biking, and scooting) and community-oriented (active plus using public transit) transportation is possible. Applying the levers of systems change, we'll see how that future is being built.

Systems-Change Strategies for Reducing Car Dependence

- Shift power to transportation-disadvantaged communities
- Build power among advocates
- Transform streets with dedicated transit infrastructure and bus rapid transit

- Transform streets and off-street land with safe, networked infrastructure for active transportation
- Reset culture through bike- and scooter-share services
- Reset culture through transit stops and stations
- Reset culture through transit agency coordination
- Reset culture through incentives and disincentives
- Reset culture through experiential education
- Pull the systems levers together around Vision Zero (municipal commitments to reduce pedestrian and cyclist fatalities to zero)
- Leverage other systems

Holding Car Dependency in Place

The transportation system has been structured around the automobile so much that it is difficult to imagine different possibilities. Big Auto, Big Oil, and Big Tech have largely dictated this system built on auto-centered land use and car culture.

Power: Big Auto, Big Oil, and Big Tech

Big Auto staked out its plan to dominate transportation concurrent with the advent of the mass production of automobiles. Allied with Big Oil and tire companies, General Motors bought out streetcar networks, the auto's main competition, and dissolved them. Once established, the auto industry used its power to solicit massive public investments into roads and, eventually, highways. Since then, we've handed over our streets and most transportation infrastructure to the automobile. More recently, we are ceding control to Big Tech in the transportation system with the rise of rideshare platforms, self-driving cars, and smart cities.

Most transportation policies and rules have been written to prop up the automobile industry. Professor Greg Shill of the University of Iowa studies the intersection of corporate power, government law, and transportation and infrastructure policy. His research uncovered the influence of Big Oil and Big Auto on laws and regulations related to land use, insurance, vehicle safety, taxes, and crime that have enabled what he calls "automobile supremacy."[10] These policies include substantial parking requirements for developments and single-family-only zoning, as discussed in chapter 4.

The lion's share of public funding for transportation supports the auto and oil industries. They have lobbied for and won public funds, such as the massive bailout for Big Auto during the Great Recession of 2008. Globally, subsidies for Big Oil were over $182 billion in 2018, not far from record highs.[11] These large subsidies have continued despite the clear links between climate change and fossil fuel burning.

Up against Big Auto and Big Oil for over a century now, public transit struggles to get adequate funding to be a viable alternative to personal vehicles. Transit infrastructure projects typically require a two-thirds vote to raise taxes and generate funding to build them. The auto, oil, and affiliated industries—notably through the Koch brothers, prominent political donors and network organizers with financial interests in automobiles, parts, gas, and asphalt—have funded successful opposition to local and state ballot initiatives for mass transit.[12] Two defeated measures include a bus and trolley network in Little Rock, Arkansas, and a $5.4 billion transit plan in Nashville, Tennessee.

Public funding for the electrification of vehicles is positive for addressing climate change over the long term but further solidifies the dominance of auto-centered corporate interests in the transportation system. Big Auto and Big Tech have successfully lobbied for subsidies that support EVs. The 2022 Inflation Reduction Act, for example, included tax credits for EV purchases and charging infrastructure and funding for manufacturing and municipal fleet conversions. In the same year, climate change legislation in California allocated $13 billion for EV incentives and several billion more for advanced manufacturing of EVs. Big Oil will not benefit, but in its place, electric utilities (discussed further in chap. 10) and technology corporations work behind the scenes with Big Auto to secure these public investments.

Corporations Uber and Lyft sit at the intersection of Big Auto and Big Tech with their ridesharing platforms. They claimed that their services would reduce car ownership and traffic. Neither has been true. Instead, the growth of rideshare has caused a decline in public transit ridership, adding more cars to the street.[13] Vehicle miles traveled have increased due to deadheading, a term that refers to the extra miles driven between dropping off one passenger and picking up another and during long commutes to city centers for low-income drivers to find passengers.

Advocates for autonomous vehicles are making the same promises. They argue that when self-driving cars are widely adopted and combined with shared mobility, millions of vehicles will be taken off the road. This outcome depends on many questionable assumptions including that people will give up ownership of cars, share rides with other passengers, and not ride in driverless cars when transit and other alternatives are available. With deadheading inherent to ridesharing, traffic congestion will worsen unless people shift to nonauto modes. Corporations behind EVs, rideshare platforms, and autonomous vehicles continue to shape our transportation system and narrative around the automobile and benefit from limited public dialogue around the drawbacks.

Land Use: Autopia

Autopia is not just a ride at Disneyland. The name encompasses how nearly every place in the United States has been designed and built around the automobile, from overall land use patterns to street and curbside space.

Suburban sprawl has been growing for decades, resulting in people living farther and farther away from job centers, retail, and other amenities. Residents in sprawl neighborhoods drive about three times as much as urban residents.[14] Supported by single-use zoning, people drive to office parks and big-box retail centers with large parking lots. Furthermore, single-family-only residential zoning excludes apartments and duplexes in many American neighborhoods, reducing density and, thus, opportunities for public transit.

Data on transportation infrastructure reveal how much land use has been dedicated to automobiles compared to other modes. As of 2022, there were 4.2 million miles of roads compared to less than 12,000 miles of transit, including commuter, heavy, and light rail in the United States.[15] Between 2010 and 2019, approximately 28,500 miles of high-capacity urban roads were built, while only 1,200 miles of transit service were constructed.[16] Highways also continue to expand. New ones are being built, such as a 75-mile, 4-lane bypass around the eastern side of Cincinnati and a 330-mile series of toll roads in southwest and central Florida. Infrastructure development continues to bolster car dependency.

New lanes and roads are proposed to relieve traffic congestion. Extensive traffic data, however, shows this only leads to more traffic.[17] In what is known as "induced demand," added road capacity encourages people to drive more often and take longer trips.

Land devoted to parking is another pillar of Autopia. The number of parking spaces often far exceeds the number of households in the same jurisdiction.[18] Garages and lots are frequently underutilized or even empty. All this space for easily parking cars encourages people to drive and allows for destinations to be far apart, making it difficult to get around any way other than by car.

Car Culture

The image of cars as an instrumental and beloved part of modern life has been propagated through marketing, advertisements, and media. It's hard to watch a televised show or event without being exposed to multiple car advertisements. The ads associate cars with things people want, like freedom, adventure, and the good life. These ads have become pervasive on websites and social media. Unsurprisingly, 65 percent of American households have at least two cars.[19]

Meanwhile, the dangers of automobiles are often hidden in the media, much to the delight of Big Auto. The roughly one hundred fatalities in the US (and one thousand worldwide) from daily car crashes do not often make the news. Yet a single train crash without fatalities or a subway shooting with a single victim makes national news. The media creates more fear around using other transportation modes when we should fear cars most.

Financial incentives, in a variety of forms, support car culture by encouraging and rewarding driving as the normal way to get around. Free parking in cities and towns is one such incentive. In his book *The High Cost of Free Parking*, urban planning professor Donald Shoup showed how free parking leads to more driving, adding to car traffic and inhibiting safe walking and biking. The tax code incentivizes driving cars from mortgage interest deductions that favor large homes in car-dominant communities to generous mileage deductions for taxpayers who use their vehicles for business. In these and other ways, government has aided and abetted car driving as a way of life.

We remain stuck in a system that makes it hard to get around without a car. Roshni Sahu shared with me why, despite her interest, taking public transportation to attend a high school program at a nearby community college was not going to work: "There was no way I could get home using the bus without a minimum 45-minute commute, long walking distances, and the risk of missing a connecting bus and waiting an hour for another. I was frustrated—it was ridiculous that a trip that was only 5 miles would have so many complications, but not surprising. I told my parents that there were no reasonable routes, and my mother resigned by saying that she was going to have to miss an hour of work every day to drive me."[20] Many people like Roshni are open and eager to using transit and other nonauto modes, yet their local transportation system does not support those choices. It doesn't have to be this way. A different vision is possible.

A Vision of Active, Community-Oriented Transportation

Public transit and active transportation have myriad benefits to society. Street space is used much more efficiently than cars. There is also substantially less cost to society than personal motor vehicles as reflected in full-cost accounting of transportation modes that includes infrastructure and externalities such as emissions. Table 6.1 provides data on these advantages of nonauto modes over car driving.

TABLE 6.1   Transportation modes comparison: Space and cost

	SPACE (NO. THAT CAN MOVE THROUGH A 10-FOOT LANE/HOUR)	COST TO SOCIETY ($ FOR EVERY $1 INDIVIDUAL SPENDS)
Car driving	600–1,600 cars	$9.20
Public transit	4,000–8,000	$1.50
Biking	7,500 bikes	$0.08
Walking	N/A	$0.01

Sources: "Designing to Move People," National Association of City Transportation Officials, April 22, 2016, https://nacto.org/publication/transit-street-design-guide/introduction/why/designing-move-people/; Christine McClaren, Caitlan Havlak, and Graeme Stewart-Wilson, "What Is the Full Cost of Your Commute?," *The Discourse*, March 26, 2015, https://thediscourse.ca/scarborough/full-cost-commute.

The cost of transportation to individuals also matters. Public and active transportation modes are a means of financial security for many Americans. Affordable transportation options are critical for families struggling to make ends meet. Even with government subsidies, EVs remain too expensive for most Americans.[21] Transportation equity and justice means moving away from automobile dependency.

The idea of freedom in the transportation system can easily be reframed. Instead, with nonauto modes, we gain freedom from not having to spend so much money on owning and maintaining a vehicle and not being relegated to so many hours of sedentary time in cars.

Safety considerations for daily travel are paramount for nearly everyone. There is safety in numbers when walking, biking, and scooting. The more people use nonauto modes, the safer streets become and the fewer lives are lost in car crashes.[22] Public transit overall is ten times safer per mile than traveling in a car, and commuter and intercity rail is eighteen times safer for passengers than being in a car.[23] Fewer cars also reduce the toll on public health from air pollution, which leads to millions of premature deaths globally every year.

Unlike cars, biking and walking promote personal health, whether the trip is to a destination or transit stop. People who started biking to work instead of driving lost an average of thirteen pounds in the first year.[24] In Blues Zones, places with the world's highest life expectancy (discussed in chap. 2), most people walk throughout the day to take care of their daily needs. Human bodies were designed to move, and movement outside boosts physical and mental health. Biking and walking release endorphins and lower stress. Since so many people sit behind desks most of the day, commutes or errands may be one of the few regular opportunities to give their bodies and minds what they need.

Nonauto modes get people out from behind windshields and thus become an opportunity to connect to community and place regularly. People are able to get closer to their physical surroundings, make eye contact, and greet one another.

In my research on transportation behavior (discussed in chap. 1), participants who commuted by bike or transit shared how much they valued the community they experienced while traveling. Some had a group they saw most days, while others enjoyed the spontaneous emergence of connecting with others on their journey.

Car-light neighborhoods also have many social benefits. People who live on quiet, walkable streets have been found to know many more neighbors than those who live on busy roads with heavy traffic.[25] The benefits of walkability include more friendships, stronger communities, and safer neighborhoods.

Active transportation can be a source of joy in people's daily lives. Carol Ting of the Pisces Foundation shares about her bike commute, "I get to enjoy fresh air, public art, and exercise. I am nourished by community, beauty, and health each day."[26]

Streets that prioritize active transportation can feel like playgrounds while still getting people to where they need to go efficiently. When people can do joyful things outside every day, their lives are enriched.

Active, community-oriented travel modes, in addition, are an important means to address some of our biggest social and environmental problems. Bringing people together through public transit and active transportation helps reduce bias and prejudices among people with different lived experiences who may not otherwise cross paths with one another. In an age of growing social divisions, this is more important than ever. Nonauto modes are also critical to addressing the climate crisis and making our cities more livable, as they significantly reduce emissions and traffic congestion. Biking and walking are pollution-free. Per-person emissions on mass transit, especially when well utilized, are much smaller than most automobile uses. Intercity buses, for example, are 550 percent more fuel efficient than cars per passenger.[27]

People's desire to get out of the car and live in walkable, bikeable, and transit-oriented communities is starting to be fulfilled again in cities and regions around the world. Systems-change strategies are helping us get there.

Systems-Change Strategies for a Place-Based Transportation System

Despite the entrenched nature of automobile dependence, movement is underway toward a system of transportation alternatives. It can be thought of as a "push" away from autos and a "pull" toward active, community-oriented modes in daily life. Empowering transportation-disadvantaged communities and building collective power among advocates are shifting power in support of nonauto modes. Transforming land use primarily means changing streets. Reallocating street space to transit, biking, and walking "pulls" people toward active transportation while "pushing" people away from car driving. Resetting culture through bike and scooter share, improved transit stops, transit coordination, incentives and disincentives, and education adds to the "pull" effect. These strategies are starting to work, especially with Gen Z. From 1983 to 2018, the percentage of eighteen-year-olds with driver's licenses decreased from 80 percent to 61 percent, and sixteen-year-olds from 46 percent to 25 percent.[28]

Shift Power to Transportation-Disadvantaged Communities

Changing the transportation system to serve people better requires sharing power, particularly with transportation-disadvantaged communities. When community members are involved in planning infrastructure change for transit, walking, and biking, they are more likely to use it. Residents' concerns about safety and accessibility for nonauto modes can be addressed when their input is valued and decision-making is shared.

Najari Smith, founder of bicycle advocacy nonprofit Rich City Rides in Richmond, California, explains the sense of ownership that develops when power is shared. "I really do appreciate having smooth paved bike lanes to ride on. But what I value more is knowing that people in the community feel like those lanes are for us, that those bike lanes are my bike lanes, and those trails are my trails. That they were made for me."[29] Planners can use guides such as Greenlining Institute's Mobility Equity Frameworks to empower community members in transportation planning.

Somewhat counterintuitively, community involvement can speed up the installation of new infrastructure. Through a pilot project, The Final Mile, 335 miles of new bike lanes were built in five cities over twenty-four months. This rapid progress in Austin, Denver, New Orleans, Pittsburgh, and Providence resulted from city officials working with community organizations, local businesses, and others in the initial planning.[30] They shifted power and moved forward quickly with broad support for the design and implementation.

Processes and results like The Final Mile may not seem possible to many planners and local government officials. Community input is often dominated by loud voices against proposed changes, drowning out those who want to see change. When people are brought into processes early, however, they are more open to change and often become supporters.

Build Power Among Advocates

Even with good community engagement processes, car-centric voices may prevail. Building collective power among advocates is also needed to overcome status quo resistance.

Transit, cycling, and walking advocacy organizations exist in many cities and regions. With limited budgets and staff capacity, they tend to focus on advocacy related to their transportation mode. The organizations often find less time to coordinate and strategically build power.

With its mission to reclaim New York City from cars, the nonprofit Transportation Alternatives is an exception and brings together all of these advocates under one roof. The organization today has over one hundred thousand supporters and reports an impact of more than one thousand bike lanes built and 150 open streets (ones fully or partially closed to cars) created.[31] The city has also built miles of dedicated bus lanes and a bus-only street, though progress on the bus lane mandate slowed down in the early 2020s. New York City has seen significant street transformation, in large part due to the coordinated pressure of transit, pedestrian, and cycling advocates.

One overarching transportation advocacy organization like Transportation Alternatives is not necessary to build collective power. It does, however, require that staff and boards at transportation nonprofits concentrate their limited resources and time on strategic partnerships (in chap. 12, strategic collaboration is discussed in detail within and across different systems).

With the growing number of people using e-bikes, e-scooters, and bike share, transportation advocates have new allies in building power to influence public policy and funding. Bike-, e-bike-, and e-scooter-share services started in 2010 in the Washington, DC, metro area. These services are now available in over 120 cities in North America. In 2022, almost one million e-bikes were sold in the US, 20 percent more than the total number of EVs sold.[32] All of these new riders need lanes and spaces to travel safely. Partnering with this expanding group of micromobility users and the companies that sell and rent to them will build more robust, better-funded coalitions in regions and cities to counteract car-dependent resistance.

Bringing potential allies of nonauto modes into transportation advocacy could shift power further to a critical mass. The case for nonauto modes can appeal to what different groups and individuals outside of the transportation field value: building community, reducing cost burdens for those struggling to make ends meet, or any of the other benefits of community-oriented, active transportation. Given the many problems car dependency creates for people, communities, and the environment, a big tent of stakeholders can be brought together to advocate for change in the transportation system.

Transform Streets with Dedicated Transit Infrastructure and Bus Rapid Transit

Public transportation needs investment so that most trips beyond walking or biking distance do not require a car. High-performing transit systems have dedicated lanes and tracks for transit. This infrastructure enables convenient, dependable, and affordable mass transit, diminishing the desire for cars. This may sound unattainable to those living with underfunded, poorly performing transit systems in the United States. Such systems, however, exist elsewhere and are expanding in the United States.

Toronto exemplifies what a dependable, convenient transit system can look like. Every major road has a bus that comes every ten minutes. Almost every person in the city is within a fifteen-minute walk of a twenty-four-hour bus route. In addition, the subway provides quick travel across the city.

Japan is well known for its excellent train system. Earlier in the chapter, Roshni Sahu explained why public transportation did not work for her where she lives in the United States. Her experience traveling in Osaka, Japan, gave her perspective on how much better it can be: "The trips were effortless: the walks from the stations to destinations were short, the transfers were quick, and the trains were efficient and on time. It was one of the first times that I enjoyed using public transit."[33] High-performing transit systems lead to higher ridership.

In places like Toronto and Japan, dedicated lanes and tracks separate car traffic from transit and support efficient and dependable service. Since building a new subway or train rail is expensive and takes years or even decades, converting existing street lanes to bus or light rail should be the priority. In the 1970s, Curitiba, Brazil, was exploring how to build public transit in the growing metropolis. At the time, constructing a new subway system was estimated to cost approximately 450 times more per mile than new bus lanes.[34] The decision was simple, and Curitiba became well known for building the first Bus Rapid Transit (BRT) system in the world, which continues to excel in getting passengers where they need to go.

Dedicated or tactical bus lanes are being implemented across the United States, from big cities such as Los Angeles and New York City to smaller cities like Everett and Cambridge in Massachusetts. In Everett, bus trip times improved by more than 20 percent.[35] In Los Angeles, one dedicated bus lane has seventy buses per hour. In San Francisco, three dedicated bus lanes improved transit reliability by 25 percent and reduced crashes that resulted in injury by 24 percent.[36] These positive outcomes led to the building of more tactical transit lanes in the city. In 2019, New York City made an entire street (14th Street) bus-only, allowing buses to travel twice the speed of other crosstown routes. More people will take transit when it is not stuck in car traffic.

Bus Rapid Transit utilizes dedicated lanes or busways. To make transit trips even faster, BRT adds features like elevated platforms, multiple doors, and prepaid tickets for quick boarding. Traffic signal priority is another element of BRT that increases bus speed and dependability. BRT has proven successful in places like Curitiba in Brazil, Bogotá in Colombia, and Guangzhou in China.

BRT is starting to take root in the United States. In 2016, Minneapolis upgraded a major bus route to BRT level. By 2018, ridership was up by 30 percent.[37] Seattle has invested in its bus system with dedicated road space, increased frequency, and clean, safe, and pleasant interiors. These changes resulted in steady increases in ridership and a 10 percent decline in commuters driving downtown between 2010 and 2018, even with a surging population and workforce.[38] Riders will come when transit works well for them.

Coordinated pressure from power shifts described earlier and political will are needed to fund dedicated public transportation infrastructure. Measures that tax rideshare services, implement downtown congestion fees, or otherwise generate revenue from automobile use can help secure funding for transit projects. In São Paolo, Brazil, a tax on rideshare companies, for example, is directed to the public transit system. BRT and dedicated bus lane measures may be more likely to pass if voters are educated about the cost-effectiveness of installing them compared to other transportation infrastructure.

Transform Streets and Off-Street Land with Safe, Networked Infrastructure for Active Transportation

When safe, networked infrastructure is installed, there is great potential to increase active transportation in cities and towns. Nearly 50 percent of car trips are three miles or less, and 20 percent are less than a mile.[39] One can walk about three-quarters of a mile or bike two or more miles in fifteen minutes. The idea of a "15-minute city," where everything one needs can be accessed within a short walk or bike ride from where one lives, has grown in popularity.

Well into the twentieth century and before the auto and oil industries changed everything, roads were safe, vibrant places for walking, biking, and other nonmotorized uses, not unlike a city park today. Bikeable and walkable cities and neighborhoods require protected lanes and space away from cars. These features need to be networked; that is, connected and located to get people where they need to go.

European and Latin American cities have long been leaders in providing safe, networked infrastructure for walking and biking. Car-free streets and zones have expanded in Madrid and other cities, which are banning cars altogether in city centers and reserving them for cyclists and pedestrians. Hamburg, Germany, banned cars on several roads and developed a network of pedestrian and bike routes linking parks and open spaces. Bogotá has a citywide cycling network approaching four hundred miles of lanes and pathways and plans to add over one hundred miles more toward its goal of 50 percent of trips made without a car.

Though not at the same scale, US cities have been investing more in bike infrastructure. Minneapolis has become one of the most bikeable cities in the United

States, with protected bike lanes and safety measures in formerly high-crash locations. Portland has earned a similar reputation with protected bike lanes and greenways that connect neighborhoods with downtown. Adding protected bike lanes in North American cities increased bike ridership on those streets by up to 171 percent.[40] This infrastructure, as mentioned earlier, also supports all types of micromobility.

Neighborhoods can be made safer and more enjoyable for walking as well. Road diets, or narrowing of roads, including bulb-outs at intersections, slow down cars and shorten distances for pedestrians to cross. Trees and lighting on sidewalks and connecting sidewalks for longer trips encourage walking.

Low-speed streets provide safe spaces for people biking as well as walking. During the 2020 pandemic, Slow Streets, discussed more in chapter 7 as a community space, were rapidly implemented in many cities. Barricades at intersections slow cars down and help prevent pass-through traffic, making it safer for people to bike, walk, and generally be out on their neighborhood streets. Popular ones in San Francisco were made permanent after the pandemic, with a plan to connect slow streets across the city and form an active transportation network.

Long-distance bikeways and bike highways connect cities and towns to the larger metropolitan area or region. Ideally, these routes are separated from cars, involving off-street pathways and on-street protected bike lanes. The Los Angeles River Path, with projected completion in 2027, will consist of thirty-two miles of trail for biking, walking, and rolling. The path is likely to be well used. It was designed with substantial input from community representatives of the eighty-five thousand people who live within a half mile and the one million people who live within three miles. Across the country, the Cross-Triangle Greenway connects the cities of Durham, Raleigh, and Cary in North Carolina. All forms of micromobility and pedestrians can also use these paths.

Reducing car parking spaces on streets is critical to building a safe, networked infrastructure for active transportation. Resistance to the removal of parking can also kill these projects. Cities like Paris show that does not have to be the case.

To accommodate an express cycling network and ten thousand new bike parking spots in Paris (also discussed in the introduction), Mayor Anne Hidalgo laid out a plan to remove more than 70 percent of on-street parking spaces for cars. Rather than end the mayor's political career, these transformations were embraced. Parisians took to cycling. In one year, from 2018 to 2019, the number of cyclists in the city rose an incredible 54 percent.[41] An additional thirty-one miles of protected bike lanes were added during the 2020–21 COVID-19 pandemic. Urban streets expert Jeff Speck shared the impact: "Sixty-one percent of cyclists polled in Paris, commuting around the streets, said they were not regular cyclists a year ago. It was the new, safe streets that caused them to be on a bike for the first time since they were kids."[42] Hidalgo was reelected in 2020 with the plan to add eighty additional miles of bike-safe (and micromobility-safe) pathways, which required the removal of additional car parking.

Flexing streets to support safe, networked active transportation is highly cost-effective compared to auto infrastructure projects. In 2018, city council member Emily Beach of Burlingame, California, asked her constituents to "compare [$16 million for forty-four] high-impact bicycle and pedestrian network improvements to the price tag of a new highway interchange ($90–160 million), the proposed Highway 101 Managed Lane Project ($500 million), or even a local parking garage ($10–20 million). For a fraction of those costs, active transportation investments help address the root cause of our traffic and parking problems."[43] Fiscally constrained governments can reduce spending on transportation while boosting car alternatives that make cities and communities better places to live. The growing use of e-scooters and e-bikes makes investments in protected bike lanes even more beneficial.

Transforming streets to be safe and multimodal becomes a virtuous cycle. Safe, connected networks for walking, biking, and scooting also support the use of public transit when access to transit stops is involved. The more people switch to non-auto modes for daily trips, the less pressure there is to protect streets and curb space for cars. Transformation in personal transportation habits can further accelerate with strategies that build an active, community-oriented transportation culture.

Reset Culture Through Bike- and Scooter-Share Services

Bike-sharing services encourage more people to bike. Cities that have rolled out bike share combined with protected, networked cycling infrastructure have seen the most significant gains in ridership.[44] The boost was particularly true in Paris and Minneapolis, where large rollouts greatly increased access to biking for those who don't own a bike. E-bike-share service can also benefit those who own regular bikes when they want to get somewhere faster or don't want to sweat. E-scooter-share adds another option.

The cost of bike share, especially e-bikes, can be high. On a couple of occasions, I've noticed that the cost of using a shared e-bike is almost equivalent to being driven the same distance in an Uber or Lyft car. For more people to be able to use bike and scooter share, the cost must be addressed.

Municipal- or community-owned bike share provides a low-cost alternative. With government support and the profit margin removed, these programs have proven to be affordable and usable by many. Boston; Washington, DC; and Montreal have publicly owned bike-share programs—the city covers 25 percent of the cost, and sponsors help bring down the price so that people across the socioeconomic spectrum can utilize the bikes.

As a cultural lever, bike- and scooter-share stations convey that those modes are valued. Stations across a city imply that in this city, people get around using active transportation. Strategically placing these stations in high-visibility locations can add a further cultural boost to cycling and micromobility.

Reset Culture Through Transit Stops and Stations

Well-designed, maintained transit stops and comfortable, attractive, and useful stations likewise send the message that taking transit is valued. They become valued neighborhood places in their own right. Recognizing their value to communities and people using public transportation, the national nonprofit Project for Public Spaces highlights exemplary stations and stops.[45] The Fruitvale Transit Village in Oakland, California, includes stores for daily needs and community programming. Beautiful art is displayed at a well-used bus stop in Nairobi, Kenya. In Northhampton, Massachusetts, a parklike bus stop attracts riders with ample seating, trees, and bike racks.

Bus stops that value and entice riders include protection from the elements and other amenities. In Minneapolis, BRT stations are well equipped with comfortable shelters, digital displays, and bike racks. Climate Resolve's bus shelter advocacy project in Los Angeles was formed to address the intense heat exposure many primarily low-income people face at bus stops that lack shelter. As a result of their advocacy, the city of Los Angeles committed to building three thousand new bus shelters on sidewalks over five years.

Mobility hubs take transit stations and stops to the next level by providing an array of services that support getting around without a car. The hubs may span a mile or two and are situated where transit stations and stops, bike lanes, pedestrian paths, and other nonauto infrastructure converge. They are designed to make accessing transportation options and switching modes easy. In Pittsburgh, fifty mobility hubs include bus and light-rail stops and e-scooter-, bike-, and car-share services. Properly designed hubs, stations, and stops improve the experience for riders and signal that noncar transportation is important.

Reset Culture Through Transit Agency Coordination

Agencies that coordinate transit regionally place riders' needs above agency autonomy. Transferring from one transit line to another can be confusing, time-consuming, and expensive. Rather than just protecting their turf, transit agencies can work together and compromise to fix the problems that riders face.

Integrated fares, automatic discounts, and a single payment card or app encourage transit riding by making trips with multiple segments easier and more affordable. In São Paolo, transit cards were integrated among the bus, train, and metro lines. Within one year, without new lines or stations, ridership increased from 2.2 to 3.5 million people.[46] In Switzerland, riders can use a mobile app, FAIRTIQ, on any of the country's 250 transit operators with a single swipe. The pricing is simple and easy to understand, based on distance traveled and not the operator. Regional coordination of transit can help build a supportive culture for increasing ridership.

Reset Culture Through Incentives and Disincentives

Incentives for active, community-oriented transportation behavior help build norms that support using those modes. Incentives can be financial or use other means to influence transportation choices. They are particularly effective when rolled out with local infrastructure improvements or timed to coincide with life's transitions, such as a new job.

Transportation Demand Management (TDM) programs run by employers and local governments promote alternatives to driving alone. In many jurisdictions, employers with a threshold level of employees are required to offer TDM benefits to employees.

Stanford University's Parking and Transportation Services runs a successful TDM program. Through the service's sustainable commute program, 64 percent of faculty, staff, and students used alternatives to driving alone in 2022, compared to 33 percent twenty years earlier.[47] Stanford offers free passes for local and regional transit services that connect to the campus and runs a free and dependable shuttle to get around campus. Locker rentals and showers are provided for bike commuters. Having emergency rides home by taxi or rental car also available gives active commuters peace of mind. These targeted investments encourage employees and students to commute car-free daily.

Parking benefit districts work on the disincentive and incentive side of resetting car culture. These specialized, community-level districts spend parking revenue funds for public services in the metered area. They ensure that a market price is charged for the private benefit of parking, making people think twice about driving. The revenue goes into sidewalks, street trees, free transit passes for residents and workers, or other means to incentivize nonauto modes.

Part of the reason for the surge in e-bike sales is financial incentive programs. Denver, Colorado, has offered $400 toward purchasing an e-bike and $1,200 for low-income residents, which inspired a statewide rebate program. Community choice energy programs (discussed in chap. 10), like Peninsula Clean Energy in San Mateo County, California, offer similar rebates.

State and federal government have also been incentivizing e-bike purchases. In 2024, the US government launched an e-bike incentive program that provides a 30 percent tax credit for the purchase price of an e-bike. States like Colorado have added large rebates for low- and moderate-income households.

Reset Culture Through Experiential Education

In 2016, I was near Palo Alto High School in California during rush hour when I witnessed something previously unimaginable to me. A couple of decades earlier, I had worked at the school. Back then, a few bikes may have been parked in the bike racks on any school day. As I waited at a traffic light that morning, I watched a couple hundred happy teens bike safely together through the intersection.

I later learned that the local Safe Routes to School (SRTS) program had trained students in bike safety starting in the second grade, with classes led by university students. SRTS is an approach that school districts and local jurisdictions can use to promote active transportation to school. Palo Alto students learned through events like bike rodeos that biking to school could be fun, healthy, cool, and safe. This culture lasted into their high school years. In 2000, about 20 percent of middle school and 10 percent of high school students biked to school. By 2019, those numbers had grown to almost 60 percent and 50 percent, respectively.[48] Giving children multiple opportunities to learn and experience biking has led to a lasting, transformative impact.

Across the bay in Richmond, California, Rich City Rides has popularized biking among low-income youth of color. The organization hosts repair workshops, a youth earn-a-bike program, and weekly group rides. Rich City Rides is building community and creating safety in numbers for kids biking on streets. Like Safe Routes to School, they are changing transportation behavior through experiential education.

Organizations can provide experiential education opportunities to help people feel confident in getting around without a car. As I found in my research on transportation behavior, part of changing one's behavior is building competence that enables and motivates new transportation habits. It can be as simple as learning to effectively use an app with real-time information on public transit schedules and routes or wearing the right bike clothing in inclement weather.

People need regular opportunities to learn new behaviors. Weekly "walking school buses" or "bike trains" in Safe Routes to School programs are a good model. These regular groups for getting to school help parents and students learn from each other and feel supported.

Experiential education instills confidence and motivation in people to get around without a car and catalyzes a cultural reset. A generation brought up with programs like Safe Routes to School will likely see active transportation as the normal way to get around daily.

Pull the Systems-Change Levers Together Around Vision Zero

In 2015, Oslo, Norway, committed to reducing pedestrian and cyclist fatalities to zero, and the city achieved it by 2019.[49] This goal, known as Vision Zero, has been adopted by cities worldwide, but none have been as successful as Oslo. That example illustrates the importance of pulling the levers of power, land use, and culture together to change the transportation system.

Discontent with the status quo had been brewing among the population, which was fed up with rising transportation injuries. With pressure, the city council and mayor's office began changing course. Power was shifted further when authority over the streets was transferred from the police to the city government, unleashing swift change. The city soon committed to reducing car traffic by one-third by 2030 and implementing the city's bicycle strategy.

Land use, specifically streets, transformed in the ensuing years. The city center became car-free. New cycling lanes and tracks sprouted across the city, including contraflow cycling on one-way streets that had previously not been allowed. The Oslo Standard for Bicycle Facilities established safety and ease of use as top priorities for designing new or modified bike infrastructure. In rapid fashion, the city implemented dedicated bus lanes, traffic restrictions on light-rail corridors, and the replacement of street parking with bike lanes. To improve pedestrian safety, the city increased the standard sidewalk width from eight to ten feet, installed curb bump-outs at intersections, reduced multilane roads to one lane in each direction, and required high-visibility crosswalks.

Consequently, car culture no longer dominates in Oslo. Speed bumps, narrowed lanes, lowered speed limits, bump-outs, and other traffic-calming measures convey that the safety of active modes is valued more than car speed. Congestion fees and increased tolls, on top of expensive gas, deter driving while providing funds for infrastructure and safety improvements. Car-centric living has rapidly faded in Oslo.

Leverage Other Systems

Place-based housing and work systems create synergies that catalyze a transition to active, community-oriented modes. The strategies to reinvent the transportation system build off of infill housing and mixed-use communities (chap. 5) that facilitate shorter daily trips and less need for cars. Having abundant local businesses within walking distance for shoppers and workers (chap. 6) further reduces the need to drive.

With their considerable collective influence on people's lives, the housing and transportation systems can also be planned together. From the onset of its BRT system, Curitiba, Brazil, built dense neighborhoods around major transit hubs. Residential buildings were clustered within three to four blocks of these hubs, making getting to highly efficient transit nearly seamless and cars less necessary. As a growing city then, Curitiba was able to plan development and transportation proactively together.

Cities around the United States are developing mixed-use, transit-oriented neighborhoods that converge place-based house, work, and transportation systems. Mixed-use neighborhood developments Mission Rock in San Francisco and Diridon Station in San Jose are being built on a central rail line with fast, electrified service that connects the two emerging neighborhoods. Parking-free residential buildings near light-rail stations with ground-floor retail are being built in many cities and quickly leased. Notably, units rent for less without the cost of parking spaces. Even Houston, a notoriously car-centric city, is jumping into the game with a neighborhood-scale development planned near downtown. The proposed project will transform warehouses and industrial spaces into a mixed-use neighborhood near transit lines, bike paths, trails, and a park.

Changing the transportation system also benefits from a place-based community space system, featured in chapter 7. As mentioned earlier, Slow Streets emerged as safe community spaces during COVID-19 but were just as useful for active transportation modes. Other community spaces that will be discussed provide the same dual purpose.

COMMUNITY SPACES

We have to believe that we're one people, one family. And we cannot turn against each other. We have to turn to each other.

—John Lewis, congressman and civil rights leader

As a child, I moved freely around my neighborhood and small city. I could roam the streets on my bike and travel independently to friends' houses from an early age. Parenting culture was different back in the 1970s and '80s. In what has become known as "free-range parenting," children were allowed to stay outside and away from their homes for hours on end. Outside of school, I found community at friends' homes, wiffle ball games on quiet streets, Cub Scouts activities, and participating in organized sports.

Not until later did I understand the privilege of my upbringing. I was fortunate to live in a place that I could regularly explore without adult supervision. I had the time and resources to participate in many activities. Many of my friends and I had backyards where we could build forts and play all sorts of games.

At the same time, being outside came with dangers. I had near misses with cars while biking. I came home after hours outdoors with trouble breathing from the exhaust-polluted air.

I also came to realize that despite my privilege, community spaces where I could be around more people were largely absent in my childhood. Getting to parks required a long bike ride or getting a car ride from a parent. Public plazas and community centers were unfamiliar to me. While I have many fond memories of sports and playtime with friends, I was not interacting much with people of different lived experiences.

Going to a large public university completely changed my connection to community life. Public plazas and parklike settings were everywhere on campus. There were countless opportunities to mix with students from different backgrounds through activities, events, and just being in these spaces together. I felt a strong sense of connection to a large, diverse community that enriched my life.

For roughly a decade after college, I lived in suburban towns that were not unlike those of my childhood. Public spaces were few and far between, and a car was usually required to get anywhere. My career, marriage, starting a family, and continued friendships provided much fulfillment and happiness, but a deeper sense of well-being was elusive.

I had been missing the feeling of being part of my local community since college. That all changed in 2004 when we moved to the Castro neighborhood in San Francisco. In this urban village, my family and I experience aspects of local community nearly every day. In addition to the local stores described in chapter 5, we have public spaces that connect people in our neighborhood. Wide sidewalks make it easy to walk around and experience the community. A park, dog park, recreation center, playground, and public plaza are all within a five-minute walk from our home. Musicians often play on the sidewalks and in the plaza. People participate in organized and informal activities at the recreation center and park. Each of these spaces has helped us connect to our community and enriched our daily lives.

* * *

Most people today do not live in neighborhoods like the Castro, where it is easy to engage with local community. Community, or fellowship with others arising from sharing and living together in one place, has been in decline for decades. In the groundbreaking *Bowling Alone: The Collapse and Revival of American Community*, political scientist Robert Putnam documented this decline in the United States since the 1970s. Putnam showed how opportunities for community life, whether at church or in a bowling league, were disappearing. He also pointed out how time spent watching television, in private vehicles, and more recently on digital devices were contributing to the decline of local community. As discussed in part 1, corporate capitalist systems have contributed to a strong inclination toward private living away from community spaces.

Those who can afford it have increasingly invested their time and money into large residences and yards, home entertainment and stuff, and private transportation. Interest in supporting investment in community spaces has consequently waned. In these ways, exclusivity based on personal wealth diminishes community life.

In contrast, low-income individuals and families have much less access to the private amenities of modern life and experience conditions that make it challenging to be out in their local communities. Pollution from industrial operations located near or in many communities of color causes respiratory diseases like asthma and threatens the overall health of people when they are outside. Toxins in the soil from prior industrial or military operations in marginalized communities add to harmful exposures when outdoors.

Extreme heat in the climate change era is another risk factor that inhibits time in community spaces. This is particularly true in historically redlined neighborhoods: ones in which residents were systematically denied mortgages and other financing services needed for home ownership, based on their race or ethnicity. A study across more than one hundred cities found that formerly redlined neighborhoods are, on average, five degrees hotter than neighborhoods not redlined.[1] These neighborhoods typically have a lot of pavement but few trees, creating a "heat island" effect that makes it dangerous to be outside.

Even when conditions permit safely going outside one's residence, parks, pedestrian zones, community centers, and other spaces are limited in many underserved communities. Low-income individuals and people of color have expressed value for the quality of life in their places more than other groups but report less access to the amenities that support it.[2] Disinvestment in community spaces has disproportionately impacted low-income communities of color.

Detachment from community comes not only at a cost to the social fabric but also to environmental and personal well-being. As more and more time is spent indoors and in cars, the rising amount of energy and stuff consumed takes an increasing toll on the environment. Social isolation also grows, and people are deprived of the health and well-being benefits of community connection. Systemic change around community spaces is needed to break the cycle of alienation from local community and mitigate its negative impacts.

All of the place-based systems in this book are designed to help regenerate community where we live. The community spaces system featured in this chapter complements the other systems and is a direct approach to building community connections in people's lives. We'll return to power, land use, and culture and see how the corporate capitalist use of these levers has restricted community spaces and harmed local community life. Fortunately, interest in safe, car-free, and vibrant public spaces is resurging across many cities and towns. We'll learn how systems-change strategies are being employed to make this vision a reality.

Systems-Change Strategies for Revitalizing Public Space for Community Connection

- Shift power to community members
- Transform land use with well-designed nearby parks
- Transform parking into parklets (mini parks) and plazas
- Transform streets into community spaces

- Transform land use with community centers
- Reset culture by activating community spaces
- Leverage other systems

What's Disconnecting People from Community

In a society where Big Tech and Big Auto influence nearly every aspect of people's lives, vital community connections can be hard to experience. Zoning and car-centric urban design have diminished physical space for community life. In addition, the media and politicians have exaggerated the dangers people face outside, fostering a culture where many fear spending time in community spaces.

Power: Big Auto and Big Tech

The economic and political power of Big Auto and Big Tech has been established in prior chapters and comes to bear on people's ability to be in local community. Viewing that power from a community space lens shows how deeply the influence of corporations has altered daily living.

In 2021 and 2022, San Francisco went through contentious political debates over whether to keep a mile and a half of a street inside Golden Gate Park as a car-free community space seven days a week. No homes, businesses, or driveways existed on the street, yet resistance to this change was fierce. Manny Yekutiel, a board member of the city's transportation authority, remarked in dismay at the pushback, "Why are there even cars in the park? It's a park! . . . Here's the world we have inherited, but we're planning for the world ahead."[3] We have inherited the world of automobile dependency, shaped by Big Auto (and Big Oil and now Big Tech) for many decades. Although most residents recognized the need to change, the future where community space without cars is valued remained elusive. A discouraging sense of powerlessness sets in when we must struggle so much just to make a section of one street in a park free of cars.

The power of Big Tech relies on keeping people inside and on screens. Spending time in community spaces interacting with one another and physical surroundings does not require technology. Big Tech's interests instead align with people finding community online and not in the places where they live. Facebook suggests that groups on its platform are "meaningful communities" even though there is no in-person interaction. Daniel Newman, a digital technology specialist, shares the corporation's real reason for focusing on groups: "The growth in focus on groups is strategic and well designed. It's keeping users on the site longer and providing rich, harvestable data for Facebook and its advertisers."[4]

Big Tech is not interested in real community spaces and will use its power to entice and keep people away from them.

Land Use: Single-Use Zoning and Car Space

Like in many communities where I've lived, single-use zoning presents formidable barriers to spending time in local communities by separating housing from other land uses, including public space. Residentially zoned areas can cover many square miles without public plazas, parks, and other community spaces. Furthermore, when people must drive everywhere, including long commutes, less time is available for community life.

Most space in cities and towns, as illustrated in chapter 6, is used for moving and parking cars and thus not conducive to social interaction. Almost entirely designed for automobiles, roads account for over 80 percent of public space in many cities.[5] In one analysis, between 44 and 65 percent of all public *and* private land in the downtown areas of four US cities—Houston, Little Rock, Milwaukee, and Washington, DC—was allocated to streets and parking for private motor vehicles.[6]

Cars on many of these roadways are driven at speeds dangerous to pedestrians and cyclists. Fast-moving vehicles deter access and interest in spending time in nearby community spaces.

About forty thousand Americans die each year in car crashes.[7] Even when traffic fatalities temporarily decreased in 2019, pedestrians and cyclists were killed in higher numbers.[8] Noise from automobiles and motorcycles also makes spending time outside in one's community less pleasant.

In places across the United States, zoning, allocation of public space to cars, and car traffic with the associated danger and noise erode community connections.

Culture: Perceptions of Danger

A decline in community life has been exacerbated by perceptions of growing threats to people in public spaces. In recent decades, concern about increasing criminal activity has created fear about going outside. Violent and property crimes, however, fell about 60 percent in the United States between 1993 and 2018.[9] Public perception of crime is at odds with this data. These misperceptions have been fueled by news outlets seeking to grab viewers' attention and politicians wishing to instill fear as part of their political strategy.[10] The abundance of time people spend on screens exposed to fearmongering politicians and news of crime incidences facilitates a retreat into private spaces.

The COVID-19 pandemic instilled additional fear about venturing out from residences. Although this was a necessary reaction to slow the spread of the virus during surges, the lasting effect of the pandemic may be individuals further removing themselves from community spaces.

The United States' acute political and social divisions add another challenge to people feeling safe and respected in community spaces. The political temperature has risen so much that many Americans are reluctant to engage with others who might have different experiences or views. The hostile environment has arisen from years of politicians and their backers instigating resentment of others, often along racial lines. In such a climate, people increasingly spend time in a small bubble of news and social media channels from the comfort of their residences and workplaces. With less time in community spaces, people encounter limited diversity of people, ideas, and lifestyles. Like perceived safety threats, these hostile divisions push people away from being in and benefiting from community life.

Despite these ominous trends, we can restore and rejuvenate community spaces grounded in the knowledge of their importance to people's lives and society. Through systems change, we can overcome the status quo and work toward safe, car-free, and vibrant community spaces in every neighborhood that rebuild community.

A Vision of Safe, Car-Free, and Vibrant Community Spaces

The Urban Institute, supported by the Knight Foundation, surveyed over eleven hundred Americans across twenty-six metro areas to better understand what attaches people to the places where they live.

The institute's *Community Ties* study found that access to arts, cultural activities, recreational areas, and safe places (to live, work, and play) supports engagement with and attachment to the local community. The sense of attachment was strongest in city centers. The research findings showed a positive correlation among spending time in local community, attachment to place, and quality of life.

To connect to place, we need community spaces where people interact and experience a range of activities together. In such settings, individuals can get to know each other and, over time, look after and help one another. Parks, parklets, plazas, wide sidewalks, libraries, community centers, and other public spaces allow people to develop social connections that enrich their lives.

Being in local community and participating in its life also reduces real and perceived threats to safety in public settings. When people spend time in community spaces, their understanding of threats such as violence and crime becomes more informed by the real world. News reports or politicians wishing to provoke fear lose their influence. People realize that there is less to be fearful about than they imagine. Furthermore, personal safety is strengthened when people connect and support one another when real threats arise.

Personal well-being is enhanced in other ways from physical surroundings that support community life. When a break is needed from work or other demands, a short walk in the neighborhood to community spaces can be a welcome and healthy reprieve. Moving outside promotes physical health, boosts positive feelings, and clears the head. Walking seven thousand to eight thousand steps (or about four miles) a day has been shown to provide substantial long-term health benefits.[11] Researchers have also found that the happiest people watch less than one hour of television daily.[12] Less time with digital entertainment and more time in local community are a recipe for feeling good.

People are more likely to get outside and resist the pull of the indoors when conditions are safe and inviting. Abundant, well-designed community spaces can entice people out of private bubbles and help rebuild a sense of local community. Features (explored later in the chapter) that help people feel secure and comfortable in public spaces should be a priority. Car-free (and car-light) design adds a layer of safety while making places more pleasant. When vibrancy is evident in community spaces, there is more reason to get out and not miss out.

Halloween demonstrates the social benefits of car spaces being flexed to community use. In many neighborhoods on this holiday evening, streets are filled with trick-or-treaters rather than moving vehicles. Adults and children can stroll through the streets with little fear and talk and laugh with one another. With kids leading the way from house to house, families greet neighbors—some they know well, others a little, and others they just met. In those moments, smiles, words, and joy are exchanged with one another, and bridges are built within the community.

Dedicated spaces that are safe, free of car danger, and activated—that is, enhanced with diverse activities and uses—are necessary to have such a "Halloween spirit" year-round. They also encourage participation in community life, which can lead to taking better care of each other and one's place.

According to the *Community Ties* report, behaviors that reinforce feelings of place attachment include connecting with diverse individuals, investing time and resources to improve the place, and choosing to stay and keep engaging and contributing. This becomes a virtuous cycle when participation in local community activities improves a neighborhood and further increases feelings of satisfaction with where one lives.

In addition to social and personal well-being, spending time outside in local community spaces benefits the environment. People drive less, use less building energy, buy more locally, and prioritize experiences rather than stuff. Time in public space is a pillar of living connected to place and benefits our collective well-being.

Systems-Change Strategies for a Local Community Spaces System

Land use, power, and culture must change to create more opportunities for community connections. Car-free parks, parklets, and plazas are needed in every neighborhood. Streets and parking can be flexed into community gathering spaces. Resetting culture to embrace these settings is facilitated by their activation. Systems change starts with empowering community members in the co-creation of public space.

Shift Power to Community Members

Like the transportation system, involving the local community in planning is the primary means to shift power in the community space system and ensure that those spaces will be well used. This approach, known as placemaking, is a collaborative process for designing and activating public space centered around the people who use it. Community members know best what they need in nearby public spaces.

Through processes that engage community members in decision-making, spaces can be designed for uses and activities that resonate with the local community. Prototyping is one approach that delivers quick improvements to public space. The community provides feedback on the prototype that informs larger projects. Co-creating community spaces with people in communities that have been marginalized can help change public settings to places where more people feel they belong.

The India Basin Shoreline Park Renovation Project in southeast San Francisco demonstrates how a resident-led, neighborhood-focused approach can bring a space alive. It started with a two-year process that led to San Francisco's first Equitable Development Plan. The plan's purpose is to ensure that the renovated park benefits the nearby residents of this historically underserved community and preserves the culture and identity of the neighborhood. The plan was developed by a leadership committee of twenty community members. Listening to other residents, they determined six areas of focus for utilizing the space: arts, culture, and identity; youth opportunities; housing security; transportation access and connectivity; workforce and business development; and healthy communities and ecology. The renovated park was designed by and for the community and is poised to be well used and strengthen the community for years to come.

Transform Land Use with Well-Designed Nearby Parks

The importance of parks in US cities and towns has long been recognized. Central Park in New York City and Golden Gate Park in San Francisco opened to the public in the nineteenth century. They are large swaths of public space within the two most dense cities in the country. Both bring thousands of people who live around them into recreational, social, and restful activities every day. These iconic, well-used parks are treasured local resources for surrounding neighborhoods, city residents, and visitors.

The Trust for Public Land popularized the idea that everyone should have a park within a ten-minute walk from their home. Most people can walk about a half mile in ten minutes. Three hundred cities nationwide have committed to ensuring everyone has safe, easy, and "within a ten-minute walk" access to a quality park. Phil Ginsburg, the general manager of San Francisco Recreation and Parks, explains that "parks are not just hard infrastructure, but they're also social infrastructure . . . [and] . . . we need to place a higher value on parks and people than we do on cars and convenience."[13] Under Ginsburg's leadership, San Francisco in 2017 became the first city in the country to meet this goal.

To address systemic inequities, parks must be clean, safe, and attractive spaces where community members want to be. The India Basin Waterfront Park, the outcome of the process described in the prior section, is situated within walking distance of about thirty-five thousand residents. Before the renovation project, it was in poor shape, polluted, and woefully inadequate in meeting community members' needs. Replacing sediment contaminated with toxins with clean soil was the first step to rejuvenating this community space. The park includes gathering spaces, picnic areas, a building for concessions and indoor programs, a boatyard and dock for water sports, fitness stations, courts, play areas, a tech hub, nature trails, and more. Safe, accessible parks with amenities designed explicitly for nearby residents, like India Basin, are critical in every community and our nation's work toward equity and justice.

Many other cities, including Oklahoma City, are also investing in parks. The Metropolitan Area Projects (MAPS), financed by a one-cent sales tax, have substantially improved the city's public realm. With funds from a third voter-approved MAPS measure, a seventy-acre park was completed between downtown and the Oklahoma River, implementing the "core-to-shore vision." Nearby and future residents, as well as downtown workers, now have access to beautiful grounds to stroll and a wide array of community gathering spots and recreational fields and courts. The parks in Oklahoma City and San Francisco, two very different political settings, show that investing in these public spaces has broad appeal.

Project for Public Spaces drills into what makes a successful or well-used park. Its research and advocacy highlight the features of comfort and image, sociability, and access and linkages.[14] Comfort and image are enhanced by well-designed and maintained landscaping, unobstructed sight lines, public art that reflects the local community, trees that provide shade, and open spaces for sunshine. Elements that promote planned and unplanned social interaction include benches, tables and chairs, and places to play different types of games. When a community space is linked to various transportation modes, it is accessible to a broader range of users and reduces car traffic and its related hazards. Successful parks break people out of private bubbles and into enjoying their community.

Transform Parking into Parklets and Plazas

In cities and towns, finding space for community requires reimagining land use. When the transportation system shifts away from cars, parking lots and spaces become places for parklets and plazas. In the center of urban living, these gathering spaces can host uses valued by the local community.

In Seattle, the Pavement to Parks program reclaims underused street space for pedestrian-oriented uses. Reinvented uses include playgrounds, activity zones, seating areas, and parklike settings. A similar program in San Francisco led to the installation of sixty-five parklets and seven street plazas at minimal cost between 2009 and 2015.[15] Small in footprint but big in impact, these parklets and plazas provide needed community space and attract people to nearby businesses. With less parking available, these spaces also encourage walking, which adds to community life.

Lakeside Landing, a plaza in a western San Francisco neighborhood, replaced an underutilized parking lot. The landing includes a nature exploration area for children, a giant octopus mural covering the former lot, a massive chess game, a pollinator garden, and seating areas. Local volunteers help maintain it. The neighborhood center is regularly activated with music performances, pop-up markets, art fairs, and other events. With the existing shops and nearby residences, a vibrant community space has sprouted to life.

Transform Streets into Community Spaces

The ubiquity of streets presents a significant opportunity to redefine, expand, and improve public space that builds community. Car-free or car-light streets can become hubs of community activity and be networked together across a city.

Temporarily closing streets to cars has surged in recent decades, starting with Ciclovía over forty years ago in Bogotá, Colombia. In this bustling city, seventy-five miles of roads are cleared of cars, buses, and motorized vehicles every Sunday. The streets become populated with as many as 1.5 million people walking, biking, roller skating, scooting, and using wheelchairs. Food, music, dancing, Zumba, and people watching further activate the car-free space. Bibian Sarmiento, who directs Ciclovía, summarizes its purpose: "Our objective is to make citizens take over the city's public space. . . . The most important thing is the social fabric that gets woven. . . . Everyone is welcome. Everyone is equal."[16]

Ciclovía started a global movement of similar weekly or monthly car-free spaces. CicLAvia in Los Angeles moves to different locations around the metro area and is billed as a temporary public park for recreation and social integration. Like in Bogotá, these car-free streets fill up with smiling, exuberant, and socioeconomically, racially diverse people. These popular events demonstrate the human need and yearning for expanded car-free community space.

Temporary alterations of streets help people imagine how they can be used for robust community life. People's perceptions change to seeing streets as a place for walking, jogging, biking, scooting, playing, and community gatherings. Streets can be places of joy, health, and community rather than the domain of cars. Seeing and experiencing the benefits of street transformations can lead to interest in changes becoming permanent. Yet temporary car-free streets like those found on Ciclovía have, for the most part, remained monthly events.

People need to see how car-free or car-light streets can fit into their daily lives to become motivated to push for their permanence. Once enough people regularly experience the benefits of these altered streets, interest and political will can tip the balance toward lasting change. Prolonged alteration of streets during the COVID-19 pandemic provided just that in multiple US cities.

A silver lining of the pandemic was the push to significantly limit cars on designated streets for months on end. These slow streets, introduced in chapter 6, allowed people to get outside in safe, socially distant ways. They were implemented in cities nationwide, from Oakland and San Francisco, California, to Columbus, Ohio, to Jersey City, New Jersey. Slow streets became valued places for neighbors to gather and interact during the pandemic.

In the most rapid, bold change to ever occur to the city's streets, San Francisco rolled out twenty-six slow streets, covering forty-five miles, during the first year of the pandemic. Shannon Hake, who managed the rollout for the city, commented that slow streets "allowed residents to reclaim public space and use it as an outdoor community center."[17] After the city put in signage and barricades at intersections, the community stepped in to install public art, add potted plants and community-designed signage and barricades, and host events. Neighborhood character made each street unique. A cellist played weekly porch concerts on one street. A local artist painted a giant street mural on another. Children rode bikes on these streets. Slow streets showed that roads can provide joyful community space.

In late 2022, after the COVID-19 pandemic emergency order was lifted, San Francisco's Municipal Transportation Authority (MTA) made more than a dozen of these slow streets permanent. Political pressure from residents played a critical role. These streets support active transportation and community building.

Barcelona is taking slow streets to the next level with superblocks. The city has been transforming nine-block grids of streets into pedestrian-first zones, providing space for children to play, people to gather, and nature to grow. Benches and planters are installed, turning sections of streets into public squares. Only residents can drive cars in the zone and must do so at six miles per hour. Barcelona hopes to create a connected network of these superblocks and green corridors, transforming the city streetscape into community space.

Car-free, pedestrian streets can also unite people across neighborhoods while supporting the local economy. Project for Public Spaces defines these as destination streets that "support retail, services, vending, events, and casual social interactions, among many other uses. Because of this rich mix of uses and activities, destination streets are also key locations where we make memories—the building blocks of a community's sense of place."[18] Destination streets have been around for decades in Europe. In Copenhagen, Stroget is a pedestrian area consisting of multiple streets with street performers, landmarks, and abundant retail that accommodates a wide range of budgets. The Latin Quarter in Paris has numerous cobblestoned pedestrian streets where street food, cafés, and restaurants abound. Carnaby Street is one of thirteen pedestrian streets in London and has over 160 shops, restaurants, bars, and cafés. These pedestrian spaces demonstrate how much streets can be transformed into vibrant community and economic spaces.

Efforts to create similar pedestrian-only streets and plazas in the United States during the 1960s and 1970s largely failed. A 2020 study by Cornell University researchers, however, found that forty-three of these pedestrian malls have survived.[19] Some, like Santa Monica's Third Street Promenade (California), Boulder's Pearl Street (Colorado), and San Diego's Horton Plaza (California), are thriving with many visitors and much economic activity. While pedestrian malls benefit from location and nearby population density, this study and a prior one also uncovered that 80 percent of the surviving ones were in cities with fewer than one hundred thousand residents.[20] Many were main street revitalizations.

The success of these pedestrian-oriented streets in diverse US locations depended on thoughtful design elements. Effective features include lots of ground-floor retail space with windows, sunshades, rain awnings, and ample seating. Vibrant, pedestrian-friendly streets, like other well-designed community settings, can foster social interactions, strengthen community, and deepen individuals' attachment to place.

Transform Land Use with Community Centers

Community spaces also include buildings where the community can gather and share resources. Indoor space is critical in inclement weather or extreme heat. Renovated or new community centers in historically underserved communities can uplift the community, provide space for community building, and offer services to residents.

In late 2022, a beautiful new community center, designed with the community, opened in southeast San Francisco, not far from the India Basin Shoreline Park described earlier. The landscaping, benches, and picnic tables outside provide a parklike space, including a nature play area for children. The interior is filled with services and programs to benefit residents, from job training provided by local nonprofits to work labs to a childcare center. People gather in a café, meeting rooms, and abundant open seating in communal areas. Photos of community leaders, past and present, decorate the walls inside, adding to its welcoming nature for residents.

Community centers that also serve as resilience hubs are becoming increasingly important as the climate crisis worsens with more frequent and intense local weather events. The Boyles Heights Art Conservatory in Los Angeles serves youth through career development services in the arts, media, and broadcast. The center can be flexed into a resilience hub, providing an air-conditioned space during heat waves and a safe space during a disaster. Wi-Fi, computers, and other technologies keep people connected during emergencies. Plans include adding solar panels and backup battery power to make the hub more resilient. Frontline communities most vulnerable to climate risks especially need these welcoming, safe, and functional spaces.

The Sogorea Te' Land Trust, based in the East Bay of the San Francisco Bay Area, is creating community resiliency centers that leverage Indigenous knowledge. Called Himmetkas ("in one place, together"), the first one built included food and medicine gardens, a seed library, water catchment and storage, first-aid supplies, and tools. Himmetkas demonstrate how Indigenous knowledge can support and deepen local resilience in a community center.

Reset Culture by Activating Community Spaces

As many prior examples demonstrate, parks, parklets, plazas, slow streets, destination streets, and community centers realize their full potential when activated. Activation includes free enhancements that entice people to stay, enjoy, and use the amenity.

Cultural events in public spaces, including parades, festivals, and performances, attract large crowds and expose people to diverse histories, traditions, and ways of seeing the world. Murals and public art are forms of activation that also interest people and promote shared experiences.

In early 2021, during the height of the pandemic, an artwork titled *Love Letters* won an annual art contest that was timed for Valentine's Day in New York City's Times Square. The installation was made of repurposed plywood and formed into two interlocking hearts with multiple spaces for the public to interact safely. Jean Cooney, director of Times Square Arts, shared, "We really wanted to expand the notion of love beyond the idea of just romantic love. It's been such an incredibly challenging year on so many levels, that we wanted to expand this idea of love to include togetherness."[21] *Love Letters* beckoned visitors to reflect on the themes of interdependence, collective resilience, and inclusivity and post their love letters on its display. Integrating public art with concern for one another builds community.

San Francisco's first Phoenix Day in 2021 demonstrated what it means to activate community space citywide. For one day, streets in neighborhoods across the city were freed from cars and "opened" for safe walking, biking, and much more. Thousands of people participated in or watched music, dance, and cultural performances. Food, games, and play spaces were plentiful. Resources for health, housing, education, and employment were shared at tables. Other features generated from neighborhood-level interest included a pop-up forest, free barbeque, and an organized community cleanup.

Community space activation can go beyond art and cultural events and promote long-lasting community connections. People can experience togetherness, solidarity, and much joy in such spaces.

The East Oakland Black Cultural Zone Collaborative transformed a city-owned, acre-plus vacant lot in Oakland, California, into a community space. Community events include peaceful rallies and a semiweekly public market featuring local, Black-owned businesses and farms. An area for children to play in helps make it a gathering space for families. The space known as Liberation Park is considered a symbol of the community's rebirth after decades of disinvestment.

Activating community spaces on an everyday basis and for special events beckons people to get outside and connect. When community members plan these activations, the commitment to being in the community solidifies.

Leverage Other Systems

Every place-based system has elements designed to increase connection to community. Mixed-use, mixed-income communities (chap. 4); local stores and work (chap. 5); active, community-oriented transportation modes (chap. 6); nature spaces (chap. 8); local farms, community gardens, and farmers markets (chap. 9); community microgrids (chap. 10); community exchanges, repair cafés, lending libraries, and secondhand stores (chap. 11) are all rooted in and foster community.

In addition, housing everyone (chap. 4) and reducing issues related to homelessness help remove barriers to people getting out in community. In 2023, there were an estimated 653,000 homeless people in the United States.[22] In many cities on the West Coast, there have been record numbers of homeless in recent years. As I've often heard living in San Francisco, observing members of this vulnerable population experiencing mental illness and openly using drugs deters "housed" people from spending time in public spaces. By reducing human suffering on the streets, a housing system for all provides for a fundamental human need and makes public space more inviting.

As evident throughout this chapter, the place-based transportation system designed around car-light living (chap. 6) is particularly catalytic in transforming land into spaces that support vital connections with community in everyday life. With less space needed for auto infrastructure, there is more opportunity to have safe, car-free, and vibrant community spaces. When a city has strong cycling, pedestrian, and public transit infrastructure networks, the potential conversion of car space to community space can grow exponentially. A study on Barcelona's superblocks, for example, found that dense cities with good public transportation could also adopt superblocks.[23] Place-based transportation systems foster community directly through active, community-oriented modes and indirectly through expanding community spaces.

Once momentum builds in this direction, people start working toward more transformative visions. A group of Berlin residents created a group called Berlin Autofrei. They are pushing for the largest car-free urban area in the world— a space larger than Manhattan circumnavigated by a circular train line. With exceptions for emergency vehicles, garbage trucks, delivery vehicles, and some car and ride sharing, the proposal is centered around car-free living. The group envisions children being able to play on the streets, anyone being able to walk and bike safely, and plenty of spaces to be outside in community.

In chapter 8, we'll explore a related, overlapping system with community spaces: nature spaces. Public space can be both community- and nature-oriented and provide the vital connections everyone needs.

NATURE SPACES

The greatest of human discoveries in the future will be the discovery of human intimacy with all those other modes of being that live with us on this planet, inspire our art and literature, reveal that numinous world whence all things come into being, and with which we exchange the very substance of life.

—Thomas Berry, *The Great Work*

At age twenty-one, I participated in a wilderness semester program in the Pacific Northwest. Before this experience, "the environment" was largely abstract to me. I was aware of frightening statistics on the degradation of forests, wetlands, coral reefs, and other natural systems. Yet I had no real sense of what was being lost.

This experience changed everything for me. Never had I connected to nature in such an intimate way. I developed a visceral bond with the land and waters and the complex ecosystems within them. I felt pain and disbelief that we would let society damage something so beautiful and necessary for life. I've been deeply concerned about the environment ever since, striving to do my part to improve the relationship between our species and the rest of the planet.

My appreciation for nature would have waned had I not stayed connected to it over the past thirty years since that seminal wilderness experience. I'm fortunate to be able to experience nature in small doses most days. I enjoy watching and hearing the birds and squirrels in our small urban backyard. Our sidewalk pollinator garden attracts bees, birds, and, on occasion, butterflies. I appreciate other sidewalk gardens sprinkled throughout our neighborhood, especially when the colors emerge during the spring bloom season. This nearby nature and paying attention to it keeps me grounded in nature and remembering that I am a part of it.

Still, it's easy to lose my felt sense of connection with nature. The pull of digital technology and indoor amenities combined with the rush of modern living make it hard to connect with nature regularly and deeply. You may also feel a strong affinity for nature and find it hard to experience it often. This feeling of disconnection has become all too common.

* * *

The time people spend in nature has drastically shrunk in recent decades. It has particularly affected children, as author and children and nature expert Richard Louv has detailed in multiple publications. In his 2005 book *Last Child in the Woods*, Louv coined the term *nature-deficit disorder*, which refers to the generational decline among children spending time outdoors and its damaging effect on their lives. As a large body of research now shows, the deficit applies to young and old alike and is taking us down a perilous path.

In corporate capitalist systems, people consume nature much more than they experience it. A study conducted by federal and state wildlife and park agencies, *The Nature of Americans National Report*, revealed how spending little time in nature has become normalized. The study's findings from a survey of twelve thousand adults illustrated a prevailing sense that the places where "people work, live and go to school generally do not encourage contact with the natural world and myriad competing priorities and activities push experiences with nature to the side."[1] Even a few minutes of daily nature connection has become elusive.

Like time in community spaces, barriers to spending time outside to connect with nature are most evident in low-income communities of color. Air, land, and water pollution are prevalent. Temperatures can be dangerously high in the summer due to the "heat island" effect, in which the prevalence of pavement increases local surface temperatures. Limited green space presents another obstacle. Whereas more than three-quarters of white people in the United States live in areas with more natural land than the US median, only one-third of Asian, Latinx, and Black people live in areas above that median threshold.[2] Limited access to nature is especially harmful to people who need the health benefits of nature to help overcome systemic health inequities.

In this chapter, we'll look at how all people can reconnect with nature through an abundant, accessible, and nearby nature spaces system. The many benefits of nature connection in people's lives are an important part of that vision. We'll first explore the power, land use, and cultural forces that keep people disconnected from nature. Systemic strategies can be employed to build a place-based nature spaces system and cure the "nature-deficit disorder." Many examples in the chapter will illustrate how that is starting to occur.

> ## Systems-Change Strategies for Revitalizing Nature for Nearby Connection
>
> - Shift power to residents and local nature-based nonprofits
> - Shift power to Indigenous groups and nature-based coalitions
> - Transform land use with renaturing cities
> - Transform land use with open space restoration and trail networks
> - Transform land use with nature-based climate adaptation
> - Reset culture through neighborhood nature restoration projects
> - Reset culture by treating nature access as a human right
> - Leverage other systems

What's Disconnecting People and Nature

The diminishment of everyday nature experiences has arisen from a confluence of systemic factors. Corporate capitalist interests, paved-over land, lack of equitable access to nearby nature, and a culture of separation from nature keep people disconnected from nature in their everyday lives.

Power: Big Auto and Big Tech (Again!)

As with community spaces (chap. 7), Big Auto's and Big Tech's power to shape systems limits the availability of local nature spaces and time spent in them. Their influence on how people have lost daily nature connection lurks through automobile dependency and digital society.

Big Auto benefits from the driveways, streets, and curbside space in new suburban developments. The auto industry has long lobbied for these developments as well as the freeways and roads that have been built to connect them with the surrounding region. As a result, the greenbelt that historically provided nearby access to nature has shrunk.

In more urban and dense neighborhoods, Big Auto's influence is seen in parking lots and spaces that crowd out urban green space. Television advertisements of SUVs driving on uncrowded roads along beautiful natural scenery convey that automobile dependency and nature are compatible. Nothing could be further from the truth when it comes to protecting and spending time in green spaces.

Big Tech strives to integrate digital technology into every aspect of people's lives. With nature, one can watch videos, webcams, screensavers, and other virtual representations. We know this virtual nature is far from a substitute for real nature. As society marches down this digital path, humanity gets ever more dis-connected from the reality of being and feeling a part of the natural world. Big Tech profits when people stay in virtual but not real nature spaces.

Land Use: Pavement and Inequitable Nature Access

Pavement is a significant impediment to connecting with nature. Creeks and native landscapes have been paved to make way for streets, parking, hardscape playgrounds and plazas, and buildings. Water is the only substance on earth used more than concrete.[3] Journalist Jonathan Watts paints a vivid picture of its mag-nitude and impact on nature: "Concrete is how we try to tame nature . . . [and] entomb[s] vast tracts of fertile soil, constipate rivers, choke habitats and—acting as a rock-hard second skin—desensitize us from what is happening outside the urban fortresses. Our blue and green world is becoming greyer by the second. By one calculation, we may have already passed the point where concrete outweighs the combined carbon mass of every tree, bush, and shrub on the planet."[4] Con-crete is so pervasive that it's difficult to imagine the plants, habitats, and water-ways that existed before they were buried.

Paved land also dramatically increases vulnerability to flooding, especially in the climate change era. Impervious surfaces like asphalt cover three-fourths of New York City. When the remnants of Hurricane Ida struck the city with flash floods in 2021, storm sewers overflowed, the subway system flooded, and several people lost their lives trapped in basement apartments.

As happened with Hurricane Katrina in New Orleans and Hurricane Harvey in Houston, the devastation to people and buildings was exponentially increased by pavement and the lack of nature to absorb runoff.

Tree canopy inequities across neighborhoods are among the many lingering effects of historical redlining of communities. Maps of tree cover across cities reveal these nature-based inequities. In Los Angeles, an affluent neighborhood in the Los Feliz area considered most suitable for investment in the 1930s by the government has 37 percent tree canopy coverage.[5] The historically redlined Pico-Union neighborhood is 17 percent covered in trees. Even though Pico-Union is only six miles from Los Feliz, it has less than half the tree canopy of that neigh-borhood. Consequently, nature connection and staying cool during heat waves are more significant challenges in Pico-Union than in Los Feliz.

Cities can fund green spaces and nature amenities in underserved communi-ties, but this can also lead to the displacement of current residents when rents and housing prices rise. Multiple studies have shown that street trees increase property values.[6] This research reflects how much people value nearby nature but also how adding more of it often leads to "green gentrification." The High Line in

New York City provides an example. This green pathway/park is used by many tourists but few longtime residents. Its creation led to rapid gentrification in the surrounding neighborhood.

Across the country, Marie Harrison, a forty-year resident of Bayview-Hunters Point in San Francisco, shares her concerns about the greening of her neighborhood: "They call it 'green' to give it a more natural kind of feel. To me, it's more or less the idea of moving folks out and replacing them with new folks. With us, in particular, it's all about gentrification."[7] When long overdue toxic cleanups occur in communities of color, existing residents rightfully ask who the cleanup is for and if they can afford to continue living there. The relationship between nature access and gentrification creates a complex dynamic that must be addressed in any solution to equitable nature connection.

Culture: Unwelcome Spaces and "Nature Is Somewhere Else"

Where nearby nature spaces exist, Black and Brown people have been excluded or not felt welcome or safe. Foothills Park, a green space in the foothills of Palo Alto, California, was closed to nonresidents of the city for fifty-one years until forced to open in 2020 by court order. The American Civil Liberties Union had sued the city for excluding from the park less affluent people of color who live in nearby cities. Also, in 2020, a white woman who feigned being threatened by a Black birdwatcher in New York's Central Park caught the nation's attention. These are just two examples of why people of color often feel unwelcome or unsafe in public green spaces. In her book *Black Faces White Spaces*, Professor Carolyn Finney detailed how slavery, Jim Crow, and racial violence led to the exclusion of people of color in nature spaces and the difficult work of undoing this legacy.

In 2001, environmental educator Randolph Haluza-Delay published a study about following up with eight urban teenagers who had been on a twelve-day wilderness-based learning experience in Alberta, Canada. His aptly named article, "Nothing Here to Care About: Participant Constructions of Nature Following a 12-Day Wilderness Program," revealed a significant disconnect between their wilderness experience and life at home. Upon their return, they did not recognize or see nature in their home communities. The teens viewed nature as undisturbed, out there, away from people, and unfamiliar. Despite its presence in their neighborhood in different forms, they concluded that nature must be elsewhere and not in their communities. This article has stuck with me years later as a profound reflection of the false human-nature dichotomy in modern culture.

With these multiple barriers at play, nature connection has become a smaller and smaller part of people's lives, and access remains riddled with inequities. A survey of twelve thousand US adults and children confirmed these trends and also found that three-quarters of adult Americans highly value contact with nature and wish to see programs that foster appreciation for nature and wildlife.[8] People yearn for nature experiences in their lives. We can restore those vital connections in everyday life with a place-based nature spaces system.

A Vision of Abundant, Accessible, and Nearby Nature Spaces

Experiencing nature every day enriches life. A participant in one of my research studies on transportation behavior shared her joy in being able to bike through an urban park on her way to work. Her most memorable experience was coming across a coyote one morning. Wildlife captivates human attention and connects deeply to something in our DNA. When she turned forty, blogger Shannon Hilson reflected on life's moments that have mattered the most to her: "The day I was walking by the beach with my friends as a teenager in the fog, saw a seal, and thought for a split second that it was a mermaid. . . . And the week a random frog lived underneath my bedroom window and made me happy every night with all his little frog noises . . . I couldn't even tell you why, but there's something magical about [these moments]—something that suggests they're what life is truly all about."[9] Nature pervades these experiences that give Shannon such meaning, delight, and wonder.

Nature connections generate feelings of awe that boost health and happiness. It taps into a sense that we're a small part of something much larger and helps put daily concerns in perspective. Feelings of awe reduce inflammation in human bodies linked to depression and can increase life satisfaction.[10] To feel awe, a person doesn't have to be in majestic natural places like Yosemite Valley. Awe can arise in everyday life in the presence of nature if one pays attention to it, as Shannon does.

A growing body of research demonstrates how and why nearby nature is so important in people's lives. An analysis of research on nature contact for humans identified twenty distinct health and well-being benefits, each backed by multiple studies.[11]

Being in nature every day enhances people's mental health in many ways. University of Michigan researchers found that twenty to thirty minutes of nature daily in urban environments significantly reduced stress levels.[12] Researchers who conducted studies in suburban communities near Chicago, Illinois, concluded that everyday nature exposure from tree-lined walkways to front-yard gardens provides a myriad of mental health benefits including improved attentional functioning and stress reduction.[13] Another research study had an even more specific finding: Vegetation cover and the presence of birds were associated with lower levels of depression, anxiety, and stress.[14] These are some of the many reasons why medical and health practitioners have started to prescribe daily doses of nature.

Nature can also provide healing for individuals and communities. A garden in West Oakland, California, was developed as a memorial amid a community beset by gun violence. Community member and musician Ezekiel McCarter reflected on the importance of the garden: "To be able to nurture life, when everything around you is seemingly chaotic and like a threat to life, is really empowering for a lot of us."[15] Nature connection helps people and communities heal from trauma.

The presence of nature enhances community. University of Illinois researchers, for example, studied the impact of trees and green space on residents in Chicago public housing.[16] They found that those with nature around their building knew more people and felt more of a sense of unity with neighbors than residents in buildings without surrounding trees and nature. In addition, those more exposed to nature near their housing were more concerned with helping each other and had stronger feelings of belonging.

Local nature can have a positive upstream benefit on the environment. Eight percent of carbon emissions[17] and 9 percent of global industrial water use[18] come from concrete production. Replacing aging cement with green space rather than new concrete is a climate-mitigation and water-conservation strategy. Trees close to buildings reduce the need for air-conditioning on hot days, reducing energy demand. Trees and vegetation also provide natural carbon sequestration. Local nature spaces benefit the global environment.

On the most fundamental level, nearby nature spaces enable us to overcome the growing alienation toward nature in today's society. With everyday nature connection, we can regain our lost sense of being a part of nature and drop the illusion that we are separate from it. When connected to nature, one is less likely to take for granted the air, water, and food that nature provides for human life. Experiencing nature is essential to being human.

Systems-Change Strategies for a Local Nature Spaces System

Nature spaces that are abundant, accessible, and nearby are needed in every neighborhood. Renaturing cities, restoring open space, and creating trail networks increase opportunities to experience nature daily. Nature regeneration also protects communities from climate change threats. Restoration projects engage people with nature and deepen their appreciation for it. Ultimately, nature access must be prioritized as a universal human right, and shifting power to residents, local nature-based nonprofits, Indigenous groups, and nature-based coalitions sets that in motion.

Shift Power to Residents and Local Nature-Based Nonprofits

Shifting power to residents, just like with community spaces, helps to ensure that nature spaces will be regularly used for nature connection. For communities of color, addressing the real fears of green gentrification is an important starting point.

Municipalities and regions can increase housing affordability and equitable nature access by decoupling greening and gentrification. The Los Angeles Regional Open Space and Affordable Housing Collaborative was formed in 2016. The partnership outlined a framework for developing parks and affordable housing together. They added affordable housing goals into the LA River Master Plan, a greening effort of a fifty-one-mile waterway that cuts across many lower-income cities in Southern California. Their first-in-the-country Displacement Avoidance Policy became part of an expenditure plan for an approved countywide parcel tax for parks and open space. The policy includes incentives, collaboration between park developers and affordable housing developers, technical assistance, and data collection and evaluation to assess the impacts of park investment on housing stability and affordability. These measures improve vital access to nature while not pushing people out of their communities and furthering inequality.

To assure residents that greening projects in their neighborhoods are being built for them and not others, community members must be involved from the start and through design and implementation. In Brooklyn, New York, longtime residents of the Greenpoint neighborhood and planners used what researchers deemed a "just green enough strategy."[19] They described the outcome as cleaning up and greening the neighborhood without triggering green gentrification. Community concerns, needs, and desires guided the process and the resulting nature space projects rather than more conventional urban design and restoration approaches. When residents are given ownership in making nature more a part of where they live, gentrifying forces can be lessened.

Local nonprofits can facilitate residents' engagement in enhancing nature in their communities. Nonprofits like Working for Northeast Trees and City Plants in Los Angeles work with teams of residents to plant trees where they are most needed in heat islands. With the support of these nonprofits, Los Angeles plans to increase tree canopy coverage by 50 percent by 2028 in neighborhoods that have been neglected, like Pico-Union featured earlier.[20] Another nonprofit, 596 Acres in New York City, worked with neighbors to create thirty-six new nature spaces on vacant lots. The city's park department now oversees many of these transformed parcels as protected green spaces.

Shift Power to Indigenous Groups and Nature-Based Coalitions

Broader commitments and funding for nature spaces can be catalyzed by sharing power with Indigenous groups and building power among nature-based organizations. Place-based, cross-sector coalitions that focus on nature and center local Native groups help shift power in support of accessible and nearby nature spaces.

Indigenous groups are our best guides for revitalizing local nature. Indigenous knowledge passed down through generations is based on living close to the land and sustaining ecosystems for millennia. San Francisco's Presidio was decommissioned as a military base and made an urban national park site in 1994. Since then, Ohlone history and practices have informed the restoration of natural lands and watersheds within it. Tribal ceremonies and celebrations are held when restoration projects are completed on this ancestral land of the Ohlone. Native plant communities have been reintroduced along with sites that allow Ohlone people to renew cultural practices. Ohlone names have been restored to unearthed creeks and other land features. Ohlone people, including park ranger Desiree Munoz, continue to shape decisions about the park.

In another part of the Bay Area, shifting power to the Amah Mutsun Tribal Band has helped protect and enhance a broad expanse of open space. The Amah Mutsun have built partnerships with public and private landowners to steward land across the coastal mountain sections of five San Francisco Bay Area counties. They work with about fifty partners and allies to protect open space from development and other threats surrounding the populous Bay Area.

Returning unceded ancestral land to Indigenous groups further shifts power and benefits local nature. In 2022, the Onondaga Nation recovered 1,023 acres of land from New York state just outside Syracuse. The land includes the headwaters of Onondaga Creek. Brine mining by the Honeywell corporation caused significant damage to the ground and water there. The intentions of the Onondaga in restoring the ecosystem were clear, as shared by Chief Tadodaho Sid Hill: "The Nation can now renew its stewardship obligations to restore these lands and waters and to preserve them for future generations yet to come. The Nation hopes that this . . . effort will be another step in healing between themselves and all others who live in this region."[21] Land recovery by Indigenous groups is not only just but also critical to regenerating nature.

Together Bay Area is a diverse coalition of over sixty Native groups, nonprofits, and public agencies in the San Francisco Bay Area working to support the health of the land across the region. In 2022, the coalition helped secure over $470 million from the State Coastal Conservancy for nature-based projects that enhance and expand access to nature for Bay Area communities. Together Bay Area built political will for nature protection and rejuvenation through media coverage, working with local legislators, and amplifying local nature conservation efforts.

In late 2022, Together Bay Area took another step toward building power by partnering twenty-five local nature-based organizations and agencies with local Native American communities through a nine-month Right Relations program. The cohort experienced Going Beyond Land Acknowledgement workshops, field trips hosted by local Native American organizations, and roundtable discussions with Native American leaders. A primary goal of the program was to catalyze collective action to restore local Native lands.

Transform Land Use with Renaturing Cities

Spurred by growing political support, local governments are investing in projects that transform land use with expanded, enhanced natural spaces in urban environments. The "renaturing cities" movement has taken hold. Designing with nature is being prioritized in urban planning. Ecosystem regeneration in urban areas includes the reintroduction of native plants that attract native insects, birds, and other wildlife.

Singapore demonstrates how cities and nature can coexist. As the second-most dense country in the world, the city-state had to carefully plan to prioritize nature. Parks, gardens, trees, and other greenery pervade the urban core of Singapore, providing opportunities for its residents to experience nature every day. The government requires green buffers around new development and green rooftops on new buildings. With this intentional design for incorporating nature, green space increased from 35.7 percent in 1986 to almost 50 percent in 2010, even as Singapore's population grew.[22] Restored wetlands, revitalized streams, and catchments naturalized with trees and plantings enable water-based nature connections. Seven nature parks provide habitat for rare and endangered species and immersive nature experiences for Singaporeans. These parks and others are connected through pedestrian and biking paths. As discussed in chapter 1, Singapore ranks as one of the happiest countries on the planet. Easy access to nature for residents is one reason why.

Some European cities are taking "renaturing" further by "rewilding" parts of their city. London took out concrete tunnels around waterways and reintroduced native plants near them. The number of bird and bat species increased dramatically. Three German cities collaborated on creating wildflower meadows across urban green spaces and saw increases in bird, hedgehog, butterfly, and bee numbers. Barcelona is installing two hundred nesting towers for bats and birds, forty beehives, and pollinating plants to attract them.

Renaturing is also happening in the United States. Over one hundred acres of land and the watershed in San Francisco's Presidio have been restored, guided by the Ohlone people and their knowledge, as discussed earlier. Adjacent to the Presidio, forty acres of asphalt at Crissy Field were transformed into tidal marsh and dune habitat along the bay. It now looks much more like the ancestral hunting and fishing grounds of the Ohlone than a former airfield. The tributaries and wetlands upstream of the tidal marsh have been unearthed, marking the first time an entire urban watershed has been revitalized. In another part of the Presidio, a small lake had succumbed to invasive fish, pollution, and sediment. The lake was dredged, cleaned, and repopulated with native fish, turtles, frogs, and mussels. Like the nearby watershed restoration, this was the first time an ancient lake ecosystem had been restored to this extent in an urban area. Native birds, insects, and other wildlife returned in droves to the Presidio and Crissy Field, including coyotes and a colony of bees not seen in nearly a century.

About fifty miles south of the Presidio, the Guadalupe River runs through San Jose. In recent years, the river channel through downtown was widened and made more natural with plantings. Before the city was built, this section of the river was a large freshwater meadow essential to the Ohlone people's way of living. Residents were barely aware of the river's existence before the revitalization effort began. A river park now runs from downtown to restored wetlands at the bay. A fourteen-mile trail winds through a forty-acre natural area with native plants, birds, and butterflies. A small number of spawning chinook salmon arrive each year, and the population could grow with further restoration. Access to the space is not without challenges. The presence of hundreds of homeless people and litter in the river illustrates how deficiencies in the housing and consumer goods systems impact the nature experience.

To maximize ecological benefits and deepen people's connection to place and nature, reintroducing native species in urban and suburban settings is essential. In his article "A Street Tree Revolution in Silicon Valley," journalist Eric Simons challenged this subregion of the San Francisco Bay Area, known for its technological innovation, to become a leader in restoring native trees. According to researchers Simons interviewed, 80 percent of the original trees in the land that is now Silicon Valley were oaks, mostly valley oaks.[23] Trees are abundant in many of the affluent suburban communities in the valley today, but very few are oaks. Native birds, mammals, and butterflies depend on the oaks. The trees also tolerate drought, absorb runoff, and sequester carbon better than most other trees. Many of the nonoak street trees were planted just after World War II. These trees are starting to die off, providing a once-in-a-generation opportunity for a large replanting of oak trees. One can imagine these native trees and the ecosystems they support becoming commonplace again. An increasing abundance of oaks could give rise to a more distinct place-based, Indigenous culture reflected in arts, education, and events.

Transform Land Use with Open Space Restoration and Trail Networks

Accessing more extensive tracts of nature, typically surrounding cities and towns or between them, requires protected open space. A land-eating sport in decline and increased interest in trails are helping transform land for more expansive nearby nature access.

Converting golf courses to open space creates a sense of wilderness within or adjacent to cities and towns. Up to eight hundred golf courses in the United States closed between 2008 and 2018, presenting an immense opportunity for rejuvenating nature on large tracts of land.[24] In a suburb outside Melbourne, Australia, land occupied by a golf course not long ago is now a wildlife sanctuary. Features include tall marsh, grassy woodlands, and open water. Next to the Santa Barbara campus of the University of California, wetlands buried by a former golf course are being restored and connected to a network of trails. These conversions allow more people to connect with biodiversity and natural habitats near where they live.

Great trails require less land conversion but can greatly expand access to nature. Signs, interpretive sites, shade structures, and other high-quality features help entice people to get on the trail. The thirty-seven-mile Razorback Greenway connects four cities in northwest Arkansas. The trail runs along a restored creek. The greenway has also brought life back to shops and restaurants along its path. Great trails increase time in nature, even when the destination is a human-made spot, and strengthen people's connection to place.

In the St. Louis region of Missouri, the Great Rivers Greenway is a network of paths and trails that make it easy for people to get out into nature. A dedicated sales tax passed in 2000 funded the building of over 128 miles of the greenway by 2022. The public agency that oversees the greenway works with partners on conservation projects along the trail network. Projects have restored woodlands, prairie, and wetlands that people now experience along the greenway's paths.

The Crosstown Trail in San Francisco, completed in 2019, provides seventeen miles of walking from the city's southeast corner to the northwest. Nature appears and inspires along the urban trail. Parkland along the bay shoreline forms the starting point, while an ocean beach lies at the end. Six connected community gardens in a low-income neighborhood, each with a different theme, are found a few miles from the start. Shortly after that, one can walk through the largest grassland in the city within the city's second-largest park. Toward the midpoint, the trail winds through a seventy-acre natural canyon for about a mile. After climbing a peak surrounded by open space, another vegetation-filled canyon with wildlife awaits. This canyon had been inaccessible until a volunteer group of mountain bikers cleared brush and built this trail section. Trails and pathways like the Crosstown across a big city help urban residents find nearby nature.

Transform Land Use with Nature-Based Climate Adaptation

Nature-based approaches needed for climate resilience also generate opportunities for people to connect with nature nearby. Tree canopy, green roofs, and other vegetation bring the heat down outside and inside buildings. Rain gardens capture storm runoff. These local nature-based solutions help protect people from climate-induced heat waves and flooding while increasing the presence of nearby nature.

Coastal regions and cities are becoming increasingly vulnerable to rising sea levels. Nature buffers are being restored in places like the town of Burlingame, California. A 9.4-acre nature and recreation park on the Burlingame shorefront is being planned. The parcel will include up to 3.5 acres of native tidal marsh habitat restoration and a transition zone between the marsh and higher land to mitigate flooding. The park will include trails as well as access to fishing and getting out in the water on kayaks and other small vessels. This project will expand nearby nature access while helping protect residents against climate change.

Digging up long-buried waterways is another way to address flooding from climate change. The Tibbets Brook, in the Bronx, New York, was diverted into sewer pipes over a century ago. When storms hit the area in 2021, the pipes overflowed and completely flooded an expressway. The city plans to unearth the waterway to reduce future flooding. This pavement-to-nature project for climate resilience will increase New Yorker's access to nature.

Reset Culture Through Neighborhood Nature Restoration Projects

Being stewards of local nature deepens our connection to place. Nature restoration projects bring communities together and people closer to nature.

In South Bend, Indiana, the city government, a local university, and a local high school collaborated on a project to revitalize a polluted waterway in a low-income Black neighborhood. The participants assessed the creek's environmental quality, removed pollutants, stabilized the creek's banks with native plants, and took other measures to prevent soil erosion. The stream is now a popular recreation site with a thriving crawfish population. The neighborhood initially resisted the restoration, fearing it might lead to gentrification. The residents remain, and bridges have been built between the community and the students who participated in the project. Since this successful restoration project, community development and nature enhancement projects have expanded around the city.

Neighborhood nature rejuvenation projects can unearth nature from pavement and interest people in paying attention to the wildlife that emerges. A mile-long creek was unearthed from concrete drainage by a community volunteer restoration project near Queensland, Australia. Fish, eels, turtles, birds, and even some kangaroos returned to the watershed. This restored creek ecosystem is on a path from a neighborhood to a local school. The wildlife often captivates children on their way to and from school.

Habitat restoration around a particular species strengthens people's connection to local nature and community. The Green Hairstreak Corridor consists of eleven restored habitat sites for the namesake butterfly spread across four natural areas in one San Francisco neighborhood. People have populated small public spaces as well as their yards with the host plants that the green hairstreak butterfly needs to survive. Thanks to this community effort and the local nonprofit Nature in the City that supports it, the green hairstreak has come back from the brink of extinction. This project has changed the neighborhood's culture. Residents feel a sense of pride about their place and saving a native species together.

Neighborhood-scale restoration projects like the Green Hairstreak Corridor project can have a ripple effect and inspire property owners to restore wild nature on their properties. Water-thirsty residential lawns pervade many US suburban communities. A native habitat restoration project in any one of these neighborhoods could get households to think differently about what could be in their yards. People get excited when native plants bring back birds and other pollinators into their yards and communities. Each lawn conversion to a native plant garden could add to the community's value for local biodiversity and have a social contagion effect.

Reset Culture by Treating Nature Access as a Human Right

Nature access for all is increasingly recognized as a human right and fundamental to human and planetary health. Much of this movement started with a focus on children and nature.

In 2012, the International Union for the Conservation of Nature adopted a resolution affirming children's rights to experience a healthy, natural world. This international conservation alliance linked the importance of connecting with nature to the fate of our planet.

Richard Louv cofounded the Children and Nature Network shortly after publishing his groundbreaking *Last Child in the Woods* in 2005. By 2023, the network, in partnership with the National League of Cities, had mobilized sixty-nine cities and communities. These places are making significant strides toward the network's vision of equitable access to nature everywhere children live, learn, and play.

Rethink Outdoors is a national initiative that launched in 2019. The funders, nonprofits, and others behind the initiative expanded the notion of a human right to nature to people of all ages. Their platform also addressed the barriers people of color encounter in safely accessing nature. They support organizations like Latino Outdoors and Outdoor Afro. These movement-building groups host hikes and encourage people to get outside regularly to promote their well-being. They are helping to make safe, enjoyable access to nature a reality for people of color.

Rights to nature also involve access to trailheads in one's region. For those without cars, transit is essential. The nature map app Outer Spatial provides users with transit trip planning to get to nearby trails. Dedicated transit service with such goals is even more critical. Trailhead Direct in Seattle transports people from downtown Seattle and light-rail stations around the metropolitan area to hundreds of miles of trails just outside the urban boundaries. The service operates on weekends and holidays from spring to fall. The federal Transit to Trails Act, introduced in 2021, would provide grants for programs like Trailhead Direct that connect underserved communities to trails and green spaces.

Leverage Other Systems

Like connection to community, every place-based system has elements designed to increase people's connection to nature. Mixed-use communities with recreational space (chap. 4), local restoration and stewardship careers and jobs (chap. 5), active transportation modes (chap. 6), community spaces with natural features (chap. 7), regional solar and wind power (chap. 11), and reduction of waste and litter (chap. 12) all help facilitate increased nature connection.

Chapter 9 focuses on regional and local food, which can connect people to nature every time they shop for food or take a bite. As we know in the abstract, nature provides the land, nutrients, climate, and water to grow our food. When individuals see and experience where their food comes from, they develop direct knowledge of nature's gifts. Growing some of their own food deepens the nature-food connection. Next, we'll explore how people can bring the abundance of nature into their lives through local and regional food systems.

FOOD

We have the power to change the way we produce, harvest, sell and consume food. We do not need the big conglomerates. More profit for farmers. More nutrition for us. Less packaging and energy use. Common sense food.

—The People's Food and Farming Alliance, November 6, 2022

Food is a central part of our daily lives. How, what, and where we eat can change much over our lifetimes and is inextricably linked with the condition of the environment. Over the years, I've shopped at all types of grocery stores, purchased organic and conventional produce, and changed my diet many times.

As my awareness of the environmental impact of food choices grew, I tried veganism in my early twenties. Without others around me doing the vegan diet, I gradually brought fish, cheese, and yogurt back into my diet. For years, I was mostly vegetarian. When we had children, chicken and fish became a more regular part of my diet.

Knowing the benefits to my body and the planet, a mostly plant-based, locally sourced diet appeals to me. I try to follow professor, food journalist, and author Michael Pollan's simple formula for healthy eating: "Eat food (i.e., whole fresh), not too much, mostly plants." Plentiful plant-based options in restaurants and lots of fresh produce in local grocery stores and restaurants make this diet possible.

Still, it's not easy to eat in these ways regularly. Organic produce almost always costs more than conventionally grown produce. There are more processed than whole foods in most grocery stores. Shopping at large corporate grocery chains is generally cheaper than at local markets. Locally grown food at restaurants and markets typically comes with a higher price tag than food grown in another country. Meat is often the centerpiece of meals at restaurants and homes.

Local, plant-based, organic food benefits personal and environmental health in many ways, but its limited availability and prices have kept it out of reach of most Americans. The food system is geared toward corporate profits, not collective well-being.

* * *

In the past half century, diets have shifted from locally grown, homemade food to globally sourced, processed, and packaged foods. With processed foods and animal products replacing traditional diets, chronic disease has soared. The globalization of food is making people sick.

In the United States, the lack of fresh, nutritious food is particularly acute in low-income communities and communities of color. The term *food deserts* is used to describe urban, suburban, and rural low-income neighborhoods with limited fresh produce and healthy groceries available at affordable prices. In 2022, 6 percent of the US population, about nineteen million people, were living in areas that had limited access to a supermarket.[1] Approximately 30 percent more people of color than white people live in food deserts.[2]

Racism has also been systemic on the food production side of the US food system. Black farmers owned 14 percent of the nation's farms in 1920.[3] A century later, however, Black people account for only 1.4 percent of farm ownership nationwide.[4] Much of the land was taken through deceptive maneuvers and discriminatory practices. Instead of a fair ownership share, people of color, mostly migrants today, experience the food production system as poorly paid, seasonal workers.

The food production system is also taking a huge toll on the environment. How food is grown and processed in the global, corporate food system has caused pervasive land and water pollution, soil and water depletion, and greenhouse gas emissions (GHGE).

Today's industrial agriculture relies on large-scale crop monoculture of genetically modified organisms (GMOs). Monoculture practices diminish soil fertility. Almost one-quarter of agricultural land areas worldwide have seen a reduction in productivity due to land degradation.[5] Over 90 percent of US-grown soybeans, corn, cotton, and canola crops are GMOs.[6] GMOs allow industrial farms to apply large amounts of chemical pesticides or herbicides, as the crops are genetically engineered to withstand them. These chemicals and the heavy use of synthetic fertilizers harm farmworkers, pollute water and land, and enter the food supply.

Most crops do not directly feed people but are used as livestock feed. Millions of cattle, pigs, chickens, and other animals grown for human consumption are confined to feedlots or windowless buildings in close quarters. These facilities are known as concentrated animal farm operations (CAFOs). The harm to people and the environment from CAFOs includes manure runoff into water bodies, air pollution, odors, spreading pathogens like salmonella that cause illnesses, and, not surprisingly, a negative impact on nearby property values.

Our food system is a primary cause of the climate crisis, biodiversity loss, and water shortages. Food and agriculture production emits around one-quarter of greenhouse gasses globally.[7] Meat and dairy products account for well over half of the emissions.[8] Excess fertilizer has run off into rivers and coastal ecosystems, leading to more than four hundred low-oxygen "dead zones" across the planet's waters.[9] Agriculture accounts for about 80 percent of water use in the United States, and most of the water is used by the meat and dairy industry.

The damage to people and the planet caused by globalized, industrialized agriculture coincides with how alienated human society has become from the food supply. Despite food being essential to survival, the modern food system separates us from the land, water, and people that produce it.

This chapter first looks at what underlies the corporate capitalist food system and its deleterious effects. We'll explore how the food system has become so globalized, centered around unhealthy diets, and difficult to change. Place-based food systems, known as foodsheds, support more planet-friendly, healthy diets and provide an alternative many people desire. This chapter highlights how systems-change levers are being applied toward this vision. These changes reconnect people with food and the nature and people that provide it.

Systems-Change Strategies for Increasing Regional and Local Food

- Shift power to local farmers and food makers
- Shift power through local hubs and land trusts
- Shift power to Black, Indigenous, and people of color (BIPOC) farmers and communities
- Transform land use with regional food plans
- Transform land use with urban agriculture
- Reset culture through farmer training
- Reset culture through healthy food incentives
- Reset culture through plant-based diet and waste reduction initiatives
- Reset culture through household and community food gardens
- Leverage other systems

Holding the Globalized Food System and Unhealthy Diets in Place

Large, multinational agriculture, chemical, and food corporations (Big Ag) exert tremendous power over the food system. Land use patterns, meat-based diets, and wasteful food practices stand in the way of a more local, sustainable, and equitable food system.

Power: Big Ag

The globalized, industrialized food system is primarily controlled by and benefits Big Ag corporations that grow, process, store, prepare, transport, and distribute food. Journalist Paul Wallich writes about corporate consolidation in this complex system: "About half the crops produced by the [world's] farms rely on seeds, fertilizers, and pesticides supplied by a mere dozen or so companies. Most of those crops are bought, traded, and transported around the world by another half dozen. . . . And when it's time for agricultural products to be processed and distributed to stores, that's another dozen or so, many overlapping with the aforementioned traders and suppliers."[10] Many farmers depend on Monsanto for Roundup herbicide and genetically engineered Roundup-resistant seeds. Chicken farmers get their chicks and feed from corporations like Tyson Foods that also distribute and sell the product.

The market concentration of Big Ag enables its interests to direct the market and secure most of the profits for themselves. From 1980 to 2020, the four largest meat-packers—Tyson, Cargill, National Beef Packing Company, and JBS—increased their market share from 36 to 85 percent.[11] With this power, they demand and get low prices from feedlots. Feedlots that have also grown and consolidated over the years put even more downward price pressure on ranchers.

Small-scale ranchers get squeezed in this system, barely surviving on razor-thin margins and often having to sell at a loss.

Big Ag uses its marketing power to deceive consumers and take market share from family farmers. Greg Gunthorp sustainably and humanely raises turkeys on his fourth-generation family farm in Indiana. A longtime retail client dropped him before Thanksgiving in 2020. The store owner explained that customers were opting for cheaper turkeys "labeled" as sustainable from corporate sellers. Gunthorp expressed his frustration: "Big Ag has co-opted and bastardized every one of our messages. When they use a fancy label with absolutely meaningless adjectives, there's just no way we can compete."[12]

Big Ag's influence on government leads to lax regulations that allow corporations to get away with misleading claims. Farmers and ranchers like Gunthorp who genuinely practice what these labels stand for lose out.

Government subsidies have long benefited Big Ag. Between 1995 and 2023, the federal government provided $523 billion in subsidies.[13] The corn, soybean, and wheat industries received almost half of that. Under the US Farm Bill, direct payments come through counter-cyclical payments triggered by low market prices, revenue assurance programs, loans with favorable terms, and disaster payments that include crop insurance. Most of these subsidies go to the largest farm operations with very little to family farmers.[14]

Agribusiness and government support for it have devastated small family farms. Between 2011 and 2018 alone, one hundred thousand farms were lost in the United States.[15] This trend has been underway for decades and has hollowed out many rural communities. Farmers who lose their land often end up working on a corporate-owned farm where most of the money flows out of the community. The image of the United States as a nation of small farmers and ranchers has been shattered.

Land Use: "Eating Up" Land

More than a third of land on the planet and three-quarters of freshwater resources are used by our one species to feed ourselves.[16] Land conversion to agriculture for global markets has cleared vast amounts of forests. From 1980 to 2000, 254 million acres of land were deforested, primarily for cattle ranching in Latin America and palm oil plantations in Southeast Asia.[17] A tripling of soybean production between 1990 and 2010 led to massive deforestation in Brazil.[18]

The most extensive use of land in the United States is pasture for cows and other grazers. Combining the pasture with cropland that produces livestock feed, 41 percent of US land is devoted to livestock.[19] This dominant land use crowds out land utilized for growing more land-efficient crops. With less meat and dairy consumption, food production would use less land and could be more easily interwoven in land closer to where people live.

Much US agricultural land does not feed Americans, and the United States imports a lot of food. The country exports over 20 percent of its agricultural products.[20] The American Midwest produces over 33 percent of the world's corn and 34 percent of the world's soybeans.[21] Even though the United States has more than enough farmland to feed all Americans, approximately 35 percent of the fruits and vegetables consumed in the United States are imported.[22] The land use is dictated by corporations seeking to expand global markets and increase profits, not feed people near where food is produced.

Farms used to encircle cities and towns like the orange groves around Los Angeles, creating bonds of mutual dependence between farming and urban communities. The global food system and suburbanization have since replaced this use of land. From 2001 to 2016, eleven million acres of agricultural land in the United

States were lost or fragmented primarily due to low-density residential development.[23] We have not only lost place-based food systems. The divides between agricultural and urban communities have grown wide and deep since then, reflected in the dangerous level of political polarization across the United States.

Culture: The American Diet

The American diet and eating practices drive the demand for so much land being used to feed people. The average American consumes almost 225 pounds of meat—beef, pork, poultry, and lamb—per year[24] and over 650 pounds of dairy.[25] Much of this food is grown far from where people consume it, as illustrated in the prior section. Meat-based meals are deeply woven into the American diet.

Fast food is a common part of the American diet. A Centers for Disease Control and Prevention study found that 36.6 percent of adults ate fast food daily.[26] Fast food is typically meat-based and reliant on national and global supply chains to keep prices as low as possible.

Food waste is also a significant cultural problem in the United States that holds the food system in place. In addition to food thrown away from restaurants, a study found that the average American household wastes 32 percent of the food it buys.[27] Food waste contributes to 24 percent of municipal waste in landfills, more than any other source.[28] Part of food culture is expecting perfect-looking fruits and vegetables, leading to "imperfect" or "ugly" produce being discarded.

The combination of high meat consumption, the prevalence of fast food, and rampant food waste makes it difficult to move away from the global food system. Without cultural change, finding enough land within most regions to sustain a place-based food system is unrealistic.

Human agriculture has existed for twelve thousand years. Only in the past century has it become globalized and industrialized with diets based on resource-intensive meat and processed foods. With food produced so far away and its origins hard to detect, people have become increasingly disconnected from where their food comes from and the people and nature that make it possible. Human history and a growing local food movement show that a different food system is feasible.

A Vision of Local Food, Regional Foodsheds, and Healthy Diets

Local food ties a person to the seasonal cycle of life. A communication from Bar 717 Ranch, a summer camp that my children attended, captured the bounty of seasonal change: "Here on the ranch, it is truly harvest season. The garden is overflowing with zucchini, cucumbers, beans, and onions. The blackberries are beginning to ripen, and a focused team of pickers can fill a Mason jar in just a few minutes. In a few weeks, we'll start the process of canning pears, apple sauce, and tomato sauce to use next year at Camp."[29] Tending to and watching food grow is oneness with nature. The connection remains beyond the harvest season when surplus food can be preserved.

In metropolitan areas, local food systems require regional foodsheds that include surrounding greenbelts and provide enough land to feed a large population. A foodshed, analogous to a watershed, refers to a geographic region that produces food for a particular population. Place-based food systems help regenerate local economies, keeping money circulating in regional foodsheds and the communities within them.

Regional foodsheds are possible in the United States. A 2020 study by researchers at Cornell and Tufts Universities found that many US metro areas could provide for all of their residents through food production within 155 miles.[30] These areas are spread across much of the country. The local potential was estimated based on seven different diets. The study assessed available agricultural land but not land that could be converted to agricultural land within regions and cities, which would add even more potential.

Diets high in plant-based foods are healthy and enable people to get all the food they need from regional foodsheds. Dan Buettner's investigations into the longest-living people found their diets revolved around the "four pillars" of grains, greens, nuts, and beans, not meat or dairy. In Nicoya, Costa Rica, one of the Blue Zones, for example, people eat meat on average five times a month and drink little to no cow's milk.[31] As highlighted earlier, growing produce for direct human consumption requires much less land than raising livestock and growing feed for livestock. Higher land productivity and improved human health are inherent to plant-based diets.

"Eating not too much," another aspect of Pollan's healthy eating mantra, reduces food waste. At the individual level, minimizing food waste can become a habit. Two personal practices are only ordering as much food as one can reasonably eat at restaurants and using up perishable items at home before they expire. At a larger scale, new companies selling imperfect, ugly produce minimize food waste. When people depend on local land for food, they become more motivated not to waste food in these and many other ways.

Plant-based diets reduce GHGE, even more so when they are based on local whole foods. Overall, emissions from plant-based foods are many times less than those from animal-based or processed foods.[32] Most of those emissions come from transport.[33] Eating local whole foods saves energy and reduces harmful emissions.

Local farmers often utilize organic, regenerative methods rather than synthetic fertilizers, pesticides, herbicides, or GMO seeds on their land. Regenerative agriculture refers to farming that improves soil health and land productivity. Farmers save money by not buying as many inputs from Big Ag. Additionally, they don't subject themselves, employees, or others to chemical pollutants. Local farmers are motivated to farm regeneratively for these reasons.

Likewise, local ranching lends itself to being humane. People do not want to live near large animal operations that crowd animals and create water, air, odor, and visual pollution. In 2018, Todd Township in Pennsylvania's Huntingdon County banned CAFOs in an effort to promote more local food production. Unconfined grazing animals also do not require large corn farms for feed and improve soil health when managed well. Such ranching practices allow ranchers to pursue other productive uses of their land and livestock.

Local farms and ranches within regional foodsheds provide opportunities for people to know where and how their food is produced. Directly experiencing the food system in these ways strengthens people's connection to nature and community. At farmers markets and through other means, community is built among consumers and food producers. Local food production helps individuals value nature and the people who feed them.

Systems-Change Strategies for a Place-Based Food System

A regional food system can be catalyzed by shifting power to local farmers, food makers, hubs, and land trusts. To address systemic racism in the system, BIPOC farmers and communities must be empowered. Transforming land use to nest agriculture in urban spaces and land across a region is possible and gaining traction. Resetting culture on the production side through farmer training and on the diet side through healthy food incentives and plant-based diet and waste reduction initiatives further helps pivot the system to be place-based. Growing food in household and community gardens can supplement the food supply and connect people more deeply to nature and its gifts.

Shift Power to Local Farmers and Food Makers

Farmers markets and community-supported agriculture (CSA) allow local farmers to sell directly to consumers. Through these exchanges, farmers don't have to share revenue with distributors, stores, and other profit-seeking intermediaries. In 2022, there were more than 8,600 local farmers markets in the United States.[34] Many occur once or twice weekly in the same community location, making it easy for customers to return frequently. Some even travel to customers. The Real Food Farm's mobile farmers' market sells local produce at wholesale prices in Baltimore's Healthy Food Priority Areas.

CSAs bring together households with a local farm or group of farms through subscriptions to produce delivery service. In this arrangement, farmers share the risks and benefits of food production with their customers. Like farmers markets, CSAs help farmers retain more revenue and pass on savings to consumers.

Even in direct sales, it's hard for local farmers to compete with Big Ag corporations subsidized by the federal government. To shift power, subsidies should end and externalities such as GHGE should be priced into food.

Researchers from the University of Oxford and the International Food Policy Research Institute proposed a carbon taxation scheme to encourage diets with less climate impact. They recommended a 40 percent tax on beef, 20 percent on milk, and 8.5 percent on poultry.[35] To have a chance politically, such taxes would need to be phased in slowly over time and not come during a time of inflation.

The savings from reduced subsidies and revenue from a carbon tax could be directed toward catalytic funding for local agriculture. The Inflation Reduction Act of 2022 provided an example. An allocation of $20 billion went to family farmers and ranchers. These food producers used this funding to improve soil health, increase crop yields, reduce fertilizer costs, increase resilience to extreme weather, and diversify income streams.

Local anchor institutions can catalyze increased demand for local food. In 2020, San Francisco's jails and public hospitals committed their $7.5 million in food purchasing to small and midsize farms and food makers in the local area. Standards included fair compensation for labor in the food chain, environmental sustainability, and animal welfare. These facilities are part of the San Francisco Bay Area Local Food Purchasing Collaborative, which includes school districts, health care institutions, and corrections facilities committed to buying local food.

Universities also leverage their market power as anchor institutions. The University of Toronto, with ninety thousand students, adopted local food standards for its food services. The University of Kentucky implemented a requirement for at least 20 percent of its school dining service to come from local farms. As of 2019, ninety-eight local farms and food businesses supply the universities' food service.[36] The national Real Food Challenge empowers college students to push their schools to buy and serve food from nearby farms, ranches, boats, and food businesses.

Shift Power Through Local Hubs and Land Trusts

Hubs bring together farmers, ranchers, and food businesses to build market power in a place-based food system. In such arrangements, local food producers share resources, purchase inputs collectively, and engage in other ways to lower costs and boost sales.

The Capay Valley Farm Shop operates as a cooperative among forty sustainable family farms in the Capay Valley between San Francisco and Sacramento in California. This hub helps farmers and ranchers with distribution, transportation, marketing, sales, packaging, and storage. Food distributed through the cooperative—assorted vegetables and fruits, flowers, herbs, nuts, grains, meats, olive oils, eggs, and honey—are each listed on its crop seasonal availability calendar. The shop generates collective market power among local food producers through these means and connects them to a dependable set of buyers who pay fair prices.

La Cocina in San Francisco is a nonprofit hub that incubates and supports local food businesses. This hub provides an affordable shared commercial kitchen space, eliminating a significant barrier to entry for the working-class food entrepreneurs it serves. It has helped women, immigrants, and people of color start over 130 businesses since 2005.[37] La Cocina has incubated locally owned cafés, restaurants, catering companies, and food-making businesses.

Land trusts build power among farmers and ranchers and ensure that profits go to family farms while regenerating nature. These trusts are organized as nonprofits for collective land management. The Marin Agricultural Land Trust (MALT) was founded in 1980 in Marin County, California, as the first farmland trust in the nation and has invested in improving soil health and water quality. Covering over fifty-five thousand acres of land, the trust includes dairy cow, beef cattle, and sheep operations; wool producers; artisan cheesemakers; egg producers; and fruit and vegetable farms. MALT farmers and ranchers are known for raising high-quality meat, dairy, and produce in regenerative ways that enhance nature.

Highlighting ranching in regional foodsheds may seem to contradict earlier arguments for more plant-based diets and their less intensive land use. Indeed, ranching and growing feed for livestock must be greatly reduced. Meat and dairy will still play a role in people's diets but need to be more limited than in the typical American diet. Furthermore, to protect the environment and provide local meat and dairy, we need to shift power to land trusts like MALT that support regenerative ranching.

Shift Power to BIPOC Farmers and Communities

A long overdue movement to restore and expand Black ownership of farms and food businesses across the United States is growing. The National Black Food and Justice Alliance includes fifty Black-led organizations and helps purchase or secure land for Black farmers. Their first assisted purchase was a 150-acre farm in Amelia County, Virginia, in 2022. With support from the alliance and local funding organizations, the farm ownership justice movement is expanding across diverse geographies.

Power is also being shifted at the state level. In New York, the Black Farmer Fund provides grants and low-interest loans to farmers and food businesses. It also works with five other BIPOC-led farming organizations in the Building Black Food Ecosystem Resilience collaborative to expand Black-owned farms across the state. The fund plans to expand across the Northeast.

Local support for BIPOC farm ownership is also needed. The Detroit Black Farmer Land Fund is helping Black residents purchase the lots they farm. Detroit has more than fifteen hundred urban farms and community gardens.[38] Most are run but not owned by Black farmers. To rectify this ownership gap, the fund had crowdsourced over $200,000 and helped seventy farmers and farm businesses buy vacant lots by 2022.[39]

Shifting power to people in the food system ultimately means food sovereignty. People, not corporations, should have more control over food production, distribution, and consumption. The needs of people for healthy and culturally relevant food choices should be at the center of the food system. Food sovereignty restores local ownership of food production and distribution and removes the system from corporate profit extraction. In the process, communities, people, and their land are reconnected.

Indigenous food systems provide a model for establishing local food sovereignty, yet Indigenous people have largely been severed from control of their food system. Many live on reservations far removed from their traditional homelands and ways of life. Long decimated and neglected, Indigenous agricultural practices are being revitalized.

The First Nations Development Institute aims to increase access to healthy food through place-based, Indigenous food systems. In its 2020 documentary *Gather*, the institute profiled growing food sovereignty among Indigenous groups nationwide. At the Apache Nation in Arizona, a chef opened an indigenous café with the support of other Apache neighbors who are growing the produce for the café. A Cheyenne rancher is helping to bring back bison in South Dakota with his daughter, who is researching the health benefits of eating bison over beef. Young adults from the Yurok Nation near the California-Oregon border are helping their people reconnect to the salmon in the Klamath River. They are winning policies like dam removal to protect the salmon habitat. All are examples of shifting power back to First Peoples through place-based food systems.

Transform Land Use with Regional Food Plans

Self-reliant, local food systems are not a fantasy from a bygone era. As highlighted earlier, there is sufficient land in most metropolitan regions in the United States to grow enough food to provide for all the people who live there. One European city has shown the way, and a growing movement in the New England region of the United States is pushing toward this vision. Regional food plans can be developed and implemented.

Following World War II, Copenhagen developed the Finger Plan, which supports multiple place-based systems including food. The fingers are five major transit corridors that connect to suburbs. The "palm" of the plan is the urban center filled with mixed-use development. Green space, including agricultural land, is protected between the fingers. As a small country, Denmark serves as the region for Copenhagen and produces almost three times as much food as its six million people need.[40] Farmer-owned cooperatives are prevalent, keeping profits with the farmers. Implementing the Finger Plan and surrounding regional food production has led to food self-reliance.

Food Solutions New England seeks to rebuild the food system to be more sustainable, just, and resilient across its six-state region. Anchored by the University of New Hampshire, the collaborative developed the New England Food Vision. The group provides a shared narrative and communications approach to promote change, convenes stakeholders, runs a leadership institute emphasizing racial equity, and coordinates regional policy advocacy. In alignment with Food Solutions, a regional food-planning partnership launched the New England Feeding New England: Cultivating A Reliable Food Supply project. The project aims to increase the amount of food produced and consumed in New England from 10 percent to 35 percent over fifteen years.

Regional food is not a trend. It has been the norm for most of human history and is essential for the health of our planet, communities, and individuals.

Transform Land Use with Urban Agriculture

Complementing farming in regional greenbelts, cities are turning underutilized land into urban farms. Tool kits like *Seeding the City* from ChangeLab Solutions help local policymakers develop land use policies for urban agriculture.

In Baltimore, Real Food Farm has a six-acre site in a park and a nearby two-acre site. Both replaced vacant lots. Fields of crops, fruit tree orchards, a sensory garden, a greenhouse, and a solar-powered walk-in refrigerator occupy the two sites. The farm provides seasonal produce to the community through a subscription program and the mobile farmer's market described earlier. It also runs a community garden with free membership for Baltimore residents and a work-share program.

Converting urban land to agriculture promotes food justice in low-income communities and communities of color. The Rainier Beach Urban Farm is an eight-acre farm in one of Seattle's lowest-income neighborhoods. Their farm stand is a "pay-what-you-can" social enterprise in which they offer $20 of produce at no cost to those in need and accept nutrition benefit funds. In Bayview Hunters Point, one of the last remaining Black neighborhoods left in San Francisco, three residents started the Loyal to the Soil farm on land described as a neighborhood dumping ground. Daily fruit and vegetable intake is low in this neighborhood, while food-related illnesses like diabetes and hypertension are high.[41] In addition to selling directly to residents, they partner with a local, Black-owned catering business that buys the farm's produce. Every community deserves a farm, especially communities that have been marginalized and disconnected from a supply of fresh, healthy food.

Citywide planning and support are needed to more fully realize the potential of urban agriculture. In concert with the Detroit Black Farmer Land Fund, the nonprofit Keep Growing Detroit (KGD) aims to make Detroit a food-sovereign city for fruits and vegetables. KGD supports community, family, school, and market food gardens across Detroit and annually engages thousands of residents in gardening and farming. Through the Garden Resource Program, KGD supports a network of gardens and farms in Detroit with seeds, vegetable transplants, and other resources. Grown in Detroit is a KGD program that sells local fruits and vegetables in farmers' markets, online, and in different retail settings.

Through its Parisculteurs initiative, Paris demonstrates how urban agricultural production can include rooftop space. Le Chambeaudie Farm is a rooftop hydroponic farm with over forty varieties of plants and herbs that are sold to local restaurants and grocery stores. In 2020, a 3.5-acre rooftop farm, Nature Urbaine, opened in southwest Paris as the largest urban farm in Europe. The farm produces two thousand pounds of organic fruits and vegetables daily during peak season. Nature Urbaine also includes small garden plots for residents to lease and a restaurant and bar on-site. Paris is finding creative ways to use urban space for farming.

Foodscapes are another way of utilizing urban land for food production. They can be thought of as urban agriculture with few boundaries. Foodscapes include growing food along roads and highways, on street medians, in public plazas, in parking lots, and in other underutilized urban spaces. The Concrete Plant Park Foodscape in New York City is situated on a former concrete factory site. Perennial plants and trees with fruits, nuts, berries, and medicinal herbs are grown here. This foodscape is part of a proposed twenty-three-mile-long foodway along the Bronx River Greenway. Calgary, Canada, has planted fruit trees and shrubs in parks and spaces across the city since 2009. In addition to the healthy, fresh food they provide, foodscapes beautify neighborhoods and public areas, encouraging people to spend time outside and connect to nature.

Reset Culture Through Farmer Training

Emma Jagoz questioned why so much food in her state of Maryland came from the West Coast and faraway places. In 2012, she decided to start Moon Valley Farm. In a podcast from the Institute for Self-Reliance, she told her story.[42] She sells produce directly through a CSA and to restaurants in her foodshed. Emma describes the connection among herself, local customers, and their food as magical. Local farming offers great rewards, but it is also a risky business.

Emma learned how to overcome challenges and manage risk in her farm business over time. She builds resilience in her farm enterprise through growing perennial crops, storage crops that can be sold year-round, and mushrooms that can grow year-round. She's figured out how to develop healthy soil and increase biodiversity for pollinators. Finding workers, financing land purchases, and investing in storage facilities and greenhouses were some of Emma's many other tasks in building her farm enterprise.

Emma advocates for greatly expanding education and training for aspiring farmers. Her story of all she had to learn illustrates why training is so essential.

Converting land to regional foodsheds and urban agriculture will do little good if there are not enough people to produce the food. Urban agricultural initiatives described earlier are investing in people and training them to farm. KGD in Detroit runs a 1.38-acre urban farm and teaching facility and trains people interested in farming on water catchment, new garden and farm development, soil testing, business development, and community organizing. The Breuil School, located in Paris's Botanical Garden, trains more than twenty-six hundred professionals and around one thousand residents yearly in urban agriculture.

Youth education and training can help build a new generation of local farmers. The Food Project in eastern Massachusetts hires 140 teens each year to grow produce across seven urban and suburban farms. The project donates much of what is grown to hunger relief organizations. Grow Dat Youth Farm in New Orleans, Louisiana, trains youth in farming and develops their leadership skills for changing the food system. The apprentice youth farmers grow crops on seven acres of New Orleans City Park farmland. They sell their harvest through a CSA program and distribute it to those in need, the participating youth, and their families. As evident in the thirty-five alums who have returned to Grow Dat for leadership programs and alumni positions, these programs are helping prepare a workforce for local agriculture.

Reset Culture Through Healthy Food Incentives

Culture must also be reset on the demand side through affordable healthy diets. Food systems in the developing world offer a good model. In his documentation of different diets around the world, photographer Greg Segal compared diets among people experiencing poverty in the United States to those in India:

> One of the surprising lessons . . . is that the best quality diets are often eaten not by the richest but the poorest. In the US, the poor are the biggest consumers of junk food because it's convenient and cheap. But in Mumbai, it costs $13 for a medium Domino's pizza, which is way beyond the means of most people. Anchal lives with her family in an 8 by 8-foot aluminum hut. Her father earns less than $5 a day, yet she eats a wholesome diet of okra and cauliflower curries, lentils, and roti which Anchal's mother makes from scratch each day.[43]

Segal further shares that a 2015 Cambridge University study found that nine of the ten healthiest diets in the world are in Africa. These diets are based on fresh vegetables, fruits, nuts, seeds, grains, fish, legumes, and very little meat or processed foods.

In contrast, the cheapest food in the US food system is often the least healthy. Culturally based diets like those in India and Africa show another way. Until the pricing for nutritious food is just, subsidies are needed for low-income Americans.

Healthy food incentive programs help low-income families afford local fresh fruits and vegetables. Introduced earlier, Real Food Farm's mobile farmers' market and the Rainier Beach Urban Farm allow customers to double their purchasing power by using federal or other nutrition benefit funds. Fresh Approach offers the same benefit through a mobile farmers' market to low-income residents across four San Francisco Bay Area counties. These programs reduce hunger, improve nutrition, and support local farms.

Reset Culture Through Plant-Based Diet and Food Waste Reduction Initiatives

Resetting culture in favor of more plant-based diets and less food waste is imperative to having enough land in a foodshed to feed a population. People have grown more aware of the environmental and health problems associated with meat-based diets and food waste, making them more open to change when it is promoted and supported. With increased awareness about the impact of beef and the expansion of plant-based alternatives, Americans now consume about a third less beef than they did in the 1970s.[44]

People need knowledge, competencies, and encouragement to shift toward plant-based diets. *Tenderly*, a vegan lifestyle online publication, provides ideas and recipes for cooking meals without meat or dairy. Social media groups like "My Healthy Plate, Our Healthy Planet," run by local nonprofit Acterra, facilitate the exchange of ideas for plant-based meals in and outside the home.

Green or Meatless Mondays encourage and support incremental diet change. When restaurants, grocery stores, schools, or other organizations promote Green Mondays, they set a social norm and context that encourages diet awareness and change. Cities from Mountain View to Emeryville in the San Francisco Bay Area have passed Green Monday resolutions. Food served at facilities, meetings, and events in these cities is plant-based on Mondays. The weekly event helps participants learn through experience how to have a plant-based diet.

Food waste reduction solutions can be targeted at specific steps in the food system. Households, grocery stores, and restaurants account for 80 percent of food waste.[45] Minimizing food waste in these three settings means less land is needed to grow food.

Through food rescue, unnecessary hunger can also be reduced. Grocery stores can donate food past its "sell by" date, which is perfectly fine to eat for a few more days. Tax write-offs based on waste reduction incentivize stores and restaurants to change their practices. Support from other organizations helps to make it happen at scale.

Food Shift, a food rescue nonprofit in Alameda, California, recovers perishable and nonperishable items from grocery stores, restaurants, and other food providers. It takes 80 percent of what it rescues and provides it to food banks and food assistance organizations. The remaining 20 percent goes to its social enterprise kitchen. This program provides on-the-job culinary training and paid apprenticeships to people who have faced barriers to employment (also boosting the local work system). Food Runners, across the bay in San Francisco, picks up excess food from catering companies after big events, grocery stores, restaurants, and corporate cafeterias. A team of mostly volunteers moves the food to agencies that feed those experiencing hunger.

At the household level, reducing food waste is a habit that can be formed and reinforced in varied settings. Zero-waste programs in schools, workplaces, and community institutions help students and others understand the importance of food waste reduction and learn how to do it. These programs encourage smaller plate sizes, composting, and other means to limit waste. It becomes second nature not to throw food waste into a garbage can.

Reset Culture Through Household and Community Food Gardens

A final cultural reset is to promote hyperlocal food production. It's important to first understand how fundamental this strategy is to reconnecting people with their food supply and its potential appeal.

I remember cofacilitating a listening session for a graduate research project with a group of first- and second-generation Vietnamese Americans when we started discussing food. To a person, the group had no interest in buying organic. Upon first hearing it, I was troubled, as it suggested what I feared: Buying organic may never be fully embraced. As I listened more, I learned that it had little to do with not understanding or appreciating organic farming methods but rather everything to do with trust. They did not trust organic labels on foods.

Looking back now, I better understand their reaction. When people are so removed from food production, how can they really know how it is grown? Local agriculture makes what has been invisible in the food system more visible. In a place-based food system, one can see farming practices firsthand or talk directly to farmers and food providers about their methods.

The listening session participants talked about how they and their families grew most of their food in Vietnam. They do not have the same amount of land where they now live in San Jose, California. Still, nearly everyone was growing vegetables on small plots at their residence.

Of all the ways to reshape the food system, none may be more powerful than each person growing some food. In household or community food gardens, you can see and feel what's in the soil, water the crops, apply organic treatments, watch growth, and reap the harvest. People know exactly what they are eating when growing food themselves, placing trust in themselves and nature.

Whether a small backyard garden, a plot of land in the community, or a small container garden in an apartment, everyone can grow food such as herbs, fruits, vegetables, or legumes. Each garden may seem like a drop in the bucket, but history shows they can add up to a lot of food. Victory gardens were popularized during World War II and supplied 40 percent of the nation's fresh vegetables.[46] Local food champion and internationally renowned chef Alice Waters describes what occurred with a nod to its potential today: "They did farms in front of the post offices, they did them in the parks, they did them everywhere they could to allow people to be fed. . . . If we really cared about feeding people in that deep way, it could be amazing."[47] Food gardens make communities more self-reliant, more cohesive as people share produce, and more life-affirming through growing food. They build a culture of connection.

People interested in food gardening need supplies and training. Local journalist Kim Dinan showed how a network of local stores in Asheville, North Carolina, provides what residents need to grow food.[48] Sow True Seeds sells over five hundred seed varieties, including heirlooms and seed-starting supplies. L.O.T.U.S Urban Farm and Garden Supply specializes in indoor growing supplies and animal feed. Fifth Season Gardens provides a variety of gardening, canning, preservation, food making, and other supplies. These stores also offer workshops to train community members on growing food. The nonprofit Garden for the Environment in San Francisco educates residents on food gardens through workshops in its public garden, online seminars, youth programs, walking tours, and a blog. To maximize the potential for hyperlocal food production and engage people in gardening, a network of community support makes a big difference.

Community gardens have been in American cities for over two hundred years, providing space for residents without land to grow food while building community. Shared gardens can be particularly important for new immigrants and refugees. They can help them establish a connection to their new place, become part of the community, maintain cultural traditions around food, and earn income. The Little Haiti Garden in Miami, for example, provides space for Haitian immigrants to produce crops from their country using traditional farming techniques. The garden offers gardening and nutrition workshops and a means for residents in this low-income community to earn money through selling the produce.

Leverage Other Systems

As evidenced in examples like foodscapes and community gardens, nearby community spaces (chap. 7) and nature spaces (chap. 8) can be utilized to grow food. Regions and neighborhoods can have thriving public spaces for recreation, community, and food production when these two systems blend with a place-based food system. More land can be used for growing food when less room is needed for cars (chap. 6).

A place-based housing system (chap. 4) includes mixed-use neighborhoods. Uses can include food production. The Alexandria Park neighborhood has social housing on eighteen acres near downtown Toronto and was redeveloped with extensive community input. As part of the revamped public space there, a local nonprofit, the Bowery Project, is repurposing vacant land into community gardens for growing food by residents.

Urban growth boundaries, discussed as a strategy for place-based housing systems, also support regional foodsheds. As discussed earlier, sprawl and development have led to a significant loss of farmland near population centers. Urban growth boundaries are a tool to protect the greenbelt from nonagricultural development.

Training people to farm or get involved in the local food production system provides a strong link between the place-based work system (chap. 5) and the food system. To regionalize and localize agriculture, a large workforce is needed.

In chapter 10, the energy system is explored. Like food, self-sufficient regional systems show much promise. Foodsheds and energysheds can coexist with solar arrays and wind turbines scattered among farms and ranches in the greenbelt.

BUILDING ENERGY

Many call simply for a technological fix: for a transition to 100% renewable energy, citing how it is technologically possible to develop sufficient renewable resources. But these calls do not specify who will develop and control that energy, to what end, or to whose benefit.

—Denise Fairchild and Al Weinrub, introduction to Energy Democracy: Advancing Equity in Clean Energy Solutions

The clean energy transformation in the United States and worldwide is underway. It gives us hope that we may be able to reduce greenhouse gas emissions (GHGE) enough to turn the tide on the climate crisis.

As of February 2024, over 4.2 million homes in the United States had rooftop solar panels.[1] In 2014, our house became one of these. Given the tax credits, incentives, and net metering rates (explained later in the chapter) at the time, it made sense financially to invest in solar for our home. The panels provided all the electricity we needed and paid for themselves about seven years after installation.

Still, like many others with solar, our home produced emissions from natural gas heating, water heating, and cooking appliances. We have slowly transitioned to electric versions of these appliances to emit less greenhouse gasses. Electrification of buildings (and vehicles; see chap. 6) is central to making the societal shift to renewable, clean energy.

We took our first electrification step about a year after installing solar. I had noticed we were getting paid little by PG&E, the investor-owned utility that controls our region's electric grid, for excess solar output. We decided to buy an electric hybrid heat pump water heater to use more of our solar panels' electricity.

It didn't all go as planned. Soon, we needed more electricity than our panels could produce. We had electric bills once again. The new water heater used much more electricity than we had anticipated. We had bought an early version of heat pump water heaters. They are more efficient now. I also discovered years later that I had overlooked the biggest factor explaining the heat pump's high energy use. A plumbing configuration was causing our water heater to work overtime. We had a circulating pump that kept constant hot water in our pipes between the water heater in our basement and our bathroom two floors above it. This mechanism allowed us to turn on the shower and get hot water almost instantly. It saved water but wasted a lot of electricity! I've since shut off the circulating pump. We're saving energy but using a little more water.

In 2024, we added electric heat pump heating, ventilation, and air-conditioning (HVAC) units to our home. These units brought our natural gas bill and emissions down to almost nothing. When our stove and oven get a little older, we will replace them with electric induction models. Then our home will be fully electrified.

To accommodate our home electric conversion, we've had to upgrade our electric service in addition to purchasing a new HVAC and water heating system. These changes are expensive. The financial cost at the household and societal level is one of the many challenges for the energy transition to renewables.

* * *

Building energy accounts for 38 percent of US GHGE—25 percent from electric power and 13 percent from burning fossil fuels for heat and cooking.[2] In 2023, US electric power was generated from 43 percent natural gas, 16 percent coal, 19 percent nuclear, and 21 percent renewables including hydropower.[3] Electricity generation has been shifting from coal and natural gas to renewables, but well over half of it still comes from coal and natural gas. Natural gas burns more efficiently than coal in generating electricity. The production and distribution of natural gas, however, emit methane, a GHGE over twenty times more potent than carbon dioxide.

The transition to renewable energy is not simply about replacing fossil fuels with solar, wind, and other renewables to meet our energy needs. How we approach this necessary energy transformation has huge implications for land use, environmental impacts, and who benefits financially. The transition also requires financial and technical support for building owners.

The major push for clean energy is focused on utility-scale electric generation projects that require hundreds of miles of high-voltage transmission lines. Many of these projects are necessary, given the scale of planned electrification. Yet they also add to energy demand in their operation. From 8 to 15 percent of energy is lost in the long-distance transmission and distribution of electricity from power plants to consumers.[4]

A large expansion of centralized, renewable power projects will reduce climate emissions but take a significant toll on the environment in other ways. Land needed for extracting the minerals, metals, and other resources that go

into solar panels, wind turbines, battery storage, other clean energy technologies, and long-distance transmission lines will grow exponentially.[5] Land and
water degradation from so much mining will continue harming nature in
developing countries and spread to other places around the globe. Industrial
production and disposal of all the infrastructure elements will further deplete
land, air, and water quality. Skeptics are right to ask what we will do with so
many used chemical-leaching batteries (from vehicles and energy storage) once
they can no longer be used. An all-in utility-scale clean energy transformation
will help alleviate the climate crisis but could easily cause great harm to ecosystems, adding to the biodiversity loss crisis.

Those with the least power have been harmed by sprawling energy infrastructure. Polluting power plants and energy infrastructure have been built
next to and through low-income communities of color for decades. The Navajo
Generating Station was the largest coal plant west of the Mississippi. It was
shut down in 2019 but leaves a legacy of pollution and harm to the community.
Despite the power plant being located on Navajo territory, many in the Navajo
Nation went without electricity. Utility-scale solar and wind won't pollute the
air, but they require a lot of land for production and transmission. If history
repeats, they won't be built near or through affluent communities with high
energy demand. The system and its harm will remain largely invisible to those
who use it the most.

We must ramp up renewable energy fast, but a centralized, long-distance
energy system can't be the only way. The proposed magnitude of utility-scale
electric projects to meet escalating energy consumption must be challenged. In
the rush to a clean energy transformation, the downsides of large-scale projects
and long-distance transmission are being downplayed. Without a rethinking of
the structure of the energy system, energy waste, environmental degradation,
and harm to communities will continue in the shadows of a vast energy infrastructure that mostly benefits corporate energy producers and utilities.

This chapter first examines what's holding our centralized, long-distance
energy system in place. To address the problems of a corporate-driven, long-
distance energy infrastructure, we need to build out household- and community-
level renewable energy projects rapidly. Blended with some utility-scale projects
around a region, harnessing enough energy within an area for all who live there
becomes possible. Prioritizing energy conservation and efficiency makes harnessing regional, renewable energy for all our energy needs something we can achieve.
These local and regional renewable energy projects combined with conservation
form the vision of the place-based energy system featured in this chapter. As with
the other systems, we'll explore how specific power shifts, land use transformations, and cultural resets can make this vision a reality.

Systems-Change Strategies for Harnessing Local and Regional Renewable Energy

- Shift power through fairer markets
- Shift power to community-driven entities
- Shift power through energy democracy
- Transform land use with local electricity production, storage, and distribution
- Transform land use with regional energyshed planning and funding
- Reset culture with net-zero building subsidies, technical assistance, and social support
- Reset culture with default, energy-efficient consumer products
- Reset culture through conservation price signals and social comparison interventions
- Reset culture through default indoor temperature settings
- Leverage other systems

Holding the Centralized, Long-Distance Energy System in Place

Switching the energy system to place-based production and conservation makes good sense. Yet Big Utilities exercise their power to resist change on these fronts. The energy system continues to be built around large, centralized power generation and long-distance transmission. A high energy use and waste culture increases energy demand and the need for more and more energy infrastructure.

Power: Big Utilities

Corporate, investor-owned utilities (IOUs), or Big Utilities, hold power in the status quo energy system. The United States' electricity market is consolidated around IOUs that control electric generation, transmission, and distribution.[6] There are roughly 168 IOUs nationwide, providing building energy to almost three-quarters of the nation's utility customers.[7]

Big Utilities influence government through lobbying efforts at state capitols and regulatory commissions across the country. Legislators have passed laws that stifle competition to utilities. These policies have helped IOUs get a guaranteed rate of return on their expenditures and retain control of the transmission grid.

Many utilities were slow to embrace renewable energy. With mounting public pressure and government requirements, they've had no choice but to source more power from solar, wind, and other renewables. Utilities generally opt for large-scale solar and wind projects with long-distance transmission over local, distributed energy generation. With their control of the grid and guaranteed rates of return on what they build, they are incentivized to construct sprawling infrastructure.

In contrast, rooftop and community solar shift ownership and profit away from Big Utilities. Consequently, they have used their power to pressure regulators in many states to limit communities and people producing their own solar energy. Policies include imposing significant fees and statewide caps on how much electricity can be generated from local sources.

California had been a leader in new community and rooftop solar installations until the regulatory body overseeing utilities bowed to pressure from the IOUs and put the brakes on local solar. In 2022, the California Public Utilities Commission decreased the rate utilities pay for excess energy from new solar panels by 75 percent. That rate was a key reason my family put solar on our roof in 2014. The drastic rate reduction led to a 90 percent drop in new solar installations from May 2022 to May 2023.[8] In 2023, the commission reduced incentives for schools, businesses, and apartment buildings to install solar panels. In 2024, the commission decreased future compensation for community solar projects. Lobbying for every one of these decisions were the state's three largest IOUs: Pacific Gas and Electric, Southern California Edison, and San Diego Gas and Electric.

Energy corporations that own multiple IOUs and other energy businesses have amassed market and political power. These corporations, like in the other systems, have been able to consolidate the electric industry while regulators looked the other way. Exelon Corporation owns six IOUs with ten million customers across five states and the District of Columbia. Exelon was permitted to take over the Washington, DC, utility shortly after making a $25 million donation to a new soccer stadium there.[9] Exelon and other energy conglomerates wield significant power with their large ownership stakes in the energy system.

IOUs and energy conglomerates use their power to seek and secure policies, regulations, and subsidies that benefit utility-scale renewables and long-distance transmission. Distributed energy loses out, along with regions' and communities' ability to control their energy supply and spur local economic activity around it.

Land Use: Sprawling Electricity Infrastructure

The dominant energy system depends on land-consuming, resource-intensive infrastructure. The United States has almost 160,000 miles of high-voltage power lines and millions more miles of low-voltage transmission and distribution lines.[10] This extensive infrastructure is necessary when energy production and consumption are so far removed from one another.

High-voltage transmission lines form the backbone of the existing electric grid, with their enormous costs of millions of dollars per mile of line passed on to consumers.[11] To accommodate utility-scale renewables, more of these lines and their interconnections to the rest of the grid are being proposed and built with the support of government subsidies.

Pattern Energy Group LP, a privately held corporation, is building SunZia Wind, the largest wind project in the Western Hemisphere. It will spread across three counties in New Mexico. It's a positive development for scaling renewable energy, and it's certainly a better direction for electricity than any fossil-fuel burning power plant.

We need wind energy but we should factor in how projects like SunZia will add to the nation's sprawling electricity infrastructure. Pattern Energy is building a new 550-mile high-voltage direct current transmission line to deliver electricity from the wind farm to a substation in Arizona. Hundreds of more miles of transmission lines will be used to get the electricity to markets in the western United States. These lines will carry enough electricity for an estimated three million Americans.[12]

Pattern Energy impressively secured $8.8 billion in loans from around twenty banks to construct the SunZia Wind and transmission line.[13] The project also benefits from tax incentives. The remaining funding for the project, $2.25 billion, is coming from a utilization of federal tax credits.

In addition to tax credits, the federal government has facilitated the expansion of utility-scale renewable projects on federal land through reduced fees. The Bureau of Land Management (BLM), in particular, is attracting projects through low fees. As of September 2024, the BLM had permitted 215 large-scale renewable projects on its lands, including the long-distance transmission lines needed to get electricity to faraway consumers.[14] Another sixty-six projects were being processed at the time. That same month, the Department of the Interior, which oversees the BLM and other public land-holding agencies, reduced fees for solar and wind projects by 80 percent,[15] helping spur hundreds of more permit applications.

It is, of course, far better for climate that these projects are not using fossil fuels. At the same time, we need to challenge how much government support for the renewable energy transition is being directed to the centralized, long-distance electricity system when much more local and regional electricity generation is possible.

Culture of High Energy Use and Waste

A high energy use and waste culture creates demand for electric power from distant locations. The steady march to living indoors with ubiquitous digital devices has increased the human appetite for energy. Expectations for tightly controlled indoor climates add further energy demand. The impact of consumerism has led to larger homes for all the stuff and even separate storage facilities, all requiring energy.

With modern indoor living, energy use easily turns into waste. It's hard to find reliable statistics, but it occurs whenever a building's occupants use energy beyond what is needed. Energy waste can include heating or air-conditioning an indoor space when no one is there; overheating or overcooling rooms; leaving computers, TVs, and other devices on or plugged in (phantom energy) when not in use; and, of course, leaving the lights on.

Water use adds to energy use. Energy is required to transport, treat, heat, and discharge water. Up to 19 percent of California's electricity, for example, is used for pumping, treating, collecting, and discharging water and wastewater.[16] In buildings themselves, hot water requires energy. Whether you're taking a shower, washing dishes, or using water another way, leaving the water tap on longer than needed is easy to do. Due to the energy-water nexus, water waste is also energy waste.

Social norms have less impact on promoting conservation when information on how one's behavior compares to others is missing. Home energy use largely takes place away from the eyes of friends, extended family, colleagues, and the public. Opportunities to influence behavior through example and social comparison are limited.

Expectations for modern indoor living, the ease of wasting energy (and water that requires energy), and the difficulty of using social comparison in energy use present significant challenges to energy conservation. As we'll explore next, a place-based energy system depends on conservation. Increasing local renewable energy will help make conservation the societal priority it needs to be.

A Vision of Local and Regional Energy Self-Reliance

A multitiered, place-based energy system offers a contrasting vision to the current corporate-driven system. In a regional, renewable energy system, the regeneration of nature, communities, and local economies is given a strong footing.

Rooftop solar, coupled with battery storage and elements that conserve energy, can power an entire building and form the foundation of a place-based, distributed energy system. This type of electricity production is ideal in metropolitan regions around Los Angeles and Denver, which have regular sunny weather. Google's Project Sunroof, however, shows that all fifty states have locations suitable for generating electricity from solar panels. With battery storage, the power can remain on at night and does not require much, if any, electricity from the grid.

Among its benefits, rooftop solar is a resilient form of energy. Following the aftermath of Hurricane Ida in 2021, New Orleans residents with rooftop solar could keep the lights on, and some even powered their neighbors' homes.[17]

Community-based electricity generation forms the next level of a place-based energy system. Community solar projects broaden access to locally generated power for renters or people who can't afford to purchase solar panels themselves. Capturing biogas from landfills, organic waste, wastewater, and animal manure is another way to generate electricity at the community level. Energy derived from organic waste also helps mitigate climate change by capturing methane that otherwise would have been released into the atmosphere.

In addition to its environmental benefits, local energy boosts local economies and community bonds. Rather than paying a large-scale utility to transmit electricity over long distances, local entities, communities, and individuals can own energy production. Bringing people together around community-scale energy generation forges new connections and ways of supporting one another.

Regional, renewable electricity production is the outer layer of a place-based energy system. Cities and communities can only generate so much energy, given their limited land and range of natural resources. A self-reliant energy system becomes more achievable when land and nature are utilized regionally. Analogous to a watershed and foodshed, a regional, renewable energyshed takes advantage of a region's natural resources and features.

In addition to solar and biogas, other clean energy sources are available in many regions. Locations throughout the Great Plains have abundant wind power. Texas, Oklahoma, Iowa, and Kansas lead the nation in wind energy production.[18] In volcanic regions like Mono County, California, electricity is generated from underground geothermal resources. Coastal areas can innovate with tidal energy sources. Small-scale hydro is possible in locations near rivers. In whatever way it is configured, an energyshed promotes regional energy independence and resilience based on its unique geography and climate.

Local and regional renewable energy production brings people closer to nature. As communities deepen their dependence on nearby renewable energy sources, the sun, wind, and other natural resources become more top of mind to people. Knowing the sun above or geothermal heat below is powering one's home connects a person intimately to these amazing natural forces.

Regional energy self-reliance on renewables can only be realized if conservation is a priority. Energy conservation speeds up the transition to renewable energy by diminishing the scale of conversion from fossil fuel–based energy.

Conservation is necessary at the household level. Building design can make it a lot easier. Net-zero, or zero-net, energy buildings produce all the energy needed for a building's occupants through onsite renewables and by employing energy efficiency and conservation measures.

Technology is inherent in net-zero buildings, but utilizing nature and structural design to heat, cool, and illuminate buildings is the foundation. Natural light and heat can be harnessed to lessen indoor energy use. Windows and skylights provide illumination in lieu of artificial lighting. Large windows allow for solar heat gain when they are south-facing, reducing heating bills on cold winter days. Trees next to buildings help keep buildings cool in the summer months. Deciduous trees do double duty by letting in solar heat and light during the winter and providing shade in the summer. All these design elements reduce energy demand and connect people to nature in subtle yet meaningful ways.

Providing energy for all who live in a region from sources within the region may seem far-fetched in today's world. Utility-scale renewable generation projects are needed, but many can be located within regional energysheds. With full utilization of local renewable energy sources and conservation aided by building design and nature, we can get close to the vision of a place-based energy system.

Systems-Change Strategies for a Place-Based Building Energy System

As a foundation for a place-based energy system, power is being shifted through mechanisms that ensure fairer markets and to community-driven entities. Land use is being transformed to accommodate building, community, and regional-level energy generation. Cultural resets that normalize and incentivize electrification and conservation are building further momentum. The potential for local renewable energy production and regional energysheds is growing.

Shift Power Through Fairer Markets

Subsidies and supportive policies for distributed local solar and other renewable energy are essential to creating fairer market competition. These measures help counteract Big Utilities' economic power and the advantages they have secured through policies and regulations.

A major reason rooftop solar initially got off the ground in the United States was financial incentives for building owners. Since 2006, households and businesses have been able to save on solar installations with a federal tax credit. With this credit, the payback period for the initial purchase of the solar panels averages seven and a half years.[19] With many systems guaranteed for twenty-five to thirty years, that translates into eighteen to twenty-three years of free electricity generation for a building. My family's decision to go solar in 2014 was based on this calculation.

The solar investment tax credit percentage was 26 percent in 2022, and it increased to 30 percent in 2023 under the Inflation Reduction Act. This boost to solar, however, benefits those with more resources. Seven in ten Americans do not have enough tax liability to benefit from the credit fully, and four in ten don't have any federal tax liability and can't receive the benefit.[20] A refundable tax credit or direct-pay tax credit would allow everyone to benefit through refunding what cannot be credited or providing a direct payment at installation rather than a future tax credit.

The exchange of electricity between a solar array and the utility's grid is known as net metering. Net metering rates are an important factor in whether local solar projects get built. This policy allows a building or community solar project to sell electricity to the grid when panels produce more than their designated users need. Credits from those sales are applied when demand exceeds local solar panel production, such as during shorter winter days. With daily and seasonal fluctuations in sun exposure, local solar panel owners rely on fair net metering prices.

Minnesota's net metering factors in costs embedded in the energy system and is fairer to community and rooftop solar owners than in many other states. Prices for rooftop solar sold back to utilities account for how solar power avoids fuel costs, offsets other power production, and doesn't pollute. Utilities need to be regulated to include fair pricing like this for buying electricity from building owners and to not impose excessive fees for using the grid. Fair net metering prices make solar more viable and a good investment.

States and the federal government can do more together to support and incentivize rooftop and community solar. As of 2021, Minnesota and six other states require electric utilities to conduct annual capacity hosting analyses to identify where the grid can accommodate additional rooftop and community solar. At the federal level, the 2022 Inflation Reduction Act included $7 billion of funding for community solar development. The state-level analyses provide the road map for the funding. This combination of state and federal action gives local renewable energy a fighting chance to compete with Big Utilities.

Cities can help create fairer markets too. The city of Minneapolis's Health Department runs a Green Cost Share program. Matching funds are available through the program for projects that save energy or add solar to commercial, industrial, multifamily, and single-family properties. Funded projects have included solar group purchases, community center solar installations, and affordable housing energy audits. Green zones, vulnerable communities that experience the cumulative effects of environmental pollution, are prioritized. Minneapolis funds the program with fees on utilities and other companies that pollute.

Shift Power to Community-Driven Entities

In addition to shifting power to local energy generation, there can be more local control in electricity purchasing. At the regional, county, and city levels, Community Choice Aggregators (CCA), municipal-owned utilities, and local cooperatives provide alternatives to Big Utilities' dominant control of the energy system.

CCAs are joint-power agencies that aggregate the energy purchases of residents, businesses, and municipal facilities at a city, county, or regional level. CCAs are not-for-profit agencies formed among multiple local governments. Community Choice Energy (facilitated by CCAs) started in 1997 in Massachusetts. By 2020, it had expanded to nine states. As a rapidly growing alternative to IOUs, CCAs help the energy system move toward local control and renewables.

In California, twenty-five city, county, or regional CCAs served more than fourteen million people by 2024.[21] Many CCAs are on track to provide 100 percent renewable energy to their customers. Additionally, several of their long-term purchase agreements are with in-state wind and solar projects, some from within the same region.

Designed to be responsible to communities and not shareholders, CCAs typically provide lower electric costs than corporate utilities. They reduce electricity costs by pooling electric loads across communities to increase purchasing power on their behalf.

The San Francisco Public Utilities Commission operates a program similar to CCAs that aggregate purchasing of affordable clean energy. The program, CleanPowerSF, sold 100 percent renewable energy to customers in 2023 for 4 percent less than the IOU with its 40 percent renewable energy mix.[22] CCAs and programs like CleanPowerSF prioritize renewable power and customers over profits. They provide a win-win for people and the environment and a mechanism for making energy sourcing more regional.

Municipal-owned utilities (MOUs) provide energy focused on customers, not shareholders and profits. Before the rise of IOUs, MOUs were the dominant form in the electric system. Despite the corporate takeover of the energy system, many MOUs, or public power utilities, remain and serve approximately one in seven Americans across forty-nine states and five US territories.[23] The largest is the Los Angeles Department of Water and Power, which has close to 1.5 million customers. Like CCAs, MOUs generally provide lower electric rates, more reliable service, and a higher percentage of renewables than IOUs.[24]

Local electric cooperatives provide power in rural areas where IOUs have not intruded. These roughly nine hundred nonprofit consumer-owned utilities provide electricity for forty-two million people.[25] Ninety-two percent of their customers live in persistent poverty counties. The cooperatives prioritize providing affordable rates. As costs have decreased for renewables, the percentage of them in cooperatives' power mix has increased. In 2023, the US Department of Agriculture allocated nearly $11 billion through the Inflation Reduction Act for rural electric cooperatives to invest in affordable, clean energy.

As these community-driven entities demonstrate, many viable alternatives exist to IOUs and energy conglomerates in the energy system. CCAs, MOUs, and electric co-ops know and serve their customers well and are fully engaged in the clean energy transformation. They provide local jobs and careers. Without faraway investors extracting profits, the wealth can be kept local. Bringing the market power of all these entities together is needed to overcome corporate power in the energy system.

Shift Power Through Energy Democracy

The energy democracy movement takes the power shift further by insisting that communities, particularly those systemically underserved, own and shape their energy. The movement, supported by the national Energy Democracy Project, seeks to challenge the corporate energy establishment and build a decentralized, community-owned energy system. Energy democracy projects are generally hyperlocal and 100 percent renewable.

Solar cooperatives are helping to operationalize the movement. Through community-owned solar, member-owners earn money or credit on the power generated and help build local wealth. With no upfront payments needed and savings of 10 to 15 percent on electric bills, these cooperatives benefit low-to-moderate-income households.[26] People Power Solar Cooperative invests in community-led energy projects. The cooperative's initial projects included three revenue-generating, cooperatively owned solar rooftop residential projects in Oakland, California. Other projects include a battery collective for sharing backup battery power with households during power emergencies. Solar cooperatives are an important path to energy democracy.

Community solar is particularly beneficial to more than half of Americans who are renters, residents of multitenant buildings, and homeowners unable to install solar panels. As of 2022, twenty states and Washington, DC, had passed community solar legislation, and almost all states had at least one project up and running.[27] New York had 728 community solar projects online by the end of 2022, the most in the nation.[28] One project in Brooklyn generates

1.2 megawatts of rooftop solar for five hundred low- and moderate-income households.

Indigenous communities are organizing around energy democracy and sovereignty. The mostly Indigenous residents of the small island of Moloka'i, Hawai'i, had to pay more than three times what the average American pays for a kilowatt hour of electricity for decades. Fed up with this drain on household income, the residents formed the Ho'ahu Energy Cooperative in 2020. As of 2024, the cooperative has received approval for two community-owned solar photovoltaic battery storage system projects. The end price for electricity will be a fraction of what it is in Hawai'i's centralized electric system.

Four thousand solar panels owned by the small tribal nation of Picuris Pueblo in New Mexico provides an existing model of energy democracy and sovereignty. In partnership with the local electric cooperative, the tribe members receive a $50 to $75 credit on their energy bills from selling the electricity they generate. The added solar capacity in this area has helped the cooperative provide nearly 100 percent daytime solar power to its thirty-three thousand customers. The cooperative also owns batteries to supplement electricity production during the night. In October 2023, the Picuris Pueblo broke ground on a new three-megawatt solar array that will feed directly to buildings. This electricity won't return to the grid and is thus another step toward energy sovereignty.

With an energy democracy approach, clean, local energy is developed and sold at rates people can afford. Revenue is earned from being a member-owner. Furthermore, local community cooperatives build resilience in an age of climate shocks and energy system breakdowns.

Transform Land Use with Local Electricity Production, Storage, and Distribution

Generating more electric power on nearby land has much potential. It starts with making use of what already exists: buildings with rooftops. A study by the National Renewable Energy Laboratory estimated that if fully deployed, rooftop solar could collectively power almost every American home.[29] The cost of solar installation dropped around 70 percent in the decade leading up to 2020,[30] changing it from a costly green purchase to a sound investment in one's building.

In addition to the potential capacity, rooftop solar power may cost less than utility-scale solar and wind farms. This research finding is contrary to what Big Utilities and energy corporations often claim about economies of scale. Researchers from Vibrant Clean Energy, a consulting firm, found that generating roughly one-fifth of the country's energy from rooftop and local solar power plus batteries would save consumers $473 billion.[31] This savings was based on estimates of what electricity would otherwise cost over thirty years. Funded partly by prosolar advocates, this study needed extra scrutiny.

Fortunately, a *Los Angeles Times* climate columnist did just that. He interviewed Jesse Jenkins of Princeton University, who was skeptical of Vibrant's study.[32] Jenkins calculated about 25 percent less rooftop solar potential than Vibrant. Both, however, agreed that there is much more cost-effective rooftop solar left to build. With financial incentives, loans, and grants for installing rooftop solar panels, this reality can be built with no new land required.

Community solar requires a change in local land use. Community solar gardens with ground-mounted panels can be situated on land in existing neighborhoods. They have been found to be more cost-effective than rooftop solar and utility-scale solar.[33] Nonprofit community solar installers like GRID Alternatives find local hosts with rooftops, parking lots, undeveloped land, or other space adequate to install sufficient solar panels to power community projects.

The combination of rooftop and community solar is giving rise to a distributed energy system. From 2021 to 2022, the number of new solar installations by utilities nationwide fell from 70 to 60 percent of the solar power market, with individuals, small businesses, and local public entities increasing energy production from 30 to 40 percent.[34] In other words, locally generated solar power grew more than large solar farms and long-distance transmission.

Land can be flexed to harvest local wind energy too. Small wind turbines, with blade diameters of thirty feet or less, can be installed on residential properties or in community wind farms. Rural properties of one acre or more are typically the best sites, with the absence of buildings or trees that may block wind.

After a tornado nearly wiped Greensburg, Kansas, off the map in 2007, the town of nine hundred people decided to rebuild green. Energy- and water-efficient buildings and grounds were a cornerstone of their plan. Energy use dropped, saving the town and residents money. Most impressively, they turned the local wind resource into an asset and built the nearby Greensburg Wind Project. The wind farm generates all the electricity the town needs.

Local geothermal resources also generate electricity for communities. In Farmington, Massachusetts, the nation's first geothermal heating and cooling neighborhood-scale system was installed. The underground system provides heating and cooling to thirty-one homes and five commercial buildings. Other similar projects are being developed in nearby cities. The US Department of Energy is helping fund some of these systems.

Self-reliance through local, distributed energy generation can expand with advances in battery storage technology. Unless hydroelectric or geothermal is locally available, battery storage is necessary to "keep the lights on" when the sun is not shining or the wind is not blowing. Batteries are commonly paired with rooftop and community solar installations. By the end of 2020, Australia had close to one hundred thousand homes with battery systems.[35] Australia is showing the world that household battery systems can be built at scale.

While boosting local energy production generally requires land use changes, the distribution of locally generated electricity requires less land than utility-scale systems. Microgrids that replace century-old electric grids connect local sources of distributed energy and allow the local system to function independently of the larger transmission grid. Large transmission poles, wires, and substations are unnecessary, helping the system use less land and blend into the community.

Traditionally used on college campuses and military operational sites, community microgrids are being deployed in communities not served well by Big Utilities. In Manipur, India, microgrids that connect solar panels and batteries have spread across villages where electricity did not exist. The tribal Blue Lake Rancheria in Northern California uses a microgrid and generates enough electricity from solar and battery storage for its community buildings to be fully "off the grid."

Local electricity production, storage, and distribution are essential elements of a place-based energy system. Regional energysheds further build the capacity to meet the energy needs of large populations.

Transform Land Use with Regional Energyshed Planning and Funding

Starting in 2022, the federal Department of Energy funded three projects through The Energyshed: Exploring Place-Based Generation funding program. The University of Vermont is researching the energyshed potential of three rural areas in the state and developing a model and tool for local decision-makers. The Launch Alaska initiative is determining three large-scale local energy projects to benefit Native Alaska communities. The Georgia Institute of Technology is creating a new metropolitan energy planning organization within the Atlanta area energyshed. These promising initiatives highlight emerging paths toward making energysheds a reality.

As discussed earlier, CCAs and municipalities have great potential to source energy from regional energysheds for their customers. Peninsula Clean Energy (PCE) secures some of its power from one geothermal plant, three wind farms, and two solar farms from counties within or adjacent to the San Francisco Bay Area region where it is located.[36] CleanPowerSF's portfolio of renewable projects includes a hyperlocal solar array in San Francisco and a large complex of geothermal power plants in adjacent counties.[37] The geothermal plants accounted for one-fifth of this type of green power in the state in 2023. That same year, CleanPowerSF developed a solar-plus storage project across the bay. In 2024, it secured almost 150 megawatts of wind energy and fifty megawatts of battery energy storage from a clean energy site, located less than 150 miles from San Francisco. Expected to come online in 2026, this project will generate enough electricity to power nearly 120,000 San Francisco homes.[38] PCE and CleanPowerSF are helping move the needle toward regional energysheds. With more regulation and customer demand for regional energy, they could go further toward this vision.

Forming a commitment to a regional energyshed spurs creativity and innovation in making the most out of nearby resources. A substantial energyshed vision was put forth by the Morris Model, a group of organizations partnering to advance sustainability in a west-central Minnesota county. One of their "Big 3" goals is to produce 80 percent renewable energy within the county for its ten thousand residents by 2030. The city of Morris has several solar arrays, a biomass gasification facility that turns crop residues from nearby farms into fuels, and wind turbines.

Large population centers still need utility-scale solar, wind, and other renewable projects. An energyshed lens in evaluating these projects raises an important question. How close can renewable energy be generated to the population that will consume it?

The SunZia Wind project, discussed earlier as the largest renewable energy project in the United States, is about 150 miles from Albuquerque, New Mexico, and 180 miles from El Paso, Texas. Those two cities' combined populations are over 1.2 million people. There are roughly another 1.5 million people in New Mexico. As mentioned earlier, Pattern estimates SunZia Wind will provide power for three million people. With battery storage and other safeguards, could Pattern generate energy for the 2.7 million people in the greater surrounding region rather than transmitting it hundreds of miles to coastal states? The existing electrical system may dictate otherwise, but these are the types of questions that need to be investigated for future utility-scale projects.

Planning for and funding local energy production, storage, and distribution combined with regional energysheds can significantly reduce the need for a centralized, long-distance electric system. Resetting culture around conservation will allow further localizing and regionalizing of the energy system.

Reset Culture with Net-Zero Buildings Subsidies, Technical Assistance, and Social Support

Net-zero buildings are rapidly becoming standard in new developments and part of existing building retrofits. Subsidies, technical assistance, and social support are helping reset culture in support of net-zero buildings that serve as a corner-stone of a place-based energy system.

Government subsidies help buildings move toward net zero. These incentives in states and cities bring down the cost of new appliances and home energy systems, reducing the time until energy savings cover the upfront costs. Nine aging apartment buildings in Brooklyn, New York, were retrofitted with all-new electric heating and cooling systems in 2021. A new surface was applied to the building exteriors to make them airtight. This revamped building system reduced energy costs by 60 to 80 percent.[39] The project was partially funded by Retrofit NY, a state government program, and notably did not displace residents during the construction.

Changing the energy system in one's home can feel overwhelming, as I shared from my own experience at the start of this chapter. There are many details, and it can be hard to find answers. Some potential changes may be unappealing. Homeowners, for example, have been reluctant to embrace the electrification of cooking, expressing a preference for cooking on gas stovetops. Not knowing where to begin and whom to contact can stifle the best of intentions.

Technical assistance can facilitate the conversion of buildings to net zero. Energy efficiency programs offered by companies and nonprofits provide comprehensive analyses of home energy use. These programs help customers find incentives to upgrade appliances and home systems. The Campaign for Fossil Free Buildings in Silicon Valley, for example, connects people to low-cost electrification plans, installers, rebates, and incentives.

Technical assistance programs that connect water and energy use are a win-win-win for energy conservation, water conservation, and customers. The Bay Area Regional Energy Network (BayREN) serves the nine-county San Francisco Bay Area. The network's Water + Efficiency Program works with utilities to support customers with "on-bill financing" for home upgrades. This mechanism allows customers to pay for the upgrades using water and energy savings on future bills. BayREN also supports multifamily property owners in energy and water upgrades and provides a one-stop online service to connect homeowners to rebates.

Social support can further help reset culture in support of electrification and conservation for a place-based energy system. The Campaign for Fossil Free Buildings deploys ambassadors who have electrified their homes to support people starting the process. Sharing positive personal experiences with induction cooktops can lead to more people purchasing them. I know I could have used more support when I stumbled through electrifying our home water heating system!

Reset Culture with Default Energy-Efficient Consumer Products

The energy efficiency of appliances and electronic goods is critical to energy conservation efforts that underpin place-based energy systems. The US Environmental Protection Agency's Energy Star program certifies products across more than seventy energy efficiency and savings categories. Utilities and local governments rely on these product certifications to design incentives for customers to buy them.

Phasing out products that do not meet Energy Star criteria and having only Energy Star appliances and goods available on the market should be the next step. With light bulbs, this is already becoming the case. Starting in 2020, LED and light bulbs with similar efficiency became the only ones allowed for sale in California, Nevada, Vermont, Washington, and Colorado. State governments could set a standard such as "all appliances, fixtures and electric-powered items meet Energy Star Criteria by 2030," with the federal government eventually adopting it.

It's easy for consumers to forget about energy efficiency when considering the many other features offered in home appliances. Making energy efficiency the default choice takes that out of the consumer's decision. It's one less thing for people to worry about when choosing expensive appliances like washing machines or refrigerators. In addition to conserving energy, people appreciate how Energy Star appliances save money on monthly electric bills.

Eliminating eco modes on washing machines, dishwashers, and other appliances and making eco mode the only setting available is another means to make energy efficiency the default choice. Eco mode should be able to get the job done and make appliances simpler and easier to use.

Electric heat pumps for heating and cooling indoor spaces and for heating water also need to become a default consumer choice. Air-source heat pump systems alternately draw warm or cool ambient air into homes. They are two to four times more efficient than conventional electric coil-only heaters. Likewise, geothermal heat pumps exchange temperatures with the soil to heat and cool a building during different seasons. Like local renewable energy, heat pumps harness the forces of nature and connect people to the local climate.

In June 2022, President Joe Biden used the Defense Production Act to increase the production of heat pumps for US homes in response to the Russian invasion of Ukraine. With Russia's dependence on natural gas exports, this was one way to reduce demand in the global marketplace. This policy sent the message that heat pumps are essential in today's world and increased their availability.

Reset Culture Through Conservation Price Signals and Social Comparison Interventions

Getting people to conserve energy as a daily practice is also needed. Energy use is multifaceted and ubiquitous in modern life. Price signals and social interventions can help nudge households and others to do a better job of reducing wasteful energy use.

Price signals are changes in price intended to change behavior. China implemented residential tiered pricing reform in most of its provinces starting in 2012. A study examined the impact on energy use across twenty-one of the provinces and found that the three-level tiered pricing reduced energy use by 6 to 7 percent.[40] Other studies, however, found little change in most households, especially more affluent ones.[41] Many of the researchers suggested modifications to the design of tiered pricing to better incentivize conservation, including more tiers and higher price increases.

Equity must be considered in any tiered pricing scheme. For low-income households, discounts should be available in the bottom usage tier. Tiered pricing with large increases or surcharges at higher consumption thresholds can target affluent households that disproportionately use the most energy per capita.

Time-of-use or time-varying-rate energy prices are another price signal strategy. These price changes can help energy use adapt to intermittent wind and solar power. Higher prices are timed when the supply is low relative to demand. This temporary price increase incentivizes changes such as running the dishwasher or washing machine and dryer to times when the energy supply is greater.

Social comparison is another research-based approach to motivate conservation behaviors. Since energy use occurs mainly in private spaces, social comparison has to be engineered. Customers can get feedback on how their energy use compares to others who live in similar homes or residences nearby. Utilities in California and other states have been required to provide this information. Initial research on some of these programs found modest but statistically significant reductions in household energy use.[42]

Another study of energy conservation behavior in hotel rooms found a specific message particularly effective in getting guests to engage in conservation behavior.[43] The message was a simply stated social norm: "The majority of guests in this room reuse their towels." This strategy could be employed at the neighborhood level with messages such as "A majority of your neighbors with similar-sized homes spend less than $50/month on heating or cooling for their home." We can think creatively about social norming messages and test them out to see their impact.

Reset Culture Through Default Indoor Temperature Settings

Given that heating and air-conditioning are the largest energy users in most American residences, resetting expectations around indoor temperatures could be a huge boon to energy conservation. *National Geographic* journalist Elizabeth Royte explains how expectations have changed and what a paradigm shift might look like: "Being a little too warm in summertime used to be something that even the affluent accepted, perhaps with the help of an iced beverage. . . . In this paradigm, the lavish chill of our conference rooms, or the 'thermal delight' that greets the sweaty pedestrian as the doors to a high-end emporium whoosh open, would become artifacts of a fleeting late 20th-century insanity."[44] Royte's descriptions reveal how energy is often wasted in cooling (or heating) large indoor spaces to excess. Reevaluating and changing these social practices reduce energy waste from overcooling and overheating buildings.

Changing expectations for indoor temperature can follow nature's lead. Tightly controlling the climate inside one's home to the same temperature year-round ignores seasonal temperature variations. With the changing seasons, buildings can be a little cooler in the winter and a little warmer in the summer.

The US Department of Energy recommends setting thermostats to 68 degrees for heating and 78 degrees for air conditioning. There may be some discomfort at first, but a pair of shorts or a sweater can help alleviate that. The increased connection to nature, which includes its seasonal variation, promotes well-being that can minimize any sense of sacrifice.

Starting with education and marketing, we could gradually move toward making the Department of Energy's indoor temperature guidelines mandatory. This substantial cultural change could be catalyzed by the vision of regional energy self-reliance, which requires strong conservation, as we have explored in this chapter. Children's show icon Mr. Rogers was known for putting on his sweater each time he entered his staged house. Modern media stars could bring the sweater back for wintertime shows and shorts for indoor summertime appearances. As a cultural norm is formed, political will could grow to support indoor temperature regulations.

Leverage Other Systems

The energy system is heavily intertwined with all the other systems. Implementing other place-based systems will help reduce energy demand to levels that local and regional resources can largely supply. Place-based housing (chap. 4) and work (chap. 5) systems, for example, support less need for travel and thus less energy overall. Nearby community (chap. 7) and nature (chap. 8) spaces entice people outside and can decrease time spent indoors using energy. Local and regional plant-based food (chap. 9) requires less production and transportation-related energy.

The transportation system (chap. 6), with its significant energy use, is the system that can be most leveraged in support of a regional, renewable energy system. As we make the societal shift to electric vehicles, expanding the electric system to charge vehicles in the same quantities as the current car fleet will require an enormous amount of energy. As discussed in chapter 6, a place-based transportation system is designed to reduce car dependence and, thus, the number of automobiles. Electricity is not needed for walking and biking, and it can be used much more efficiently to power public transportation, e-bikes, and e-scooters.

In the next chapter, we'll explore building a place-based consumer goods system. Like food (chap. 9), less distance from production to consumption means less transport energy.

CONSUMER GOODS

> The capitalist monster that commodifies everyone and everything sells us down the river and alienates us, because alienated, isolated and insecure people make such good consumers. Connected, grounded, rooted, soulful people make terrible consumers but great citizens.
>
> —Rebecca Solnit, speaking on the *Outrage and Optimism* podcast

It's hard not to feel compelled to buy new clothing, household items, and other stuff in a consumerist culture like the United States. Over the years, I've bought my share of new apparel, sports equipment, and outdoor gear. My wife and I have purchased new furniture, household accessories, and other items for our home. Some of it has come and gone. Like many Americans, we have containers in our garage to hold extra stuff and seasonal items like winter jackets and holiday decorations.

In our dominant consumer culture, it takes rethinking and resolving not to keep buying new goods. Finding alternatives to buying new is not always easy, but options exist. Concerned about consumerism's environmental and social impacts, I've tried to change my consumption habits over time. Local stores and high-quality goods have helped me to reduce my consumption footprint.

I've found ways to buy secondhand and treasure more of what I have. A couple of secondhand clothing stores within a mile of my house have a great selection of good-quality clothing. Over the past five years, about half the clothing I've bought has come from these stores. For the few new items I buy, I opt for clothing that will last and is made from recycled materials. Likewise, we have treasured furniture items that have been in our home for over two decades.

Plastic packaging is one of the environmental costs of consumerism and something I've also sought to reduce. I have not found ways to avoid it altogether, but I have eliminated it from bathing and shaving products. A local market co-op, Rainbow Grocery (see chap. 5), sells bar soap, shampoo, conditioner, and shaving soap. They all work well, last, and require no plastic bottles.

With these practices, I sometimes feel like a fish swimming upstream in the consumerist river. Yet up until the last fifty years, these practices and many others that support the treasuring, sharing, and reuse of consumer goods were commonplace.

* * *

Over the past half century, mass production and the corporatization of manufacturing and retail have led to an explosion of material goods. This has led us to think there is no limit to what we can consume. We've also been bombarded with messages that suggest happiness can be derived from the accumulation of stuff.

Research has found that buying stuff, particularly online, creates an endorphin rush but not lasting happiness.[1] As introduced in chapter 3, consumerism keeps people on the "hedonic treadmill," searching for happiness without increasing it. This treadmill has led to an accumulation of so many consumer goods that many homes cannot hold all of them. Ninety percent of the world's self-storage inventory is in the United States, where 5 percent of the world's population lives.[2]

Clothing exemplifies the extent to which consumerism and material waste have taken hold in society and degraded the environment. The editors of *Nature Climate Change* summarized their analysis of research on the clothing industry and its environmental impact: "There are [approximately] 20 new garments manufactured per person each year [worldwide]. And we are buying 60% more [in 2018] than we were in 2000. . . . A large proportion of clothing manufacturing occurs in China and India, countries which rely on coal-fueled power plants. . . . Around 5% of global [carbon] emissions come from the fashion industry. . . . Almost 60% of all clothing produced is disposed of within a year of production ending in a land-fill or incineration."[3] The volume and frequency of buying clothes have increased so much that we now refer to it as "fast fashion." New clothing lines appear every few weeks, and clothes purchased not long ago pile up or are discarded.

Making it hard to confront the impacts, the clothing and overall consumer goods systems are complex and often hidden from consumers. Researchers and environmental nonprofit leaders John C. Ryan and Alan Durning uncovered the global journey of consumer goods in their book *Stuff: The Secret Life of Everyday Things* back in 1997. Their chapter on a pair of Nike Air Jordan shoes brought to life how little most of us know about how consumer goods are assembled in the global economy.[4] Leather from cows in Texas made up much of the upper shoe. Rubber from Saudi oil and benzene from a coal factory in Taiwan composed the sole inputs. The pressurized air component was made in the United States. The shoes were assembled in South Korea. The shoebox was made in a mill in New Mexico, and the tissue paper within it came from Sumatran rainforest trees.

Durning and Ryan emphasize how nearly every step in the shoe production chain is located where environmental and labor standards are the least stringent.

Heavily polluted rivers in South Korea result from tanning chemicals. The factories are hot, crowded, and filled with toxic fumes. Workers endure long hours and earn so little that it takes over a month to make the equivalent of one pair of shoes. Meanwhile, consumers of these shoes don't see and often have little awareness of these impacts on people and the planet.

We know that the mass consumption of material goods has required the extraction of natural resources worldwide, adding to habitat loss and the biodiversity crisis. What is less well recognized is the relationship between consumerism and the climate crisis. The use of energy in the extraction of materials and manufacturing of consumer goods generates considerable greenhouse gas emissions (GHGE). Embodied carbon analyses in which emissions are traced along the entire production process reveal the amount for different consumer products. For example, researchers found that manufacturing one smartphone requires the energy equivalent of running a refrigerator for a year.[5] Due to high levels of consumption and embodied carbon emissions, consumer goods are the second-largest source of GHGE for the average American.[6]

The regular disposal of products adds to the environmental toll. Worldwide, around two-thirds of the over one hundred billion tons of extracted resources that go into consumer products are thrown away every year.[7] In the United States, the average person generates five pounds of trash daily.[8] Much of the waste stream is packaging materials.

Single-use plastics have become ubiquitous in packaging materials as well as many consumer goods. They provide convenience but at a high cost. Forty percent of plastic produced is found in single-use packaging material.[9] More than one million plastic beverage bottles are sold every minute around the world, and this is expected to nearly double by 2030.[10] Plastic is made from oil and fossil fuels, placing increased demand on extracting those fuels with collateral damage to nature.

Plastic pollution has become a global crisis. Only about 9 percent of plastic is recycled globally.[11] Most of it ends up in landfills or as litter. In the oceans, plastics break down into fine particles. These microplastics harm ocean life and end up in human bodies through food, air, and water. They pose health risks that we are just beginning to understand.[12]

The production of cheap, seemingly limitless consumer goods relies on exploiting nature and labor and a vast waste stream. Global corporations control almost every part of the system. The profit-taking by corporations drains money from local economies.

For a livable planet, we must reckon with consumerism. In this chapter, we'll unpack what is holding it in place. A place-based alternative to the global consumer goods systems is one in which consumer goods are regionally made and recirculated. Despite many challenges, we can move toward this vision through systems change and chip away at consumerism's dominant influence on society. This chapter explores this necessary transition and shows how systems-change levers are being applied to regenerate local economies, community bonds, and nature depleted by the global consumer goods system.

Systems-Change Strategies for Making and Recirculating Local and Regional Consumer Goods

- Shift power through regulating advertisements and marketing claims
- Shift power through single-use plastic bans
- Shift power through circular economy policies and business networks
- Transform land use with local manufacturing and makerspaces
- Transform land use with regional makingsheds and fibersheds
- Reset culture through local rental businesses and lending libraries
- Reset culture through secondhand stores and community exchanges
- Reset culture through repair cafés and "right to repair" laws
- Reset culture through the slow consumerism movement
- Leverage other systems

Holding the Global Consumer Goods Systems and Consumerism in Place

Although the promise of a less material lifestyle appeals to many, Big Retail corporations and advertisers use their influence to keep the drumbeat of consumerism going. The Big Plastic industry puts its weight behind these efforts and obstructs reform to limit disposable waste. Land use connected to the global supply chain inhibits transitioning to a place-based consumer goods system. Additionally, cultural forces such as planned obsolescence and one-click shopping keep people locked into the global, corporate consumer goods system.

Power: Big Retail and Advertising

Environmentalist and author Paul Hawken poses a fundamental question about consumer choices: "Does it serve human needs or manufacture human wants?"[13] If we look honestly at material goods consumption in society, it's apparent that we have gone way beyond fulfilling needs, and a seemingly infinite number of wants have been manufactured.

Big Retail and the global consumer goods manufacturers that supply them have used their considerable marketing and advertising budgets to manufacture wants. Research shows that materialistic values and goals grow with exposure to advertising.[14] It puts a person in a state of always wanting something more. This mindset of constant dissatisfaction sets a person up to be a good consumer. Ads tell him what his "problem" is and what product will "solve" it.

Advertising on the internet, social media, television, print, and billboards surrounds people every day. The average person in the United States is exposed to four thousand to ten thousand advertising messages daily.[15] Many of these ads are simply a brand logo on a piece of clothing or food item. Research, however, has shown that brands made familiar through frequent exposure strongly influence people's choices.[16] Corporate retailers continuously send messages that encourage people to keep buying products and ensure consumption remains front and center in their minds.

Advertisements often feature the latest version of products, stating or implying that you must have it. The latest iPhone, the newest car model, or a revolutionary razor for shaving are examples of how advertising induces feelings of wanting something new, even when what one has works perfectly fine. "Fast fashion" advertising suggests that the next new clothing trend or item will impress others and boost one's self-image. Pervasive advertising creates a desire to keep up with everyone else by purchasing new consumer goods.

In the digital realm, advertising has become more sophisticated and effective in targeting specific groups of people and their preferences. Monica Peart, forecasting director for eMarket, describes how Amazon mines data to support advertisers in capturing customers: "The platform is rich with shoppers' behavioral data for targeting and provides access to purchase data in real-time. This type of access was once only available through the retail partner, to share at their discretion. But with Amazon's suite of sponsored ads, marketers have unprecedented access to 'shelves' where consumers are shopping."[17] In addition, much advertising is now done through influencers on social media. Amazon pays influencers to get people to buy products on Amazon. They rarely disclose the relationship when talking up products, but you can always find the link to Amazon in their posts. Advertising continues to change and evolve, becoming more intrusive, stealthy, and manipulative online.

"Green product" advertising is another tactic to keep people buying new items. These ads can lead people to think they can buy stuff with little to no environmental impact. Products marketed as "green" can be marginally more beneficial than nongreen alternatives. They still, however, use up natural resources, generate emissions in their production, and end up in the waste stream. More often than not, "green product" advertising gets people to buy or use products they do not need.[18] This advertising puts a spin on purchasing new products but does little to alter the underlying consumerism and trained attachment to stuff.

Power: Big Plastic

With so many consumer goods being made and packaged with plastics, corporations involved with plastics have collectively developed significant economic and political power. Big Plastic is an industry that overlaps with several other sectors, notably Big Oil, gas, and large chemical corporations that provide the inputs and manufacture the plastics. The oil and gas industries see plastic production as a way out of climate change–driven reductions in the use of fossil fuels for energy. They are counting on enormous increases in plastic production to provide a lifeline for their profits.[19] Corporations in the consumer goods system that make and sell products with disposable plastic make up another wing of Big Plastic. With so many powerful interests behind Big Plastic, it's no wonder it's everywhere.

Big Plastic corporations seek preferential treatment from the government. They have delayed or stopped plastic bag and plastic bottle bans and restrictions in the United States.[20] The industry's answer to reducing plastic pollution has been recycling, fully knowing that the plastic recycling rate has been less than 10 percent for years. They ignore the reality that communities, rivers, and oceans are awash in plastic pollution across the globe.

The plastic industry also leverages the US government's influence on other countries. The industry group, for example, instigated the US effort to reverse Kenya's plastic bag ban and its pledge to limit imports of plastic garbage.[21] Their lobbyists work hand in hand with US trade representatives to pressure Kenya and other governments to change their policies on plastic.[22] Big Plastic works closely with the government to secure and continually expand its market.

Land Use: Global Footprint

The consumer goods system is entangled in a complex, global supply chain. Ryan and Durning's tale of how Nike shoes are made takes place across five countries—Korea, Indonesia, Taiwan, the United States, and Saudi Arabia—and three continents.

The on-the-ground footprint of the global consumer goods system includes all the land mined, deforested, and otherwise exploited for raw materials and the production facilities concentrated in the Global South. The clothing industry supply chain, for example, is dispersed worldwide through farms (cotton), ranches (wool and leather), oil wells and pipelines (polyester and other clothing materials), and factories.

Land use in the global consumer goods system also includes a vast network of shipping and storage facilities. Ports, airports, warehouses, and shipping centers have large footprints and continue to expand all over the planet. Additionally, the constant movement of goods takes up a lot of road space, adding to the system's footprint.

Consumer Culture: Planned Obsolescence and One-Click Shopping

In addition to Big Retail's advertising and marketing, the large amount of consumer goods that become quickly obsolete and the ease of one-click shopping have helped create a culture of rampant material consumption.

Planned obsolescence is a business strategy in which consumer goods are made to become outdated and need replacement. A survey of fifteen hundred American households found that 50 percent of toys had stopped working or were broken within thirty days of purchase.[23] Finding replacement parts or repair services can be difficult. Electronics from printers to coffee makers have been programmed to stop working.[24] Computers and other digital devices often become incompatible with new software versions or new accessories like chargers and headphones.[25] A replacement part for a good may be as expensive as buying a whole new product. All these tactics incentivize the buying of new stuff.

One-click shopping with speedy delivery has made consuming new stuff even more central to everyday life. Clicking on items that arrive within one or two days has rapidly become how people expect to shop. In 2019, 1.5 million packages were delivered daily in New York City alone, and about 15 percent of households received a package every day.[26] By 2024, daily Amazon package deliveries in the city had increased to two million.[27] Corporate online platforms have caused the frequency of shopping and the amount of consumer goods in households to skyrocket.

The societal value placed on convenience helps explain the growing sales of Amazon and Big Retail online. Introduced in chapter 3, Professor Tim Wu's "tyranny of convenience" helps explain the rise of one-click shopping over shopping at local stores: "Clicking on a product from the comfort of your couch seems more convenient [than going to a local store]—and that impression of ease can have more influence on our behavior than better service, quicker acquisition, and lower prices."[28] Wu raises the question: At what cost are we prioritizing convenient and frequent shopping in our lives?

In this rapid transition to online shopping, we are acquiring more consumer goods but losing community connections, local stores, and the satisfaction of sharing and treasuring well-made products. Many people are feeling that something is amiss. A vision of bringing the consumer goods system back closer to where people live and reigning in consumerism is growing in appeal.

A Vision of Locally and Regionally Made and Recirculated Consumer Goods

A place-based consumer goods system shrinks the role of consumption in people's lives and puts it back in balance with nature, community, and deeper life satisfaction. The system encourages differentiating between human needs and wants, offering the opportunity to live more simply with fewer material goods.

Regional supply chains and local manufacturing produce goods reflective of local culture and natural resources. Producing all the goods consumed in a region within that region requires business practices and consumer behaviors that don't rely on so much new stuff.

Recirculating goods reduces the resources that go into consumer goods and the associated waste. Regional or local circular economies focus on keeping materials and products in use and maintaining their value. For example, local manufacturers can use materials from used goods to make new products.

Buying secondhand items recirculates consumer goods. In many cities, it's not hard to build a fashionable wardrobe entirely from secondhand clothing stores. Purchasing used books and household items, from kitchenware to furniture, are other ways to reduce the consumption of new goods and prevent waste.

Sharing and repairing items that are expensive or infrequently used also reduces overconsumption. Power tools and rarely used kitchen appliances, for example, can be shared among neighbors and friends. Items in disrepair or in need of maintenance can be fixed if built that way. Sharing and repairing consumer goods provides opportunities for building community and conserving natural resources.

A place-based consumer goods system changes people's relationship to material goods. It goes from one of acquisition and accumulation to one of gratitude and respect for the resources that make them. In a regional consumer goods system, people are nudged to be more mindful of where and what they buy, how they use things and share, and their waste.

The benefits to personal well-being of owning and having less stuff are multifaceted. Less time spent shopping and organizing consumer goods helps a person focus her energy on what matters the most for happiness and well-being: experiences, time with friends and family, and being connected to community and nature. It nurtures simplicity and removes clutter from one's life, boosting mental capital. Finding ways to reduce the consumption of new stuff brings an additional level of satisfaction, with a sense of doing one's part to conserve natural resources and reduce pollution and landfill. Buying fewer material goods also saves money that can be put toward financial security.

Being less a consumer of stuff and more connected to place charts a course toward more sustainable and meaningful ways of living.

Systems-Change Strategies for a Place-Based Consumer Goods System

Cultural resets that prompt sharing, repairing, and reusing goods are foundational to changing the consumer goods system. Slowing down consumption overall is a movement aimed at digging up the roots of consumer culture. When land use shifts to local and regional manufacturing and making, reliance on global products decreases and the potential to treasure goods and conserve resources increases. Shifting power away from Big Retail and diminishing consumerism can be assisted by regulating advertisements and marketing claims. Bans on plastics and circular economy policies shift power from Big Plastic and Big Retail to local actors engaged in recirculating goods and materials locally. Applying the systems-change levers in these ways can create a place-based consumer goods system in which people get what they need, protect the environment, and support local economic growth.

Shift Power Through Regulating Advertisements and Marketing Claims

Regulation of advertising could help reduce the harmful effects consumerism and the corporations peddling it are having on people and the environment. Due to public health concerns, restrictions on tobacco and junk food advertising have been implemented in many places and show that it can be done.

With the urgent need to address the climate crisis, restricting advertisements for products with high carbon emissions can also be justified in the name of public health. The Fossil Free Advertising group in the Netherlands successfully lobbied the Amsterdam city council to ban advertising for high-carbon goods in 2020 and is now seeking a national ban. Cities in the United Kingdom, including North Somerset, Liverpool, and Norwich, followed suit and passed similar prohibitions on ads at city-managed sites such as bus stops and billboards. Stockholm and other cities in Europe have since joined this growing movement.

Regulation could be more directly aimed at consumer goods by restricting the use of the often misleading "green product" label. The Swedish Consumer Agency has taken companies to court for misleading claims. In 2023, the agency convicted a dairy company for falsely claiming that its products were climate-neutral.

What if Amazon's claims were brought under scrutiny?

Amazon presents itself as a leader in sustainability and a good steward of the environment. The corporation doesn't, however, account for the exponential growth in packages it delivers to customers. In their emissions calculations, Amazon and other Big Retail corporations do not include the embodied carbon emissions in all the products they sell and deliver. Additionally, Amazon's sustainability claims ignore the environmental impact of its continual building and deployment of warehouses, data centers, large-haul trucks, and rapid-delivery trucks.

Amazon also claims to be becoming "Earth's best employer," yet its warehouse employees engage in repetitive, fast-paced, and often dangerous work. They are paid around minimum wage and are increasingly being laid off as robotic technology replaces them.

On the community front, Amazon states that it strengthens communities. In reality, Amazon may be "Earth's biggest community destroyer." As documented in this book and elsewhere, its growth has come at the expense of communities nearly everywhere through the closure of local businesses unable to compete with Amazon's unfair business practices.

Regulating partial truths and misleading messages is not simple, and agreeing on where to draw the line can be challenging. An alternative could be funding for high-profile counter-advertising that tells a more complete picture of corporations like Amazon and their actual impact.

Shift Power Through Single-Use Plastic Bans

With Big Plastic's vested interest in consumerism and the global consumer goods system, power must be shifted away from it. Banning single-use plastics reduces Big Plastic's market size and related power.

Disposable plastic bags can be easily replaced with other materials and, most importantly, reusable cloth bags. Some prohibitions are outright, while others require consumers to pay a fee to get one. As of 2023, ten US states have adopted such bans.[29]

Full plastic bag bans should be the goal. Many people continue using plastic bags even when they have to pay for them. Many of these partial bans result in stores selling thicker, reusable plastic bags, which do more harm than regular plastic bags if they are not reused. If a person doesn't bring a bag to a store one day with a complete ban, he will quickly learn not to forget bags in the future. People will complain but can adapt.

Single-use plastic water bottles should also be banned. Environmentally minded cafés and markets already offer drinking water in paper or aluminum containers. These packaging materials are more recyclable and less persistent in the environment than plastics. Just like reusable bags, reusable bottles are becoming more commonplace. High safety standards for tap water must be met to enact a plastic bottle ban.

Shift Power Through Circular Economy Policies and Business Networks

Circular economy policies provide another means of pulling the power shift lever. Catalyzed by these policies, local businesses and organizations that share, repair, and repurpose products grow in power. Big Retail and multinational manufacturing corporations lose influence as demand for their products decreases.

A city or county can issue a local resolution to set direction for a circular economy. The resolution acknowledges existing circular practices in the jurisdiction, such as electronic repair services. The city or county commits to expanding circular practices with a zero-waste goal. To gain traction, the resolution can designate a lead agency or official, call for an assessment of existing resources and waste streams, and set up an exploration of business and job opportunities that would support a circular economy.

Amsterdam aspires to be the world's first circular city by 2050. One policy strategy has been called the Denim Deal. This entails making denim jeans and other apparel locally and with recycled material. Denim repair shops keep jeans in use, while recycling collection points close the material loop.

Circular economies can also be enacted at the regional level through networks of businesses. The ReUse Corridor connects eight rural counties across Ohio, Kentucky, and West Virginia in Appalachia and demonstrates the potential of regional circular economies. Power has shifted to diverse local economic actors in this economically distressed region.

The corridor is helping to revitalize the regional economy by making waste a valued resource. Local economic activity has picked up with a new supply chain of reused and recycled goods and materials from within the region. Fifty small businesses and three hundred jobs were created in ten years.[30]

ReUse Corridor network members host collection events regularly. The materials are sent to various reuse and recycling facilities within the region. As new organizations join the corridor, new materials are added to the circular stream. Mattresses, electronic scraps, textiles, plastic film, and compost are some of the many products and materials now recirculated.

Transform Land Use with Local Manufacturing and Makerspaces

With support, local manufacturing and making businesses can expand and produce new goods (with as much recycled or salvaged content as possible) for nearby residents. Focusing on needs, the scale of manufacturing and making is much less than the global consumer goods system has led us to believe is necessary.

Manufacturing facilities and makerspaces can be situated in cities and towns and help fill empty storefronts. As they expand and the demand for global consumer goods declines, they can be located on land vacated by ports, airports, shipping centers, and warehouses.

Organizations in Los Angeles are building an ecosystem for local making. Make It In LA is a volunteer-run nonprofit in Los Angeles. It is a one-stop shop for local entrepreneurs, linking them to resources, accelerator programs, makerspaces, entrepreneur communities, and government incentives. Make It In LA supports those interested in starting manufacturing businesses and retail or wholesale companies that want to use local suppliers. A partner organization, LA Original, highlights creative makers and artists who make products in LA and connects consumers to them. An independent Los Angeles business, COMUNITYmade, designs and sells shoes made in a nearby factory. The company's headquarters also serve as a community space.

Makers Valley Partnership (MVP) is a nonprofit in a neighborhood in the inner city of Johannesburg, South Africa. Creative entrepreneurs who live and work in the MVP include artisans, urban gardeners, carpenters, shoemakers, metal- and woodworkers, and clothing designers. The MVP is increasing the supply of local products while providing economic opportunity in a low-income urban neighborhood.

Advanced technology can facilitate a more complete local product–making ecosystem. Three-dimensional (3D) printers are widely available and being deployed for commercial product manufacturing. Adidas uses 3D printing to make some lines of its athletic shoes. 3D printing requires much less space than traditional factory manufacturing, making it easier for manufacturers to produce things locally. Imagine ordering shoes from a local 3D manufacturing business and then walking a few blocks to pick them up or having them delivered through a local delivery service. Continued advances in 3D printing may soon lead to a true renaissance in local manufacturing, providing local jobs and serving local consumers.

Transform Land Use with Regional Makingsheds and Fibersheds

Targeted regional land use is needed to round out the production side of a place-based consumer goods system. The concepts of makingsheds and fibersheds help us envision what is possible.

A makingshed (a term not yet in the current lexicon) consists of manufacturers and makers who use regionally sourced materials and labor and sell their products within the region. It is essentially a regional version of Makers Valley, described in the prior section. Makingsheds leverage circular economy practices that recycle, reuse, and repurpose materials to sustain natural resources that they depend on within the region. Manufacturers and makers can form associations or cooperatives to share production facilities and sell to local retail stores.

Fibersheds support a regional textile economy that combines growing and milling fiber from crops and animals, weaving, dyeing, and sewing to make clothing. An organization in Northern California named Fibershed is helping develop a regional fiber system focusing on soil and environmental health. Its membership-based network includes farmers, ranchers, designers, sewers, weavers, knitters, felters, spinners, mill owners, and natural dyers. Fibershed producers certify that all fiber, botanic dye, and labor are sourced within Northern California to become a member.

Fibersheds are part of a growing movement based on transforming land for regional clothing and textile production. The Piedmont Fibershed seeks to develop a regional fiber economy within a two-hundred-mile radius of Durham, North Carolina. The Three Rivers Fibershed extends over a 175-mile radius of Minneapolis across portions of Minnesota, Wisconsin, Iowa, and South Dakota. Each emerging fibershed celebrates its region's natural resources and people in producing locally sourced clothes and textiles.

Land used by the global sourcing and trade of consumer goods can pivot to use for makingsheds and fibersheds relatively easily. Agricultural land may require little change if the region has been exporting crops. The transition is to instead direct crops to clothing (and food) production for consumers within the region. Shipping and storage facilities used in the global consumer goods system can be flexed into processing and distribution facilities for regional goods.

Guided by Indigenous wisdom, making- and fibersheds generate respect for and reciprocity with nature. Like with foodsheds and energysheds, these regional consumer goods systems depend on what is locally available. Manufacturers and makers are confronted with limits to natural resources and must carefully steward them to fulfill human needs in a sustainable way. Land use changes support this cultural reset that can spread to other businesses, organizations, and consumers.

Reset Culture Through Local Rental Businesses and Lending Libraries

Resetting culture to support a place-based consumer goods system involves centering community, sharing, and resource conservation. Rental businesses and lending libraries can reshape culture in these ways and decrease the production of new goods.

Local sporting goods and outdoor stores in most cities and towns provide a model for rental businesses being part of a place-based consumer goods system. These stores support the sharing of goods through rental services. Last Minute Gear in San Francisco rents camping supplies and outdoor gear and also maintains a library of donated gear that can be borrowed for free. Sports Basement, a locally owned set of stores in the San Francisco Bay Area, rents equipment for snow sports, biking, camping, backpacking, water sports, tennis, outdoor events, and even picnics.

Like camping gear, many tools are only needed once or twice a year. Community tool cooperatives or tool lending libraries can fill this need. These lending services prevent community members from having to buy tools they rarely use for carpentry, landscaping, car repair, cleaning, electrical, and other projects. The Denver Tool Library stocks over five thousand tools and lends them to members who pay $100 annually for the service and access to workshops and classes. Community tool cooperatives also bring neighbors together to share ideas, skills, and knowledge and help each other with projects.

The lending library in Berkeley, California, is part of its actual public library system. In addition to tools, it lends out cooking equipment like bread makers, food processors, and canning materials. The tool lending catalog is easily searchable on the public library's website. Attaching lending libraries to places people otherwise visit increases opportunities for people to use them.

Lending libraries can include all sorts of items, as the Share Shed, also known as a Library of Things, in Devon, United Kingdom, demonstrates. The mobile library travels weekly through Devon and surrounding towns to provide easy access to things people occasionally need. The over 350 items in the Share Shed include drills, gazebos, chocolate fountains, carpet cleaners, dehumidifiers, and hedge trimmers. For a small annual donation on a sliding scale, residents become members and can rent items weekly for a small fee. Share Shed reports that its 3,100-plus members have saved over 420,000 English pounds since its inception.[31] When people have easy access to rental businesses and lending libraries that save them money, they are motivated to use these services.

Reset Culture Through Secondhand Stores and Community Exchanges

Secondhand stores and community exchanges add another layer of recirculating goods in a place-based consumer goods system. When people no longer need or want an item in good condition, they can sell it to a secondhand store or bring it to a community exchange. Access to these stores and exchanges helps foster a culture of buying less new stuff.

Buying secondhand, or thrifting, is experiencing a generational transformation. Millennials and Gen Z are buying used goods over new items two and a half times more than previous generations.[32] The apparel resale market is growing around twenty times faster than the new apparel market.[33] The growth is expected to continue, doubling the market size in less than five years.

Secondhand apparel or clothing thrift stores are easy to find in many cities. They are particularly numerous in cities and towns with colleges and universities. A trio of students from Vanderbilt University wrote a guide to their favorite thrift stores in Nashville for clothes shopping.[34] They were inspired to get out and see all these stores to build their dream wardrobe at prices they could afford. Their list included nine stores, all within about three miles of campus. Three of the stores were within close walking distance. Abundant, accessible secondhand stores make buying used clothing easy and fun.

Secondhand stores sell many other types of goods. Nonprofit SCRAP in San Francisco has been a depot for secondhand arts, crafts, and educational supplies since 1976. In Portland, Oregon, Tool Shed Ted's is a popular spot to buy used hammers, rakes, shovels, ladders, and other home and garden tools. Octogenarian and owner of the tool shed, Ted Hill, ran a vintage shop in the building for a couple of decades before turning it into a tool shop over thirty years ago.

Community exchanges are another way to extend the life cycle of consumer goods. These nonmonetized exchanges emphasize interaction and community building while efficiently redistributing the societal abundance of material goods.

The Buy Nothing Project supports forming and self-organizing neighborhood groups around a "hyper-local gift economy." The project connects people to neighborhood groups on its app. Members of a neighborhood group post things they no longer need or want and acquire items for free from other members. The rules are simple: no buying or selling, and all pickups and drop-offs must occur within the group's jurisdiction. Ten years after launching in 2013, the Buy Nothing Project was engaging 7.5 million members across 128,000 communities with the support of 13,000 volunteers.[35] The rapid growth of the network reflects the yearning for community, protecting the environment, and steering away from consumerism.

In-person community events are also great ways to promote interaction among neighbors and exchange material goods. The nonprofit GrowNYC supports Stop'N'Swap events across the city. Volunteers sort through donated items at each swap and organize them on tables. In one 2019 event alone in the Queens borough, 5,064 pounds of items were donated, and about 81 percent of that volume was acquired by new owners.[36] The Friends of Duboce Park in San Francisco hosts an annual tag sale in the park in which neighbors donate goods from their closets and garages. The items are sold at bargain prices at the one-day event, and the proceeds go toward park improvement.

Reset Culture Through Repair Cafés and "Right to Repair" Laws

Repair cafés provide another direct way to reduce the purchasing of new consumer goods. These pop-up events counter corporate manufacturers' and retailers' planned obsolescence strategies. Local repair cafés utilize volunteers with a knack for repairing things. The volunteers fix broken items brought in by nearby residents. Repairing goods that have served a person well allows the person to treasure them longer and avoid buying new stuff.

Building on a tradition of periodic repair events around the world, Martine Postma started the first repair café in Amsterdam in 2009. There are now more than two thousand local repair cafés across the globe, many of which are supported by the Repair Café Foundation that Postma started.[37] At a repair café, clothes, furniture, electric appliances, bicycles, toys, and other items can be repaired for free. These cafés also provide instructions on how to make repairs, increasing the capacity of community members to repair things.

Libraries provide settings for repair cafés. The Elkridge Library in Howard County, Maryland, hosts a repair café as part of its overall support for helping people share and treasure material goods. The library rents tools and provides a makerspace for patrons to repair and create goods. Likewise, the San Francisco Public Library hosts events to fix bikes and clothing.

In addition to saving resources and preventing waste, repair cafés and events foster community bonds. At the quarterly pop-up repair café in Palo Alto, California, the ringing of a handbell signals a successful repair. The joy of repairing something in community is felt by all present.

Despite all of these efforts, many products are difficult to repair because of planned obsolescence, computerization of goods, and manufacturers limiting access to parts, tools, and service information. The Repair Café Foundation gathers data on hard-to-repair products to provide input on policy changes such as "right to repair" legislation. These laws require companies to manufacture products for easy repair.

"Right to repair" laws are being proposed and garnering support. In 2023, New York made electronic devices repairable by law. "Right to repair" laws can catalyze more repair cafés, events, and businesses and strengthen the culture around making goods last.

Reset Culture Through the Slow Consumerism Movement

A slow consumerism movement is also taking place, and it can inspire people to want less new stuff and to reduce waste. Slow fashion, for example, is simply slowing down the frequency of clothes purchasing and buying fewer, more durable items. The movement helps people create a pause before buying something new for one's wardrobe. At such a moment, a person can reflect on a clothing item's durability, feel to their skin, and how many times they might wear it.

Emma Kidd started the fashion detox challenge in which participants refrained from buying clothes for ten weeks. This challenge, launched in 2019, involved one hundred undergraduate students majoring in fashion. The student participants didn't purchase new clothing for a trimester, wrote a weekly blog, and demonstrated quick adaptation to creative, sustainable clothing behaviors.

Using the KonMari Method is a trend that supports the slow consumerism movement. Started by Marie Kondo, the method has become an extremely popular way for people to tidy up their homes and let go of items that no longer bring them joy. The logical extension is not to go out and buy more stuff but to treasure what you have.

Minimalism has also been gaining attention and deters consumerism. Joshua Fields Millburn and Ryan Nicodemus have reached twenty million people through their books, blog, podcast show, and documentary on minimalism. They explain the benefits of minimalism: "Minimalism is a tool that can assist you in finding freedom. . . . Freedom from the trappings of the consumer culture we've built our lives around. . . . We tend to give too much meaning to our things forsaking our health, our relationships, our passions, our personal growth, and our desire to contribute beyond ourselves."[38] Minimalism may be too big of a leap for many people today. However, its merits, as popularized by Milburn, Nicodemus, and others, are growing in appeal to many dissatisfied with society's emphasis on accumulating stuff.

Ultimately, the cultural reset involves identifying less and less as consumers. Letting go of consumerism helps people feel less separated from the people and places around them. Experiences over material goods take people in the direction of connection to community, nature, and each other, promoting more lasting happiness.

Leverage Other Systems

Other place-based systems help reduce the consumption of material goods. The transportation, nature, and community space systems (chaps. 6–8) provide the antidote to consumerism. Safe biking and walking infrastructure and abundant, attractive, and activated public spaces entice people to get outside and have meaningful and fun experiences. As discussed throughout this book, these types of experiences provide a more lasting sense of happiness and can replace the more short-term dopamine boosts people get from shopping.

The regional character of the place-based food and building energy systems (chaps. 9 and 10) is similar to that of the consumer goods system and presents potentialities for synergizing these systems. Planning for these systems together builds collective power among advocates in pushing for land use that integrates energy, food, and consumer goods systems across a region. The systems can form a circular economy that minimizes energy, food, and material waste and conserves resources. Additionally, agriculture is the basis of the food system (chap. 10) and the clothing and textile segment of the consumer goods system. Agriculture can be utilized in the region to maximize benefits to both.

Part 3

CATALYZING PLACE-BASED SYSTEMS CHANGE

Just when the caterpillar thought the world was over, it became a butterfly.

—Chuang Tzu, Taoist philosopher

As part 2 demonstrated, there are many ways systems-change strategies are building momentum toward and creating place-based systems. Many examples in part 2 showed the systems-change levers in action and their impact on places and how people live. You may have wanted more details from some of these examples or have been curious about how these changes get set in motion and then realized.

Part 3 fills that gap and provides the "how" of systems change, which lies in the work of systems-change catalysts. Place-based systems change is elusive without employing the four featured catalysts: strategic collaboration among organizations, systems-oriented government, place-based education, and personal change. Collectively, these catalysts pull the levers of systems change synergistically.

Bringing organizations together through strategic collaboration (chap. 12) is essential. Successful collaboratives enact change themselves, build power, and pressure government to make policy and funding decisions supportive of place-based systems. To enact systems change, local governments must not only respond to the demands of collaboratives but also be reorganized into systems-oriented government (chap. 13).

Building a place-based society that lasts requires education and personal change. As another catalyst, place-based education (chap. 14) prepares hearts and minds for the society we need while engaging students in real-world projects that help build place-based systems now. Part 3 and this book conclude with a focus on personal change (chap. 15). Every one of us can be a catalyst in our personal and professional lives. When we attach a systems mindset to changing ourselves, we increase our ability to be effective catalysts.

STRATEGIC COLLABORATION

> If one tree fruits, they all fruit—there are no soloists. Not one tree in a grove, but the whole grove; not one grove in the forest, but every grove; all across the county and all across the state. The trees act not as individuals, but somehow as a collective. Exactly how they do this, we don't yet know. But what we see is the power of unity. What happens to one happens to us all. We can starve together or feast together. All flourishing is mutual.

—Robin Wall Kimmerer, "The Council of Pecans," *Braiding Sweetgrass*

Since 2016, my professional life has involved designing, facilitating, evaluating, and researching place-based collaboration at the city, county, regional, and state levels. In this chapter, I'll share examples and insights from that work and explain how place-based collaboration can catalyze systems change.

I came to this work after researching transportation behavior and sustainability more broadly. It became clear that many organizations strategically working together were required to change the systems holding harmful human behavior patterns in place. Since then, I've been fortunate to help groups of place-based organizations collaborate in ways that shift power, transform land use, reset culture, and leverage other systems. Some collaboratives have worked well and continue to thrive, while others struggled to get off the ground or lost momentum. Through it all, I've learned much about what is needed for effective strategic collaboration and how it can be a powerful catalyst for systems change.

* * *

Bringing organizations together around systems change is critical to addressing big problems, but it is not easy work. Inertia, politics, and status quo resistance can squash the belief that change is possible. If collaborative work can get over these hurdles, formidable challenges and uncertainty still await.

Nonprofit leaders, staff, and others invested in social change also suffer from collaboration fatigue. Many have spent considerable time in a past collaboration that did not lead to the desired change. After a successful event jointly planned by a group of community-based organizations in a project I supported, the host organization suggested that the collaboration continue and build toward larger goals. One of the executive directors immediately reacted by stating that it was unnecessary and that their organization was already doing the work. There was a lot to unpack in the statement, but one thing was clear: There can be intense wariness of collaboration.

If a group is trying to start a collaborative, they can better convince others to join if they can articulate how it will differ from previous collaborations. Through my work and utilizing research and analyses by others who support collaborative efforts, I have discovered conditions that lead to effective, efficient, and impactful place-based collaboration.

Essential Conditions for Place-Based Collaboration

There are a variety of useful frameworks that identify conditions for success in collaboration, such as the well-used Collective Impact framework. I've applied, adapted, and expanded on these frameworks across projects. Through those iterations, I developed the *Essential Conditions for Place-Based Collaboration* (see table 12.1).

TABLE 12.1   Essential conditions for place-based collaboration

Community partnership	Structure the collaborative process and decision-making to include community leaders and members as equal partners
Trusting, valued relationships	Prioritize the cultivation of relationships built on trust and value
Shared, place-based vision	Establish a vision around improving a place that brings diverse stakeholders and perspectives to the cause and inspires them to stay committed with a network mindset
Systems-change strategies	Integrate systems-change levers into collaborative strategies
Alignment with coordination	Frequently discuss, assess, and improve alignment across stakeholders; enable aligned action through coordination
Shared accountability	Determine and regularly use metrics that assess progress with strategies and overall impact; seek feedback on processes and the health of relationships
Joint governance with backbone support	Employ structure for participation and decision-making with clearly defined roles; provide backbone staff with time to facilitate, coordinate, and monitor the collaboration

Many well-intended collaboratives (or coalitions or alliances) have failed to have the desired impact that motivates continued participation. Some collaboratives become learning networks where participants share common interests, build relationships, and learn from each other. Although these networks can benefit participants, they fall short of collective action and catalyzing systems change. The seven conditions outlined in this chapter turn collaboration into systems-level impact.

The foundation for these conditions is a belief in the collective power that can emerge from a strategic partnership. We'll first explore the idea of collective power in strategic collaboration and then examine the conditions for place-based collaboration that depend on this cornerstone.

Collective Power

We must find new avenues to overcome political and social divisions that support the status quo and build collective power. Emily Kawano, codirector of the Wellspring Cooperative Corporation, and Julie Matthaei, cofounder of the US Solidarity Economy Network, explain the transformation that can occur through the metaphor of how a butterfly comes to be: "When a caterpillar makes its cocoon, it starts to form imaginal cells, each with the potential to become a part of the emergent butterfly. At the beginning, the caterpillar's immune system perceives them as alien and kills them off. But as they find each other and clump together, they gain strength and together build a butterfly."[1] We can find each other in the places where we live, build ties, and work together toward a shared transformative purpose like imaginal cells.

A shared understanding of the myriad benefits of altering a system can form connections among organizations and people who don't typically cross paths. Changing the transportation system, for example, has benefits that appeal not just to transportation advocates but also to organizations working on housing, community life, public health, social justice, education (travel to and from school), and more. Alliances that unite organizations across areas of concern are essential to building sufficient power to overcome the status quo and make lasting change.

San Francisco Children and Nature started in 2016 and still thrives today with its focus on low-income children's access to nature in the city. As the original facilitator of the collaborative, I witnessed firsthand how it came together. The desire to equitably improve nature connection for children and youth in San Francisco engaged stakeholders from different fields and lines of work. The government agencies and nonprofits involved came from parks and recreation, public health, urban planning, formal education, youth development, environmental education, and the mayor's office. The intersection of children, nature, equity, and making the city a better place to live has been a winning formula for building collective power.

The collective push of San Francisco Children and Nature's partners has resulted in a measurable impact on the ground. As of 2024, twenty-one early childhood education play spaces were fully renovated for nature connection, over twelve thousand people had been engaged in hands-on nature programming, more than sixteen hundred tree stumps were repurposed for nature play, and nearly three hundred early childhood educators had been trained in nature-based education.[2] The collaboration has helped inspire a "renaturing" citywide movement with an ambitious goal of San Francisco's land being 30 percent biodiverse green space by 2030.

Building enough collective power for impact may be easier to achieve than we think. A growing number of studies suggest a relatively low threshold of involvement in creating a tipping point for making societal change. Experimental research by Professor Damon Centola and colleagues found that the majority's opinion can change when around 25 percent of group members adopt a social norm.[3] In *Full Ecology*, authors Mary Clare and Gary Ferguson shared research that shows when about 10 percent of the population decides there is a better way, a tipping point for cultural change can occur.[4] Even more encouraging, Harvard University political scientist Erica Chenoweth argued that engaging 3.5 percent of a population could lead to a win, citing historical studies of what it took to overthrow dictatorships.[5] Although these tipping points do not signify complete systems change, they suggest that building power that leads to systems change is within reach.

Placed-based organizations pulling together can build sufficient power to change the status quo in their communities, cities, and regions. Within the collaborative, power must also be shifted and equitably distributed, which brings us to the first essential condition of place-based collaboration: community partnership.

Community Partnership

Community leaders and members need to be equal partners with local government, institutions, and other organizations in the collaborative process and decision-making. It is the right thing to do and necessary to achieve systems-level impact. The population a place-based coalition or collaborative intends to impact can be considered the community. Sharing power with organizations and people from communities who have been the least served by the existing system should be a priority for any collaboration.

Applying a place-based systems lens to community partnership helps identify specific populations to include in a collaborative. A housing systems alliance
involves people vulnerable to displacement (chap. 4). A business and work system collaborative includes local businesses, workers, and community financial
institutions (chap. 5). A food system coalition involves Black, Indigenous, and
people of color, whether as farmers, community members, or both (chap. 10).

Place-based systems will require changes to lifestyles and daily choices, so
involving community in leading this change is critical. Revamped system elements such as public transit, nature spaces, or microgrids are more likely to be
used and improve people's lives when the community helps shape them. However, due to decades of disinvestment and broken promises, communities of color
and low-income communities may be reluctant to participate.

As an outside facilitator, I helped guide the start of a collaborative that was to
decide the future of a 135-acre urban nature parcel in northeast Oklahoma City.
We formed a steering committee of about a dozen members, three of whom were
leaders from the historically Black community that bordered the property.

In the first meeting, I laid out a plan for community engagement in which
I would facilitate listening sessions via Zoom and we would use that input to
develop a shared vision. That plan quickly vanished. One member voiced concern about the speed and format of these processes, and others agreed. I grew
concerned about the growing scope of the project and losing control of the process. I worried about how we would get to a shared vision for the property.

Although I had worked on community engagement and building trust among
stakeholders in many projects, I had to listen, learn, and pivot to help advance
this one. The three community leaders requested a meeting with the project
coordinator and me. In our conversation, they shared their frustrations over historic underinvestment in their neighborhood and how the few developments
that had taken place were imposed on their community. They had been asked to
share their input and ideas multiple times and saw nothing happen repeatedly.
There was no reason to think this would be different. They added that something
did not seem particularly right with this project. The elephant in the room turned
out to be me! I, a white male from San Francisco, had been hired by a foundation
to facilitate the process. They felt that the plan for the property had already been
decided and that I was there to shepherd it through a faux process.

At first, I didn't know what to do. But then, in partnership with one of the
community leaders, we overhauled the process. At the next steering committee
meeting, the three community leaders shared the history of disinvestment and
systemic racism experienced by their community and their concerns about the
current process. We decided to change my role and the project outcome. I would
not conduct listening sessions. The shared vision would be more of an articulated

statement of shared interests from the institutions, organizations, and individuals on the steering committee. Once more funding was secured, consultants from the community would conduct the listening sessions, gather input, and compare it to the steering committee's ideas.

We wanted to avoid an unnecessary gap between the community and the committee's ideas for the property. We recruited more community leaders to join the committee. From then on, half of the committee came from the local community.

In this process, we integrated what collaborative leaders Jennifer Blatz, Byron White, and Professor Mark Joseph call *community authority*. In their article on the topic, they reflected on shortcomings in integrating equity and inclusion in their past partnerships and how they rectified it in ongoing collaboratives. As they shared, community authority is not an either-or proposition; instead, "institutional leaders must empower residents and grassroots leaders as peers with shared authority, shared responsibility, and shared accountability. . . . Neither an institutional solution that shuts out community authority nor a community organizing model that does not effectively deploy institutional assets can realistically effect transformational change."[6] In the northeast Oklahoma City collaborative, we struck a balance between community and institutional membership. We had to alter the power imbalances with intention and move slowly to build trust. In the process, community experience and voice were brought to the center.

Place-based collaboration thrives when those most impacted by proposed projects are empowered to help shape them from start to finish. My hope for the 135-acre parcel of land in northeast Oklahoma City is that it meets the needs and reflects the wishes of the surrounding community. The community deserves an ample, accessible public space shaped by local needs and culture.

Trusting, Valued Relationships

Collaboration has been recognized as critical to social change for some time, but less so the role of relationships in it. A focus on building strong relationships keeps people motivated and engaged in a collaborative. It's hard to move the needle on social change without investing in relationships.

Trust and value are the foundation of successful place-based collaboratives. Trust building requires open discussion, clear intentions, and staying committed for the long run. Convening people around an important local issue can spark new conversations and ideas that permeate the daily work of organizations and individuals. When this level of involvement materializes, the value for one another increases.

Author adrienne maree brown shows what a murmuration of starlings teaches us about the importance of trusting, valued relationships in accomplishing something together:

> We move as a murmuration, the way groups of starlings billow, dive, spin, dance collectively through the air. . . . Here's how it works in a murmuration . . . each creature is tuned in to its neighbors, the creatures right around it in the formation. . . . Each creature is shifting direction, speed, and proximity based on the information of the other creatures' bodies. There is a deep trust in this: to lift because the birds around you are lifting, to live based on your collective real-time adaptations. . . . Imagine our movements cultivating this type of trust and depth with each other, having strategic flocking in our playbooks.[7]

When we center the cultivation of relationships in place-based collaboration, we can become a murmuration and go far together.

I've been fortunate to witness firsthand collective trust and value emerge and grow in place-based collaboration. When this occurs, collaboratives develop a self-sustaining power that leads to action and impact.

In 2018, I facilitated a two-day retreat with a group representing about fifteen animal welfare organizations across Oklahoma. Their shared concern was the needless euthanasia of cats and dogs in animal shelters. Before the retreat, many participants shared stories with me of past conflicts among organizations and remaining scars within the animal welfare community. This effort had to feel different to rebuild trust and value for one another. Through exercises and activities, they discovered they had much in common. They shared deep ties to Oklahoma, a desire to make it a better place for people and animals, and an understanding of why Oklahoma had one of the highest euthanasia rates for shelter pets in the country.

The group left the retreat feeling that something was different and that maybe they could work together effectively to address this complex problem. Led by this coalition that became known as Common Bonds, Oklahoma increased the save rate from 70 to 80 percent in three years, saving tens of thousands of dogs and cats. They set a shared goal of a 90 percent save rate. The positive relationships and teamwork have created a yearning to stay together beyond achieving their shared goal of decreased euthanasia. They committed to working together toward a broader vision. The partners want to help all communities in Oklahoma value the human-animal bond and embrace the connection between animal well-being and the quality of life in their communities.

Trusting, valued relationships can be elusive. In one collaboration I supported, a large nonprofit was reluctant to engage in discussion and seemed more of an observer than a participant. There had been a long-standing conflict between its leadership and that of another in the group. The nonprofit viewed the collaborative as a competitor, not as something to uplift all involved toward greater impact.

Organizational egos are a regular threat to effective collaboration. When an organization thinks it can be "the hero," its leadership and staff fail to value other participants. In return, the other organizations don't trust the "hero-motivated" organization. Collaborative participants, instead, must adopt a network mindset in which giving credit to others and subsuming organizational ego below the shared vision becomes the norm. Organizations that cannot participate in this way leave the collaborative, which happened in the above case.

Place-based collaboratives can help us restore faith in each other, community, and local institutions and develop collective efficacy. At their core, they build trust and value for one another, increasing our collective ability to change systems. The emphasis on competition and individuality shaped by capitalism, however, often gets in the way of the natural flow of collaboration. Other conditions are needed for place-based collaboration to counter these powerful forces and succeed.

Shared, Place-Based Vision

An effective shared, place-based vision motivates participation, cooperation over competition, and long-term commitment. The stakeholders who formed San Francisco Children and Nature had a rich exchange of ideas from the onset, leading to a vision they all could embrace: Nature for Every Child, Every Day. This shorthand for the vision became a citywide call to action. A shared, place-based vision for a collaborative lies at the intersection of place and addressing the issue(s) that brought organizations together. This combination can lead to a vision that serves as a "big tent," inspiring more to the cause and many to stay committed.

The vision of Berlin Streets for Everyone, an alliance of transportation, urban planning, and environmental policy organizations, is apparent in its name, with the addition of "for a people-friendly and climate-friendly Berlin." It further delineated its vision with a shared goal to halve the number of cars on Berlin's streets over ten years by 2030. The alliance's vision mobilized a wide swath of Berlin organizations and residents to register districts across Berlin for car-free streets.[8] Its demands have grown to include eliminating most automobile use in the fifty-five-square-mile city center. This additional vision spawned another group, Berlin Autofrei (discussed in chap. 7). Berlin Streets for Everyone aims to win transportation and community spaces systems change in its city, and its ambitious vision is mobilizing many organizations and additional coalitions.

A facilitated process helps ensure that all participants contribute to finding common ground in a vision. There must be time to hear and learn from diverse perspectives about current realities and aspirations for change. Discussing and bridging ideas can create a vision that helps stakeholders imagine what might be possible through collective action. The shared vision can acknowledge the present while providing a picture of a highly desired future. For example, car-oriented city streets could be reimagined into interconnected corridors for biking, scooting, and walking. The transformed street network could connect people to local businesses, schools, and nature and community spaces. An ambitious vision may never be fully achieved, but it motivates stakeholders to continue in its pursuit.

Developing a common vision brings stakeholders together in a less competitive, more cooperative spirit. A vision for improving the quality of life in a place can unify organizations and individuals across fields, sectors, and lived experiences in a particular region, county, city, or community.

Systems-Change Strategies

Meaningful movement toward a shared vision will be difficult if it is not grounded in systems-change levers. Part 2 provided many systems-change strategies based on these levers. Collaboratives that cut across multiple systems can apply the levers in creative, synergistic ways to increase the impact on their place.

Integrating the systems-change levers into collaborative strategies challenges stakeholders to think big and clarifies that collaboration is essential to creating a more transformative level of change. No organization can shift power, transform land use, reset culture, or leverage other systems alone in a place, but these things become possible by working together.

As with developing the shared vision, the diverse experiences of stakeholders from different fields and the community provide the collective insight to understand where and how to change systems. Devising collaborative strategies through a systems lens surfaces the conditions that produce and hold in place the problem(s) stakeholders are seeking to address. From such deliberation, systems-change strategies emerge.

When I work with groups at this stage, I lead them through a brainstorming activity. They first generate ideas about human behaviors related to the problems they seek to address and what behaviors they wish to see instead. With a large collaborative focused on helping victims of domestic violence, for example, ideas for problematic behaviors included keeping things in secrecy, living in fear, and being overpowered. The desired behaviors were utilizing services, belonging to a community, and feeling empowered. Participants then thought about how to use the systems-change levers to change the problematic behaviors into desired behaviors. For this collaboration, strategies emerged that included shifting power to the communities with the most domestic violence incidents, transforming land use through a new shelter with added space and programming, and resetting culture through expanding and improving services for children, families, and youth.

Partners may wish to focus on the most relevant and doable lever as a starting point in smaller collaborations. I saw this play out in five different city-school district teams in a countywide Safe Routes to School fellowship program I helped facilitate. Each team initially employed one lever to increase the number of students biking and walking to school in their jurisdiction. One team shifted power through robust community engagement at schools. Two teams changed land use through quick-build projects for pedestrian safety near schools. The other two teams reset culture through, respectively, an "Every Kid Deserves a Bike" program and the creation of walk- and bike-to-school maps. Collectively, these five teams built a foundation for systems change with one lever. When combined with other systems-change strategies going forward, small collaboratives have the potential to change the larger system and related human behavior.

In 2022, a coalition of organizations in San Francisco successfully organized to keep cars off a mile-and-a-half section of a street inside Golden Gate Park. This street section had become known as the JFK Promenade and was made car-free during the COVID-19 pandemic. Making it permanently car-free required defeating a measure placed in front of San Francisco voters to return the promenade to cars.

Local nonprofits joined forces in support of a permanent JFK Promenade. The city's Recreation and Parks Department played an important supporting role. This partnership employed systems-change strategies in the lead-up to the vote.

- It enlisted residents through neighborhood events and partnered with other community organizations and groups. This effort built collective power and helped shift power away from a powerful arts museum and other status quo groups that wanted cars to return to the street.
- Land use was transformed to include large seating areas throughout the promenade with varied amenities, including a community book library, ping-pong table, pianos, music stages, and a beer garden. Street murals and large sculptures were placed along the promenade.
- Culture was reset by activating the space and people having positive experiences walking, biking, skating, sitting, and otherwise being on the car-free street. Children and youth had ample room to learn how to ride bikes, roam safely, and play.

The strategies to shift power, transform land use, and reset culture were intentional and impactful. The measure was clearly defeated, with 65 percent of voters opposing it. The JFK Promenade became a permanent car-free, vibrant community space. Systems-change strategies set a collaborative effort on the path to overcoming systemic barriers that often thwart transformative change.

Alignment with Coordination

To implement a shared vision and systems-change strategies, alignment and coordination among stakeholders are necessary. Regularly discussing, assessing, and improving alignment is helpful to ensure that participating organizations are rowing in the same direction. Coordination can drive aligned action in which each partner's strengths determine their role and how they can best contribute to the collective effort. A saying that captures this important dynamic is "Do what you do best and connect to the rest."

With the Save JFK Promenade campaign, each organization took on unique responsibilities and regularly coordinated with the others. SF Bike helped with community organizing and bringing groups together around the same message. Walk SF helped organize events, rallies, and tabling in public places to educate the public. It gathered over ten thousand postcards from residents for delivery to San Francisco supervisors. Kid Safe SF led the political campaign logistics and fundraising. The Recreation and Parks Department made the physical changes that turned the street into a promenade and vibrant community space. Each organization focused on its strengths and did so in an intentional way to complement each other and build a successful movement.

* * *

Within a month of winning the ballot box, the city approved sixteen permanent Slow Streets (community spaces with only local, slow-car traffic allowed, as described in chap. 8) and another car-free street. A People's Slow Streets campaign led by the Save JFK nonprofit organizations, a senior and disability advocacy group, a citywide parks alliance nonprofit, and neighborhood groups from underserved communities helped push through these expansive wins. The impact of collaborative alignment and coordination to Save the JFK Promenade shows how a win can catalyze systemic change.

Shared Accountability

The time and energy to align and coordinate among stakeholders may wane if results are not regularly measured and assessed. Participants are motivated when they see tangible progress and are more likely to contribute if they have a sense of accountability to one another.

Shared accountability is often one of the most challenging parts of collaboration. Performance metrics help measure progress, but getting organizations to agree on them can be a struggle and is just the first step. Data must then be collected, and it can be hard to obtain in a format useful to stakeholders. Once data is captured, an analysis is needed to make sense of it and adapt strategies.

Keeping it simple is imperative. A key performance metric or two overall and for each collaborative strategy should suffice. I learned this the hard way with San Francisco Children and Nature. Guided by a national support organization, we devised a comprehensive list of different ways to measure nature connection for children and neighborhood nature elements. The amount of data was way too much for the collaborative to gather and seemed to contribute more to paralysis than action! Wishing to move forward, the working groups in the collaborative started planning and implementing aligned action without metrics. After all groups had gained traction and better defined what they would do, a narrowed-down list of metrics emerged: the number of nature exploration play spaces, educators trained in nature-based education, and people engaged in hands-on nature programming.

Having learned from this experience, I helped Common Bonds in Oklahoma develop a narrower set of performance metrics from the beginning. As discussed earlier, the overall metric was the save rate for shelter cats and dogs. Each working group determined its performance metric, which included the number of spay/neuter clinics and programs, district captains and community advocates, and shelters reporting data on their save rate. There was mixed success in gathering and utilizing this data due to shifting priorities and other challenges. In a process to modify the collaborative's strategy, three new working group–level metrics—certified communities, engaged government entities, and engaged animal shelters—were identified with criteria to measure each. These fit better with what each working group was doing and with systems-change strategies for resetting culture (communities adopting attitudes and behaviors), shifting power (pressure on government) and transforming land use (animal shelters).

In a place-based collaborative, accountability is about change at the collective level, whether in a neighborhood, city, county, region, or small state. Metrics are not used for specific interventions but are more holistic, intended to measure proxies for systems change. Changing what is measured for performance at certain junctures is almost inevitable due to the complex nature of the problems being addressed and evolving dynamics in the collaborative.

Joint Governance with Backbone Support

As a final condition, effective place-based collaboration requires well-designed governance and backbone support for overseeing and implementing the other conditions. Thoughtfully designed structure for participation and decision-making builds on and reinforces an equal partnership with the community and the cultivation of trusting, valued relationships. Clearly defined governance and roles help turn a shared vision and systems-change strategies into aligned, coordinated action with shared accountability.

A study of twenty-five well-established collective impact initiatives found backbone support to be instrumental for initiatives in achieving success and having an impact on target populations.[9] Backbone staff, such as a network facilitator, are particularly effective when frequently touching base with stakeholders, connecting stakeholders, and facilitating meetings where all perspectives are valued. All this work is done to advance the collaborative vision and strategies.

Governance structures vary depending on the size of the collaborative, available funding, and how much alignment and coordination are needed. As fully operational collaboratives aimed at place-based systems change, the two collaboratives profiled in this chapter have similar governance structures. Joint governance involves a steering committee that sets, aligns, and coordinates strategies and working groups that shape and implement the strategies. Common Bonds also has an advisory council to bring in perspectives from other fields on its work to jointly improve animal and community well-being. Most importantly, both collaboratives have a full-time director who wakes up each working day to focus on shepherding the collaborative effort. A backbone support organization—a foundation in one and a government agency in the other—funds and hosts the backbone staff.

ChangeScale was a collaborative for environmental education across the San Francisco Bay Area with a director and program coordinator for backbone support. Starting in 2012, ChangeScale provided well-attended forums, workshops, and other events, convening those interested in increasing environmental literacy in schools and other settings across the region. In addition, ChangeScale facilitated five local partnerships. Each partnership included a school district and local environmental education providers such as waste management businesses and parks agencies. They jointly worked to advance environmental literacy from kindergarten through twelfth grade. Many of these partnerships made considerable progress in expanding opportunities for place-based environmental learning in local schools.

In 2020, what had been an impactful, well-organized collaborative sadly imploded. ChangeScale experienced its first backbone staff transition in 2018 with a new director and program coordinator. Over time, communication and coordination between the backbone staff and the steering committee started to break down. These issues led to diminished trust and a lack of alignment among the stakeholders. The steering committee chair, director, and coordinator collectively resigned. The collaborative soon after went dormant, revived itself for a while, and has now ended.

Ultimately, there was an important lesson about governance in what happened. In its first six years, ChangeScale relied heavily on the director and coordinator and a few early leaders from the steering committee to move forward and progress. Those early committee leaders had mostly left before the staff leadership transition. The new director and coordinator were given significant autonomy without steering committee members being actively engaged. When the committee started to pay more attention, they expressed concerns over the direction of the collaborative, and trust began to wane. In the end, too much autonomy was given to the backbone staff, and too little communication and shared decision-making took place. Joint governance, or shared responsibility, with regular communication among partner organizations and backbone staff is critical for long-term success.

Effective governance and backbone support capitalize on participants' time and contributions. Well-facilitated meetings by backbone staff or partners leave participants energized, clear on the next steps, and growing in trust and value for one another.

Place-Based Collaboration for Regeneration

Place-based collaboration can be organized in ways that cut across systems and thus promote well-being across more aspects of people's lives and with broader potential to regenerate nature, community, and local economies. This fuller ecosystem approach incorporates two or more of the systems discussed in part 2, expanding possibilities for changing how people live and stemming our interrelated crises.

Place-based collaboration can start in one system and branch out to others. The Northern Manitoba Food, Culture, and Community Collaborative is helping build local food systems with the goal of community-led food security for the Indigenous people of northern Manitoba, Canada. Their collective work has broadened into the consumer goods system, focusing on locally produced goods and services for local use. Working with community partners to relearn traditional ways of local self-reliance is catalyzing community economic development and regional resilience across the food, consumer goods, and work systems.

The Seattle Good Business Network runs several initiatives that incorporate multiple systems. True to its name, the network advances local business and work opportunities. Seattle Restored turns vacant storefronts and windows into local pop-up shops and art installations. Seattle Made supports its seven hundred urban manufacturer and producer members, boosting the place-based work and consumer goods systems. The Sustainable Business and Circular Economy program brings community stakeholders and organizations together to address another aspect of localizing the consumer goods and work systems. The Good Food Economy and Good Kitchens initiatives connect food producers and businesses across the regional food system and promote local food consumption. The network shares the philosophy that binds its many initiatives: "With local ownership comes local accountability—local owners care about our place, just like we do. When we choose and cultivate diverse, local resources—food, energy, raw materials, finance, and other locally made goods and services—we develop a deep respect for and connection to the natural and human resources of our place."[10] Dozens of partners come together to change the work, consumer goods, and food systems to make it possible for people in Seattle to live increasingly connected to place. They are regenerating nature, community, and local economies in the process.

Drawdown Marin was formed in 2018 in Marin County, just north of San Francisco. It is a countywide collaborative to help drive down greenhouse gas emissions (GHGE) and prepare for climate change impacts. With the focus on a comprehensive county approach to climate, its collective work intersects with building energy, transportation, and food systems. Through a community-driven planning process involving more than 150 people, Drawdown Marin established a vision, mission, values, and six focus areas: renewable energy, transportation, buildings and infrastructure, local food and food waste, carbon sequestration, and climate-resilient communities. Six working groups were formed around these priority areas. By 2021, four projects—Zero Emissions Vehicles, Community Resilience Hubs, Marin Biomass Project, and the Marin Carbon Farming Initiative—had secured over $2 million in funding. In addition, two community-led projects that address GHGE and serve frontline communities were funded. Encouraged by the ability of Drawdown Marin to pull organizations and people together into meaningful action, the county government launched a climate action plan with ambitious 2030 goals and equity at the center.

As a final example, the Sustainable Neighborhood Action Program (SNAP) pairs a regional conservation authority with municipalities and community leaders across the Toronto, Canada, region to implement multiple place-based systems. Residents, businesses, groups, and institutions work within neighborhood or city networks to speed up the implementation of climate action and resiliency measures. With SNAP's support, the networks develop action plans. These local partnerships build momentum through quick-start local demonstration projects such as naturalized landscaping, rain harvesting, and renewable energy installation. Over time, SNAP supports larger projects in building energy efficiency retrofits and behaviors, renewable energy, urban forests, green infrastructure, water conservation, stormwater reuse in buildings, food production, and rainwater harvesting. SNAP catalyzes change across many systems—nature spaces, building energy, and food—in one region, neighborhood by neighborhood.

Breaking down silos among organizations and groups opens possibilities for systems change to make our places and world better. We get beneath the symptoms and break down the alienation that plagues our society and the ability to progress in addressing crises. As David Brooks puts it, "Trust is built and the social fabric is repaired when people form local relationships around shared tasks."[11] We can make significant progress toward place-based systems through strategic, place-based collaboration.

Aligning government to place-based systems is another means for catalyzing systems change and is the subject of chapter 13. Place-based collaboratives can exert their collective power to make government embrace and use its many tools to support place-based systems change.

SYSTEMS-ORIENTED GOVERNMENT

Creating a great city is not a technical or financial issue; it's an issue of political will. We need to put our money where our mouths are. There is no shortage of money; there is a lack of political will to bring it into alignment with our values and vision for our community. This is key.

When you say "no" to something, you say "yes" to something else. . . . We need to [understand] that if we're saying "no" to housing density, we're saying "yes" to sprawl, or that if we say "no" to a bike lane on our street, we're saying "yes" to air pollution.

—Gil Penalosa, 8 80 Cities

Emily Beach served on the Burlingame City Council for nine years. Burlingame is a suburban city of thirty thousand people in San Mateo County, about sixteen miles south of San Francisco. Emily now serves as the chief communications officer for the San Mateo County Transit District. She brings a strong commitment to local living, inclusivity, and sustainability to her public service.

Emily's life is centered on community connections. She and her family walk to parks from their house. Emily frequently gets around by bike or on foot and shops locally. She appreciates how Burlingame is set up with homes close to one another, walkable neighborhoods, and two downtown districts. Emily likes how these land uses facilitate people getting to know their neighbors and community members around the town. As a local leader, she seeks ways to enrich people's connections with the community, each other, and the environment.

As a local leader, Emily champions safe, convenient, and cost-effective alternatives to cars. Her case for bike and pedestrian infrastructure's cost-effectiveness compared to automobile infrastructure was described in chapter 6. During her tenure as Burlingame mayor, the city adopted its first-ever Bicycle-Pedestrian Plan. The plan included thirty new miles of bike infrastructure and eighty-two pedestrian improvements.

Emily has been an advocate for improving the local community spaces system. She supported Burlingame closing its two downtown streets to cars during COVID-19 in 2020. Emily wrote about it in an editorial: "We made a bold decision to close Burlingame Avenue and Broadway to cars, an unimaginable experiment a year ago. In addition to providing space for social distancing and commerce, we learned that creating pedestrian promenades—prioritizing people over automobiles—enhanced safety, vibrancy, and community."[1] Although these alterations were temporary, both streets remain vibrant with pedestrian priority and slow car traffic. Emily's advocacy for safe, engaging public spaces paid off in helping shepherd a vision for a new downtown square. This new community-gathering space is being built on a former parking lot in the Burlingame Avenue retail district. The planning process for the square was anchored in robust community engagement and input processes that helped galvanize the political will to make it happen.

Emily was also deeply involved in updating the City of Burlingame's general plan in 2019. The update promotes transit-oriented development with mixed-use zoning and affordable housing. Nature spaces that increase access to nearby nature and promote climate resilience were also part of the plan, as reflected in a shoreline park project in the city described in chapter 8. These are significant changes. As discussed in chapter 4, proposed changes to land use and the housing system, especially in suburban communities like Burlingame, often encounter fierce status quo resistance.

Emily's commitment to transportation systems change has led her to serve on six transportation-related regional and county boards, committees, and task forces. She understands how to work across jurisdictions to reduce car dependency. When Emily was the chairperson for the San Mateo County Transportation Authority, she helped direct investments in transit and bike networks that allow people to travel from city to city without a car. She served on the county's transportation demand management agency for over eight years. The mission of this agency is to reduce drive-alone vehicle trips. Emily has been a consistent, effective leader in her many public roles for transportation systems change.

* * *

Having highly engaged, visionary, yet grounded leaders like Emily is critical to place-based systems change. We need local government leaders who can help catalyze systems change that enables people to live more connected to place.

This chapter explores the essential role of government in realizing place-based systems. Aligning local government departments, planning, policy, and expenditures with place-based systems increases the likelihood of developing and sustaining those systems. Regional governance and federal and state governments play important supportive roles in making this happen. Political leaders who are systems change–oriented, like Emily Beach, help get the ball rolling and keep it on course.

Systems Change–Oriented Political Leadership

Before discussing the political leaders who make a difference with changing systems, it's important to acknowledge a fundamental challenge. Electing leaders willing to change systems can be difficult. Corporate and other large donors often get in the way of electing these visionary, courageous leaders. As discussed throughout this book, these powerful interests largely benefit from the status quo. More often than not, they seek to fund the campaigns of politicians who will keep current systems intact.

Campaign finance reform and conflict-of-interest regulation (discussed in chap. 3) are necessary to address these persistent political obstacles to systems change. The size of campaign donations and lobbying to further corporate dominance must be strictly limited. At the same time, we cannot wait for this scale of political reform to occur. As laid out in chapter 12, organizing coalitions of local groups and people in support of place-based systems change can help build up a voter base to challenge the status quo. Working on political reform and coalition building gets communities on the path to electing visionary, systems change–oriented leaders over status quo politicians.

When elected officials and other government leaders are committed to systemic change, place-based transformation previously thought impossible happens. It's not easy work. These leaders must persevere through challenges like local resistance to additional housing. In some cases, they may not get reelected or lose their job, but the changes they helped put in place remain.

The hostile reaction to a proposal to build 315 apartments in the affluent suburb of Lafayette, California, was shared in chapter 4. The proposed project included sixty-three affordable units and was next to a regional transit station.

The resistance to the project was eventually overcome, thanks to one government leader's courage and sacrifice. Steven Falk, Lafayette's city manager for almost twenty-nine years, understood the San Francisco Bay Area's housing supply crisis. He was concerned about its disproportionate impact on low-income families and individuals and people of color. Falk was fed up with the pushback and decided to take a stand in favor of the proposal. The backlash was intense, leading to a reprimand for Falk from the city council. Yet he did not give up. Falk eventually got people to see his side of the issue and deftly maneuvered through the political process. In 2020, the Lafayette City Council voted 4 to 1 to approve the apartment project.

This was a big win for a place-based housing system, but the fallout from the controversy eventually led to Falk's resignation. In his letter of resignation, he wrote, "All cities—even small ones—have a responsibility to address the most significant challenges of our time: climate change, income inequality, and housing affordability. I believe that adding multifamily housing at the BART station is the best way for Lafayette to do its part, and it has therefore become increasingly difficult for me to support, advocate for, or implement policies that would thwart transit density. My conscience won't allow it."[2] Every leader needs to make their own calculation. Falk was willing to risk his job. He showed that city leaders do not need to give in to vocal pressure and helped tip the balance toward the project's approval. Falk has since taught at the University of California, Berkeley, and served as interim city manager in cities near Lafayette. These cities and university students are now benefiting from his housing system change experience, expertise, and courage.

Anne Hidalgo was elected the city of Paris's first woman mayor in 2014 and reelected in 2020. The dramatic transformation of Paris's streets (see introduction and chap. 6), revitalization of community and nature spaces along the Seine River and through urban gardens (see introduction), expansion of urban food production (see chap. 9), and efforts to build more affordable housing and fifteen-minute neighborhoods (see introduction) have all happened under her leadership. It wasn't easy work. Hidalgo and her team encountered a campaign of strong resistance from the status quo, especially those habituated to driving cars. However, many other residents were excited about the changes, especially after experiencing some of the initial projects. Hidalgo was able to stay the course and make significant changes across transportation, food, nature spaces, and community spaces systems in a rapid fashion.

Enrique Peñalosa was the mayor of Bogotá, Colombia, from 1998 to 2001 and 2016 to 2019. He oversaw Bogotá's transition from a dangerous, violent, corrupt city to one that cultivated its residents' well-being. Peñalosa and his team transformed land into community spaces with a network of parks and pedestrian plazas and new libraries, schools, and nurseries. Under his leadership, the city catalyzed transportation systems change. They made significant investments in bike infrastructure and bus rapid transit. Highway expansion stopped, fuel taxes increased, and drivers could not commute by car more than three days a week. Car dependency dropped across the city.

In Charles Montgomery's book *Happy City*, Peñalosa explained his motivation for leading these changes: "We need to walk, just as birds need to fly. We need to be around other people. We need beauty. We need contact with nature. And most of all, we need not be excluded. We need some sort of equality."[3] This quality-of-life vision inspired residents to support big changes, including shifting away from car use. Bogotá has become a safer, healthier, and happier place to live, with more inclusive, equitable communities.

Leaders like Beach, Falk, Hidalgo, and Peñalosa helped catalyze shifts in power, land use transformations, and cultural resets across multiple systems. In doing so, they made their places better for people, communities, nature, and local economic activity. They helped grow support for systems change by focusing on the well-being of all residents (or, in the case of Falk, the well-being of people who deserved to live in Lafayette).

* * *

Visionary leaders can help local government strategically apply the systems-change levers. However, they will struggle to create lasting change unless government is oriented around place-based systems. Otherwise, it's like trying to fly a new plane on an old engine. Given the complexity and slow-moving nature of government, this may be the most radical idea in this book. Moving in this direction, however, creates the durable foundation we need for government to be a systems-change catalyst.

Government bureaucracy, policy, and processes have become complicated and cumbersome. It's hard to find a clear purpose or direction in governments with so many specialized structures (see the two cities in table 13.1 as examples) and functions. The organization and processes of government need to be disrupted (note, this does not mean decimated like the Trump administration and Elon Musk attempted to do in 2025).

Place-based systems provide a means of integrating structure, planning, policies, and funding around essential goals. Government oriented around the systems that shape how we live (the eight place-based systems featured in chaps. 4–11) would both simplify and bring coherence to its operations. The goal of place-based systems to improve people's well-being and regenerate nature, communities, and local economies can serve as a unifying purpose to build alignment and synergies among all parts of a government. For shorthand, we'll refer to the unifying purpose as well-being and regeneration. Orienting government around place-based systems increases its potential to catalyze systems change.

Systems-Oriented Structure

Well-prepared, hardworking, and skillful leaders and staff can be found throughout local government. The work they do, however, is often siloed into specialized functions. I've worked with government agencies with ambitious plans that get quickly stymied by other agencies or departments. What typically ensues is a lost sense of agency and a retreat from trying to make meaningful change. The emphasis on specialization presents a significant barrier to transformative change catalyzed by government.

Large city governments have become known for their complicated, unwieldy bureaucracies. Perhaps no city exemplifies this more than my home city of San Francisco.

The City and County of San Francisco have over 180 different entities for a city with a population of approximately nine hundred thousand. In 2023, the city government included fifty-three departments, fifty-six boards and commissions, and seventy-four advisory bodies.[4] San Francisco is unique in combining two levels of government, city and county, into one. The city and county also run large enterprise departments like the airport and port. Nonetheless, the government structure of San Francisco is absurdly complex. While this structure might quite possibly have the most government entities per capita in the country, most other large cities are also mired in bureaucracy. Amid such a structure, the default becomes working in narrow silos and missing synergistic opportunities for greater impact on systems and people's lives.

Smaller cities and towns have less complicated bureaucracies but are still highly departmentalized. Burlingame, where Emily Beach served on the city council, has seventeen departments for a city with 31,000 residents.[5] The town is one of twenty cities within San Mateo County. The county government is composed of thirty-two departments.[6] When combining city and county government, Burlingame is overseen by forty-nine departments.

Despite the range in government structure and population size, these two cities and their respective county governments share one thing in common with each other and local governments across the United States: many silos without a coherent framework. What if rather than a complicated web of city and county departments, divisions, agencies, and commissions, local government could be efficiently organized for a positive systemic impact on people's lives?

Local government structured around place-based systems provides a way. Aligning structure with place-based systems simplifies the structure and keeps it aimed at promoting well-being and regeneration. Fewer departments and silos would help government leaders and employees more effectively work with each other. A structure organized around place-based systems that relate most directly to people's lives would also make government more accessible to residents.

Flexing and combining place-based systems to encompass and integrate the work of city and county governments could lead to the following departments: Housing and Community Development; Economic and Workforce Development; Transportation; Public Spaces; Food and Agriculture; Building Energy; and Circular Economy. Table 13.1 shows how our two examples of local government—Burlingame and San Francisco—could be incorporated into these proposed place-based system departments.

Four core departments round out local government's essential functions and support effective governance. These proposed departments are Administrative and Legal Services, Public Safety, Family and Health Services, and Oversight and Accountability (see the bottom of table 13.1). These core departments form a foundation for the government on which a systems-oriented structure can be built.

Adding in the seven place-based system-aligned departments mentioned above, a local government would entail less than a dozen departments. The context would determine whether the departments would be at the city, county, or both levels. For example, San Francisco has a city agency and a county authority overseeing transportation. Whether those remain separate would depend on whether the current division gets in the way of meaningful change and effective operation of the local transportation system.

TABLE 13.1 Systems-oriented structure

DEPARTMENT (TYPE)	SAN FRANCISCO, CALIFORNIA (CITY AND COUNTY)	BURLINGAME, CALIFORNIA + SAN MATEO COUNTY[a]
Housing and community development (housing system)	Planning; Mayor's Office (Housing and Community Development); Community Investment and Infrastructure; Homelessness and Supportive Housing; Rent Board; Short-Term Rentals; Building Inspection; Historic Preservation; Treasure Island Development; Human Services Agency (Housing and Shelter)	Community Development; Planning; Building Code Compliance *Housing; County Manager (Project Development); Public Health (Environmental Health Services-Housing); Sustainability (Livable Communities-Home for All; Waste Reduction-Construction & Demolition)*
Economic and workforce development (local business and work system)	Economic and Workforce Development; Small Business; Arts, Entertainment, and Film Commissions; Grant for the Arts; Cannabis; Public Health (Environmental Health, Inspections); Human Services Agency (Benefits and Family Support); Financial Empowerment; Adult Probation	Economic Development *Human Services Agency (Employment Services); Public Health (Environmental Health Services, Body Art, Massage, Food Businesses); Sustainability (Green Business)*
Transportation (transportation system)	Municipal Transportation Agency; County Transportation Authority; Airport; Port	Public Works *Sustainability (Livable Communities-Active Transportation, Commute Alternatives; Climate Change-EV Charge Up)*
Public spaces (community spaces system and nature spaces system)	Recreation and Parks; Public Works; Community Challenge Grants; Library; Animal Care and Control; Port (Recreation); War Memorial; Museums; Mayor's Office (Neighborhood Services)	Parks and Recreation; Public Works; Library *County Parks; County Manager-Community Affairs (Community Engagement); Public Health (Environmental Health Services-Water Protection and Land Use; Public Pools); Library; Sustainability (Climate Change-Sea Change SMC)*

(continued)

TABLE 13.1 (continued)

DEPARTMENT (TYPE)	SAN FRANCISCO, CALIFORNIA (CITY AND COUNTY)	BURLINGAME, CALIFORNIA + SAN MATEO COUNTY[a]
Food and agriculture (food system)	Human Services Agency (Food Assistance); Recreation and Parks (Urban Agriculture); Public Health (Environmental Health-Agriculture)	*Agriculture, Weights and Measures; Sustainability (Waste Reduction-Composting/ Community Gardens)*
Building energy (building energy system)	Public Utilities Commission; Environment; Building Inspection (Energy Conservation)	Public Works; *Sustainability Sustainability; Peninsula Clean Energy*
Circular economy (consumer goods system)	Environment (Zero Waste and Toxics & Health); Port (Maritime-Shipping); Public Health (Environmental Health)	Sustainability *Public Health (Environmental Health Services-Hazardous Materials, Household Hazardous Waste, Pollution Prevention, Medical and Solid Waste); Sustainability (Waste Reduction)*
Administrative and legal services (core)	City Administrator (most of the 62 divisions); Board of Supervisors; Mayor's Office; Treasurer-Tax Collector; Attorney, Courts and Jury (multiple entities); Committee on Information Technology; City Hall Events; Human Resources; Employee Retirement System; Elections; Assessor-Recorder; Law Library; Civic Engagement and Immigrant Affairs	Finance; Clerk; Human Resources; City Manager; City Attorney *Board of Supervisors; Assessor, County Clerk-Recorder and Chief Elections Officer; Coroner; County Counsel; County Managers Office/Clerk of the Board; Court; District Attorney; Private Defender; Probation; Human Resources; Information Services; County Manager-Community Affairs (Immigrant Services); Revenue Services*
Public Safety (core)	Fire; Police; Sheriff; Emergency Management	Fire; Police; Sheriff *Public Safety Communications*
Family and health services (core)	Public Health (Health Network; City Clinic; Behavioral Health; Maternal, Child and Adolescent Health; Gender Health; Emergency Medical Services; Disease Prevention Control; HIV Health; Healthy SF) Human Services Agency (Early Care and Education; Child Care and Family Services; Disability and Aging Services; Health Service System; Benefits and Family Support); Mayor's Office on Disability; Children, Youth and Families; Child Support Services; First 5; Juvenile Probation; Public Health (children and youth-related community partnerships); liaison function with School District	*Human Services Agency; Public Health (multiple service divisions) Child Support Services; Human Services Agency (Children & Family); Public Health (Family Health programs); Sustainability (Climate Change-Youth Climate Ambassadors; Waste Reduction-Education & Schools)*
Oversight and accountability (core)	Controller; Board of Appeals; Civil Grand Jury; Civil Service Commission; Ethics Commission; Police Accountability; SF Gov TV; Elections Commission	Controller

TABLE 13.1 (*continued*)

DEPARTMENT (TYPE)	SAN FRANCISCO, CALIFORNIA (CITY AND COUNTY)	BURLINGAME, CALIFORNIA + *SAN MATEO COUNTY*[a]
Integrated across departments	Human Rights Commission; Immigrant Rights Commission; Status of Women; Environment (Climate Change)	*Sustainability (Climate Change)*

[a] County departments are italicized, city departments are not

The Economic and Workforce Development Department, aligned with the local business and work system, can serve as an anchor in bringing departments together. As explored in the "Leverage Other Systems" section of chapter 5, the local business and work system connects directly to all the other place-based systems. Each of the other systems requires and generates local jobs and careers. In San Francisco, many commissions, departments, and agencies have a slice of workforce and economic development. In other cities, this function of government can be incomplete and underfunded. By making it one of the departments in a systems-oriented government, Economic and Workforce Development can get the attention, integration, and funding it needs to be a driver of place-based systems change.

A systems-oriented government structure would shift paradigms and catalyze more holistic change. Placing airports within a Transportation Department, for example, may help localities think more broadly about transportation within and to/from their city or county. Building and running train and bus stations are much cheaper than airports. Working with other jurisdictions and state and federal government to support long-distance rail and bus services may be a smarter investment than expanding an airport. This shift would also be significant in reducing greenhouse gas emissions. As another example, a more expansive view of public space occurs when parks and recreation, public works, community spaces like the library, and animal welfare are integrated into a Public Spaces Department.

Transitioning to Place-Based Systems Departments

Consolidating departments, especially in a large city with a complex bureaucracy, is difficult to accomplish. Such efforts have failed due to how expensive, disruptive, and rife with conflict the consolidation process can be.[7]

An interim step is to retain existing departments and agencies but group them into jointly funded and managed clusters. In this scenario, department leaders and staff across the government would frequently meet to pursue shared goals.

A Public Space cluster in San Francisco, for example, would regularly convene with Recreation and Parks, Public Works, Community Challenge Grants, Library, Animal Care and Control, Port, War Memorial, Museums, and Neighborhood Services (in the mayor's office). These departments and entities have worked together on projects in different combinations. These efforts, however, have not added up to a holistic place-based system in which people in every neighborhood have access to safe, car-free, and vibrant community and nature spaces. A cluster with this type of shared goal could galvanize a more focused, actionable approach necessary for systems change.

Reviving Food and Agriculture in Local Government

Whether as a cluster or department, Food and Agriculture is not a part of most local governments today. It's touched on here and there in different government departments but rarely as a core element of local governance structure.

Before the rise of agribusiness, local governments paid attention to and supported local agriculture. Once agriculture markets shifted to national and global scales, the food and agricultural functions of local government largely ceased.

Growing awareness around the importance of healthy, local food and food security to well-being and regeneration is reviving interest in food and agriculture and resurfacing it as an important local government function again. The nonprofit Chicago Food Policy Action Committee, for example, advocates for a city Department of Food Policy to coordinate and communicate food policies and improve the food security and health of residents.

Belo Horizonte, a large city in Brazil, provides a fully developed model for instituting Food and Agriculture Departments in local government. The city declared food a right of citizenship in 1993. A city agency was formed with a cross-sector council that included residents. The agency led several changes. It allocated public space for local farmers' markets and expanded school meal programs using whole food from local growers. The agency partners with local farmers to distribute and sell produce at fixed prices to low-income neighborhoods. People's Restaurants serve thousands of residents daily with low-priced, locally grown food. Farmers have profited, with intermediaries largely eliminated from the market. Hunger has decreased dramatically.[8] Funding the agency and its programs required less than 2 percent of the city's annual budget, and the transition took less than ten years. Belo Horizonte shows that shifting from a corporate-based to a place-based food system is possible when government structure supports and aligns with that goal.

Doing Away with Special Departments

The alignment of government departments with place-based systems and their purpose of well-being and regeneration reduces the need for other special departments or offices. In progressive cities and counties, offices and commissions for sustainability, environment, community resilience, justice, equity, and other well-being goals have been established and grown in recent years (see the last row in table 13.1). Unfortunately, these well-intended departments and offices add more layers of bureaucracy and create more opportunities for silos. Worse yet, they marginalize themselves by not being integrated into core government functions. Their activities can be perceived as being outside of normal government operations, undermining the purposes for which they were originally formed.

Another approach is to have a chief officer position(s) in a jurisdiction's core Administrative and Legal Services Department. The 100 Resilient Cities initiative of the Rockefeller Foundation has hired and trained chief resilience officers (CROs) in all the cities in its network. The CRO reports to the city's chief executives and is the city's point person for resilience building. The officer works across government departments to break down internal divisions, reduce duplicative work, and increase synergies. The CRO also works with external stakeholders from the private sector, nonprofits, and civil society to create broader alignment and support for community resilience. These types of positions can help drive systems change by bringing together stakeholders within and outside government around a common goal.

Reducing Demands on Government Through Prevention Supported by Place-Based Systems

Another benefit to organizing local government around place-based systems is that demand for safety, health, and social services may diminish and consequently require less public spending. What leads people to destructive or criminal behavior is complicated, but unmet needs related to financial security, connection and belonging, and health help explain it. A local government organized around helping people thrive locally through place-based systems is a means of deterring unsafe behavior in communities. Additionally, local governments that prioritize active transportation, local and healthy food, nearby nature access, community spaces, and local recreation create preventive health conditions and reduce the need for expensive public health services. Place-based system structures offer an intelligent approach to government that can provide more of what people need to live and thrive locally while reducing bureaucracy and expensive government services.

Bringing Departments Together Around a Unifying Purpose and Common Approach

A systems-oriented structure, of course, is not a panacea. Silos can develop within any department and among departments. Transportation, for example, utilizes lots of public space, particularly in the form of streets. If the Transportation and Public Space Departments do not form a close working relationship, transportation and public space system changes may be minimal. When all departments are focused on the purpose of well-being and regeneration, synergies across and within departments can more easily be built. Elected and department leaders, with the eyes of voters on them, will need to elevate the unifying purpose and hold staff and stakeholders accountable to it regularly.

Departments can further increase the effectiveness of their collective effort to improve well-being and regenerate nature, community, and local economies with systems-change strategies. Like effective collaboratives described in chapter 12, developing and implementing strategies around shifting power, transforming land use, resetting culture, and leveraging other systems will greatly increase the government's capacity to contribute to the creation of place-based systems. The systems-change levers form the common approach that, in addition to the unifying purpose, increases the effectiveness of government and its potential to catalyze transformative change.

The effort and energy required to keep everything connected, especially for those used to working in narrow specialties, will be substantial initially. Shifting the mindset and culture to one of coherence and regular strategic collaboration will take time. Connectors in each department who embrace and understand the unifying purpose and common approach can lead the way and help keep the wheels of government turning in the same direction. As the connectors engage others, mindsets and culture within government begin to shift. The systems-oriented approach starts to permeate government.

Systems-Oriented Planning

In concert with reorganizing and simplifying government structure, local governments can undertake more unified planning approaches around place-based systems. For instance, separate climate, environmental justice, sustainability, and equity plans have become increasingly common in local government. With planning aligned to place-based systems and their unifying purpose of well-being and regeneration, those important goals can instead be embedded in county and city general plans, bringing them into the central functioning of government.

The Shortfalls of Climate Action Planning

Cities across the United States have adopted climate action plans. With the climate crisis worsening, local governments have also declared climate emergencies to shorten the timeline to achieve zero emissions and accelerate action toward resilience. Yet with all these plans and a sense of urgency, greenhouse gas emissions have continued to increase, and the inequitable impacts of the climate crisis have grown.

In the 2021 report "The State of Local Climate Planning," a group of climate-planning professionals shared their concerns about local climate action approaches being siloed. They explained that "climate planning has typically been led by sustainability staff and issue experts with varying degrees of linkage to other citywide plans and agencies. . . . While adopting standalone climate plans has strongly signaled elected official support for addressing climate, it has also sometimes left climate isolated from other core local government functions and disciplines as well as from community-based organizations."[9] This analysis raises the question of why we have local climate action plans. We need general plans from local governments that integrate climate action across government rather than separate, standalone climate action plans.

Aligning General Plans to Place-Based Systems

In California and other states, counties and cities are required to have a general plan that serves as a blueprint for meeting the community's long-term vision through action. There are nine mandated elements in California's general plans: land use, circulation, housing, conservation, open space, noise, safety, environmental justice, and air quality as well as optional elements such as economic development and recreation. Local governments are given latitude in presenting and organizing elements in their general plan. For example, California's guidance stresses the elements' interrelated nature and encourages jurisdictions to consolidate statutory requirements into fewer elements. This flexibility provides an opportunity for systems-oriented planning. Table 13.2 demonstrates how California city and counties can organize their general plan elements around the systems-oriented government structure framing from the prior section.

TABLE 13.2 General plan elements

SYSTEMS-ORIENTED (HYPOTHETICAL)	CA GENERAL PLAN (2022)
Housing and community development (housing system)	Economic Development[a] Environmental Justice Housing Land Use
Economic and workforce development (local business and work system)	Circulation Economic Development[a] Environmental Justice Land Use
Transportation (transportation system)	Air Quality Circulation Economic Development[a] Environmental Justice Land Use Noise
Public spaces (community spaces system and nature spaces system)	Conservation Economic Development[a] Environmental Justice Land Use Open Space Recreation[a]
Food and agriculture (food system)	Air Quality Conservation Economic Development[a] Environmental Justice Land Use
Building energy (building energy system)	Air Quality Conservation Economic Development[a] Environmental Justice Land Use
Circular economy (consumer goods system)	Air Quality Conservation Economic Development[a] Land Use
Safety (core)	Safety (police, fire, etc.)

[a] Element not required by CA law

Integrating the systems-oriented departments with the elements of a general plan aligns government structure and planning into a stronger catalyst for systems change. The place-based systems framing, like for structure, makes planning more concrete and directly relevant to people's lives through housing, work, transportation, public space, food, building energy, and consumer goods.

The systems-oriented reframing of plan elements unlocks a more holistic approach to planning than California's existing configuration of elements. The element of environmental justice can be weaved throughout the general plan, reflecting its importance as a societal goal. Economic development applies to all the place-based systems. Rather than a standalone item, integrating it across the plan prioritizes the regeneration of local economies across all departments and elements. Reflecting the primary causes of greenhouse gasses and other air pollutants, the air pollution element can be addressed across the Transportation, Food and Agriculture, Building Energy, and Circular Economy (Consumer Goods) Departments.

For a plan to have an impact, something must result from it. That may seem like an obvious statement. Unfortunately, those involved in planning processes know that many plans gather dust. To avoid wasting a good plan, tangible results need to occur. For government, this typically starts with changing policy and funding streams.

Systems-Targeted Policy and Funding

Supportive local policy and funding, tied to systems-oriented departments and plans, are critical to the implementation of place-based systems. A system-specific resolution (like for circular economies discussed in chap. 11) signals a shift in direction for government and can get the ball rolling toward systems change. Resolutions establish the need and urgency for the change and set commitments for making it happen. Specific policies and funding then put the resolution into action.

Circular economy policies in European and US cities are supporting the implementation of a place-based consumer goods system with additional benefits to the local business and work system. Policies in Paris have led to refurbishing and repair workshops, reusing furniture from private companies, bulk sale shops, and reusing building materials with training support. Lisbon has established repair shops that train and provide jobs for students and unemployed people. Austin, Texas, and New York City have established online platforms that facilitate the reuse of materials. These policy-driven developments are resetting culture in the consumer goods system and strengthening the local business and work system.

On the funding side, San Francisco has expanded and enhanced public space with support from local bond measures passed by voters. The 2020 Health and Recovery Bond, approved by 71 percent of voters, included $239 million for improvements to neighborhood parks (including the India Basin Waterfront Park featured in chap. 7), citywide parks, recovery parks for physical and mental health, and playgrounds. The measure also funds small neighborhood projects, trails, urban agriculture sites, and plazas. These investments are helping to transform land use and change the community spaces, nature spaces, and local food systems.

Despite all the progress that local government can make toward developing place-based systems through structure, planning, policy, and funding, it will fall short of transformative change without regional governance and state and federal government support. These last two sections explore how these higher levels of government can help by directing their substantial resources to place-based systems, checking corporate power and influence, and removing other barriers to place-based systems change.

Regional Governance

Although much government authority exists at the county and city level to catalyze local change, regions are an essential part of the equation. The place-based food, energy, consumer goods, and transportation (public transit) systems depend on regional resources and strategy.

As an important part of place-based transportation systems, public transit benefits from regional coordination and governance. Federal and state laws have required regional transportation plans for decades. To execute these plans, regions have established governing bodies that develop these plans and direct state and federal funds to projects.

In California, eighteen metropolitan planning organizations (MPOs) provide governance and coordination for regional transportation. The Metropolitan Transportation Commission (MTC) has been the San Francisco Bay Area's MPO since 1970. The MTC provides planning, funding, coordination, and technical assistance to the region's 101 cities, nine counties, and twenty-seven transit agencies.

The MTC has helped the Bay Area develop elements of a place-based transportation system through plans that prioritize public transit, biking, and walking. The agency exerts influence through being the conduit for more than $1 billion in federal and state transportation funding each year. Funding has been directed to land use transformation through infrastructure investments and also to programs like Safe Routes to School (described in chap. 6) that reset culture. In 2023, the MTC also endorsed a comprehensive plan to better coordinate public transportation for riders across the region's many transit agencies and is making some headway.

MPOs provide a governing model for regional food, energy, and consumer goods systems. As mentioned in chapter 10, the Georgia Institute of Technology is working on a plan for a metropolitan energy planning organization to oversee and facilitate the implementation of an Atlanta area energyshed. With regional governance, important steps can be taken to move toward the vision of foodsheds, energysheds, makingsheds, and fibersheds.

The Role of State and Federal Government

Place-based systems benefit from local control and regional governance but also need much support from federal and state governments. Most tax revenue is collected at these two levels of government. Consequently, their budgets dwarf those of local government and regional bodies. The federal government also plays an important role in curbing corporate power, which helps shift power to local businesses and other entities aligned with place-based systems. When local governments somewhat paradoxically create barriers to place-based systems change (see, for example, homeowner resistance in chap. 4), state government oversight and policies are needed.

Directing Funding and Resources to Place-Based Systems

The federal government's funding and resources are needed for regions, counties, and cities to enact place-based systems change. In 2021, the $1.2 billion Infrastructure Investment and Jobs Act provided $550 billion for new investments and programs. Hundreds of billions were allocated to transportation and energy infrastructure. Significant parts went to automobile, truck, and air travel infrastructure and long-distance energy transmission, eroding rather than supporting place-based systems. At the same time, however, historic amounts of funding were provided to state and local governments for passenger rail, public transit, and pedestrian and bike facilities.

The US Department of Transportation's Reconnecting Communities Initiative (depicted in chap. 4) is a smaller but more targeted use of federal resources for place-based systems change. The almost $1B in funding is being used for freeway demolition to restore communities and housing that had been eliminated by the freeways. In addition to boosting local housing systems, these land use transformations are increasing community amenities for nature (nature spaces system), recreation (community spaces system), and food access (food system). Such funding can catalyze multiple place-based systems at once while also making long-overdue reparations for past harms.

State governments can help fund place-based systems like transportation. The California Department of Transportation was an auto infrastructure–oriented body for much of its history. It has shifted to a multimodal approach. The agency adopted a statewide bike and pedestrian plan in 2017 and has funded well over $1 billion in bicycle and pedestrian projects through its Active Transportation Program. Bike paths, lanes, sidewalks, and programs that encourage shifting modes are now regularly funded. The combination of infrastructure and program investments is helping transform land use and reset culture away from car dependency and toward place-based transportation systems.

Changes to existing laws are also necessary to allow funding to go more directly to place-based systems change. Federal and state laws, for example, prohibit airport taxes and fees from being used for public transit. These significant revenue sources could support high-speed rail and regional transit that, in addition to facilitating general mobility, get people to airports. If planned and executed well, this would reduce the demand for air and car travel. Less funding would then be needed for highway and airport expansion, where much public funding continues to be spent.

If well-being and regeneration are prioritized, infrastructure and other federal and state government funding could be flexed more to transform land use in support of place-based systems. Road and bridge funding, for example, could be directed to transit, bike, and pedestrian uses. Energy infrastructure funding could include local and regional generation with conservation incentives.

Shifting Power Through Regulations, Enforcement, and Taxation

As explained in chapter 5, after a four-decade lapse of regulation and enforcement, the federal government finally reasserted itself in combating corporate consolidation starting in 2020. Under the Biden Administration, the Federal Trade Commission (FTC) and its chair, Lina Khan, returned to enforcing anti-merger and antitrust laws and regulations.

Unsurprisingly, corporations pushed back hard. In 2024, corporate leaders lobbied Kamala Harris, the Democratic candidate for president, to replace Lina Khan as chair.[10] Curbing corporate power will continue to be a difficult political struggle. If we are to enact place-based systems and boost local economies, the federal government must stay the course of unwinding and preventing corporate consolidation.

Think tanks and advocacy organizations are providing a playbook for taking on corporate power at the federal level and returning it to localities and regions. The analyses and recommendations of the Institute for Local Self-Reliance (ILSR) helped inform the systems-change strategies presented in local business and work (chap. 5), food (chap. 9), energy (chap. 10), and consumer goods (chap. 11) systems described in this book. The ILSR also provides helpful guidance for restricting corporate power across the board through regulation, enforcement, and taxing.

The ILSR understands that partial measures may do little to check corporate power and regenerate local economies. In its comments to the FTC and the Department of Justice's Antitrust Division regarding merger guideline updates in 2022, the institute argued that the government must ban mergers by corporations that already dominate a market or are in highly concentrated markets. Specifically, the ILSR recommended merger evaluations based on the goal of decentralized, competitive markets; guardrails for mergers that protect suppliers (farmers, etc.) and their income from being driven down by corporations exerting their buying power; and scrutiny of vertical mergers that block other businesses from any part of the supply chain. These types of measures are essential to shift power to local businesses and other entities that help form place-based systems.

Since the 1970s, with the rise of procorporate federal policies, corporations have been able to avoid much taxation. In their joint report, *Tax Dodging Is a Monopoly Tactic*, the ILSR's Stacy Mitchell and the Roosevelt Institute's Susan Holmberg explain how Amazon grew its market power from tax dodging. By locating its headquarters in Washington, a state without sales tax, Amazon avoided collecting sales tax nearly anywhere for over two decades after its founding in 1995. In 2018, the Supreme Court finally overruled this unfair tax advantage of Amazon and other corporate online retailers. In addition, Amazon sought and received $4.8 billion in development subsidies for new warehouses from 2012 to 2022. Like other corporations, Amazon has also avoided corporate taxes through shell companies in other countries that provide tax havens. As recently as 2021, Amazon paid no European income taxes and avoided over $5 billion in US taxes through these schemes.[11] Corporations like Amazon have benefited immensely from sophisticated tax maneuvers. These unfair tax advantages make it difficult for small businesses to compete and local economies to thrive, eroding the potential for place-based systems.

Government reform of taxation policies and their enforcement is necessary for the local business and work system to have a fighting chance. Regional food, energy, and consumer goods place-based systems also require a fair playing field in which corporations in those fields do not get tax advantages over local farms, energy producers, manufacturers, and other place-based businesses.

Removing Local Barriers to Place-Based Systems Change

Place-based systems change also requires that state and federal government remove local barriers that get in the way. A 2020 California law, for example, helped fast-track bike, bus, and light-rail projects by temporarily exempting them from environmental reviews. Local procar groups and individuals who did not want changes to streets had been using the long, drawn-out environmental review process to delay and sidetrack these projects.

State governments play a vital role in combating local resistance to mixed-income and mixed-use housing development needed for a place-based housing system. As described in chapter 4, rezoning policies are one tool that the state government can use.

In the early 2020s, California finally started holding local governments accountable for providing adequate and affordable housing. Beginning in 2022, local jurisdictions were required to submit housing plans that fulfill their allocation of the state's needed 2.5 million housing, including one million affordable units for low-income families. The allocations were not new, but enforcement was strengthened. The consequence of losing state housing funds has forced localities to follow through on meeting their allocations for new housing. With ramped-up oversight, localities have begun approving housing developments previously denied. The long-awaited approval of the housing project in Lafayette, California, discussed earlier, was assisted by this increased state pressure.

*　*　*

When governments at all levels act in ways like those depicted in this chapter, they become catalysts for place-based systems change and changing how people live. Pushed by and in partnership with coalitions and collaboratives (chap. 12), the centering of society around people's well-being and regeneration of nature, community, and local economies gains momentum.

Education, like collaboration and government, plays an essential role in catalyzing systems change. Every day across the United States, nearly fifty-five million children and youth attend school.[12] Schools thus represent a huge opportunity to grow place-based systems now and in the future. Chapter 14 explains place-based education and its potential for spurring systems change.

PLACE-BASED EDUCATION

> **The goal of the revolution [in education] is the reconnection of young people with their own habitats and communities. The classroom is the ecology of the surrounding community, not the confining four walls of the traditional school. The pedagogy of the revolution is simply a process of organized engagement with living systems and the lives of people who live by the grace of those systems.**
>
> —David Orr, Oberlin College professor, *A Sense of Wonder for Young Minds*

In chapter 1, I shared my journey from a public school educator to a researcher and consultant for place-based systems change. At the onset of that transition, I reviewed research on environmental education in schools.

For years, I had believed that formal education was an essential force in changing society for the better. My research goal was to better understand how environmental literacy could become a more integrated aspect of schooling. That pursuit didn't last long. I learned from research studies that building environmental awareness and knowledge did little to change human behavior and, thus, society.

As I flexed my research into studying broader community change, it felt like I was giving up on education. That was hard for me to digest after spending seventeen years working in the public school system. I now realize I was only stepping away from traditional, classroom-based education. Over the past century, this dominant approach in K-12 schools has not led students to become invested in the change needed to avert worsening planetary crises.

Since my time in K-12 education, I've worked on many projects involving a different approach to education. From these experiences and related research, I've discovered the great promise of place-based education (PBE) in contributing to systems change.

Most importantly, PBE enriches the student education experience and improves learning outcomes. Reflecting on my experience teaching, this became clear to me. The times students were most engaged and excited about learning was when I was using elements of PBE.

* * *

In PBE, student learning extends well beyond classroom walls. Students learn firsthand about systems in their communities, cities, and regions, and work to improve them. They also develop the skills, knowledge, and competencies to continue working on place-based systems change after their time in school.

In this chapter, we'll explore what PBE is and what it looks like in relation to different systems. Unpacking PBE this way helps us understand how it can propel place-based systems change now and in the future. We'll then examine multiple ways to elevate the role of PBE in our educational system so that it can reach its potential as a systems-change catalyst.

Place-Based Education

The Center for Place-Based Learning and Community Engagement defines place-based education as "immers[ing] students in local heritage, cultures, landscapes, opportunities and experience, using these as a foundation for . . . subjects across the curriculum."[1] PBE integrates school, community, and local nature, blurring the lines arbitrarily drawn among them. Community members and organizations closely engage with the school. The school melds into the surrounding landscape and communities, extending benefits to all involved.

PBE offers educational opportunities that build bridges among subject areas rooted in the real world. Education reformers Tom Vander Ark and Andrew Meyers offer an example of interdisciplinary learning through a PBE approach:

> Consider logarithms. Most people remember taking a quiz on logs at some point and then instantly forgetting what they were. But what if a math teacher told students they had to learn logarithms to determine the pH of a solution in science class? The science teacher could make the concept of pH emotionally resonant by setting up a project to, say, measure the environmental health of a local river.
>
> The humanities teacher could have students consider the history of industrialization and the role humans have played in polluting the river. And finally, the class could canoe down the river with paddles they built in art class, taking samples and observing local wildlife.[2]

Students gain mastery in specific subjects in ways that help them understand larger issues and better get to know the place where they live. This real-world pedagogy engages students' minds and hearts, leading to integrated and lasting knowledge.

PBE is an umbrella term for many types of education. Environmental education, outdoor learning, project-based learning, problem-based learning, service learning, and experiential learning form a rich tapestry of PBE. As this list indicates, there are many ways to apply PBE to student learning. A school or school district can identify what PBE practices it might already be utilizing and build out a fuller PBE program from there.

Through PBE, students are given opportunities to address real community problems. Using Vander Ark and Meyers's earlier example, students could participate in or even organize a river cleanup. They might develop an outreach campaign to educate community members about the river and its pollution. In combination with any of these activities, students may decide to participate in city council meetings and advocate for policies to prevent further river pollution. In whatever way it unfolds, students are empowered through acquiring knowledge and skills relevant to a local problem and trying to help solve it.

As students become change agents through PBE, K-12 education becomes a catalyst for place-based systems change. In return, as the systems become more place-based, they provide more opportunities for students to learn from their place.

Transportation (chap. 6), community spaces (chap. 7), nature spaces (chap. 8), food (chap. 9), and energy (chap. 10) are five systems that particularly stand to benefit from this reciprocal relationship. They directly connect PBE to changing the systems that shape how people live and underlie our societal crises. In the next section, we'll learn about community, nature, transportation, food, and energy-based education and how these PBE approaches can catalyze systems change.

Community-Based Education

Community-based education helps students learn firsthand about issues affecting their community's well-being. In the process, they develop skills and become motivated to take action.

PBE experts David Sobel and Gregory Smith compiled several examples of PBE that illustrate how students improve and help create community spaces through community-based learning.[3] Students at an elementary school in North Portland, Oregon, developed a plan to redesign and clean up their vandalized school playground and adjoining park. In the Llano Grande region of Texas, students interviewed community members, many of whom migrated from Mexico. They then set up a public exhibit and event to share their knowledge. Community-based education is a powerful tool for improving students' sense of self-efficacy and community spaces at the same time.

The Growing Up Boulder program involved students in designing improvements to a local community space in this Colorado city of one hundred thousand people. A partnership among the city, local school district, and local university engaged close to 225 young people, ages four through sixteen, in community-based education.[4] The children and youth participated in a visioning process for the Civic Area, a prominent public space with a creek in the city's downtown area.

After learning about community space design, the students recommended that the Civic Area provide space for nature play with creek access, active play, and hanging out and eating with friends. They also concluded that increased sight lines across the creek and art and cultural representations would help make it a safe, welcoming place for more people. The city adopted many of the students' specific recommendations, including a reclaimed tree house, a small wetland, safe creek access elements, food trucks, and lots of nature. When children and youth help plan community spaces like this, they, the whole community, and nature benefit.

Nature-Based Education

Nearby nature provides an excellent medium for PBE. Outdoor learning can happen in any place during any season. Despite the harsh winter climate, schools in Vermont and Norway have students learning outside year-round. Nature-based learning can also take place in the most urban of settings, as illustrated in this example: "Our first-grade students have been immersed in learning about the Mission neighborhood. One of the themes they observed and identified was nature in the neighborhood. They visited gardens, parks, and green spaces. They identified concerns they have about nature and created projects to become allies for animals and nature. You can see their letters and posters on the wall outside their classroom, and they have also created a few PSAs [public service announcements]."[5] This nearby nature-based education project occurred at my children's former elementary school in a dense urban neighborhood in San Francisco. Student observations and experiences in local nature turned into advocating for improving the nearby nature spaces system.

Watersheds provide an orientation for studying and caring for local ecosystems within a nature-based education approach. Every place is part of a watershed, even if it is damaged or hidden. The Students and Teachers Restoring a Watershed (STRAW) program works with San Francisco Bay Area schools to combine nature-based education with service learning. The students learn about their local watershed, clean debris from streams, and restore native habitats. Watershed-based education can involve schools in places without current surface water bodies. Schools can partner with place-based organizations that seek to uncover and restore local streams buried under pavement (see efforts featured in chap. 8).

The STRAW program shows that nature-based education can benefit local nature spaces and biodiversity. A study in Japan found that two conservation PBE projects led to biodiversity improvements, including increases in indicator species.[6] Nature-based education can help improve nearby nature spaces and motivate students to be lifelong stewards of local nature.

Transportation-Based Education

Transportation-based education helps students develop active transportation skills and habits while furthering the development of place-based transportation systems. Safe Routes to School (SRTS), introduced in chapter 6, is an excellent example of transportation-based education that promotes both goals.

SRTS was launched in 2005 with federal funds. By 2019, local SRTS programs were active in 426 locations across rural (22 percent), suburban (38 percent), and urban (40 percent) areas in forty-four states and Washington, DC.[7] As explained in chapter 6, SRTS programs align well with systems-change strategies. Students who lead and participate in these programs help pull the systems-change levers.

In walk audits, for example, students and other school stakeholders study the streets and sidewalks surrounding a school. They identify places where it feels unsafe or uncomfortable to walk or bike. From this process, students contribute to recommendations for improving infrastructure around the school. They may then work to get school district and city decision-makers to design and install new infrastructure, helping transform land use to support active transportation.

Cultural resets around traveling to and from school also result from students' participation in SRTS programs. Students, for example, gain bike riding skills and confidence through "bike rodeos" and learn safe ways to cross streets on "walking school buses" (introduced in chap. 6). As students walk and bike to school more, their visibility helps build a cultural norm around walking and biking that can push the larger community to follow suit.

Our Voice, a citizen science project housed at the Stanford University School of Medicine, exemplifies how SRTS can change student travel mode choices. The Our Voice team helped a school in Santa Clara County, California, build out a Safe Routes program. The project's Discovery Tool phone app and other methods helped a group from the school identify safety issues around the school related to both infrastructure and behavior. The children then collaborated with city and school staff on several changes that increased the percentage of children walking and biking to the school from 5.3 to 30 percent.[8]

Making walking and biking safer and more accessible for students enables other residents who live in those neighborhoods to travel locally with less car use. If enough schools get involved in a city, opportunities to expand infrastructure and culture supportive of reducing car dependency can grow across the jurisdiction. In my work with SRTS, I have seen city staff involved in SRTS programs extend street changes from the schools into other neighborhoods. Transportation-based education plays an important role in changing transportation systems.

Food-Based Education

Food-based education has been expanding across US schools and supporting the growth of place-based food systems. This realm of PBE connects students to where their food comes from and involves them in growing it. Food-based education can occur on school grounds or in the surrounding community. It also can connect schools with their regional foodsheds.

The nonprofit Edible Schoolyard Project, founded by chef Alice Waters in 1995, started in partnership with the King Middle School in Berkeley, California. The schoolyard, kitchen, and cafeteria at the school were transformed to provide delicious school meals from scratch for all students in the district. They sourced ingredients from the school garden and local farmers and ranchers. The school garden became a setting for teaching science and humanities. By 2017, over 5,800 edible schoolyard programs existed across all US states and territories and seventy-five countries.[9] Edible schoolyards transform land use to enrich student learning and boost local food systems.

At the city level, the Detroit School Garden Collaborative supports students in growing fruits, vegetables, and edible flowers. The collaborative partners with the city's school district to supply fresh produce for student meals from over eighty school gardens. Utilizing these school gardens and a two-acre urban farm, students learn about growing food, healthy eating, and sustainability.

California Food for California Kids (CFCK) is a network of over 140 public school districts supported by the nonprofit Center for Ecoliteracy. CFCK helps the food operations in all these districts provide students with fresh, locally grown food. The center supports teachers in providing students with learning opportunities about food and sustainable living. The curriculum is free to teachers and connects the classroom, cafeteria, and school garden. CFCK food–based educational activities include taste tests, cooking demo events, hands-on learning in gardens, and farmer visits.

Food-based education intimately connects students to nature and their food. Through these programs, students grow up with an understanding of a place-based food system as a healthier and possible alternative to the global, corporate-run food system. In the process, place-based food systems are expanded with school gardens and local farms and ranches that supply schools with food.

Energy-Based Education

Energy-based education engages students in learning how energy is produced and developing the know-how to save energy. Energy conservation and local renewables are often part of energy-based education and two essential components of a place-based energy system.

In an AP Environmental Science course at Rocky Mountain High in Fort Collins, Colorado, students learned about energy issues and how conservation is an integral part of the solution. They then designed and led a project that reduced the school's electricity consumption by 50 percent over six years.[10]

The nonprofit Climate Action Pathways (CAPS) works with school districts to lower their energy costs and greenhouse gas emissions (GHGE). The organization hires, trains, and supports high school interns to work on these energy savings projects. In its first year, CAPS helped Porterville Unified School District in California's Central Valley save $320,000 in energy bills and reduce GHGE by 13 percent across its twenty schools.[11]

Energize Schools, a project of the nonprofit Strategic Energy Innovations (SEI), provides a curriculum that teaches K-12 students about energy auditing, solar design, and renewable energy. Through webinars with professionals and other resources, the project supports students in developing career skills for the clean energy economy. Students can earn Sustainability Certificates in solar design, green buildings, and zero-net energy. Energize Schools also runs a bilingual Energy Challenge across California. This competition engages students in taking action to conserve energy in their schools. In these ways, Energize Schools is building capacity for students to advance place-based energy systems.

Projects in classes like AP Environmental Science and organizations like CAPS and SEI that partner with schools connect student learning to local renewable energy and conservation practices. In turn, students help bolster place-based energy systems.

Place-Based Education Across Multiple Systems

As the above examples indicate, PBE can be adapted in many ways. These adaptations include blending PBE across multiple systems.

The Neinas Dual Language Learning Academy in Detroit, Michigan, turned nearby urban blight into thriving gardens for outdoor learning. Parents and teachers were concerned about pollution from idling trucks in a parking lot next to their school. They convinced the city to purchase the lot. With support from community partners, they turned it into a garden and nature sanctuary. In this space, students plant and grow vegetables and native plants. They spend time observing and interacting with the ecosystem they created.

A blighted building was subsequently removed across the street, providing another opportunity to transform land use and expand PBE. Seeing the abandoned lot across the street, the students surveyed the community about potential uses. They developed 3D models of their proposal for a "nature escape" park there. With the support of the adults, the students raised money and secured volunteers to install the park.

The Neinas Academy and its students provide a model that weaves together community-based, nature-based, and food-based education. Their ambition and efforts are helping expand these place-based systems while engaging students in transformative learning and action.

Making the Case for Place-Based Education

Place-based education catalyzes growth in place-based systems with benefits to communities and nature. For PBE to be widely adopted in schools, however, it must improve educational outcomes, particularly for students who have struggled in school. To better assess how PBE impacts student learning, it's important to understand the current dominant mode of schooling and its shortcomings.

Traditional, classroom-based education has been the norm in the US school system for over a century. Education reformers Vander Ark and Meyers explain that it often fails to engage or inspire students: "Most schools expect students to sit silently while the teacher fills them up with facts. Everyone learns the same subject, the same way, on the same schedule. Classrooms are centered on teachers, rather than students. Topics are siloed—math class, science class and so on—and students are rarely afforded the time and resources to follow their passions. Students routinely cram before tests and then forget the information almost as soon as they put their pencils down."[12] This portrait of traditional education is true for too many of the nearly fifty-five million children[13] in the United States' K-12 public schools.

Learning in schools generally takes place indoors, removed from students' lived experiences. Students learn from reading texts, listening to lectures, watching videos, being on computers, and classroom discussions. Many teachers try to connect curriculum to children's lives through creative questions and lessons, but that almost always occurs inside classroom walls. Learning experiences that engage students emotionally and cognitively are elusive. The daydreaming or distracted student portrayed in movies and television is the unfortunate reality in the traditional educational system.

Examples of PBE shared in this chapter show how it offers a better way of engaging students in learning. The real-world, student-driven nature of PBE instills interest and passion in learning. In one study, a teacher reflected on incorporating a place-based approach: "In my twenty years of teaching before using the environment-based approach, I heard 'Why are we learning this? When are we going to finish?' And now when we are out in the field and sorting macro-invertebrates, for example, I have to make them stop after four hours for lunch. And then they say, 'We don't want to.'"[14] As this teacher's experience and my own from a few decades ago validate, PBE makes learning school subjects fun and interesting to students. Rather than learn secondhand from a lecture or reading, students learn firsthand through their own experiences.

In addition to getting students more engaged in learning, PBE has been found to improve student outcomes across a variety of measures. Environmental education (EE) is a well-researched area of PBE. Similar to but more expansive than nature-based education, EE serves as a good proxy for the larger field of PBE.

Led by Stanford University's Nicole Ardoin, a group of university researchers across the country analyzed 119 peer-reviewed studies. Their meta-analysis showed that EE improved students' academic performance.[15] One of the studies conducted on a large sample of K-12 schools in California found that students in environment-based educational programs improved academic performance across subject areas.[16] This research, supported by the California Department of Education, found that students in these programs outperformed students in traditional education standardized tests 80 percent of the time in language arts, 77 percent of the time in social studies, 67 percent of the time in science, and 65 percent of the time in math.

In the twenty-first century, students need to develop a variety of skills to succeed in college and their careers. In the review of 119 peer-reviewed studies, students' ability to grasp and retain new information, critical thinking, confidence, autonomy, and leadership were also significant outcomes of environmental education.[17] Related to PBE and environmental education, other research has demonstrated that time spent learning in nature improves both focus and imagination in children.[18] PBE prepares students with essential skills and creativity.

PBE reduces inequities in education by benefiting students who typically struggle in the classroom. A study of low-income elementary schoolers across the country found that time spent learning from real phenomena outside led to increased academic achievement.[19] A middle school teacher in upstate New York integrating PBE into her curriculum describes how PBE promotes equity: "I have students with a variety of learning styles and learning abilities. The hands-on aspect was an equalizer. The kids who have trouble learning, and the kids who are super advanced—they're all having the same discussions. There's more collaboration and engagement."[20] During an outdoor lesson on transpiration from leaves on a tree, a middle school teacher in Los Angeles noticed students who were less engaged in the classroom asking questions, collaborating, and offering ideas, reflecting an in-depth understanding of the science.[21] Educational outcomes validate these observations and insights.

Place-based education is a "win-win-win" for students, communities, and the environment. Students get to know their place better and become invested in its health and sustainability. They develop valuable skills, knowledge that lasts, and an understanding of how they can make a positive difference. PBE is powerful student learning and helps build place-based systems that support well-being and regeneration.

* * *

Despite all the benefits to students and their communities, PBE has remained mainly at the margins of K-12 education due to multiple barriers.

- Testing has become more and more a cornerstone of formal education. Tests and preparing for them take up much school time, leaving less time for experiential and project-based learning.
- Technology-based instruction is another impediment to PBE. Students learn more on screens than in their communities or nearby nature.
- The amount of asphalt on school grounds and in surrounding communities makes it harder to access nature as a medium for learning.

Testing, technology, and asphalt are large industries with powerful corporations. These industries have helped shape K-12 education and benefit when schools stay dependent on their resources. These three features of K-12 education present obstacles to implementing PBE.

Education reform itself is also complex and difficult. PBE requires change on many levels. Teachers have to change their instructional practices and become comfortable and effective in teaching in settings outside their classroom. Administrators need to develop a deep understanding of how PBE works to best support teachers in changing curriculum and instruction. Parents and students, as the customers of K-12 education, must learn about PBE practices and how they can support its implementation. School districts and schools also need to forge partnerships with local organizations that can support PBE in nearby parks and other community settings. Changing K-12 education to PBE is no small endeavor.

Schools and school districts need strong motivation to adopt PBE and effectively transition to it. Fortunately, that motivation is brewing. Growing environmental and social crises have elevated interest in educating students on how to take on these challenges now and in their careers and lives. This critical time in human history has opened the door for PBE. School systems are partnering with organized networks of local organizations, reinventing educator training, transforming schoolyards, and supporting whole-school reform efforts to adopt and spread PBE. Changes in state policies present opportunities to scale PBE. The moment for PBE to take hold in K-12 education may be here.

Partnering with Organized Networks of Local Organizations

Instead of the testing and technology industries, local organizations can be the primary educational partners of schools and support the adoption of PBE. Place-based organizations help students deepen their knowledge about important issues evident at the local level. Working with teachers, local organizations provide place-based learning opportunities and action projects that complement classroom instruction.

To build out a complete PBE program, schools need the support of multiple organizations. PBE can expand and thrive when community partners and a school or school district create a formal network in support of student learning.

The Rachel Marshall Outdoor Learning Laboratory project in Keene, New Hampshire, shows what's possible when local organizations partner with a school district to provide a PBE learning progression across grades.[22] With support from the city parks and recreation department, a local university, a local stewardship organization, and their teachers, students designed a plan to restore a three-acre riparian corridor. Students conducted field research, interviewed residents, and wrote articles about the project in the town's weekly newspaper. They restored the natural corridor by enhancing wildlife habitat and installing native plants. Projects involved all grade levels. For example, third graders built a butterfly garden, and high school students participated in a bird banding project. They restored the landscape so well that it turned into a city park. Spurred on by this success, the learning laboratory expanded to all two thousand acres of public land in Keene.

Learning Landscapes is a collaborative that serves schools throughout the Feather River Watershed in northern California. With the support of public agencies and private landowners, every school in the watershed has a nature preserve within a ten-minute walk from the school. Students learn through an interdisciplinary curriculum taught on these lands known as the Outdoor Core. The program serves twenty-five hundred students annually with students from one school district participating in nine to fifteen outdoor learning experiences.[23]

The Alameda Unified School District in the San Francisco Bay Area developed and implemented a comprehensive plan for place-based learning. Initially, a loose grouping of independent organizations provided assorted community-based educational opportunities. With support from a local science center and ChangeScale, a regional environmental education collaborative (introduced in chap. 12), the organizations supporting PBE transformed into a well-organized network that integrated systemically into the district's education program for all students. Angela Vergara, a program manager at the local county's waste management agency, expressed the following about the renewed partnership: "Being invited to be at the district table like this is unique. We are networking and building stronger relationships with other community partners. It helps morale, showing we are not alone."[24] With organizations enthusiastically involved with the school district as equal partners, abundant opportunities for PBE now exist for students across the district. PBE learning experiences are organized in a progression from kindergarten to twelfth grade. A map of walking field trips was developed for each school site. Student learning takes place along the bay, in the nearby hills, and at community sites like the local waste management center. With support from community partners, school gardens at elementary schools, nature centers at high schools, and school-based waste management projects have become key features of on-campus PBE across the school district.

Reinventing Educator Training

When teachers become comfortable and competent in teaching outdoors and in the community, opportunities for PBE expand and deepen. Administrators also must know how to best support teachers in this work on and off campus, including oversight for green schoolyards and streamlined field trip processes.

Organizations and collaboratives are providing training to help administrators and teachers implement PBE at their schools. The nonprofit Green Schoolyards America delivers professional development to help district and school administrators develop, implement, and utilize green schoolyards for student learning. Their offerings include an annual institute for school principals. The Learning Landscapes program, described in the prior section, provides teachers with training on place-based instruction at the nearby nature preserves. The professional development involves learning from teachers with PBE experience and local scientists.

Training that leads to substantive change in instruction needs to be ongoing. Support organizations are helping school districts deliver regular PBE professional learning opportunities. The Southeast Michigan Stewardship Coalition trains teachers to support students in investigating local environmental justice issues. The teachers learn how to instruct in ways that enable students to understand the interconnectedness of social and ecological problems in their communities and take action to address them as "citizen-stewards." The California Environmental Literacy Initiative (CAELI) partners with statewide subject matter networks to provide intensive professional learning programs for teachers. Summer institutes connected to workshops during the school year help teachers integrate environment-based learning into science, history-social science, health, arts, and other subjects.

Relevant, substantive, and ongoing PBE training enables administrators and teachers to put place at the center of teaching and learning in their schools.

From Asphalt to Green Schoolyards

PBE, particularly anything involving nature, does not happen easily on asphalt. It's nearly ubiquitous, however, in communities and schools. In the middle to late twentieth century, blacktop, a type of asphalt, became the default surface for children's outdoor recreational space and proliferated across US school grounds, parks, and playgrounds.

Asphalt is problematic in many ways. Children are more easily injured on it than on other surfaces. It disconnects children from the nature buried and stifled underneath it. With escalating climate change, blacktop is dangerous in extreme heat. Researchers recorded school asphalt temperatures of 145 degrees, hot enough to cause severe burns, in a school in the Los Angeles metropolitan area.[25] Asphalt-covered schoolyards are disproportionately located in low-income neighborhoods of color that also often lack nearby nature spaces that could be used for PBE.

The era of asphalt in schools may be ending. Green, or living, schoolyards with gardens, trees, and other natural features are sprouting up in schools nationwide. They provide places for students to play, get the restorative benefits of nature, grow food, and learn across subjects. They are a natural fit for PBE methods. Once life starts flourishing on school grounds, it opens endless opportunities for student wonder and enrichment.

In 2001, a group of committed leaders formed the Green Schoolyards Alliance in San Francisco. When a modernization bond for the city's school district was being planned, this group lobbied for the inclusion of green schoolyards and gardens. That vision became a reality when the bond measure passed. A nonprofit, Education Outside, grew out of the initial alliance and played a critical role in activating school gardens and living schoolyard elements for student learning through a corps of trained garden educators. Over 90 percent of schools in the district implemented active green schoolyard elements on their campus.

Landscape architect Sharon Danks guided the San Francisco schoolyard transformation. In 2013, she founded Green Schoolyards America (mentioned earlier for its training of administrators in schoolyard PBE) to support the expansion of living schoolyards across California and the country. Sharon is an ambassador for the many benefits of green schoolyards to students and society. As Sharon explains, water agencies want unpaved land to reduce runoff, multiple city and county agencies are working on climate resilience, and school districts want kids to have engaging, enriching learning experiences.[26] Green Schoolyards America brings together these stakeholders and others to support removing asphalt and making nature spaces on school campuses. The organization's twenty-year goal is to have green schoolyards in all ten thousand public schools in California. In her award-winning book *Asphalts to Ecosystems*, Sharon uses examples from 150 schools in eleven countries to show how to design and build natural schoolyards.

Supporting Whole-School Reform

PBE can take off in schools when networks of local organizations, educator training, school campus greening, and other school practice changes come together in a whole-school-reform approach. This seemingly tall order is starting to happen with the support of county offices of education in California.

The San Mateo County Office of Education (SMCOE) supports twenty-three school districts on the peninsula just south of San Francisco. In 2017, the office established the state's first-ever county-level Environmental Literacy and Sustainability Initiative (ELSI). The initiative's use of the 4Cs Whole System Framework for Environmental and Climate Action in Schools reads like a blueprint for PBE. The 4 C's of campus (greening facilities and operations), curriculum (PBE instruction through training teachers), community (partnerships with organizations), and culture (school sustainability practices led by students) add up to whole-school reform.

ELSI is recognized as a model program because it empowers administrators, teachers, and students to implement PBE. ELSI provides administrators with tools, support, and flexibility to green their facilities and operations and implement outdoor classrooms. They are supported through yearlong fellowships and a school partnership network that provides technical assistance. Teachers have been trained through workshops and fellowships to design and implement PBE curriculum. Students participate in a year-long youth climate ambassador program in which they conduct a community impact project. ELSI also hosts an annual youth summit to educate and empower students to act. Schools that make meaningful changes are recognized through awards and recognition programs.

With its success in changing school and classroom practices, the ideas from ELSI have spread to other county offices of education (COE) in California, with at least six other COEs investing in a similar initiative as of 2022. State-wide, CAELI and the nonprofit Ten Strands run multiple programs to support this expansion, including a COE Innovation Hub. The hub supports a state-wide community of practice for administrators interested in environmental and sustainability initiatives from over thirty of California's fifty-eight COEs. These programs and efforts build capacity across the school system, empowering stakeholders to focus more on PBE and less on testing and traditional classroom-based education.

Centering Place-Based Education in Education Policy

K-12 education is primarily overseen and funded at the state level, so state policy supporting PBE is critical. State curriculum standards and frameworks guide what students learn in schools. They have been modified in multiple states to incorporate environmental literacy and sustainability in ways that expand PBE.

In 2018, Wisconsin became one of the first states to adopt curriculum standards for environmental literacy and sustainability. These standards are anchored in PBE by being organized around students developing and connecting with a sense of place. The curriculum has students explore ecological principles in nature and community and engage in the design and implementation of stewardship projects.

Maryland has an environmental literacy high school graduation requirement. Students work toward it through comprehensive, interdisciplinary environmental education programs across their K-12 years. The requirement is anchored in five overarching standards. The first of those involves students investigating environmental issues and taking local action. Like Wisconsin, Maryland has elevated the role of PBE in its schools through curriculum standards.

Many states have adopted the Next Generation Science Standards (NGSS) for their science curriculum. An emphasis across the standards is that students learn the practices of being a scientist or engineer. Hence, the NGSS encourages learning in local contexts where students can do scientific field studies, engage in engineering projects, and otherwise learn outside the classroom.

With state policy changes like these, top-down pressure is applied to schools to implement PBE. Organized networks and educator training help prepare schools and teachers for these changes. As green schoolyards replace asphalt, PBE becomes easier to implement. Whole-school-reform efforts provide the most substantial foundation for PBE. The momentum in these areas gives hope for a sea change in education.

* * *

As an educator, researcher, and consultant, I've worked with many of the people and organizations profiled in this chapter. I've witnessed and supported school districts, schools, nonprofit organizations, and government agencies providing great PBE experiences for students on campuses and in communities and the outdoors. PBE offers rich learning opportunities for students, promotes deep connections to place, and improves student achievement, communities, and the environment at the same time.

Shifting to PBE is necessary in the twenty-first century. The transformation in education positively impacts students and their learning and is a lasting force for change in the systems that shape how people live. Place-based systems expand when schools and communities support students in local projects that make a difference, whether it's an energy conservation program or an edible schoolyard. Place-based education also shifts mindsets, attitudes, identities, and behavior, fostering personal change that aligns with place-based systems change.

In chapter 15, we'll explore the relationship between personal change and systems change. Personal change represents the final catalyst of place-based systems change.

PERSONAL CHANGE

Find your place on the planet. Dig in and take responsibility from there.

—Gary Snyder, poet

I often wonder whether our society can make the monumental shift to reorienting our lives around the places where we live with the support of place-based systems. Those who benefit from corporate capitalism resist change at every step with their disproportionate power. Multinational corporations are large employers—Walmart and Amazon alone employ almost four million people.[1] Tens of millions of Americans have invested their retirement in corporations. Everyone relies on corporations in at least some way as a consumer. It's hard to change systems and how people live when the tentacles of corporations are nearly everywhere and have made us dependent on them. Yet if we strive to regenerate nature, community, and local economies, we have no choice but to steer sharply away from corporate capitalism and toward the places where we live.

As I've attempted to illustrate in this book, there is hope through shifting power, transforming land use, resetting culture, and leveraging systems together to change systems in our places. We can pull these levers and realize systems change through strategic collaboration, systems-oriented government, and place-based education. Through these catalysts, systems can be and are being changed to enable the right relationships and behaviors in people's lives for well-being and regeneration.

One more important catalyst is needed to create lasting transformation: that is you and everyone else reading this book. Personal change and systems change go hand in hand. Changing systems is much easier if we row our lives in the same direction. As social creatures, how we live matters. When enough people begin to live in certain ways, it spreads to others. There is synergy between personal change and systems change.

In this chapter, we'll examine the process of personal change and how we can each be a catalyst for place-based systems change. It is not about changing one behavior at a time; it's a deeper and broader process of centering our relationship with place in our lives. Growing our sense and knowledge of place provides a foundation and helps us develop place-based identities. Conscious place-based living can flow from such an identity and become a model for others. Living connected to place also involves participating in the building of place-based systems. As more and more of us prioritize place in our lives and live accordingly, we move collectively toward well-being and regeneration.

Deepening Sense and Knowledge of Place

Getting to know our place sounds so simple, yet it's become hard to do with the constant hustle and distraction of modern life. Living under corporate capitalist systems, we have lost much knowledge of the places where we live.

Indigenous wisdom orients us toward regaining knowledge of our places. As discussed in other chapters, community, nature, and connectedness are central to Indigenous value systems based on living close to nature and each other. Indigenous groups worldwide convey that we are all connected through the web of life. We can feel that every day when we pay attention to and deepen our connection to what surrounds us.

With more knowledge of a place, our separation from it diminishes. Our sense of being a part of it expands. To counteract the push toward placelessness, we can start by simply taking more time to pay attention to our place.

Knowing a place involves slowing down and observing its human-made and natural features. Social psychiatrist Dr. Mindi Fullilove visited 178 main streets worldwide for her book *Main Street: How a City's Heart Connects Us All*. Fullilove developed methods for people to learn more about these central hubs of activity in their places. She explains one practice that she calls "Stroll and Scroll": "During the walk, you are enjoying the weather, the people, the buildings, and the unexpected. You can use your phone to take photos, if you like, and a small piece of paper or a map to write some notes. . . . There is lots to see on a Main Street: look for the age of buildings, the kinds of store windows, places you'd love to visit, the 'collection of main things' like the library, grocery store, and movie theater."[2] Fullilove's advice is simple yet revolutionary. We have stopped paying much attention to the world just outside our door. Even just a few minutes of "strolling and scrolling" can become building blocks for recovering our sense of place.

Applying Fullilove's methods to everyday life awakens us to the present challenges as well as the beauty, resilience, and promise in our communities. We may discover local businesses nearby that we didn't know existed. We may observe bees pollinating native plants, wildflowers blooming, or small plants taking root through cracks on an empty lot. We will see birds and hear their chatter. More than we might expect, we will see people helping others. The more we are present in our communities, the deeper our connection to and appreciation for it becomes.

With place-based knowledge, we can envision steps to take that will make our place better for people and nature. It may be getting to know our watershed and doing what we can to conserve and protect it. It could be learning about local food availability and supporting local grocery stores, farmers' markets, and restaurants that provide it.

Between knowledge and action, however, lies an important mediator. Identity influences whether we adopt a sustained connection to place and let it shape how we live.

Developing Place-Based Identities

Identity influences human choices and behavior, as it helps answer the question: Am I the kind of person who does this? It's predictive of various behaviors, from buying organic food[3] to exercising.[4] The more we identify with certain groups or ideas, the more likely those groups or ideas are to influence our decisions and how we live.

Political tribalism has increasingly shaped identities and the identity-behavior connection in the United States. The polarization is reflected in views and actions related to the climate crisis. On one side, the crisis is real, urgent, and requires significant action. The other side has downplayed the issue and suggested people can't do much about it. Political-based identity and its influence on behavior became apparent during the COVID-19 pandemic. Whether you wore a mask or got the vaccine was influenced by your political affiliation.[5] We seek to act in accordance with how we identify ourselves, and stark lines have been drawn around those identities, leading to behaviors that stand in direct conflict with one another.

Place-based identities provide another way to shape our behavior. By deepening our knowledge and sense of place, we can see ourselves more as part of our place than belonging to any political group or other affiliation. Rather than identities that pull us apart, identifying with our places can bring us together. It can lead to behavior choices that may differ significantly from those guided by political identities.

Identifying strongly with the place where one lives can lessen or even subsume divisive identities. A person may have a place-based identity *and* a political identity that questions or denies climate change. If the individual's identity is strongly influenced by her relationship to place, she will be more prone to live locally and in ways that have less impact on climate. It doesn't matter why someone adopts a place-based, low-impact lifestyle; what matters is that they do. Place-based identities can serve as encompassing identities that move society in a more positive direction.

With a place-based identity, we may start to look at everything differently. Public space becomes an opportunity for rich interaction with each other and nature. Space for cars and big box retail feels lifeless. We see cars more as a danger and polluter that interferes with community and nature than a way to get around daily. Food, energy, and water use become meaningful rituals to connect with nature and those who harvest them. Our places become ones of discovery, connection, and meaning every day.

Place-based identities can cut across one's neighborhood, city, and region and align with living connected to place at these different scales. Seeking to buy food and consumer goods sourced from the region may emanate from an affinity and pride in one's place. Identifying with one's neighborhood encourages shopping at local businesses and spending time in nearby community and nature spaces. Walking and biking within one's community and city reinforce identity at those levels, while longer rides on public transit may fit with one's regional identity. Over time, with a flexible place-based identity, living connected to place whenever possible becomes almost automatic.

Still, the constant presence of corporate capitalist influences makes it hard to have a place-based identity and live accordingly. We have to sink into our desire for connectedness and decide to prioritize it in our lives.

Conscious Place-Based Living as a Light for Others

A place-based identity can evoke feelings of connectedness that help guide our choices. We may feel a disconcerting sense of separation when in cars or on screens. Active transportation and local community and nature spaces become the antidote we seek instead. We may reduce our attachment to consumer goods and instead desire more experiences that connect us to our surroundings and other people. Artist Hans Hoffman stated, "The ability to simplify means to eliminate the unnecessary so that the necessary may speak."[6] That "necessary" is nature, community, and connectedness.

We are more motivated to use and waste less energy, food, and stuff in daily life when we are connected to the natural resources and people that provide them. We come to know the sun, wind, soil, water, plants, and animals that nourish us, keep us comfortable, and provide for our other needs. Farmers, makers, renewable energy technicians, and all the people who help transform nature into what we need also become known to us. Our feelings of gratitude motivate us to live in ways that regenerate nature, community, and local economies.

Indigenous wisdom guides us to live in regenerative ways. Robin Wall Kimmerer, in *Braiding Sweetgrass*, describes the traditional ecological knowledge of Indigenous people through the Honorable Harvest, which teaches: "Take only what you need. Never take more than half. Leave some for others. Harvest in a way that minimizes harm. Use it respectfully. Never waste what you have taken. Sustain the ones who sustain you and the Earth will last forever."[7] Respect and reciprocity with nature, as Kimmerer explains, are elusive if we are not directly connected to the land for our needs. If we depend more on local nature and community, Indigenous wisdom can pervade our world again. It puts us in the right relationship with nature, community, and our places.

We will find ourselves at the crossroads between corporate capitalist and place-based ways. In our lives, the choice presents itself often.

The winter holidays allow one to peer at the crossroads and decide on a direction. The corporate capitalist path leads us to focus on shopping, wrapping gifts, anticipating material gifts from others, and exchanging gifts. The place-based pathway opens other possibilities. Annual holiday traditions can be more about slowing down, feeling the changing seasons, and deepening connection to place. Family and friends will likely be part of the holidays either way, but what we pay attention to and experience together will differ.

Halloween is another opportunity to decide on a direction for how we experience an annual ritual. With corporate capitalism's influence, the likely focus will be on buying new costumes from Amazon or other Big Retailers. For children, the accumulation of candy may be the main priority. Author and well-being leader Tamar Lechner explains Halloween from a more place-based perspective: "Halloween is a time where we come together outside regardless of the weather and spend time walking together. . . . Trick-or-treating allows for a slow walk outdoors where you have no goal other than to enjoy the evening. Take notice of the sounds and smells as you enjoy time outside."[8] When we spend time outside during the Halloween season and pay attention, we can experience the changing seasons with crisp air and fall colors on trees. A jack-o'-lantern can extend the holiday and nature's gifts if we extract and roast the seeds. If the pumpkin is carved the day before, we may be able to remove the pulp and cook it too. With conscious place-based living, every holiday is an opportunity to connect to and treasure the gifts of nature and community.

From these moments, we can start to imagine what living connected to place might be like in its fullest expression: living in mixed-use, mixed-income communities; seeking work that is part of one's place; getting to know local store and restaurant staff and owners; walking regularly in one's neighborhood; biking across town; navigating public transit with ease; spending time in local nature and public spaces; engaging in community activities; eating food from local farms and growing some of our own; powering homes with nearby and regional renewable energy; and treasuring and sharing consumer goods made from natural resources and people in one's region. These placed-based ways of living require supportive systems, but when we move in this direction by changing how we live, we help form those systems.

In corporate capitalist systems, the odds are heavily stacked against those without power and nature as a whole. Yet every time we choose to conserve, buy locally, travel without a car, or reach out to community members in need, we nudge systems in a different direction. No one suggests that an individual can do this alone. Those who are ready need to act and show others that living connected to place is possible and desirable.

When we live in alignment with a place-based identity, we change the context for others as at least one reference point on how one might live. It's human nature to bristle at even the hint of being told how to live. Anchoring one's behavior in intrinsic values around connectedness, community, and nature and talking about it as such can be more inviting to others. It's the difference between saying, "I rarely drive a car because of climate change" and "I enjoy walking in my community and seeing my neighbors." The first statement may come across as "You should too if you care enough," while the second statement is rooted in a sense of community that is more appealing.

In *Change: How to Make Big Things Happen*, author and researcher Damon Centola shows that everyone has more power than they might think. He posits that individual changes matter not because they add up to a complete solution but because they shift the zeitgeist that leaders and influencers integrate into their work and messages.[9] A virtuous cycle can begin when institutions such as local government are influenced by people willing to change their lives. Then, those institutions facilitate systems change, leading to more people adopting similar changes in how they live. It's not an "either-or" but changing ourselves and systems together, anchored in evolving place-based identities.

Participating in the Building of Place-Based Systems

In addition to how we live, we can join others and push directly for systems change to make it possible for more people to live connected to place. Advocating for more housing and mixed-use zoning is critical so that more people live close to the amenities they need in their daily lives. Demanding local ordinances that protect small local businesses is another one. Pick any system or combination that interests you and find one way to get involved. You can help move the needle on what is needed to change how people live. Each of us, connected and committed to our places, can help build place-based systems.

Lydia Francis was recognized as the San Francisco Bicycle Coalition's 2021 Bike Champion of the Year. Lydia took up biking in San Francisco during the COVID-19 pandemic. She describes how taking most trips by bike has impacted her: "Biking has given me a deeper sense of belonging here in San Francisco—both to the literal geography of this place and the people I meet while exploring on two wheels."[10] After learning the ins and outs of buying, maintaining, and riding a bike, Lydia became a teacher to new riders. She coaches people who are new to biking and helps them find used bikes. Lydia regularly organizes themed group rides with friends. She has found ways to live more connected to her place through biking and is spreading her passion and knowledge to others. By providing a supportive social context, Lydia is helping reset culture and change the transportation system in her city.

Ray Leon, the mayor of the small town of Huron in California's Central Valley, leads and inspires systemic change that makes his place better for nature and people. He grew up in Huron, attended the University of California, Berkeley, and returned to his hometown upon graduation. Leon sparked the city's development of a solar microgrid and storage project. He has helped advance plans for a two-hundred-acre hemp farm to provide good-paying jobs for growing and processing hemp fiber and seed oil. Leon explains why he promotes local agriculture and takes on agribusiness in his community: "All this [agriculture] is bringing in incredible revenues to the area. But very little of it reaches the people who make it possible—the people who work in agriculture. And we need to change that."[11] He facilitated a vanpool for farmworkers, saving them hundreds of dollars annually. He also has led the installation of electric vehicle chargers for those vans and other vehicles. Leon started a downtown tree-planting project. He is working to establish a three-thousand-acre nature preserve near town that can bring in conservation and carbon sequestration dollars and employ local people and youth. Working with others, Leon has helped shift power and move land use toward place-based systems in energy, food, transportation, nature spaces, and work.

The emergence of slow streets in San Francisco, described in chapter 7, demonstrates how people can influence the community spaces system. Barriers at intersections that restrict car traffic initially created slow streets, but they needed much more to become spaces for community gathering. Local journalist Ricardo Cano explained how residents who became self-appointed mayors, or caretakers, of these streets made the difference.[12] They look after the barriers, facilitate enhancements with art and plantings, organize events, and liaise with city agencies. Andrew Casteel, "comayor" of Sanchez Street with Yuko Shah, explains their role and motivation: "We just do what we can to make sure that the street is safe, that people want to visit, that it's fun and it's beautiful because it's the people getting out there and using the slow street that keeps . . . that stronger sense of community alive."[13] Casteel and other slow street mayors successfully advocated for permanent slow streets. Two other comayors, Jessica Jenkins and Molly Hayden of Page Street, worked to get San Francisco's first community parklet built. The parklet is located at a street intersection and includes seating, a free library, and a garden. The slow street mayors have helped transform land use and reset culture on streets in support of local, vibrant community.

These place-based systems-change leaders have inspired me. Although I have lived connected to place in many ways for years, I have been less involved in participating in systems-change efforts in my neighborhood and city.

At the start of 2024, I joined the San Francisco Bicycle Coalition's board. This citywide nonprofit is helping to shift power in support of a citywide network for biking and rolling. This network of protected bike lanes, slow streets, and other infrastructure is expanding and will transform land use. The coalition also educates and trains people of all ages in urban biking, helping to reset culture.

At the neighborhood level, I've begun working with neighbors to form a Vision Zero group (see chap. 6 for more information on Vision Zero). We are advocating for safer pedestrian and biking infrastructure at places where cars have injured people. We also know these changes will encourage more people to bike, walk, and use transit. We are building power by engaging with other neighborhood groups and being part of the citywide Vision Zero Coalition.

It's taken me a while to engage in these local systems-change efforts. The personal rewards have been many: getting to know my community better, forming deeper bonds with neighbors and city residents, and participating in something bigger than myself to help make my place better. I am motivated to stay involved and do what I can to further these efforts.

The examples of the slow street mayors, Ray Leon and Lydia Francis, are inspiring, but not everyone will or can take the initiative to act locally and help change systems as they do. Many of us, though, can participate in a local project. Joining a monthly neighborhood cleanup, for example, improves community space and builds relationships with fellow community members. Nature restoration activities and community tree plantings are ways to improve the local nature spaces system. Helping to maintain a community food garden adds to the local food system. Participating in a community swap event supports a place-based consumer goods system. Community-building activities can enhance any place-based system.

The more people work on building place-based systems, the more place-based living and all its benefits can be realized across society. Systems dominated by corporate capitalism are not inevitable when we stand up for nature, community, and our places. Whenever I meet someone working to improve their region, county, or city, my sense of hope grows for the just, sustainable world we want and need. The climate, biodiversity loss, inequality, and social breakdown crises aren't going away without us working to change ourselves and our systems. The change we need is possible if we act daily with intent and build a movement together for place-based systems and ways of living.

There will be plenty of doubters, status quo resistance, and the challenge of trying to see beyond present circumstances. But we must remember that we have created the current systems. Although we can't alter them easily, there is hope when we participate in change from a systems lens and concentrate efforts on shifting power, transforming land use, resetting culture, and leveraging other systems.

Moving Collectively Toward Well-Being and Regeneration

To fully confront the social and environmental crises we face, we desperately need points of unification. While so much continues to push us apart, one thing can bring us together like nothing else: a shared love of and engagement with the place where we live. Connectedness, community, and reciprocity with nature are part of our genetic makeup, shaped over millennia. We can find this deeper part of our humanity in our places. Issues that have divided us lose their power as we come together to help our places better nourish people's lives and those of our nonhuman kin. It is the path to well-being and regeneration.

Place-based systems and living connected to place allow us to move away from the false and damaging nature-human society dualism. The belief that all humanity, life, and matter are fundamentally "one" is found across Indigenous cultures. Writer, filmmaker, and activist Julian Brave NoiseCat of the Canim Lake Band Tsq'escen explains: "We are not alone. We have relatives. We are, in fact, all related and not just us humans. The other than human world shares some of our DNA too. If we remember that, maybe we will recognize that our fates are also interrelated. . . . In some important way, place determines who and what we are. . . . Remember that we all come from somewhere and that those places and the place called Earth need us to fight for them."[14] Connected to place, we feel a more profound dependence on and shared affinity for nature and community. As we sink further into place, the "other" in people and nature fades, and the illusion of separation diminishes. We become awakened to how interconnected we are and the importance of acting as "one" to care for ourselves and all of life.

Once we get beyond separation and see and feel ourselves in everything around us, we are on the path to healing people and the planet. When we change systems to regenerate nature, communities, and local economies, we regenerate society and ourselves. No technology will fix our broken world. Only we can, by changing systems and living rooted in our places and oneness.

Cultivate a place-based identity with a deep and sustained connection to the place where you live. Change begins at home, and place is your home. May you find happiness, meaning, and hope in your place and in helping make it better for all who live there, human and nonhuman.

Acknowledgments

I first want to thank my life partner, Lisa, for her love and unwavering support. I could not have written this book without you. You mean the world to me. I deeply appreciate my parents, Richard and Susan Biggar, who raised me to believe in myself and pursue my dreams. My dad was a loving father and avid book reader. I've written this book in his memory. To my mom, brother Rob, sister Lauren, and children Kat and Jack, I'm grateful for your continued love and support.

The idea for this book was seeded under the mentorship of Nicole Ardoin at Stanford University. Her openness, enthusiasm, and thoughtfulness helped me find ways to weave my passions into my research. Nicole also provided opportunities for me to research place-based systems change and collaboration. Guided by her expertise in environmental behavior, my research laid the foundation for this book.

While at Stanford, I benefited from the work of many great thinkers and researchers. Raymond DeYoung and Steven and Rachel Kaplan were particularly influential. Though I never met them, their research and understanding of the relationship between context and human behavior quietly guided my writing.

When I started exploring the idea of a book, I received great advice from experienced writers and editors. Jim Burke, a prolific author and outstanding educator, helped me understand how to start writing a book. Jim and I worked together at a high school for six years, and I'm so glad we've stayed in touch.

I also had formative conversations with Hannah Love, a former editor at the University of California Press. Her guidance and early enthusiasm for the book were a big boost. I also interviewed Hannah and wrote a profile of how she lives connected to place.

I would never have been able to write this book without support from Jess Beebe of Waxwing Studio. Jess's years of experience editing and working in the book publishing industry were invaluable to me as a first-time author. She helped tremendously with the initial manuscript development and dispensed expert guidance through the process of finding the right publisher.

I owe a debt of gratitude to colleagues and friends with specialized knowledge in chapter topics. Thank you, Chris Batson (housing), Shane Hampton (local business and work), Mike Sallaberry (transportation), Kristin Haukom (transportation), Phil Ginsburg (public space), Scott Sampson (nature), Lydia

Wendt (clothing production), Sara Zimmerman (circular economies), Ben Cook (renewable energy), and Ben Rosenfield (local government), for lending your time and expertise to reviewing book chapters.

I had the pleasure of interviewing many inspiring people who live connected to place in my writing process. Some of their stories are included in this book, while others are featured in my blog series, *Profiles in Living Connected to Place* (www.connectedtoplace.com/ctpprofiles). In addition to Hannah and others mentioned below, they are Nic Jay Aulston, Juan Miguel Arias, T. R. Amsler, Chalida Anusasananan, Leslie Parra, Anthony Khalil, Rebecca Au, Lucian Beebe, Bill Kelly, Brett Korsgaard, Roshni Sahu, Joshua Spodek, Tina Syer, Wanda Stewart, Emily Beach, Sharon Danks, and Annie Burke.

In my consulting projects, I've worked with many effective, caring people who have helped me better understand place-based systems change and how to make it work in the real world. I won't be able to thank everyone here, but the following are a few. I want to thank Damien Raffa, who connected me to my first place-based systems-change and collaboration project, San Francisco Children and Nature. Damien was a great partner on that project and also the subject of one of my *Profiles in Living Connected to Place*. I'm grateful to the late Louisa McCune of the Kirkpatrick Foundation for partnering on many place-based collaborative projects and to Kelly Burley, the outstanding director of one of those projects, Common Bonds. I benefitted a lot from working with Maria Durana, the impactful director of San Francisco Children and Nature, and her review of the strategic collaboration chapter. I'm thankful to Andra Yeghoian for our work together on education partnerships and her review of the place-based education chapter. Finally, I'd like to thank Theresa Vallez-Kelly, the superb Safe Routes to School Coordinator in San Mateo County, California, who has embraced the place-based systems change approach in a city government-school partnership program that she leads and I help support.

Finally, thank you, Kitty Liu and Cornell University Press, for publishing this book. Your belief in my work and guidance in improving the manuscript are greatly appreciated.

Notes

INTRODUCTION

1. Dodai Stewart, "Parisians Are Choosing Bikes over Cars. Will New Yorkers Do That, Too?," *New York Times*, August 26, 2024, https://www.nytimes.com/2024/08/26 /nyregion/street-wars-bike-lanes-paris.html.

2. "Ten Years of Transformation of Paris, A Look Back at the Major Achievements," City of Paris, 2024, last modified March 25, 2024, https://www.paris.fr/pages /dix-ans-de-transformation-de-paris-au-service-des-parisiennes-et-des-parisiens-26671.

3. Mark Sutton, "TfL Economic Benefits of Cycling Paper a Home Run for Investment Case," *Cycling Industry News*, August 15, 2019, https://cyclingindustry.news/tfl -economic-benefits-of-cycling-paper-a-home-run-for-investment-case/.

4. Hans Bruyninckx, "Bend the Trend: Pathways to a Liveable Planet as Resource Use Spikes," *United Nations Environment Programme Global Resources Outlook* (2024), https:// wedocs.unep.org/20.500.11822/44901.

5. Jean-Paul Rodrigue, "World Energy Consumption 1965–2020," in *The Geography of Transport Systems*, 6th ed. (Routledge, 2024), https://doi.org/10.4324/9781003343196.

6. Ivan Grujic, Jovan Doric, Nadica Stojanovic, and Oday I. Abdullah, "Numerical Analysis of Hydrogen Fueled IC Engine," *19th Conference on Thermal Science and Engineering of Serbia*, October 2019, https://www.researchgate.net/publication /337898468_Numerical_analysis_of_hydrogen_fueled_IC_engine#pf1.

7. "It's 2024, How Many Cars Are There in the World," Which Car, accessed September 23, 2024, https://www.whichcar.com.au/news/how-many-cars-are-there-in-the-world.

8. Jeff Davis, "VMT Back to Pre-COVID Level in 2023, but Still Lags per Capita," *Eno Center for Transportation*, February 9, 2024, https://enotrans.org/article/vmt-back -to-pre-covid-level-in-2023-but-still-lags-per-capita/.

9. Tom Randall, "American Cars Are Developing a Serious Weight Problem," *Bloomberg*, August 8, 2023, https://www.bloomberg.com/news/articles/2023-08-08/american -cars-are-developing-a-serious-weight-problem.

10. Tim Bakke, "How Much Square Footage Do I Need for a New Home," The Plan Collection, October 6, 2023, https://www.theplancollection.com/blog/how-much-square -footage-do-i-need-for-a-new-home.

11. A. J. Jacobs, "Trying to Live a Day Without Plastic," *New York Times*, updated June 20, 2023, https://www.nytimes.com/2023/01/11/style/plastic-free.html.

12. Hannah Ritchie, Max Roser, and Pablo Rosado, "Meat and Dairy Production," *Our World in Data*, last revised December 2023, https://ourworldindata.org/meat-production.

13. Mehzabeen Mannan and Sami G. Al-Ghamdi, "Indoor Air Quality in Buildings: A Comprehensive Review on the Factors Influencing Air Pollution in Residential and Commercial Structure," *International Journal of Environmental Research and Public Health* 18, no. 6 (2021): 3276, https://doi.org/10.3390/ijerph18063276.

14. Camryn Smith, "Screen Time Statistics," Allconnect, February 23, 2024, https:// www.allconnect.com/blog/screen-time-stats.

15. Emma Elsworthy, "Average Adult Will Spend 34 Years of Their Life Looking at Screens, Poll Claims," *Independent*, May 11, 2020, https://www.independent.co.uk/life

-style/fashion/news/screen-time-average-lifetime-years-phone-laptop-tv-a9508751.html.

16. Robert A. Manduca, "The Contribution of National Income Inequality to Regional Economic Divergence," *Social Forces* 98, no. 2 (2019), https://doi.org/10.1093/sf/soz013.

17. Peter H. Kahn Jr. "Special Issue: Children and Nature," *Ecopsychology* 10, no. 4 (2018), https://www.liebertpub.com/toc/eco/10/4.

18. "People Should Balance Busyness with Self-Reflection," Stanford University, August 23, 2018, https://news.stanford.edu/stories/2018/08/people-balance-busyness-self-reflection.

19. John Helliwel, *Understanding and Improving the Social Context of Well-Being* (National Bureau of Economic Research, 2012).

20. Caleb Cohen, "500+ Connections: Networking Inundation, Addiction & Delusion," Decision Lab, March 4, 2019, https://thedecisionlab.com/insights/business/500-connections-inundation-addiction-and-delusion-in-social-and-professional-networking.

21. Brad Plumer and Lisa Friedman, "What Trump 2.0 Could Mean for the Environment," *New York Times*, July 16, 2024, https://www.nytimes.com/2024/07/16/climate/trump-epa-regulation.html.

22. Jacques Leslie, "How Climate Change Is Disrupting the Global Supply Chain," *Yale Environment 360*, March 10, 2022, https://e360.yale.edu/features/how-climate-change-is-disrupting-the-global-supply-chain.

23. David Brooks, "The Localist Revolution," *New York Times*, July 20, 2018, https://www.nytimes.com/2018/07/19/opinion/national-politics-localism-populism.html.

24. Ashlie D. Stevens, "Raise Chickens? Make Preserves? Why Americans Are Flocking to Urban Homesteading Activities," *Salon*, April 2, 2020, https://www.salon.com/2020/04/02/backyard-chickens-gardens-canning-preserves-urban-homesteading/.

25. Maya MacGuineas, "Capitalism's Addiction Problem," *Atlantic*, March 6, 2020, https://www.theatlantic.com/magazine/archive/2020/04/capitalisms-addiction-problem/606769/.

26. Donella H. Meadows, *Thinking in Systems* (Chelsea Green, 2008), 2.

27. "Transition Groups Near Me," Transition Network, accessed September 26, 2024, https://transitionnetwork.org/transition-near-me/.

28. "Welcome to Cittaslow International," Cittaslow International, accessed September 26, 2024, https://www.cittaslow.org/.

29. "7 Essential Ingredients," Transition Network, accessed September 26, 2024, https://transitionnetwork.org/do-transition/starting-transition/7-essential-ingredients/.

1. CHANGING HOW WE LIVE

1. Myles Allen et al., *Global Warming of 1.5°c: An IPCC Special Report on the Impacts of Global Warming of 1.5°c Above Pre-Industrial Levels and Related Global Greenhouse Gas Emission Pathways*, Intergovernmental Panel on Climate Change, 2018.

2. "Global Electricity Review 2024," Ember, accessed May 8, 2024, https://ember-energy.org/latest-insights/global-electricity-review-2024.

3. International Energy Agency, "Trends in Electric Cars," *Global EV Outlook 2024: Moving Towards Increased Affordability*, IEA, 2024, https://www.iea.org/reports/global-ev-outlook-2024/trends-in-electric-cars.

4. International Energy Agency, *World Energy Outlook 2023*, IEA, October 2023, https://www.iea.org/reports/world-energy-outlook-2023.

5. Raymond De Young and Thomas Princen, *The Localization Reader* (MIT Press, 2012), xix.

6. Craig Welch, "The Future of Driving Is Here—And It's Electric," *National Geographic*, October 2021, https://www.nationalgeographic.com/magazine/article/the-future-of-driving-is-here-and-it-is-electric-feature.

7. Dionne Searcey and Eric Lipton, "Hunt for the 'Blood Diamond of Batteries' Impedes Green Energy Push," *New York Times*, November 29, 2021, https://www.nytimes.com/2021/11/29/world/congo-cobalt-albert-yuma-mulimbi.html.

8. Anthony Barnosky et al., "Approaching a State Shift in Earth's Biosphere," *Nature* 486 (2012): 52–58, https://doi.org/10.1038/nature11018; Tom Crompton, "Weathercocks and Signposts: The Environment Movement at a Crossroads," *World Wildlife Fund* (2008), https://assets.wwf.org.uk/downloads/weathercocks_report2.pdf; Thomas Dietz and Paul Stern, *New Tools for Environmental Protection: Education, Information, and Voluntary Measures* (National Academies Press, 2002); Elizabeth Shove, "Beyond the ABC: Climate Change Policy and Theories of Social Change," *Environment and Planning A* 42, no. 6 (2010): 1273, https://doi.org/10.1068/a42282.

9. Jared Diamond, "High Consumption by Some Nations Puts All of Us at Risk," *National Geographic*, December 2018, https://www.nationalgeographic.com/magazine/article/inequality-rich-poor-essay-jared-diamond.

10. Hiroko Tabuchi, "Lifestyle Emissions of the Rich and Famous," *New York Times*, November 13, 2019, https://www.nytimes.com/2019/11/13/climate/one-thing-we-can-do-balance-our-energy-demand.html.

11. Christopher Jones and Daniel Kammen, "A Consumption-Based Greenhouse Gas Inventory of San Francisco Bay Area Neighborhoods, Cities and Counties: Prioritizing Climate Action for Different Locations," University of California, Berkeley, 2015, https://escholarship.org/uc/item/2sn7m83z.

12. "Carbon Footprint Factsheet," Center for Sustainable Systems, University of Michigan, 2022, https://css.umich.edu/publications/factsheets/sustainability-indicators/carbon-footprint-factsheet.

13. "What Is Your Carbon Footprint?," *Nature Conservancy*, 2019, https://www.nature.org/en-us/get-involved/how-to-help/carbon-footprint-calculator/.

14. "New Analysis Shows Cities Have Bigger Opportunity to Reduce Global Emissions If They Address Consumption—C40 Cities," C40 Cities, July 10, 2023, https://www.c40.org/news/new-analysis-shows-cities-have-bigger-opportunity-to-reduce-global-emissions-if-they-address-consumption/; Christopher Jones and Daniel Kammen, "A Consumption-Based Greenhouse Gas Inventory of San Francisco Bay Area Neighborhoods, Cities and Counties: Prioritizing Climate Action for Different Locations, University of California, Berkeley, 2015, https://escholarship.org/uc/item/2sn7m83z; Chris Goodall, *How to Live a Low-Carbon Life: The Individual's Guide to Tackling Climate Change* (Earthscan, 2010); Seth Shulman and Jeff Deyette, *Cooler Smarter: Practical Steps for Low-Carbon Living* (Island, 2012).

15. Christiana Figueres and Tom Rivett-Carnac, *The Future We Choose: Surviving the Climate Crisis* (Knopf, 2020).

16. Richard Louv, "Telling a Powerful Tale," *Our Planet*, no. 2 (2018): 32–33, https://doi.org/10.18356/2fc8212e-en.

17. "2020 Had the Largest Single-Year Carbon Emissions Drop in History. But Will It Last?," *Science Alert*, January 3, 2021, https://www.sciencealert.com/world-might-have-hit-peak-carbon-emissions-last-year-others-think-it-was-a-blip.

18. "Climate Change in the American Mind: Beliefs & Attitudes, Spring 2024," Center for Climate Change Communication, July 16, 2024, https://www.climatechangecommunication.org/all/climate-change-in-the-american-mind-beliefs-attitudes-spring-2024/.

19. Raymond DeYoung, "New Ways to Promote Proenvironmental Behavior: Expanding and Evaluating Motives for Environmentally Responsible Behavior," *Journal of Social Issues* 56, no. 3 (2000): 509–26, https://doi.org/10.1111/0022-4537.00181.

20. Stephen Kaplan, "New Ways to Promote Proenvironmental Behavior: Human Nature and Environmentally Responsible Behavior," *Journal of Social Issues* 56, no. 3 (2000): 491–508, https://doi.org/10.1111/0022-4537.00180.

21. "Americans' Stress, Worry and Anger Intensified in 2018," Gallup, April 25, 2019, https://news.gallup.com/poll/249098/americans-stress-worry-anger-intensified-2018.aspx.

22. Robert H. Shmerling, "Why Life Expectancy in the US Is Falling," Harvard Health, October 20, 2022, https://www.health.harvard.edu/blog/why-life-expectancy-in-the-us-is-falling-202210202835.

23. "U.S. Health Care Spending Highest Among Developed Countries | Johns Hopkins Bloomberg School of Public Health," Johns Hopkins Bloomberg School of Public Health, January 7, 2019, https://publichealth.jhu.edu/2019/us-health-care-spending-highest-among-developed-countries.

24. "Life Expectancy by Country and in the World (2024)," Worldometer, 2024, https://www.worldometers.info/demographics/life-expectancy/.

25. Anne Case and Angus Deaton, *Deaths of Despair and the Future of Capitalism* (Princeton University Press, 2020).

26. Benedict Carey, "Is the Pandemic Sparking Suicide?," *New York Times*, May 19, 2020, sec. Health, https://www.nytimes.com/2020/05/19/health/pandemic-coronavirus-suicide-health.html.

27. "Hawaii Tops U.S. in Wellbeing for Record 7th Time," Gallup, February 27, 2019, https://news.gallup.com/poll/247034/hawaii-tops-wellbeing-record-7th-time.aspx.

28. John Helliwell et al., "Environments for Happiness: An Overview," World Happiness Report, March 20, 2020, https://worldhappiness.report/ed/2020/environments-for-happiness-an-overview/.

29. Allyson Chiu, "Americans Are the Unhappiest They've Ever Been, U.N. Report Finds. An 'Epidemic of Addictions' Could Be to Blame," *Washington Post*, March 21, 2019, https://www.washingtonpost.com/nation/2019/03/21/americans-are-unhappiest-theyve-ever-been-un-report-finds-an-epidemic-addictions-could-be-blame/?noredirect=on.

30. Jean Twenge, "The Sad State of Happiness in the United States and the Role of Digital Media," World Happiness Report, March 20, 2019, https://worldhappiness.report/ed/2019/the-sad-state-of-happiness-in-the-united-states-and-the-role-of-digital-media/.

31. Bu Zhong, Yakun Huang, and Qian Liu, "Mental Health Toll from the Coronavirus: Social Media Usage Reveals Wuhan Residents' Depression and Secondary Trauma in the COVID-19 Outbreak," *Computers in Human Behavior* 114 (January 2021): 106524, https://doi.org/10.1016/j.chb.2020.106524.

32. Jody Aked et al., "A Report Presented to the Foresight Project on Communicating the Evidence Base for Improving People's Well-Being," New Economics Foundation, 2008, https://neweconomics.org/uploads/files/8984c5089d5c2285ee_t4m6bhqq5.pdf.

33. "20 Habits for a Healthier, Happier Life," Blue Zones, January 4, 2018, https://www.bluezones.com/2018/01/20-habits-healthier-happier-life/.

34. John Wasik, "How to Be Happy Without Earning More," University of Chicago Booth School of Business, 2018, https://www.chicagobooth.edu/review/how-be-happy-without-earning-more.

35. Andrew T. Jebb, Louis Tay, Ed Diener, and Shigehero Oishi, "Happiness, Income Satiation and Turning Points Around the World," *Nature Human Behaviour* 2, no. 1 (January 2018): 33–38, https://doi.org/10.1038/s41562-017-0277-0.

36. Christian Krekel and George MacKerron, "How Environmental Quality Affects Our Happiness," in World Happiness Report 2020, ed. John F. Helliwell, Richard Layard, Jeffrey Sachs, and Jan-Emmanuel De Neve (New York: Sustainable Development Solutions Network), https://worldhappiness.report/ed/2020/how-environmental-quality-affects-our-happiness/#fnref30.

37. Naomi Imatome-Yun, "Where Are the Happiest Cities in America?," Blue Zones, October 18, 2017, https://www.bluezones.com/2017/10/happiest-cities-america/.

38. Kara Shaughnessy, "Despite Perils, Decide to Hope," *National Geographic*, October 2018, https://www.zinio.com/publications/national-geographic-interactive/2820/issues/40 5155.

39. Stephen Kaplan and Rachel Kaplan, "Creating a Larger Role for Environmental Psychology: The Reasonable Person Model as an Integrative Framework," *Journal of Environmental Psychology* 29, no. 3 (September 2009): 329–39, https://doi.org/10.1016/j .jenvp.2008.10.005; Anja Kollmuss and Julian Agyeman, "Mind the Gap: Why Do People Act Environmentally and What Are the Barriers to Pro-Environmental Behavior?," *Environmental Education Research* 8, no. 3 (2002): 239–60, https://doi.org/10.1080/13504620220145401; Wesley Schultz, "Knowledge, Information, and Household Recycling: Examining the Knowledge-Deficit Model of Behavior Change," in *New Tools for Environmental Protection: Education, Information, and Voluntary Measures*, ed. Paul Stern and Thomas Dietz (National Academy Press, 2002), 67–82; Linda Steg and Charles Vlek, "Encouraging Pro-Environmental Behaviour: An Integrative Review and Research Agenda," *Journal of Environmental Psychology* 29, no. 3 (2009): 309–17, https://doi.org/10.1016/j.jenvp.2008.10.004.

40. Auden Schendler, "Worrying About Your Carbon Footprint Is Exactly What Big Oil Wants You to Do," *New York Times*, August 31, 2021, sec. Opinion, https://www.nytimes .com/2021/08/31/opinion/climate-change-carbon-neutral.html.

41. Rebecca Solnit, "Big Oil Coined 'Carbon Footprints' to Blame Us for Their Greed. Keep Them on the Hook," *Guardian*, August 23, 2021, https://www.theguardian.com /commentisfree/2021/aug/23/big-oil-coined-carbon-footprints-to-blame-us-for-their -greed-keep-them-on-the-hook.

2. PLACE-BASED SYSTEMS, WELL-BEING, AND REGENERATION

1. "Public Transport Must Double in Cities over next Decade to Meet 1.5°c Target—C40 Cities," C40 Cities, January 25, 2022, https://www.c40.org/news/public-transport -cities-decade-1-5c-target/.

2. Christopher Jones and Daniel Kammen, "A Consumption-Based Greenhouse Gas Inventory of San Francisco Bay Area Neighborhoods, Cities and Counties: Prioritizing Climate Action for Different Locations," Escholarship.org, December 17, 2015, https:// escholarship.org/uc/item/2sn7m83z.

3. Marguerite Holloway and George Etheredge, "When There's No Heat: 'You Need Wood, You Get Wood,'" *New York Times*, February 19, 2021, sec. Climate, https://www .nytimes.com/2021/02/19/climate/wood-banks-winter-maine.html.

4. Dan Buettner, "Blue Zones of Happiness Author Dan Buettner on Denmark, Costa Rica and Singapore," *National Geographic Magazine*, October 16, 2017, https://www .nationalgeographic.com/magazine/article/worlds-happiest-places.

5. Buettner, "Blue Zones of Happiness."

6. "Singapore," Biophilic Cities, accessed October 30, 2024, https://www.biophiliccities .org/singapore.

7. "Where Are the Happiest Cities in America?," Blue Zones, October 18, 2017, https://www.bluezones.com/2017/10/happiest-cities-america/.

8. Ayenat Mersie and Ami Vitale, "For Kenya's Orphaned Elephants, Goats to the Rescue," *National Geographic Magazine*, August 12, 2021, https://www.nationalgeographic .com/animals/article/kenyas-orphaned-elephants-goats-to-the-rescue.

9. Movement Generation, *A Strategic Framework for a Just Transition from BANKS and TANKS to COOPERATION and CARING*, 2017, https://movementgeneration.org /wp-content/uploads/2016/11/JT_booklet_Eng_printspreads.pdf, 4.

10. "About Us—Regenerative Communities Network," Regenerative Communities Network, accessed October 30, 2024, https://www.regencommunities.net/about-us/.

11. Robert Steuteville, "Biggest Suburb Gets a New Downtown as Walkable Becomes Legal," Congress for the New Urbanism, October 21, 2021, https://www.cnu.org/public square/2021/10/21/biggest-suburb-gets-downtown.

12. Jesse Sherry, "The Impact of Community Sustainability: A Life Cycle Assessment of Three Ecovillages," *Journal of Cleaner Production* 237, no. 10 (November 2019): 117830, https://doi.org/10.1016/j.jclepro.2019.117830.

13. "Las Ecoaldeas Como Alternativa Ecológica," Iberdrola, accessed October 30, 2024, https://www.iberdrola.com/sustainability/ecovillages-alternative-ecological -communities.

14. "Merwedekanaalzone | Gemeente Utrecht," City of Utrecht, 2024, https://www .utrecht.nl/wonen-en-leven/bouwprojecten-en-stedelijke-ontwikkeling/bouwprojecten /merwedekanaalzone.

15. Robert Steuteville, "Building Community through Transportation," CNU, September 2020, https://www.cnu.org/publicsquare/2020/09/01/building-community-through -transportation.

16. Daniel Herriges, "Our Self-Imposed Scarcity of Nice Places," Strong Towns, November 3, 2021, https://www.strongtowns.org/journal/2021/11/3/our-self-imposed -scarcity-of-nice-places.

3. THE PATH TO PLACE-BASED SYSTEMS CHANGE

1. Doug McKenzie-Mohr, "New Ways to Promote Proenvironmental Behavior: Promoting Sustainable Behavior: An Introduction to Community-Based Social Marketing," *Journal of Social Issues* 56, no. 3 (January 2000): 543–54, https://doi.org/10.1111/0022 -4537.00183; Martha C. Monroe, "Two Avenues for Encouraging Conservation Behaviors," *Human Ecology Review* 10, no. 2 (2003): 113–25, https://www.jstor.org/stable /24706961; Carmen Tanner, "Constraints on Environmental Behaviour," *Journal of Environmental Psychology* 19, no. 2 (June 1999): 145–57, https://doi.org/10.1006/jevp.1999 .0121.

2. "IBISWorld—Industry Market Research, Reports, and Statistics," IBIS World, 2024, https://www.ibisworld.com/global/industry-trends/biggest-industries-by-revenue/.

3. WSJ staff, "Five Tech Giants Just Keep Growing," *Wall Street Journal*, May 1, 2021, sec. Tech, https://www.wsj.com/articles/five-tech-giants-just-keep-growing-11619841644.

4. Andrea Murphy and Matt Schifrin, eds., "Forbes 2024 Global 2000 List—The World's Largest Companies Ranked," *Forbes*, June 6, 2024, https://www.forbes.com/lists /global2000/#72f5ef24335d.

5. Jacob S. Hacker and Paul Pierson, *Let Them Eat Tweets: How the Right Rules in an Age of Extreme Inequality* (Liveright, 2021), 67.

6. Hacker and Pierson, *Let Them Eat Tweets*, 55.

7. Annette Becker and Lessano Negussie, "Bloomberg—Are You a Robot?," *Bloomberg*, April 30, 2018, https://www.bloomberg.com/news/articles/2018-04-30/copenhagen -architect-jan-gehl-takes-on-smart-cities.

8. Erle C. Ellis et al., "Anthropogenic Transformation of the Biomes, 1700 to 2000," *Global Ecology and Biogeography* 19, no. 5 (June 2010): 589–606, https://doi.org/10.1111 /j.1466-8238.2010.00540.x.

9. Hannah Ritchie and Max Roser, "Half of the World's Habitable Land Is Used for Agriculture," Our World in Data, February 16, 2024, https://ourworldindata.org/global -land-for-agriculture.

10. Tim Wu, "The Tyranny of Convenience," *New York Times*, February 16, 2018, https://www.nytimes.com/2018/02/16/opinion/sunday/tyranny-convenience.html.

11. Elizabeth Shove, "Converging Conventions of Comfort, Cleanliness and Convenience," *Journal of Consumer Policy* 26, no. 4 (December 2003): 395–418, https://doi.org/10.1023/a:1026362829781.

12. John Wasik, "How to Be Happy Without Earning More," University of Chicago Booth School of Business, 2018, https://www.chicagobooth.edu/review/how-be-happy-without-earning-more.

13. Roger Cohen, "Boris Johnson and the Coming Trump Victory in 2020," *New York Times*, December 13, 2019, https://www.nytimes.com/2019/12/13/opinion/uk-election-trump-2020.html.

14. Maya MacGuineas, "Capitalism's Addiction Problem," *Atlantic*, March 6, 2020, https://www.theatlantic.com/magazine/archive/2020/04/capitalisms-addiction-problem/606769/.

15. "Where Are the Happiest Cities in America?," Blue Zones, October 18, 2017, https://www.bluezones.com/2017/10/happiest-cities-america/.

16. Eduardo Gudynas, "The Good Life: Each Region as Self-Sufficient as Possible," Both ENDS (blog), June 6, 2012, https://www.bothends.org/en/Whats-new/Blogs/The-Good-Life-Each-region-as-self-sufficient-as-possible/.

17. Liz Canning, "Motherload" (Motherload Films, 2019), www.motherloadmovie.com.

4. HOUSING

1. J. K. Dineen, "These S.F. Neighborhoods Have High Eviction Rates, but Little Help from the City," *San Francisco Chronicle*, June 6, 2021, https://www.sfchronicle.com/local/article/The-missing-middle-These-S-F-16226448.php.

2. Chris Neiger, "The Typical Monthly Rent Is $1,988. Here's How Much It's Increased since 2020," *The Ascent by The Motley Fool*, April 29, 2024, https://www.fool.com/the-ascent/personal-finance/articles/the-typical-monthly-rent-is-1988-heres-how-much-its-increased-since-2020/.

3. Eric McGhee, Marisol Cuellar Mejia, and Hans Johnson, "California's Renters," Public Policy Institute of California, February 27, 2024, https://www.ppic.org/blog/californias-renters/.

4. Megan Henney, "US Home Prices Have Surged 47% since the Start of 2020," FOX-Business, May 13, 2024, https://www.foxbusiness.com/economy/us-home-prices-have-surged-47-since-start-2020.

5. Mikayla Bouchard, "Transportation Emerges as Crucial to Escaping Poverty," *New York Times*, May 7, 2015, https://www.nytimes.com/2015/05/07/upshot/transportation-emerges-as-crucial-to-escaping-poverty.html.

6. Michael Gerrity, "20 Largest Brokerage Firms Handle 55 Percent of All US Home Sales," *World Property Journal*, April 8, 2021, https://www.worldpropertyjournal.com/real-estate-news/united-states/irvine/real-estate-news-t3-sixty-2021-enterprise-20-report-top-10-real-estate-brokers-in-america-realogy-holdings-keller-williams-realty-remax-homeservices-o-12462.php.

7. Daniel Herriges, "Fixing Finance for Small-Scale Development," Strong Towns, October 21, 2021, https://www.strongtowns.org/journal/2021/10/21/fixing-finance-for-small-scale-development.

8. Alexander Ferrer, "Over Two Thirds of All Los Angeles Rentals Are Now Owned by Speculative Investment Vehicles. What Does That Mean for Tenants? | KNOCK," Medium, March 10, 2021, https://medium.com/groundgamela/los-angeles-rental-speculation-4022d16a0d28.

9. Herriges, "Fixing Finance for Small-Scale Development."

10. Stephen Wheeler, "Why We Need to Reimagine Our Cities" (University of California Press, 2022), https://www.ucpress.edu/blog-posts/58468-why-we-need-to-reimagine-our-cities.

11. Stephen Menendian et al., "Single-Family Zoning in the San Francisco Bay Area," Othering & Belonging Institute, October 7, 2020, https://belonging.berkeley.edu/single-family-zoning-san-francisco-bay-area.

12. Donald Shoup, "Cutting the Cost of Parking Requirements," *ACCESS Magazine*, no. 48 (spring 2016): 26–33, https://www.accessmagazine.org/wp-content/uploads/sites/7/2016/05/access48-webprint_cuttingthecost.pdf.

13. Chris Batson, interview by author, December 20, 2023.

14. Lisa Prevost, "Town after Town, Residents Are Fighting Affordable Housing in Connecticut," *New York Times*, September 4, 2022, sec. Real Estate, https://www.nytimes.com/2022/09/04/realestate/connecticut-affordable-housing-apartments.html.

15. Binyamin Appelbaum, "Opinion | Much Ado About a Little More Housing," *New York Times*, August 1, 2019, https://www.nytimes.com/2019/08/01/opinion/montgomery-county-housing.html.

16. Peter Bergman et al., "Creating Moves to Opportunity: Experimental Evidence on Barriers to Neighborhood Choice," *American Economic Review* 114, no. 5 (May 1, 2024): 1281–1337, https://doi.org/10.1257/aer.20200407.

17. "Mountain View, CA," Niche, April 5, 2024, https://www.niche.com/places-to-live/mountain-view-santa-clara-ca/.

18. "Oak Park, IL," Niche, accessed October 30, 2024, https://www.niche.com/places-to-live/oak-park-cook-il/.

19. "Columbia, MD," Niche, August 19, 2024, https://www.niche.com/places-to-live/columbia-howard-md/.

20. Robert A. Manduca, "The Contribution of National Income Inequality to Regional Economic Divergence," *Social Forces* 98, no. 2 (March 25, 2019), https://doi.org/10.1093/sf/soz013.

21. Joe Cortright, "America's Most Diverse Mixed Income Neighborhoods," City Observatory, June 18, 2018, https://cityobservatory.org/admin/.

22. Erika Pinto, "Housing for Everyone, the Danish Way," SPUR, August 31, 2022, https://www.spur.org/news/2022-08-31/housing-for-everyone-the-danish-way.

23. Alexander Thompson and Jocelyn Yang, "Community Land Trusts Make Housing Affordable," *YES! Magazine*, May 2, 2022, https://www.yesmagazine.org/economy/2022/05/02/affordable-housing-community-land-trusts.

24. Daniel Herriges, "Where Did All the Small Developers Go?," Strong Towns, October 18, 2021, https://www.strongtowns.org/journal/2021/10/18/where-did-all-the-small-developers-go.

25. Daniel Herriges, "A New Generation of Town Makers," Strong Towns, October 20, 2021, https://www.strongtowns.org/journal/2021/10/20/a-new-generation-of-town-makers.

26. Herriges, "A New Generation of Town Makers."

27. "Biden Administration Trying to Reverse Racist Effect of Infrastructure Projects," *NBC News*, February 22, 2022, https://www.youtube.com/watch?v=wLF0mmPhM6w.

28. "Biden-Harris Administration Announces First-Ever Awards from Program to Reconnect Communities," US Department of Transportation, February 28, 2023, https://www.transportation.gov/briefing-room/biden-harris-administration-announces-first-ever-awards-program-reconnect-communities.

29. "Inner Loop East Project," City of Rochester, New York, 2017, https://www.cityofrochester.gov/departments/des/inner-loop-east-project.

30. David Mamaril Horowitz, "1,100-Unit Balboa Reservoir Development Agreement Approved by Board of Supervisors," Ingleside Light, August 15, 2020, https://www.inglesidelight.com/1100-unit-balboa-reservoir-development-agreement-approved-by-board-of-supervisors/.

31. "Parking Mandates Map," Parking Reform Network, accessed October 30, 2024, https://parkingreform.org/resources/mandates-map/.

32. Robert Steuteville, "Reforming Parking by Changing One Word," Congress for the New Urbanism, July 11, 2024, https://www.cnu.org/publicsquare/2024/07/11/reforming-parking-changing-one-word.

33. Emma Goldberg, "What Would It Take to Turn More Offices into Housing?," *New York Times*, December 27, 2022, sec. Business, https://www.nytimes.com/2022/12/27/business/what-would-it-take-to-turn-more-offices-into-housing.html.

34. Goldberg, "What Would It Take to Turn More Offices into Housing?"

35. Goldberg, "What Would It Take to Turn More Offices into Housing?"

36. Sujata Srivastava et al., "Exploring the Viability of Office-to-Residential Conversion in San Francisco's Changing Real Estate Market from Workspace to Homebase," October 2023, https://www.spur.org/sites/default/files/2023-10/SPUR_From_Workspace_to_Homebase.pdf.

37. Kenneth Chan, "Squamish Nation Moves Vancouver Forward with Transformative Senakw Project | Urbanized," *Daily Hive*, February 5, 2021, https://dailyhive.com/vancouver/senakw-squamish-first-nation-vancouver-rental-housing-development.

38. James Brausell, "Analysis: California's Single-Family Zoning 'Killer' Barely Making a Dent so Far," Planetizen.com, 2021, https://www.planetizen.com/news/2023/01/121105-analysis-californias-single-family-zoning-killer-barely-making-dent-so-far.

39. "Case Study: Transforming East Lake: Systematic Intentionality in Atlanta," America's Promise Alliance, accessed October 31, 2024, https://purposebuiltcommunities.org/wp-content/uploads/2016/09/Americas-Promise_EastLake_CaseStudy_2014_03-1.pdf.

40. Brausell, "Analysis: California's Single-Family Zoning 'Killer.'"

41. "Housing Our Education Workforce: How AB 2295 Will Facilitate Development of School Employee Housing on District Property," SPUR, September 2, 2022, https://www.spur.org/events/2022-09-27/housing-our-education-workforce-how-ab-2295-will-facilitate-development-school.

42. J. K. Dineen, "'No Slums in the Sunset': Backlash over Affordable Housing Development Intensifies in Western S.F. Neighborhood," *San Francisco Chronicle*, January 19, 2021, https://www.sfchronicle.com/bayarea/article/Slum-charges-fly-in-fracas-over-affordable-15880321.php.

43. Chris Batson, interview by author, November 26, 2023.

44. Sarah Holder, "No, Really. Building More Housing Can Combat Rising Rents," *Bloomberg*, November 20, 2023, https://www.bloomberg.com/news/articles/2023-11-20/does-building-new-housing-cause-gentrification.

45. "Our Impact," California YIMBY, August 13, 2024, https://cayimby.org/our-impact/.

46. David Goldstein, "Does Every Car Need 8 Parking Spaces? Ride-Sharing Can Save Emissions by Reducing Parking, Too," NRDC, March 9, 2015, https://www.nrdc.org/bio/david-b-goldstein/does-every-car-need-8-parking-spaces-ride-sharing-can-save-emissions-reducing.

47. Will Chilton and Baird Bream, "The High Cost of Free Parking," *Vox*, July 19, 2017, https://www.vox.com/videos/2017/7/19/15993936/high-cost-of-free-parking.

5. LOCAL BUSINESS AND WORK

1. Walmart, "How Many People Work at Walmart?," Walmart, accessed October 30, 2024, https://corporate.walmart.com/askwalmart/how-many-people-work-at-walmart.

2. Naveen Kumar, "How Many Employees Does Amazon Have (2014–2024)," DemandSage, October 11, 2024, https://www.demandsage.com/amazon-employees/.

3. Charles Passy, "Here's Why More Americans Than Ever Now Shop at Amazon," MarketWatch, October 7, 2024, https://www.marketwatch.com/story/heres-why-a-whopping-83-of-american-households-now-shop-at-amazon-07bed254.

4. Kennedy Smith, "Adopt Dollar Store Restrictions—Institute for Local Self-Reliance," Institute for Local Self-Reliance, March 23, 2023, https://ilsr.org/articles/dollar-store-restrictions/.

5. Michael Corkery and Andrea Bruce, "Will a Dollar General Ruin a Rural Crossroads?," New York Times, June 2, 2023, https://www.nytimes.com/2023/06/02/business/dollar-general-ebony-virginia.html.

6. Stacy Mitchell, "We Need a Popular Front to Overthrow Corporate Rule. Small Businesses Are Key," The Forge, March 22, 2022, https://forgeorganizing.org/article/we-need-popular-front-overthrow-corporate-rule-small-businesses-are-key.

7. Chris Gaetano, "More Americans Work at Big Firms Than Small Ones," NYS Society of CPAs, April 7, 2017, https://www.nysscpa.org/news/publications/the-trusted-professional/article/more-americans-work-at-big-firms-than-small-ones-040717.

8. Terry Bennett, comments at Eureka Valley Neighborhood Association meeting, October 2020.

9. Stacy Mitchell and Ron Knox, "Boxed Out: How Big Retailers Are Flexing Their Supply Chain Power to Kill Off Small Businesses," Institute for Local Self-Reliance, May 24, 2024, https://ilsr.org/articles/boxed-out/.

10. Stacy Mitchell and Ron Knox, "Issue Brief: How Amazon Exploits and Undermines Small Businesses, and Why Breaking It Up Would Revive American Entrepreneurship," Institute for Local Self-Reliance, June 16, 2021, https://ilsr.org/articles/fact-sheet-how-breaking-up-amazon-can-empower-small-business/.

11. Seairra Jones, "Main Street vs. Big Box Stores: A Western North Carolina Analysis," Strong Towns, September 13, 2022, https://www.strongtowns.org/journal/2022/9/13/mainstreet-vs-chain-stores-a-western-north-carolina-analysis.

12. Pat Garofalo, "Maine Took on Big Box Stores, and Won," Public Seminar, May 9, 2022, https://publicseminar.org/2022/05/maine-took-on-big-box-stores-and-won/.

13. Jonathan O'Connell et al., "More Than Half of Emergency Small-Business Funds Went to Larger Businesses, New Data Shows," Washington Post, December 2, 2020, https://www.washingtonpost.com/business/2020/12/01/ppp-sba-data/.

14. Luke Goldstein, "Small Businesses Rise to Fight Wall Street," The American Prospect, February 7, 2023, https://prospect.org/power/2023-02-07-small-business-credit-card-fees/.

15. Charlie Thaxton, "The Hidden Price of Cashless Retail," Fortune, April 3, 2019, https://fortune.com/2019/04/03/cashless-stores-retail-amazon-go/.

16. Tim Wu, "The Life and Death of the Local Hardware Store," New York Times, November 22, 2019, sec. Opinion, https://www.nytimes.com/2019/11/22/opinion/sunday/small-business-economy.html.

17. "Amazon Warehouse Locations—An Ultimate Guide," SaasAnt, February 16, 2024, https://www.saasant.com/blog/amazon-warehouse-locations/.

18. Kenneth P. Vogel et al., "Mnuchin Paved Way for U.S.P.S. Shake-Up," New York Times, August 22, 2020, https://www.nytimes.com/2020/08/22/business/economy/dejoy-postmaster-general-trump-mnuchin.html.

19. Vogel et al., "Mnuchin Paved Way for U.S.P.S. Shake-Up."

20. Heather Knight, "'It's Insulting': Amazon Is Sponsoring S.F.'s Small Business Week—And Retailers Are Upset," San Francisco Chronicle, May 12, 2023, https://www.sfchronicle.com/sf/bayarea/heatherknight/article/small-business-week-amazon-18089471.php.

21. Henning Strubelt, "Shop Local, Local Materials, and Local Budgets," *Encyclopedia of the UN Sustainable Development Goals*, January 1, 2020, 579–89, https://doi.org/10.1007/978-3-319-95717-3_78.

22. Charles Marohn, "The Numbers Don't Lie," Strong Towns, October 12, 2020, https://www.strongtowns.org/journal/2020/10/11/the-numbers-dont-lie.

23. "Economic Impact Analysis: A Case Study Local Merchants vs. Chain Retailers," Civic Economics, December 2002, http://nebula.wsimg.com/e4710ded56a36d7d e033984b21a7ee02?AccessKeyId=8E410A17553441C49302&disposition=0&allowori gin=1.

24. "State of Retail," Independent Shopkeepers Association, 2023, https://isaok.org/stateofretail.

25. Stacy Mitchell, "Small Pharmacies Beat Big Chains at Delivering Vaccines. Don't Look so Shocked," *Washington Post*, February 5, 2021, https://www.washingtonpost.com/outlook/small-pharmacies-beat-big-chains-at-delivering-vaccines-dont-look-so-shocked/2021/02/05/6bb307ec-671b-11eb-886d-5264d4ceb46d_story.html.

26. Wu, "The Life and Death of the Local Hardware Store."

27. Yuliya Parshina-Kottas et al., "What the Tulsa Race Massacre Destroyed," *New York Times*, May 24, 2021, sec. U.S., https://www.nytimes.com/interactive/2021/05/24/us/tulsa-race-massacre.html.

28. Parshina-Kottas et al., "What the Tulsa Race Massacre Destroyed."

29. Kennedy Smith, "Small Business's Big Moment," Institute for Local Self-Reliance, January 24, 2022, https://ilsr.org/articles/report-small-business-big-moment/.

30. Nick Stumo-Langer, "There's Nothing Magical about Vermont (Episode 46)," Institute for Local Self-Reliance, May 17, 2018, https://ilsr.org/articles/vermont-is-magic-blp-episode-46/.

31. Rob Hopkins, From What Is to What If: Unleashing the Power of Imagination to Create the Future We Want (Chelsea Green, 2020), 153–54.

32. "About Us," Faire, accessed October 31, 2024, https://www.faire.com/about.

33. "An Update to Faire's Pricing in North America," Faire, May 17, 2023, https://www.faire.com/blog/selling/north-america-pricing-update/.

34. Kennedy Smith, "Stop Dollar Store Proliferation in Your Community: A Strategy Guide," Institute for Local Self-Reliance, February 28, 2023, https://ilsr.org/articles/dollar-store-strategy-guide/.

35. "Collective Impact," Mainstreet America, 2023, https://mainstreet.org/our-network/collective-impact.

36. "Collective Impact."

37. Sam Kraft, "Bring Back Corner Stores to Create a Connected, Equitable City," *Seattle Times*, June 25, 2021, https://www.seattletimes.com/opinion/bring-back-corner-stores-to-create-a-connected-equitable-city/.

38. Christina Campodonico, "SF Garages Give Local Artists & Artisans Space to Chase Dreams," *San Francisco Standard*, February 28, 2022, https://sfstandard.com/2022/02/28/sf-garages-give-creatives-space-to-chase-dreams/.

39. "Highlighted Business Actions," Local Futures, 2019, https://actionguide.localfutures.org/themes/business.

40. Kathleen Davis, "The Case for Shopping Local (Infographic)," NBC News, July 27, 2013, https://www.nbcnews.com/id/wbna52598711.

41. "Stats and Facts," American Public Power Association, accessed October 31, 2024, https://www.publicpower.org/public-power/stats-and-facts.

42. "Mission and History," GRID Alternatives, accessed October 31, 2024, https://gridalternatives.org/who-we-are/mission-history.

43. Patrick Sisson, "Car-Free Living Takes off in Car-Centric Cities," *Bloomberg*, March 14, 2023, https://www.bloomberg.com/news/articles/2023-03-14/can-car-free-living-succeed-in-cities-built-around-the-automobile.

44. Mark Sutton, "TfL Economic Benefits of Cycling Paper: A Home Run for Investment Case," *Cycling Industry News,* August 15, 2019, https://cyclingindustry.news/tfl-economic-benefits-of-cycling-paper-a-home-run-for-investment-case/.

45. "The Benefits of Riding Your Bike to Work: A Win-Win for Employees and Employers—Peachtree Creek Greenway," Peachtree Creek Greenway, May 17, 2024, https://peachtreecreek.org/the-benefits-of-riding-your-bike-to-work-a-win-win-for-employees-and-employers/.

6. TRANSPORTATION

1. Romic Aevaz, "2018 ACS Survey: While Most Americans' Commuting Trends Are Unchanged, Teleworking Continues to Grow, and Driving Alone Dips in Some Major Cities," The Eno Center for Transportation, October 19, 2019, https://enotrans.org/article/2018-acs-survey-while-most-americans-commuting-trends-are-unchanged-teleworking-continues-to-grow-and-driving-alone-dips-in-some-major-cities/.

2. Andrew Gross, "Think You're in Your Car More? You're Right. Americans Spend 70 Billion Hours Behind the Wheel," AAA NewsRoom, February 27, 2019, https://newsroom.aaa.com/2019/02/think-youre-in-your-car-more-youre-right-americans-spend-70-billion-hours-behind-the-wheel/.

3. "Consumer Expenditures—2023," US Bureau of Labor Statistics, September 25, 2024, https://www.bls.gov/news.release/cesan.nr0.htm.

4. Elizabeth Stampe, "Moving San Mateo County Forward: Housing and Transit at a Crossroads" (Transform and Housing Leadership Council, June 2018), https://hlcsmc.org/wp-content/uploads/2018/06/HLC2018-MovingReport-v7web-1.pdf.

5. "How Many Cars Are There in the World in 2024?," Hedges & Company, accessed October 31, 2024, https://hedgescompany.com/blog/2021/06/how-many-cars-are-there-in-the-world/.

6. Ivan Penn and Eric Lipton, "The Lithium Gold Rush: Inside the Race to Power Electric Vehicles," *New York Times*, May 6, 2021, sec. Business, https://www.nytimes.com/2021/05/06/business/lithium-mining-race.html.

7. Brad Plumer, Nadja Popovich, and Blacki Migliozzi, "Electric Cars Are Coming. How Long Until They Rule the Road?," *New York Times*, March 10, 2021, sec. Climate, https://www.nytimes.com/interactive/2021/03/10/climate/electric-vehicle-fleet-turnover.html.

8. Post Opinions Staff, "Opinion: Here Are 11 Climate Change Policies to Fight for in 2019," *Washington Post*, January 2, 2019, https://www.washingtonpost.com/news/opinions/wp/2019/01/02/feature/opinion-here-are-11-climate-change-policies-to-fight-for-in-2019/?noredirect=on&utm_term=.a5b720441567.

9. Alec Tyson and Brian Kennedy, "How Americans View Future Harms from Climate Change in Their Community and around the U.S.," Pew Research Center Science & Society, October 25, 2023, https://www.pewresearch.org/science/2023/10/25/how-americans-view-future-harms-from-climate-change-in-their-community-and-around-the-u-s/.

10. Gregory H. Shill, "Car Crashes Aren't Always Unavoidable," *Atlantic*, July 9, 2019, https://www.theatlantic.com/ideas/archive/2019/07/car-crashes-arent-always-unavoidable/592447/.

11. Watura Matsumura and Zakia Adam, "Fossil Fuel Consumption Subsidies Bounced Back Strongly in 2018—Analysis," IEA, June 13, 2019, https://www.iea.org/commentaries/fossil-fuel-consumption-subsidies-bounced-back-strongly-in-2018.

12. Hiroko Tabuchi, "How the Koch Brothers Are Killing Public Transit Projects Around the Country," *New York Times*, June 19, 2018, https://www.nytimes.com/2018/06/19/climate/koch-brothers-public-transit.html.

13. Clyde Hughes, "After Taking on Taxis, Ride-Share Services Now Challenging Public Transit in U.S.," UPI, January 8, 2019, https://www.upi.com/Top_News/US/2019/01/08/After-taking-on-taxis-ride-share-services-now-challenging-public-transit-in-US/5281546857951/.

14. "What Is Sprawl Development?," Greenbelt Alliance, November 22, 2016, https://www.greenbelt.org/blog/what-is-sprawl-development.

15. "System Mileage within the United States | Bureau of Transportation Statistics," Bureau of Transportation Statistics, accessed October 31, 2024, https://www.bts.gov/content/system-mileage-within-united-states.

16. Laura Bliss, "Behind the Gains in U.S. Public Transit Ridership," *Bloomberg*, January 13, 2020, https://www.bloomberg.com/news/articles/2020-01-13/behind-the-gains-in-u-s-public-transit-ridership.

17. Jason Schaefer, "Reducing Traffic or Inducing It?," Strong Towns, November 20, 2015, https://www.strongtowns.org/journal/2015/11/20/reducing-or-inducing-traffic.

18. Angie Schmitt, "American Cities Are Drowning in Car Storage—Streetsblog USA," Streetsblog, July 12, 2018, https://usa.streetsblog.org/2018/07/12/american-cities-are-drowning-in-car-storage#new_tab.

19. Jeff Sparrow, "The Car Culture That's Helping Destroy the Planet Was by No Means Inevitable," Literary Hub, November 27, 2019, https://lithub.com/the-car-culture-thats-helping-destroy-the-planet-was-by-no-means-inevitable/.

20. Roshni Sahu, "Public Transportation: An American Necessity," March 2020, Junior English term paper, Middle College, San Mateo Union High School District.

21. Jack Ewing, "Electric Cars Too Costly for Many, Even with Aid in Climate Bill," *New York Times*, August 8, 2022, sec. Business, https://www.nytimes.com/2022/08/08/business/energy-environment/electric-vehicles-climate-bill.html.

22. P. L. Jacobsen, "Safety in Numbers: More Walkers and Bicyclists, Safer Walking and Bicycling," *Injury Prevention* 9, no. 3 (September 1, 2003): 205–9, https://doi.org/10.1136/ip.9.3.205.

23. Veronica Vanterpool, "Public Transit: An Undervalued, Effective Vision Zero Strategy," Vision Zero Network, September 4, 2018, https://visionzeronetwork.org/public-transit-an-undervalued-effective-vision-zero-strategy/.

24. James Partlow, "19 Bike to Work Day Facts," Washington, DC, Department of General Services, accessed October 31, 2024, https://dgs.dc.gov/dgs-blog/19-bike-work-day-facts.

25. "Revisiting Donald Appleyard's Study," Cockburn Association, June 27, 2023, https://www.cockburnassociation.org.uk/news/revisiting-donald-appleyards-study/.

26. Carol Ting quoted by Pisces Foundation, X (formerly Twitter), January 2, 2020, https://x.com/PiscesFdn/status/1212811818231402497.

27. Bryn Culbert, "What Is the Most Eco-Friendly Way to Travel?," Wanderu, July 23, 2023, https://www.wanderu.com/blog/most-sustainable-way-to-travel/.

28. Alex Healey, "A Growing Trend Among Teens Could Mean Fewer Drivers on the Road," Jerry, Inc., June 27, 2022, https://getjerry.com/insights/growing-trend-among-teens-could-mean-fewer-drivers.

29. Sarah Trent, "A Blueprint for More Equitable Transportation Planning," Next City, April 2, 2018, https://nextcity.org/urbanist-news/a-blueprint-for-more-equitable-transportation-planning.

30. Yasmin Garaad, "How Five U.S. Cities Built 335 Miles of Bike Lanes in 24 Months," Next City, August 24, 2022, https://nextcity.org/urbanist-news/how-five-u.s.-cities-built-335-miles-of-bike-lanes-in-24-months.

31. Transportation Alternatives, accessed October 31, 2024, https://transalt.org/.

32. "Active Transportation and Micromobility," US Department of Energy—Alternative Fuels Data Center, accessed October 31, 2024, https://afdc.energy.gov/conserve/active -transportation.

33. Sahu, "Public Transportation."

34. Nick Grossman, "Curitiba Bus Rapid Transit System," Project for Public Spaces, April 10, 2006, https://www.pps.org/places/curitiba-bus-rapid-transit-system.

35. "Best Practices in Implementing Tactical Transit Lanes," UCLA Institute of Transportation Studies with Funding from the California Department of Transportation (Caltrans) SB1 Research Fund, February 2019, https://www.its.ucla.edu/wp-content/uploads /sites/6/2019/02/Best-Practices-in-Implementing-Tactical-Transit-Lanes.pdf.

36. Laura Bliss, "To Build a Better Bus Lane, Just Paint It," *Bloomberg*, March 1, 2019, https://www.bloomberg.com/news/articles/2019-03-01/how-tactical-transit-lanes -help-buses-beat-traffic.

37. Angie Schmitt, "The Twin Cities Figured Out the Formula for Increasing Bus Ridership," Streetsblog.org, April 30, 2018, https://usa.streetsblog.org/2018/04/30/minneapo lis-figured-out-the-formula-for-increasing-bus-ridership.

38. Laura Bliss, "Why Seattle Is America's Bus-Lovingest Town," *Bloomberg*, May 11, 2018, https://www.bloomberg.com/news/articles/2018-05-11/seattle-has-a-4-step-plan -to-building-bus-ridership.

39. Post Opinions Staff, "Opinion: Here Are 11 Climate Change Policies to Fight for in 2019."

40. "Equitable Bike Share Means Building Better Places for People to Ride," National Association of City Transportation Officials, July 2016, https://nacto.org/equitable-bike -share-means-building-better-places-for-people-to-ride/.

41. "Increase in Paris Cycle Lanes Leads to Dramatic Rise in Bike Commuting," Transport & Environment, January 17, 2020, https://www.transportenvironment.org/articles /increase-paris-cycle-lanes-leads-dramatic-rise-bike-commuting.

42. Jake Blumgart, "Vehicles Are Still Firmly in Control of City Streets," Governing, August 3, 2021, https://www.governing.com/community/vehicles-still-firmly-in-control-of-city -streets.

43. Emily Beach, "Sustainable Transportation Solutions," *San Mateo Daily Journal*, February 27, 2018, https://www.smdailyjournal.com/opinion/guest_perspectives/sustainable -transportation-solutions/article_1c59ad6a-1b63-11e8-8d3d-87b9b44e2459.html.

44. "Equitable Bike Share Means Building Better Places for People to Ride," National Association of City Transportation Officials, July 2016, https://nacto.org/equitable-bike-share -means-building-better-places-for-people-to-ride/.

45. Yumika Takeshita, "Great Public Spaces: Expecting More of Transit Stops & Stations," Project for Public Spaces, April 2, 2020, https://www.pps.org/article/great-public-spaces -expecting-more-of-transit-stops-stations.

46. Sergio Avelleda, guest, "The Future of Urban Transport," Outrage and Optimism, https://www.outrageandoptimism.org/episodes/urban-transport-future?hsLang=en.

47. "Transportation 101 Series: Why Do We Send an Annual Commute Survey?," Stanford University Transportation, 2023, https://transportation.stanford.edu/news/transportation -101-series-why-do-we-send-annual-commute-survey.

48. "Safe Routes to School," City of Palo Alto, 2023, https://www.cityofpaloalto.org /Departments/Transportation/Safe-Routes-to-School.

49. Anine Hartmann and Sarah Abel, "How Oslo Achieved Zero Pedestrian and Bicycle Fatalities, and How Others Can Apply What Worked," The City Fix, October 13, 2020, https://thecityfix.com/blog/how-oslo-achieved-zero-pedestrian-and-bicycle-fatalities -and-how-others-can-apply-what-worked/.

7. COMMUNITY SPACES

1. Brad Plumer and Nadja Popovich, "How Decades of Racist Housing Policy Left Neighborhoods Sweltering," *New York Times*, August 24, 2020, sec. Climate, https://www.nytimes.com/interactive/2020/08/24/climate/racism-redlining-cities-global-warming.html.

2. "Community Ties: Understanding What Attaches People to the Place Where They Live," Knight Foundation, May 20, 2020, https://knightfoundation.org/reports/community-ties-understanding-what-attaches-people-to-the-place-where-they-live/.

3. Manny Yekutiel, Twitter (now X), March 23, 2022, https://x.com/manny_yekutiel/status/1506666814478028806.

4. Salvador Rodriguez, "Mark Zuckerberg Shifted Facebook's Focus to Groups after the 2016 Election, and It's Changed How People Use the Site," CNBC, February 16, 2020, https://www.cnbc.com/2020/02/16/zuckerbergs-focus-on-facebook-groups-increases-facebook-engagement.html.

5. "How to Make Streets into Great Public Spaces," Mobycon, accessed October 31, 2024, https://mobycon.com/updates/how-to-make-streets-into-great-public-spaces/.

6. Charlie Gardner, "Old Urbanist: We Are the 25%: Looking at Street Area Percentages and Surface Parking," Old Urbanist, December 12, 2011, https://oldurbanist.blogspot.com/2011/12/we-are-25-looking-at-street-area.html.

7. Timothy Moore and Heidi Gollub, "Fatal Car Crash Statistics 2023," *USA Today*, August 9, 2023, https://www.usatoday.com/money/blueprint/auto-insurance/fatal-car-crash-statistics/.

8. Luz Lazo, "Traffic Fatalities Are Down in the U.S., but More Pedestrians and Bicyclists Are Being Killed, Officials Say," *Washington Post*, October 22, 2019, https://www.washingtonpost.com/transportation/2019/10/22/traffic-fatalities-are-down-us-more-pedestrians-bicyclists-are-being-killed-officials-say/.

9. John Gramlich, "What the Data Says About Crime in the U.S.," Pew Research Center, April 24, 2024, https://www.pewresearch.org/short-reads/2024/04/24/what-the-data-says-about-crime-in-the-us/.

10. Maggie Koerth, "Many Americans Are Convinced Crime Is Rising in the U.S. They're Wrong," FiveThirtyEight, August 3, 2020, https://fivethirtyeight.com/features/many-americans-are-convinced-crime-is-rising-in-the-u-s-theyre-wrong/.

11. Gabby Landsverk, "Forget 10,000 Steps—Here's How Much You Should Walk a Day," *Business Insider*, July 7, 2021, https://www.businessinsider.com/walking-10000-steps-for-health-not-science-based-in-marketing-2021-7.

12. "How to Live Longer, Better: Discovering the Blue Zones," Blue Zones, accessed October 31, 2024, https://www.bluezones.com/live-longer-better/#section-6.

13. Benjamin Schneider, "The Mayor of San Francisco's Parks," San Francisco Examiner, August 26, 2022, https://www.sfexaminer.com/news/the-city/the-mayor-of-san-francisco-s-parks/article_29652866-2326-11ed-ac28-9f4504610330.html.

14. "How to Make Streets into Great Public Spaces."

15. "Case Study: Pavement to Parks; San Francisco, USA," Global Designing Cities Initiative, accessed October 31, 2024, https://globaldesigningcities.org/publication/global-street-design-guide/streets/pedestrian-priority-spaces/parklets/case-study-pavement-to-parks-san-francisco-usa/.

16. Alma Guillermoprieto, "Bogotá, Colombia's Ciclovía Bans Cars Every Sunday, and People Love It," *National Geographic*, March 27, 2019, https://www.nationalgeographic.com/environment/article/bogota-colombia-ciclovia-bans-cars-on-roads-each-sunday.

17. Shannon Hake, interview by author, June 2021.

18. "How to Make Streets into Great Public Spaces."

19. Samantha Matuke, Stephan Schmidt, and Wenzheng Li, "The Rise and Fall of the American Pedestrian Mall," *Journal of Urbanism: International Research on Placemaking and Urban Sustainability* 14, no. 2 (July 22, 2020): 129–44, https://doi.org/10.1080/17549 175.2020.1793804.

20. Nate Berg, "The Secret to Revitalizing Urban Downtowns," Fast Company, September 15, 2020, https://www.fastcompany.com/90549564/the-secret-to-revitalizing-urban -downtowns.

21. Max Reyes, "Celebrating Valentine's Day in a Pandemic," *Bloomberg*, February 10, 2021, https://www.bloomberg.com/news/features/2021-02-10/celebrating-valentines -day-in-a-pandemic.

22. "Homeless People in the U.S. 2007–2018," Statista, September 5, 2024, https://www .statista.com/statistics/555795/estimated-number-of-homeless-people-in-the-us/.

23. Sven Eggimann, "The Potential of Implementing Superblocks for Multifunctional Street Use in Cities," *Nature Sustainability* 5 (March 3, 2022), https://doi.org/10.1038 /s41893-022-00855-2.

8. NATURE SPACES

1. "U.S. Study Shows Widening Disconnect with Nature, and Potential Solutions," *Yale Environment 360*, April 27, 2017, https://e360.yale.edu/digest/u-s-study-shows-wid ening-disconnect-with-nature-and-potential-solutions.

2. Alejandra Borunda, "People of Color 3x More Likely to Live in 'Nature Deprived' U.S. Neighborhoods," *National Geographic*, July 29, 2020, https://www.nationalgeo graphic.com/science/article/how-nature-deprived-neighborhoods-impact-health-peo ple-of-color.

3. Jonathan Watts, "Concrete: The Most Destructive Material on Earth," *Guardian*, February 25, 2019, https://www.theguardian.com/cities/2019/feb/25/concrete-the -most-destructive-material-on-earth.

4. Watts, "Concrete."

5. Alejandro Borunda, "Los Angeles Confronts Its Shady Divide," *National Geographic*, June 17, 2021, https://www.nationalgeographic.com/magazine/article/los-angeles -confronts-its-shady-divide-feature.

6. Patrick Barkham, "Introducing 'Treeconomics': How Street Trees Can Save Our Cities," *Guardian*, August 15, 2015, https://www.theguardian.com/cities/2015/aug/15 /treeconomics-street-trees-cities-sheffield-itree.

7. Pendarvis Harshaw, "Bay Nature Magazine: Does Green Gentrification Push People Out?," *Bay Nature*, September 2018, https://baynature.org/article/do-parks-push -people-out/.

8. "US Study Shows Widening Disconnect with Nature, and Potential Solutions," YaleEnvironment360, April 27, 2017, https://e360.yale.edu/digest/u-s-study-shows-wide ning-disconnect-with-nature-and-potential-solutions.

9. Shannon Hilson, "8 Life Lessons I've Learned at 40-Something That I Wish I'd Known at 20-Something," Medium, The Post-Grad Survival Guide, July 5, 2020, https:// medium.com/the-post-grad-survival-guide/8-life-lessons-ive-learned-at-40-something -that-i-wish-i-d-known-at-20-something-d7d1b0617eff.

10. Ashley Abramson, "Filling Your Summer Calendar? Slow Your Roll," *New York Times*, May 14, 2021, https://www.nytimes.com/2021/05/14/well/filling-your-summer -calendar-slow-your-roll.html.

11. Howard Frumkin et al., "Nature Contact and Human Health: A Research Agenda," *Environmental Health Perspectives* 125, no. 7 (July 24, 2017), https://doi.org/10.1289/ehp 1663.

12. MaryCarol R. Hunter, Brenda W. Gillespie, and Sophie Yu-Pu Chen, "Urban Nature Experiences Reduce Stress in the Context of Daily Life Based on Salivary Biomarkers," *Frontiers in Psychology* 10, no. 1 (April 4, 2019), https://doi.org/10.3389/fpsyg.2019.00722.

13. R. De Young et al., "Some Psychological Benefits of Urban Nature: Mental Vitality from Time Spent in Nearby Nature," in *Advances in Psychology Research*, ed. A. M. Columbus (Nova Science, 2017), 93–120, https://deepblue.lib.umich.edu/handle/2027.42/136087.

14. Daniel T. C. Cox et al., "Doses of Neighborhood Nature: The Benefits for Mental Health of Living with Nature," *BioScience* 67, no. 2 (January 25, 2017): biw173, https://doi.org/10.1093/biosci/biw173.

15. Justin Phillips, "I Found 'Eden' in West Oakland. It's Surrounded by Trauma," *San Francisco Chronicle*, July 11, 2021, https://www.sfchronicle.com/bayarea/justinphillips/article/I-found-Eden-in-West-Oakland-It-s-16305317.php.

16. Rebekah Coley, William Sullivan, and Frances Kuo, "Where Does Community Grow?: The Social Context Created by Nature in Urban Public Housing," *Environment and Behavior* 29, no. 4 (1997), https://doi.org/10.1177/001391659702900402.

17. Johanna Lehne and Felix Preston, "Making Concrete Change Innovation in Low-Carbon Cement and Concrete," *Chatham House Report*, June 2018, https://www.chathamhouse.org/sites/default/files/publications/2018-06-13-making-concrete-change-cement-lehne-preston-final.pdf.

18. Sabbie A. Miller, Arpad Horvath, and Paulo J. M. Monteiro, "Impacts of Booming Concrete Production on Water Resources Worldwide," *Nature Sustainability* 1, no. 1 (January 2018): 69–76, https://doi.org/10.1038/s41893-017-0009-5.

19. Harshaw, "Bay Nature Magazine."

20. Borunda, "Los Angeles Confronts Its Shady Divide."

21. "The Onondaga Nation, in Unprecedented Land Back Moment, Regains 1,023 Acres of the Land from New York State," *Onondaga Nation*, July 1, 2022, https://www.onondaganation.org/uncategorized/2022/land_back_1023_acres/.

22. "Singapore: The First City in Nature?," Center for Liveable Cities, September 2017, https://www.clc.gov.sg/research-publications/publications/digital-library/view/singapore-the-first-city-in-nature.

23. Eric Simons, "A Street Tree Revolution in Silicon Valley," *Bay Nature*, January 2, 2018, https://baynature.org/article/a-street-tree-revolution-in-silicon-valley/.

24. "When Private Golf Courses Land in the Rough, Communities Tee Up Public Parks," Trust for Public Land, April 17, 2018, https://www.tpl.org/blog/when-private-golf-courses-land-rough-communities-tee-public-parks.

9. FOOD

1. "Communities with Limited Food Access in the United States," Annie E. Casey Foundation, August 4, 2024, https://www.aecf.org/blog/communities-with-limited-food-access-in-the-united-states.

2. Allison Karpyn et al., "The Changing Landscape of Food Deserts," *UNSCN Nutrition* 44 (2019): 46–53, https://pmc.ncbi.nlm.nih.gov/articles/PMC7299236/.

3. Hiroko Tabuchi and Nadja Popovich, "Two Biden Priorities, Climate and Inequality, Meet on Black-Owned Farms," *New York Times*, January 31, 2021, sec. Climate, https://www.nytimes.com/2021/01/31/climate/black-farmers-discrimination-agriculture.html.

4. Tom Philpott, "White People Own 98 Percent of Rural Land. Young Black Farmers Want to Reclaim Their Share," *Mother Jones*, June 27, 2020, https://www.motherjones.com/food/2020/06/black-farmers-soul-fire-farm-reparations-african-legacy-agriculture/.

5. "UN Report: Nature's Dangerous Decline 'Unprecedented'; Species Extinction Rates 'Accelerating,'" United Nations, May 6, 2019, https://www.un.org/sustainabledevelopment/blog/2019/05/nature-decline-unprecedented-report/.

6. Laura Reiley, "Perspective | Five Myths about Corn," *Washington Post*, August 9, 2019, https://www.washingtonpost.com/outlook/five-myths/five-myths-about-corn/2019/08/09/14242b1c-b9ea-11e9-a091-6a96e67d9cce_story.html.

7. Hannah Ritchie, Max Roser, and Pablo Rosado, "Environmental Impacts of Food Production," Our World in Data, 2022, https://ourworldindata.org/environmental-impacts-of-food.

8. Hannah Ritchie, "Food Production Is Responsible for One-Quarter of the World's Greenhouse Gas Emissions," Our World in Data, 2019, https://ourworldindata.org/food-ghg-emissions.

9. "UN Report: Nature's Dangerous Decline 'Unprecedented.'"

10. Paul Wallich, "Everything You Always Wanted to Know about Big Ag," IEEE Spectrum, May 30, 2013, https://spectrum.ieee.org/everything-you-always-wanted-to-know-about-big-ag.

11. Peter S. Goodman and Erin Schaff, "Record Beef Prices, but Ranchers Aren't Cashing In," *New York Times*, December 27, 2021, sec. Business, https://www.nytimes.com/2021/12/27/business/beef-prices-cattle-ranchers.html.

12. Andrew Jacobs, "Lawsuits over 'Misleading' Food Labels Surge as Groups Cite Lax U.S. Oversight," *New York Times*, September 7, 2021, sec. Science, https://www.nytimes.com/2021/09/07/science/food-labels-lawsuits.html.

13. "EWG's Farm Subsidy Database," Environmental Working Group, accessed November 1, 2024, https://farm.ewg.org/region.php?fips=00000&progcode=total.

14. "Farm Subsidy Primer," Environmental Working Group, accessed November 1, 2024, https://farm.ewg.org/subsidyprimer.php.

15. Alana Semuels, "'They're Trying to Wipe Us off the Map.' Small American Farmers Are Nearing Extinction," *Time Magazine*, November 27, 2019, https://time.com/5736789/small-american-farmers-debt-crisis-extinction/.

16. "UN Report: Nature's Dangerous Decline 'Unprecedented.'"

17. "UN Report: Nature's Dangerous Decline 'Unprecedented.'"

18. Wallich, "Everything You Always Wanted to Know about Big Ag."

19. Dave Merrill and Lauren Leatherby, "Here's How America Uses Its Land," *Bloomberg*, July 31, 2018, https://www.bloomberg.com/graphics/2018-us-land-use/.

20. "Agricultural Trade," USDA Economic Research Service, accessed November 1, 2024, https://www.ers.usda.gov/data-products/ag-and-food-statistics-charting-the-essentials/agricultural-trade/.

21. Sherrie Wang et al., "Mapping Twenty Years of Corn and Soybean across the US Midwest Using the Landsat Archive," *Scientific Data* 7, no. 1 (September 15, 2020), https://doi.org/10.1038/s41597-020-00646-4.

22. David Roberts, "This Company Wants to Build a Giant Indoor Farm Next to Every Major City in the World," *Vox*, April 11, 2018, https://www.vox.com/energy-and-environment/2017/11/8/16611710/vertical-farms.

23. Adam Wernick, "US Lost 11 Million Acres of Farmland to Development in Past 2 Decades," The World from PRX, July 31, 2020, https://www.pri.org/stories/2020-08-07/us-lost-11-million-acres-farmland-development-past-2-decades.

24. Adriana Valcu-Lisman, "Per Capita Red Meat and Poultry Consumption Expected to Decrease Modestly in 2022," USDA Economic Research Service, April 15, 2022, https://www.ers.usda.gov/data-products/chart-gallery/gallery/chart-detail/?chartId=103767.

25. Rachel French, "Dairy Consumption Hits Record Highs Despite Fluid Milk Dip," *Supply Side Food and Beverage Journal*, January 8, 2024, https://www.supplysidefbj .com/market-trends-analysis/us-cheese-consumption-breaks-records-while-dairy -milk-continues-decline.

26. Cheryl Fryar et al., "Fast Food Consumption Among Adults in the United States, 2013–2016," CDC, October 2018, https://www.cdc.gov/nchs/products/databriefs /db322.htm.

27. Yang Yu and Edward C. Jaenicke, "Estimating Food Waste as Household Production Inefficiency," *American Journal of Agricultural Economics* 102, no. 2 (January 23, 2020): 525–47, https://doi.org/10.1002/ajae.12036.

28. United States Environmental Protection Agency, "Sustainable Management of Food Basics | US EPA," US EPA, accessed November 1, 2024, https://www.epa.gov /sustainable-management-food/sustainable-management-food-basics.

29. Bar 717 Ranch, Summer 2020 Newsletter.

30. Julie E. Kurtz et al., "Mapping U.S. Food System Localization Potential: The Impact of Diet on Foodsheds," *Environmental Science & Technology* 54, no. 19 (September 14, 2020): 12434–46, https://doi.org/10.1021/acs.est.9b07582.

31. Dan Buettner, "For a Long Life, These Are Foods to Live By," *National Geographic*, December 17, 2019, https://www.nationalgeographic.com/magazine/article /these-traditional-diets-from-the-blue-zones-can-lead-to-long-lives-feature.

32. Dorothy Neufeld, "The Carbon Footprint of the Food Supply Chain," Visual Capitalist, February 10, 2020, https://www.visualcapitalist.com/visualising-the-greenhouse -gas-impact-of-each-food/.

33. Neufeld, "The Carbon Footprint of the Food Supply Chain."

34. "About Farmers Markets," Farmers Market Coalition, accessed November 1, 2024, https://farmersmarketcoalition.org/education/qanda/.

35. Marco Springmann et al., "Mitigation Potential and Global Health Impacts from Emissions Pricing of Food Commodities," *Nature Climate Change* 7, no. 1 (November 7, 2016): 69–74, https://doi.org/10.1038/nclimate3155.

36. Lela Nargi, "The University of Kentucky's Long Road to Sourcing 'Local' Food," Civil Eats, February 26, 2019, https://civileats.com/2019/02/26/the-university-of-kentuckys-long -road-to-sourcing-local-food/.

37. "Business List," La Cocina, accessed November 1, 2024, https://www.lacocinasf .org/bornatlacocina.

38. Jena Brooker, "In Detroit, a Push to Help Black Farmers Purchase Land," Grist, October 26, 2021, https://grist.org/agriculture/in-detroit-a-push-to-help-black-farmers -purchase-land/.

39. Carey Byron, "Black Farming Projects Look to Restore Historical Land Losses," *YES! Magazine*, August 26, 2022, https://www.yesmagazine.org/economy/2022/08/26 /black-farming-historical-land-losses.

40. "Denmark Country Commercial Guide—Agricultural Sector," US International Trade Administration, January 20, 2024, https://www.trade.gov/country-commercial -guides/denmark-agricultural-sector.

41. Soleil Ho, "In Bayview, a New Farm Aims to Take a More Equitable Spin on California Farm-to-Table Cuisine," *San Francisco Chronicle*, July 31, 2020, https://www .sfchronicle.com/restaurants/article/An-upstart-organic-farm-in-the-Bayview-hopes -to-15440891.php#photo-19734502.

42. "Local Farms Key to Healthy and Resilient Food Systems—Episode 140 of Building Local Power," Institute for Local Self-Reliance, November 25, 2021, https://ilsr.org /articles/moon-valley-farm-episode140/.

43. Jessica Stewart, "Interview: Kids around the World Photographed Surrounded by Their Weekly Diet," *My Modern Met*, June 20, 2019, https://mymodernmet.com/daily-bread-gregg-segal-interview/.

44. Jillian Mock and John Schwartz, "What If We All Ate a Bit Less Meat?," *New York Times*, August 21, 2019, https://www.nytimes.com/2019/08/21/climate/what-if-we-all-ate-a-bit-less-meat.html.

45. Sarah Taber, "Perspective: Farms Aren't Tossing Perfectly Good Produce. You Are," *Washington Post*, March 8, 2019, https://www.washingtonpost.com/news/posteverything/wp/2019/03/08/feature/farms-arent-tossing-perfectly-good-produce-you-are/.

46. Tejal Rao, "Food Supply Anxiety Brings Back Victory Gardens," *New York Times*, March 25, 2020, sec. Food, https://www.nytimes.com/2020/03/25/dining/victory-gardens-coronavirus.html.

47. Editorial Staff, "What Comes After the Pandemic?," *California Magazine* (Cal Alumni Association), January 6, 2022, https://alumni.berkeley.edu/california-magazine/summer-2020/what-comes-after-pandemic/.

48. Kim Dinan, "Local Garden Supply Stores Keep Asheville Growing," *Mountain Xpress*, December 8, 2018, https://mountainx.com/living/local-garden-supply-stores-keep-asheville-growing/.

10. BUILDING ENERGY

1. Ara Agopian, "How Many Americans Have Solar Panels in 2024?," *Solar Insure*, February 3, 2024, https://www.solarinsure.com/how-many-americans-have-solar-panels.

2. "Sources of Greenhouse Gas Emissions," US Environmental Protection Agency, October 22, 2024, https://www.epa.gov/ghgemissions/sources-greenhouse-gas-emissions.

3. US Energy Information Administration, "What Is U.S. Electricity Generation by Energy Source?," US Energy Information Administration, February 29, 2024, https://www.eia.gov/tools/faqs/faq.php?id=427&t=3.

4. Jacques Schonek, "How Big Are Power Line Losses?," *Schneider Electric Blog*, March 25, 2013, https://blog.se.com/energy-management-energy-efficiency/2013/03/25/how-big-are-power-line-losses/.

5. "Mineral Requirements for Clean Energy Transitions—The Role of Critical Minerals in Clean Energy Transitions," IEA, accessed November 1, 2024, https://www.iea.org/reports/the-role-of-critical-minerals-in-clean-energy-transitions/mineral-requirements-for-clean-energy-transitions.

6. John Farrell, "How Big Utilities Are Impeding Clean Energy, and What We Can Do About It," Institute for Local Self-Reliance, January 2021, https://cdn.ilsr.org/wp-content/uploads/2021/01/SLPG_Electricity.pdf.

7. "Investor-Owned Utilities Served 72% of U.S. Electricity Customers in 2017," US Energy Information Administration, August 15, 2019, https://www.eia.gov/todayinenergy/detail.php?id=40913.

8. Julie Cart, "Policy Change in California Has Slashed New Solar Installations by 80%," *San Francisco Chronicle*, February 3, 2024, https://www.sfchronicle.com/climate/article/solar-panel-power-california-18644945.php.

9. John Farrell, "Mergers and Monopoly: How Concentration Changes the Electricity Business," Institute for Local Self-Reliance, October 31, 2017, https://ilsr.org/articles/electricity-mergers-and-monopoly/.

10. "U.S. Electricity Grid & Markets," US Environmental Protection Agency, January 10, 2022, https://www.epa.gov/green-power-markets/us-electricity-grid-markets.

11. Farrell, "How Big Utilities Are Impeding Clean Energy."

12. "SunZia Wind," Pattern Energy, accessed November 1, 2024, https://patternenergy.com/projects/sunzia-wind/.

13. Gail Rajgor, "Pattern Closes 'Groundbreaking' $11bn Financing Deal for Sun-Zia," *Wind Power Monthly*, January 11, 2024, https://www.windpowermonthly.com/article/1857069/pattern-closes-groundbreaking-11bn-financing-deal-sunzia.

14. "Renewable Energy," Bureau of Land Management, accessed November 1, 2024, https://www.blm.gov/programs/energy-and-minerals/renewable-energy.

15. Sean Wolfe, "Interior Finalizes Rule to Cut Solar and Wind Fees up to 80% on Public Land, Permits New Projects," *Renewable Energy World*, April 12, 2024, https://www.renewableenergyworld.com/policy-regulation/interior-finalizes-rule-to-cut-solar-and-wind-fees-up-to-80-on-public-land-permits-new-projects/#gref.

16. Claudia Copeland and Nicole Carter, "Energy-Water Nexus: The Water Sector's Energy Use," Congressional Research Service, 2017, https://sgp.fas.org/crs/misc/R43200.pdf.

17. Halle Parker, "Rooftop Solar Systems Survived Hurricane Ida; in Blackout, Some Powered Neighbors, Too," NOLA.com, September 13, 2021, https://www.nola.com/news/environment/article_3cf5e99e-11af-11ec-a7b0-1f16a8fc2f09.html.

18. "Wind Energy by State (August 2021)," *Choose Energy*, October 4, 2024, https://www.chooseenergy.com/data-center/wind-generation-by-state/.

19. Vikram Aggarwal, "Solar Payback Period: How Soon Will They Pay Off?," *Energy Sage*, September 3, 2024, https://www.energysage.com/solar/understanding-your-solar-panel-payback-period/.

20. Ryan Shea and Russell Mendell, "Congress Cannot Ignore Residential Solar Tax Credit Inequities," Rocky Mountain Institute, October 14, 2021, https://rmi.org/congress-cannot-ignore-residential-solar-tax-credit-inequities/.

21. "Homepage," California Community Choice Association, accessed November 1, 2024, https://cal-cca.org/.

22. "Rates," CleanPowerSF, June 21, 2023, https://www.cleanpowersf.org/rates.

23. "Stats and Facts | American Public Power Association," American Public Power Association, accessed September 1, 2023, https://www.publicpower.org/public-power/stats-and-facts.

24. "Stats and Facts | American Public Power Association," American Public Power Association, accessed November 1, 2024, https://www.publicpower.org/public-power/stats-and-facts.

25. "Electric Co-Op Facts & Figures," National Rural Electric Cooperative Association, April 10, 2024, https://www.electric.coop/electric-cooperative-fact-sheet.

26. Susan Shain, "One Thing You Can Do: Join a Community Solar Project," *New York Times*, September 25, 2019, https://www.nytimes.com/2019/09/25/climate/nyt-newsletter-climate-strikes-protests.html.

27. Maria McCoy, "The State(s) of Distributed Solar—2022 Update," Institute for Local Self-Reliance, April 23, 2023, https://ilsr.org/articles/the-states-of-distributed-solar-2022/.

28. Katelyn Weisbrod, "Community Solar Is About to Get a Surge in Federal Funding. So What Is Community Solar?," *Inside Climate News*, February 23, 2023, https://insideclimatenews.org/news/23022023/inside-clean-energy-community-solar/.

29. Pieter Gagnon et al., "Rooftop Solar Photovoltaic Technical Potential in the United States: A Detailed Assessment," National Renewable Energy Laboratory, January 2016, https://www.nrel.gov/docs/fy16osti/65298.pdf.

30. "Documenting a Decade of Cost Declines for PV Systems," National Renewable Energy Laboratory, February 10, 2021, https://www.nrel.gov/news/program/2021/documenting-a-decade-of-cost-declines-for-pv-systems.html.

31. Christopher Clack et al., "A New Roadmap for the Lowest Cost Grid," Vibrant Clean Energy LLC, December 1, 2020, https://www.vibrantcleanenergy.com/wp-content/uploads/2020/12/WhyDERs_ES_Final.pdf.

32. Sammy Roth, "How Rooftop Solar Could Save Americans $473 Billion," *Los Angeles Times*, January 7, 2021, https://www.latimes.com/environment/newsletter/2021-01-07/how-rooftop-solar-could-save-americans-473-billion-dollars-boiling-point.

33. John Farrell, "Report: Is Bigger Best in Renewable Energy?," Institute for Local Self-Reliance, September 30, 2016, https://ilsr.org/articles/report-is-bigger-best/.

34. McCoy, "The State(s) of Distributed Solar."

35. Livia Albeck-Ripka and Ivan Penn, "How Coal-Loving Australia Became the Leader in Rooftop Solar," *New York Times*, September 29, 2020, sec. Business, https://www.nytimes.com/2020/09/29/business/energy-environment/australia-rooftop-solar-coa.html.

36. "Power Sources," Peninsula Clean Energy, accessed December 3, 2023, https://www.peninsulacleanenergy.com/power-sources/.

37. "Energy Sources," CleanPowerSF, accessed December 3, 2023, https://www.cleanpowersf.org/energysources.

38. "SFPUC Commits to Largest Wind Development in CleanPowerSF History," San Francisco Public Utilities Commission, October 23, 2024, https://www.sfpuc.gov/about-us/news/sfpuc-commits-largest-wind-development-cleanpowersf-history.

39. Patrick Sisson, "New York's Real Climate Challenge: Fixing Its Aging Buildings," *New York Times*, December 29, 2020, sec. Business, https://www.nytimes.com/2020/12/29/business/new-york-passive-house-retrofit.html.

40. Min Wang and Xiumei Yu, "Impact of Tiered Pricing Reform on China's Residential Electricity Use," *China Economic Quarterly International* 1, no. 3 (September 2021): 177–90, https://doi.org/10.1016/j.ceqi.2021.08.001.

41. Chuanwang Sun, "An Empirical Case Study about the Reform of Tiered Pricing for Household Electricity in China," *Applied Energy* 160 (December 15, 2015): 383–89, https://doi.org/10.1016/j.apenergy.2015.09.030.

42. Hunt Allcott, "Social Norms and Energy Conservation," *Journal of Public Economics* 95, nos. 9–10 (October 2011): 1082–95, https://doi.org/10.1016/j.jpubeco.2011.03.003.

43. Noah J. Goldstein, Robert B. Cialdini, and Vladas Griskevicius, "A Room with a Viewpoint: Using Social Norms to Motivate Environmental Conservation in Hotels," *Journal of Consumer Research* 35, no. 3 (October 2008): 472–82, https://doi.org/10.1086/586910.

44. Elizabeth Royte, "Too Hot to Live: Millions Worldwide Will Face Unbearable Temperatures," *National Geographic*, June 17, 2021, https://www.nationalgeographic.com/magazine/article/too-hot-to-live-millions-worldwide-will-face-unbearable-temperatures-feature.

11. CONSUMER GOODS

1. Susan Weinschenk, "Shopping, Dopamine, and Anticipation," *Psychology Today*, October 22, 2015, https://www.psychologytoday.com/us/blog/brain-wise/201510/shopping-dopamine-and-anticipation.

2. "Self-Storage: U.S. Vs Rest of the World 2018," Statista, accessed November 1, 2024, https://www.statista.com/statistics/984719/self-storage-inventory-usa-vs-rest-of-the-world-2018/.

3. Editors, "The Price of Fast Fashion," *Nature Climate Change* 8, no. 1 (January 2, 2018): 1–1, https://doi.org/10.1038/s41558-017-0058-9.

4. John C. Ryan and Alan Thein Durning, *Stuff: The Secret Life of Everyday Things* (Northwest Environment Watch, 1997), 26–32.

5. James Suckling and Jacquetta Lee, "Redefining Scope: The True Environmental Impact of Smartphones?," *International Journal of Life Cycle Assessment* 20, no. 8 (June 10, 2015): 1181–96.

6. David Friedman, Union of Concerned Scientists, Suzanne Shaw, Seth Shulman, Jeff Deyette, Brenda Ekwurzel, Margaret Mellon, and John Rogers, *Cooler Smarter: Practical Steps for Low Carbon Living* (Island Press, 2012).

7. Robert Kunzig, "Here's How a 'Circular Economy' Could Save the World," *National Geographic*, February 18, 2020, https://www.nationalgeographic.com/magazine/article /how-a-circular-economy-could-save-the-world-feature.

8. Alana Semuels, "What Happens Now That China Won't Take U.S. Recycling," *Atlantic*, March 5, 2019, https://www.theatlantic.com/technology/archive/2019/03/china-has -stopped-accepting-our-trash/584131/.

9. Laura Parker, "Fast Facts About Plastic Pollution," *National Geographic*, December 20, 2018, https://www.nationalgeographic.com/science/article/plastics-facts-infographics -ocean-pollution.

10. Rachel Ramirez, "Plastic Water Bottle Sales Boom with 1 Million Sold Every Minute," Advocate Channel, March 17, 2023, https://advocatechannel.com/plastic-water -bottle-sales-boom-1-million-sold-every-minute.

11. OECD, "Plastic Pollution Is Growing Relentlessly as Waste Management and Recycling Fall Short, Says OECD," OECD, February 22, 2022, https://www.oecd.org/en/about /news/press-releases/2022/02/plastic-pollution-is-growing-relentlessly-as-waste -management-and-recycling-fall-short.html.

12. Jillian Mock, "Microplastics Are Everywhere, but Their Health Effects on Humans Are Still Unclear," *Discover Magazine*, January 11, 2020, https://www.discovermagazine .com/health/microplastics-are-everywhere-but-their-health-effects-on-humans-are -still.

13. Paul Hawken, interview by Rob Hopkins, *From What Is to What If*, episode 44, https:// www.robhopkins.net/2022/06/21/from-what-if-to-what-next-episode-forty-four/.

14. Tim Kasser et al., "Badvertising: Advertising's Role in Climate and Environmental Degradation," December 3, 2020, https://www.badverts.org/latest/new-report-exposes -advertisings-role-in-driving-climate-amp-ecological-breakdown.

15. Ron Marshall, "How Many Ads Do You See in One Day? Get Your Advertising Campaigns Heard," Red Crow Marketing, September 10, 2015, https://www.redcrowmarketing .com/blog/many-ads-see-one-day/.

16. Andrew Simms, "The Advertising Industry Is Fuelling Climate Disaster, and It's Getting Away with It," *Guardian*, October 11, 2021, https://www.theguardian .com/commentisfree/2021/oct/11/advertising-industry-fuelling-climate-disaster-con sumption.

17. Hamza Shaban, "Digital Advertising to Surpass Print and TV for the First Time, Report Says," *Washington Post*, February 20, 2019, https://www.washingtonpost.com /technology/2019/02/20/digital-advertising-surpass-print-tv-first-time-report-says/.

18. Trevor Zink and Roland Geyer, "There Is No Such Thing as a Green Product (SSIR)," *Stanford Social Innovation Review*, Spring 2016, https://ssir.org/articles/entry /there_is_no_such_thing_as_a_green_product.

19. Katie Brigham, "How the Fossil Fuel Industry Is Pushing Plastics on the World," CNBC, January 29, 2022, https://www.cnbc.com/2022/01/29/how-the-fossil-fuel-industry -is-pushing-plastics-on-the-world-.html.

20. Tik Root, "Inside the Long War to Protect Plastic," Center for Public Integrity, May 16, 2019, https://publicintegrity.org/environment/pollution/pushing-plastic/inside-the -long-war-to-protect-plastic/.

21. Hiroko Tabuchi, Michael Corkery, and Carlos Mureithi, "Big Oil Is in Trouble. Its Plan: Flood Africa with Plastic," *New York Times*, August 30, 2020, sec. Climate, https://www.nytimes.com/2020/08/30/climate/oil-kenya-africa-plastics-trade.html.

22. Tabuchi, Corkery, and Mureithi, "Big Oil Is in Trouble."

23. Avital Andrews, "Netflix for Toys," *Sierra*, September 8, 2015, https://www.sierraclub.org/sierra/2015-6-november-december/green-biz/netflix-toys.

24. Gaia Vince, "The High Cost of Our Throwaway Culture," BBC, November 29, 2012, https://www.bbc.com/future/article/20121129-the-cost-of-our-throwaway-culture.

25. John Harris, "Planned Obsolescence: The Outrage of Our Electronic Waste Mountain," *Guardian*, April 15, 2020, https://www.theguardian.com/technology/2020/apr/15/the-right-to-repair-planned-obsolescence-electronic-waste-mountain.

26. Matthew Haag and Winnie Hu, "1.5 Million Packages a Day: The Internet Brings Chaos to N.Y. Streets," *New York Times*, October 27, 2019, https://www.nytimes.com/2019/10/27/nyregion/nyc-amazon-delivery.html?smid=nytcore-ios-share.

27. "3 Ways Amazon Packages Are Delivered in Densely Populated Areas like New York City," About Amazon, March 1, 2024, https://www.aboutamazon.com/news/transportation/amazon-delivery-new-york-nyc.

28. Tim Wu, "Opinion | The Tyranny of Convenience," *New York Times*, February 16, 2018, https://www.nytimes.com/2018/02/16/opinion/sunday/tyranny-convenience.html.

29. Sultan Khalid, "10 States That Banned Plastic Bags," Yahoo! Finance, June 1, 2023, https://finance.yahoo.com/news/10-states-banned-plastic-bags-114109220.html.

30. Neil Seldman, "How the ReUse Corridor Is Creating Wealth from Waste in Appalachia," Institute for Local Self-Reliance, March 21, 2021, https://ilsr.org/articles/how-the-reuse-corridor-is-creating-wealth-from-waste-in-appalachia/.

31. "Homepage," Share Shed—A Library of Things, accessed November 1, 2024, https://www.shareshed.org.uk/.

32. Marcia Layton Turner, "Used Clothing Resale Is a Rising Opportunity for Retailers Large and Small," *Forbes*, March 30, 2020, https://www.forbes.com/sites/marciaturner/2020/03/30/used-clothing-resale-a-rising-opportunity-for-retailers-large-and-small/?sh=1b3876fe5c72.

33. Lauren Thomas, "Resale Market Expected to Be Valued at $64 Billion in 5 Years, as Used Clothing Takes over Closets," CNBC, June 23, 2020, https://www.cnbc.com/2020/06/23/thredup-resale-market-expected-to-be-valued-at-64-billion-in-5-years.html.

34. Daniela Aguilar, Nate Downey, and Lexie Perez, "A Vanderbilt Student's Guide to Thrifting Treasures in Music City," *Vanderbilt Hustler*, December 18, 2023, https://vanderbilthustler.com/2023/12/17/a-vanderbilt-students-guide-to-thrifting-treasures-in-music-city/.

35. "About," Buy Nothing Project, accessed November 1, 2024, https://buynothingproject.org/about/.

36. Eduardo Garcia, "Three Things You Can Do: Swap, Share and Donate," *New York Times*, August 7, 2019, https://www.nytimes.com/2019/08/07/climate/nyt-climate-newsletter-swap.html.

37. June Bell, "Make It Work," *Stanford Magazine*, 2020, https://stanfordmag.org/contents/make-it-work-repair-cafe.

38. Joshua Fields, "What Is Minimalism?," The Minimalists, November 16, 2010, https://www.theminimalists.com/minimalism/.

12. STRATEGIC COLLABORATION

1. Emily Kawano and Julie Matthaei, "System Change: A Basic Primer to the Solidarity Economy," The Next System Project, July 31, 2020, https://thenextsystem.org/learn/stories/system-change-basic-primer-solidarity-economy.

2. "Homepage," SF Children & Nature, accessed August 18, 2024, https://sfchildrennature .org/.

3. Damon Centola et al., "Experimental Evidence for Tipping Points in Social Convention," *Science* 360, no. 6393 (June 7, 2018): 1116–19, https://doi.org/10.1126/science .aas8827.

4. Mary Clare and Gary Ferguson, *Full Ecology* (Heyday, 2021).

5. Erica Chenoweth, "It May Only Take 3.5% of the Population to Topple a Dictator—With Civil Resistance," *Guardian*, February 1, 2017, https://www.theguardian.com /commentisfree/2017/feb/01/worried-american-democracy-study-activist-techniques.

6. Jennifer Blatz, Byron White, and Mark Joseph, "Elevating Community Authority in Collective Impact," Stanford Social Innovation Review, Winter 2019, https://ssir.org /articles/entry/elevating_community_authority_in_collective_impact.

7. adrienne maree brown, *Emergent Strategy: Shaping Change, Changing Worlds* (AK, 2017), 71.

8. Olivia Logan, "Berlin Could Be Car Free in Summer 2023," IamExpat, January 14, 2023, https://www.iamexpat.de/lifestyle/lifestyle-news/berlin-could-be-car-free-summer -2023.

9. Sarah Stachiowiak and Lauren Gase, "Does Collective Impact Really Make an Impact?," Stanford Social Innovation Review, August 9, 2018, https://ssir.org/articles /entry/does_collective_impact_really_make_an_impact.

10. "About Us," Seattle Good Business Network, accessed November 1, 2024, https:// seattlegood.org/about-us/.

11. David Brooks, "A Really Good Thing Happening in America," *New York Times*, October 8, 2018, https://www.nytimes.com/2018/10/08/opinion/collective-impact-community -civic-architecture.html.

13. SYSTEMS-ORIENTED GOVERNMENT

1. Emily Beach, "Celebrating Local Innovation and Resilience," *San Mateo Daily Journal*, December 21, 2020, https://www.smdailyjournal.com/opinion/other_voices /celebrating-local-innovation-and-resilience/article_087d17b0-4341-11eb-afa0-f7ef19 52d160.html.

2. Conor Dougherty, "Build Build Build Build Build Build Build Build Build Build Build Build Build Build," *New York Times*, February 13, 2020, sec. Business, https://www .nytimes.com/2020/02/13/business/economy/housing-crisis-conor-dougherty-golden -gates.html.

3. Charles Montgomery, *Happy City: Transforming Our Lives Through Urban Design* (Penguin Books, 2013), 4.

4. Josh Koehn, "Only 1 Person at SF City Hall Knows the Answer to This Simple Question," *San Francisco Standard*, July 6, 2023, https://sfstandard.com/2023/07/06 /only-1-person-at-sf-city-hall-knows-the-answer-to-this-simple-question/.

5. "Departments," City of Burlingame, accessed November 2, 2024, https://www .burlingame.org/101/Departments.

6. "Departments," County of San Mateo, accessed November 1, 2024, https://www .smcgov.org/departments.

7. Ben Rosenfield, city controller of San Francisco, interview by author, June 14, 2023.

8. Anita Makri, "How Belo Horizonte's Bid to Tackle Hunger Inspired Other Cities," *Nature Index*, September 28, 2021, https://www.nature.com/nature-index/news/how -belo-horizontes-bid-tackle-hunger-inspired-other-cities.

9. Michael Armstrong et al., "The State of Local Climate Planning," May 2021, https:// farallonstrategies.com/wp-content/uploads/2021/09/State-of-Local-Climate-Planning -FaraStrat-5-21-2021.pdf.

10. Andrew Ross Sorkin et al., "The Stakes Behind the Fight over Lina Khan's Future at the F.T.C.," *New York Times*, July 26, 2024, https://www.nytimes.com/2024/07/26/business/dealbook/behind-the-democrats-fight-over-lina-khans-future.html.

11. Stacy Mitchell and Susan Holmberg, "Tax Dodging Is a Monopoly Tactic: How Our Tax Code Undermines Small Business and Fuels Corporate Concentration," Institute for Local Self-Reliance, March 2023, https://ilsr.org/wp-content/uploads/2022/10/ILSR-RI-Tax-Dodging-is-a-Monopoly-Tactic-Issue-Brief-2023.pdf.

12. https://nces.ed.gov/fastfacts/display.asp?id=372.

14. PLACE-BASED EDUCATION

1. "What Is Place-Based Education?," Promise of Place, accessed November 1, 2024, https://promiseofplace.org/what-is-pbe/what-is-place-based-education.

2. Andrew Meyers and Tom Vander Ark, "In Age of Lyft, Uber, Our Education System Is Stuck on a Horse and Buggy," Fox Business, March 7, 2019, https://www.foxbusiness.com/technology/in-age-of-lyft-uber-our-education-system-is-stuck-on-a-horse-and-buggy.

3. David Sobel and Gregory Smith, "Building a Three-Legged Stool of Academic Achievement, Social Capital and Environmental Quality," in *Place-Based Education: Connecting Classrooms and Communities*, ed. David Sobel (Orion, 2013).

4. Victoria Derr and Emily Tarantini, "'Because We Are All People': Outcomes and Reflections from Young People's Participation in the Planning and Design of Child-Friendly Public Spaces," *Local Environment* 21, no. 12 (February 19, 2016): 1534–56, https://doi.org/10.1080/13549839.2016.1145643.

5. Highlight from the Classroom: Nature in the Neighborhood Videos in CDS Coop newsletter, January 15, 2020.

6. Hiromi Kobori, "Current Trends in Conservation Education in Japan," *Biological Conservation* 142, no. 9 (September 2009): 1950–57, https://doi.org/10.1016/j.biocon.2009.04.017.

7. Sara Zimmerman and Michelle Lieberman, "The Safe Routes to School Program Census Project 2019 National Program Assessment Report," *Safe Routes Partnership*, 2020, https://www.saferoutespartnership.org/sites/default/files/resource_files/national_srts_census_report_final.pdf.

8. "Safe Routes to School—Santa Clara County," Stanford Medicine Our Voice, accessed November 2, 2024, https://med.stanford.edu/ourvoice/our-projects/united-states/SafeRoutesSantaClara.html.

9. "Mapping the Movement," The Edible Schoolyard Project, November 2, 2017, https://edibleschoolyard.org/network.

10. Chelsea Schelly et al., "How to Go Green: Creating a Conservation Culture in a Public High School Through Education, Modeling, and Communication," *Journal of Environmental Education* 43, no. 3 (January 2012): 143–61, https://doi.org/10.1080/00958964.2011.631611.

11. "CAPS Creating a Cleaner and Greener Porterville," Porterville Unified School District, January 13, 2022, https://pathways.portervilleschools.org/apps/news/article/1553139.

12. Meyers and Vander Ark, "In Age of Lyft, Uber, Our Education System Is Stuck on a Horse and Buggy."

13. "Back-to-School Statistics," National Center for Education Statistics, accessed November 1, 2024, https://nces.ed.gov/fastfacts/display.asp?id=372.

14. Julie (Athman) Ernst and Martha Monroe, "The Effects of Environment-Based Education on Students' Critical Thinking Skills and Disposition Toward Critical Think-

ing," *Environmental Education Research* 10, no. 4 (November 2004): 507–22, https://doi.org/10.1080/1350462042000291038.

15. Nicole M. Ardoin et al., "Environmental Education and K-12 Student Outcomes: A Review and Analysis of Research," *Journal of Environmental Education* 49, no. 1 (September 29, 2017): 1–17, https://doi.org/10.1080/00958964.2017.1366155.

16. Gerald Lieberman, Linda Hoody, and Grace Lieberman, "The Effects of Environment-Based Education on Student Achievement," State Education and Environment Roundtable, March 2000, http://www.seer.org/pages/research/CSAP2000.pdf.

17. Ardoin et al., "Environmental Education and K-12 Student Outcomes."

18. Chuck Collins et al., "Nature Is the World's Most Powerful Classroom," Bay Nature, April 30, 2020, https://baynature.org/2020/04/30/the-worlds-most-powerful-classroom-no-tech-support-required/.

19. Collins et al., "Nature Is the World's Most Powerful Classroom."

20. Andrew Schneller et al., "A Case Study of Indoor Garden-Based Learning with Hydroponics and Aquaponics: Evaluating Pro-Environmental Knowledge, Perception, and Behavior Change," *Applied Environmental Education and Communication* 14, no. 4 (2015), https://doi.org/10.1080/1533015X.2015.1109487.

21. Erika Remedios, "Why Does Teaching Science Beyond the Classroom Matter?," Ten Strands, April 8, 2019, https://tenstrands.org/ed/why-does-teaching-science-beyond-the-classroom-matter/.

22. Sobel and Smith, "Building a Three-Legged Stool of Academic Achievement."

23. "Connecting Kids to Nature | Learning Landscapes," Feather River Land Trust, accessed November 2, 2024, https://www.frlt.org/our-work/program-to-connect-kids-to-nature/.

24. Angela Vergara, interview with author, July 23, 2017.

25. Alejandra Reyes-Velarde, "Playground Asphalt Sizzles to 145 Degrees in Extreme Heat Waves. Parents Demand School Shade," *Los Angeles Times*, September 1, 2022, https://www.latimes.com/california/story/2022-09-01/school-playgrounds-sizzle-in-california-extreme-heatwaves.

26. Sharon Danks, interview by author, October 6, 2020.

15. PERSONAL CHANGE

1. "Companies Ranked by Number of Employees," Companies Market Cap, accessed November 1, 2024, https://companiesmarketcap.com/largest-companies-by-number-of-employees/#google_vignette.

2. Mindi Fullilove, "A Score for Main Street," accessed November 2, 2024, https://universityoforange.org/wp-content/uploads/2020/10/A-score-for-main-street-1019.pdf.

3. Moira Dean, Monique Raats, and Richard Shepherd, "The Role of Self-Identity, Past Behavior, and Their Interaction in Predicting Intention to Purchase Fresh and Processed Organic Food," *Journal of Applied Social Psychology* 42, no. 3 (August 11, 2011): 669–88, https://doi.org/10.1111/j.1559-1816.2011.00796.x.

4. Yannis Theodorakis, "Planned Behavior, Attitude Strength, Role Identity, and the Prediction of Exercise Behavior," *Sport Psychologist* 8, no. 2 (June 1994): 149–65, https://doi.org/10.1123/tsp.8.2.149.

5. "Republicans, Democrats Move Even Further Apart in Coronavirus Concerns," Pew Research Center, June 25, 2020, https://www.pewresearch.org/politics/2020/06/25/republicans-democrats-move-even-further-apart-in-coronavirus-concerns/.

6. GoodReads, Hans Hoffman quotes, https://www.goodreads.com/quotes/70138-the-ability-to-simplify-means-to-eliminate-the-unnecessary-so.

7. Robin Wall Kimmerer, "Braiding Sweetgrass," in *Braiding Sweetgrass: Indigenous Wisdom, Scientific Knowledge and the Teachings of Plants* (Milkweed, 2013).

8. Tamar Lechner, "Why We Love Halloween—And It's Not the Candy," Presence, October 14, 2016, https://presence.app/blogs/personal-growth/why-we-love-halloween-and-its-not-the-candy.

9. Damon Centola, "The Snowball Effect," Hidden Brain Media, April 6, 2023, https://hiddenbrain.org/podcast/the-snowball-effect/.

10. Nairi Azaryan, "2021 Bike Champion of the Year!," San Francisco Bicycle Coalition, April 20, 2021, https://sfbike.org/news/2021-bike-champion-of-the-year/.

11. Glen Martin, "As Water Runs Low, San Joaquin Valley Adapts to a Drier Future," *California Magazine*, February 15, 2022, https://alumni.berkeley.edu/california-magazine/2021-winter/as-water-runs-low-san-joaquin-valley-adapts-to-a-drier-future/.

12. Ricardo Cano, "S.F.'s Most Popular Slow Streets Have One Thing in Common: Self-Appointed 'Mayors,'" *San Francisco Chronicle*, January 24, 2023, https://www.sfchronicle.com/sf/article/slow-streets-mayor-17737262.php#photo-23396455.

13. Cano, "S.F.'s Most Popular Slow Streets Have One Thing in Common."

14. Julian Brave Noise Cat, "Remembering Who We Are and Our Relations," Bioneers, September 29, 2022, https://bioneers.org/remembering-who-we-are-and-our-relations-with-julian-brave-noisecat/.

Index

3D printing, 23, 202
"15-minute cities", 113
50 Simple Things You Can Do to Save the Earth, 30
100 Resilient Cities initiative, 237
596 Acres in New York City nonprofit, 143
2020 World Happiness Report, 28
2022 Inflation Reduction Act, 105, 179–180

Accessory Commercial Units (ACUs), 97–98
Accessory Dwelling Units (ADUs), 78
Acterra nonprofit, 166
Active Hope: How to Face the Mess We're in with Unexpected Resilience and Creative Power (Macy and Johnstone), 29
addiction to stuff
  dopamine effect, 53, 59, 208
  effect on happiness, 37, 192
  needs *vs.* wants, 194–199
  self-storage inventory, 192
  waste, 41
administrative regulations
  federal regulation of corporate power, 244–245
  See also zoning regulations
advertising, 8, 53, 98, 154, 194–196
  billboards, 39, 195, 200
  car culture, 106, 138
  public service announcements, 250
  regulation of, 199–200
affluence
  and climate crisis, 22
  within corporate capitalist systems, 41
  the "good life", 23, 25, 106
affordable housing. *See* mixed-income communities
aging parents and grandparents, 39, 78
agriculture. *See* farms and agricultural land
air-conditioning, 53, 87, 133, 142, 176, 189
air pollution, 1, 122, 137, 152–153, 253
  during COVID-19, 24
  vision of active, community-oriented transportation, 107–109
air travel, 55, 197, 235, 243, 244
Alameda, California, 166, 258

Alberta, Canada, 140
Albuquerque, New Mexico, 185
alcohol abuse, 26
Alexandria Park neighborhood, 168
alienation, 3–4
Almost Everything: Hope Noted (Lamott), 29
Alphabet/Google, corporate influence, 50, 93
Amah Mutsun Tribal Band, 144
Amazon
  advertising and marketing, 195, 200
  data mining, 195
  employment statistics, 263
  market dominance, 50, 83, 84, 86–88, 91, 93–96, 195
  package delivery statistics, 197
  as "small business champion", 87–88
  tax advantages, 245
  working conditions, 200
Amelia County, Virginia, 161
American Booksellers Association, 95
American Express, 88
American Independent Business Alliance, 98
American Innovation and Choice Online Act, 93
American Rescue Plan Act (ARPA), 91
Amsterdam, 31, 199, 201, 206
anchor institutions, explained, 92
antimerger and antitrust laws, 55, 90–91, 95, 244
anxiety and stress, 26, 141, 142
Apache Nation, 161
Appalachia, 201
Apple, corporate influence, 50
apps
  Buy Nothing Project, 205
  Discovery Tool, 251
  to facilitate public transit, 116–118
  Outer Spatial, 150
Ardoin, Nicole, 255
art, public, 116, 129, 130, 132, 134
art galleries, 98
artificial intelligence, 21
Arvada, Colorado, 96
Asheville, North Carolina, 168
Asphalts to Ecosystems (Danks), 260

asthma, 122
Atlanta, Georgia, 78, 184, 242
The Atlantic, 53
Austin, Texas, 88, 110, 241
automobiles. *See* cars/automobile industry
awe, feelings in nature, 141

backbone support organizations, 222–224
Balboa Reservoir Project, 75
Baltimore, 159, 162, 163
Bank of America, 87
banking industry, corporate power, 49, 66
Barcelona, 97, 132, 135, 146
bath products, 53
bats, 145, 146
Batson, Chris, 79
batteries, 21, 22, 103, 133, 172, 176–178,
    181–185
Bay Area Rapid Transit (BART) system,
    101, 230
Bay Area Regional Energy Network
    (BayREN), 186
Bayview-Hunters Point, 140, 163
Beach, Emily, 115, 227–228, 232
beef consumption/cattle industry, 152, 155,
    156, 160, 166
bees, 145, 146
Belo Horizonte, Brazil, 236
belonging. *See* connectedness
Bennett, Terry, 84
Berkeley, California, 76, 204, 252
Berlin Autofrei, 135, 218
Berlin Streets for Everyone, 218
bicycles and biking, 1, 39, 58, 80, 97, 100, 101,
    118, 243, 245, 269
    accidents involving pedestrians and cyclists,
        114, 119
    advocacy organizations, 110–111
    bike paths and bike lanes, 31, 110, 111, 114,
        116, 119
    bike racks/bike parking, 77, 116
    "bike rodeos", 251
    bike shares, 56, 111, 115–116
    "bike trains", 118
    connectedness, 20
    e-bikes and e-scooters, 111, 115, 117, 118
    long-distance bikeways connecting cities
        and towns, 114
    networked infrastructures for, 113–115
    space and cost of transportation modes
        (table), 108
    strategies for reducing car dependence
        (table), 103

students biking to school, 1, 118, 220,
    251–252
Biden Administration, 90, 187, 244
Big Ag. *See* food and food production
Big Auto. *See* cars/automobile industry
Big Oil and Gas. *See* oil and gas companies
Big Plastic. *See* plastics industry
Big Real Estate. *See* real estate developers
Big Retail. *See* consumer goods
Big Tech. *See* technology companies
Big Utilities. *See* energy consumption
"big tent" vision, 55, 111, 218
biking. *See* bicycles and biking
billboards, 39, 195, 200
biodiversity, 3, 4, 147, 149, 153, 164, 172, 193,
    251, 271
biogas capture, 177
BIPOC (black, indigenous, and people of
    color) communities. *See* marginalized
    communities
birds, 24, 140, 142, 145, 146, 149, 257
black, indigenous, and people of color
    (BIPOC) communities. *See* marginalized
    communities
Black Faces White Spaces (Finney), 140
Blatz, Jennifer, 216
*Blue Zones Habits for a Happier, Healthier
    Life,* 27
Bogotá, 112, 113, 131, 230
book stores, 88, 89, 92–93
Bookshop.org, 92–93
Boston, Massachusetts, 115
bottles, plastic, 191, 193, 196, 201
Boulder, Colorado, 39, 132, 249
boundaries, urban growth, 57, 65, 74, 169
Bowery Project, 168
*Bowling Alone: The Collapse and Revival of
    American Community* (Putnam), 122
Boyles Heights Art Conservatory, 133
Braiding Sweetgrass (Kimmerer), 267
branding of products, 195
Breuil School, 99, 164
brine mining, 144
brokerage firms, residential real estate
    market, 66
Bronx, New York, 148, 164
Brooklyn, New York, 143, 181–182, 186
Brooks, David, 9, 226
brown, adrienne maree, 217
Buettner, Dan, 29, 38
Buffalo, New York, 43, 75
Buffalo Whole Food and Grain Company,
    82, 89

Build South Bend, ecosystem for housing development, 72
Building Black Food Ecosystem Resilience collaborative, 161
building codes and fees, 67
building energy. *See* energy consumption
bulb-outs and bump-outs, 114, 119
Bureau of Land Management (BLM), 175
Burlingame, California, 44, 115, 148, 227–228, 232
Burt, Justine, 99
business districts, local, 56, 83, 89, 95, 96–97
Business for Local Living Economies, 98
busing/bus systems, 52, 112–119
   bus rapid transit (BRT), 112–113, 116
   environmental reviews, bus projects, 245
   integrated transit cards, 116–117
   intercity buses, 109
   stops and shelters, 116, 199
   "walking school buses", 118, 251
   See also transportation/transit
butterflies, 136, 145, 146, 149, 213, 257
Buy Nothing Project, 205–206
buying local, 6, 8, 82–84
   vs. Big Retail, 49–50
   business districts, 56, 83, 89, 95, 96–97
   co-opting of term *local,* 87
   community building/social hubs, 89
   rebuilding place-based systems, 90–91
   systems-change strategies, 88–90
   table of strategies, 84
   wage averages, local *vs.* corporate retail, 89

CAFOs (concentrated animal farm operations), 152–153
Calgary, Alberta, 164
California Employee Ownership Act in 2022, 94
California Environmental Literacy Initiative (CAELI), 259
California Food for California Kids (CFCK), 252
Cambridge, Massachusetts, 112
campaign financing, 50–51, 56, 229
Campaign for Fossil Free Buildings, 186
Campodocino, Christina, 98
Canning, Liz, 58
Capay Valley Farm Shop, 160
carbon/greenhouse gas emissions, 153, 170, 225, 239
   carbon footprint, 22, 23, 31
   carbon sequestration, 142, 225, 269
   carbon tax, 159

consumer goods, production of, 192, 193, 199, 200
   and individual behavior, 20–24, 30
   K–12 curriculum, 253
   transportation-related emissions, 64
Cargill, 154
cars/automobile industry, 52, 101, 102
   advertising, 138, 195
   amount of land used for moving and parking cars, 125
   autonomous vehicles, 50–51, 102, 104, 105
   Big Auto, 7–8, 49, 104, 106–107, 124, 138–139
   Big Oil, 7–8, 49, 104–105
   car culture, 3, 104–107, 266
   car-free/car-light living, 127, 131, 134, 218, 220–221, 227–228
   car-sharing, 105, 115, 116
   crashes, 102, 107, 108, 112, 125
   drive-alone vehicle trips, 228
   electric vehicles (EVs), 21, 102, 103, 105
   housing and mixed-use communities, transforming space for cars into, 74–76
   number of cars in U.S., 102
   social and public health crisis, 102
   space and cost, transportation modes comparisons (table), 108
   strategies for reducing car dependence (table), 103
   traffic, 105, 106, 119, 125
   work commutes, 64
   See also highways and streets; oil and gas
Cary, North Carolina, 114
Castro neighborhood, San Francisco, 63, 83, 95, 122
catering companies, 166
cattle industry, 154, 155
   feedlots, 152–153
   holistic livestock management, 42
   pastureland, 155
   wool and leather, 197
   See also meat
cell phones, computers, television screens, and other electronic devices, 7–8, 49
   advertising, 195
   effect on community, 122, 124, 126
   nature, virtual representations of, 138–139
   planned obsolescence, 197
   screentime, 3, 10, 26, 53
Center for Ecoliteracy, 252
Center for Place-Based Learning and Community Engagement, 248
Centola, Damon, 214, 268

Central Park, NYC, 129, 140
Change: How to Make Big Things Happen
    (Centola), 268
Change Lab Solutions, 162
ChangeScale, 223–224, 258
Chelsea Convenience Hardware, 89
Cheyenne, Wyoming, 161
Chicago, Illinois, 34, 70, 141, 142, 236
chicken farming. *See* meat
chief resilience officers (CROs), 237
children
    childcare, 78, 94, 133
    Children and Nature Network, 150
    infant formula, 42
    San Francisco Children and Nature, 213–
        214, 218, 222
    walking and biking to school, 1, 118, 220,
        251–252
    See also education, place-based; young
        people
China, 112, 188, 192
Choice Neighborhoods, 78
CicLAvia, 131
Ciclovía, 131
Cincinnati, 106
circular economy policies, explained, 201–202
cities' role in creating place-based systems. *See*
    government
"citizen-stewards", 259
Citizens United vs. FEC, 50
City Plants nonprofit, 143
cleanliness/cleaning products, 52–53
CleanPower SF, 184–185
click bait, 53
Cliff's Variety Store, 83, 84
Climate Action Pathways (CAPS), 253
climate crisis, 21–23, 31, 103, 104, 123, 193,
    265–266
    clean energy transformation, harm to
        ecosystems from, 172
    food production, effect of, 153
    limiting change to 1.5 degrees Celsius, 22
    limiting to 1.5 degrees Celsius, 36
    place-based solutions, 36–37
    regeneration, path to healing, 271–272
    vision of active, community-oriented
        transportation, 107–109
Climate Resolve, 116
clothing and textiles
    clothing designers, 202
    clothing stores, 83
    fast fashion, 195
    fibersheds, explained, 203–204

secondhand stores and community
    exchanges, 205
slow fashion, 207
statistics on production of, 192
used, 60, 191–192
See also consumer goods
coal, 171, 172, 192
cobalt, 21, 103
coffee shops/coffee roasters, 83, 97, 98
cohousing, 39, 45, 46
collaboration, 55–56, 211–226
    accountability, 221–222
    alignment and coordination among
        stakeholders, 221
    community partnership, 214–216
    vs. egos, competition, and individuality, 218
    equality of partners, 214–216
    essential conditions for place-based
        collaboration (table), 212
    governance and backbone support, 222–224
    inertia/wariness, 211–212
    performance metrics, 222
    power, 213–214
    strategies, 219–221
    trust, 216–218
    vision, 218–219
Columbia, Maryland, 70
Columbus, Ohio, 131
Common Bonds, Oklahoma, 217, 222, 223
community authority, explained, 216
community benefit districts (CBDs), 95
community choice aggregators (CCAs),
    180–181
community gardens, 23, 45, 202
    education across multiple systems, 253–254
    food systems, 158, 161, 163, 167–168
    and resilience, 38
    urban revitalization, 43, 147
    well-being, 39
community resilience, explained, 37
Community Resilience Hubs project, 225
community spaces, 6–7, 11, 14, 121–135
    car-free/car-light design, 127
    corporate power (table), 49
    COVID-19, effect of, 126
    cultural resets, 134
    distance from homes, 129
    environmental benefits, 128
    government structures to support
        (tables), 233, 240
    and homeless people, 135
    influence of Big Auto and Big Tech
        (table), 49

land use transformation, 129–130, 133
leveraging other systems, 80–81, 135
parking lots and spaces, transformation, 130
perceived danger, 125–126
in place-based *vs.* corporate systems
    (table), 35
planning, 128–129, 134
power shifting, 124–125, 128–129
regeneration, virtuous cycle, 6–7, 11, 14
strategies for creating/revitalizing, 128–135
strategies for creating/revitalizing
    (table), 123
streets, transformation, 131–133, 243
vision, 126–128
volunteer maintenance of, 130
well-being factors, 40
community-supported agriculture (CSAs),
    158–159, 164
Community Ties study, 126, 127
commuting to work, 20, 23, 52, 64, 90,
    125, 230
mixed-use communities, 69–70
in place-based systems, 44, 101, 102,
    105–109, 113, 117
systems-oriented government, 230
worker-owned cooperatives, 94
comparative advantage concept, 57–58
Compass realtor firm, 66
COMUNITYmade, 202
concentrated animal farm operations
    (CAFOs), 152–153
concrete, 139, 142, 144, 149, 163, 240
Concrete Plant Park Foodscape, 163
condominiums, 63
congestion fees, 113, 119
Congo, 21
connectedness, 20, 24, 25, 27
vs. alienation, 3–4
collective power from inclusivity, 55–56
and hope, 30
"oneness", 25
well-being factors, table, 28
consumer goods, 30, 37, 50, 191–210
advertising, 194–196, 199
Big Retail, 49–50
corporate capitalist systems, 49
corporate power (table), 49
cultural resets, 204–208
government structure, systems-oriented
    (table), 234
"green products", 195–196, 200
leveraging other systems, 208
minimalism, 207

online purchases. *See* online shopping
planned obsolescence, 197–198
power shifting, 199–202
repairing *vs.* replacing, 198, 201,
    204, 207
sharing, 45, 198, 201, 204
strategies for creating place-based systems,
    199–208
strategies for making/recirculating (table),
    194
vision, 198–199
well-being factors, 40
See also advertising; retail
convenience in American culture, 52–54, 197
cooking equipment, 83, 170, 171, 186
Cooney, Jean, 134
cooperatives, 55, 213–214
electric cooperatives, 180–182
food and agriculture, 160, 162
housing cooperatives, 65, 71–72
independent businesses and worker
    cooperatives, 88–90, 93–95
makingsheds and fibersheds, 203–204
repair projects, 204
Copenhagen, 31, 39, 132, 162
core government departments, 233, 240
CORE MVMT studio, 82–83
"core-to-shore vision", 130
corn production, 152, 155, 158
Cornell University, 132
corporate capitalism, 7–10
comparison of systems (table), 35
and status quo, 48
corrections facilities, food purchasing, 159
Costa Rica, 38, 39, 42, 43, 157
Costco, 87
counties' role in creating place-based systems.
    See government
COVID-19 pandemic, 8, 9, 24, 26, 37, 42, 76,
    77, 82, 86, 89, 91, 114, 120, 126, 131, 132,
    220, 227, 265, 269
Credit Card Competition Act, 91
credit cards, 86, 88, 91
creeks and streams, 139, 148–149
crime
    perceived danger in public spaces, 125–127
    prevention, 237
    statistics, 78, 79
Crissy Field, 146
Cross-Triangle Greenway, 114
Crosstown Trail, 147–148
crosswalks, 95, 119
cryptocurrency, 21

culture, creating conditions to shape choices
    and habits, 10–13, 30–32
  systems-change framework (diagram), 14
Cupertino, California, 44–45, 74
Curitiba, Brazil, 112, 119–120

dairy products, 25, 42, 153, 155–157, 159, 160,
    166, 200
Daly City, California, 79
Dank, Sharon, 260
Danville, California, 78
data centers, 21, 87
data mining, 86, 195
"deadheading", 105
Defense Production Act, 187
deforestation, 155, 196
Denim Deal, 201
Denmark, 31, 38, 39, 71, 132, 162
Denver, Colorado, 110, 117, 176, 204
depression, 5, 26, 141, 142
destination streets, explained, 132
Detroit, Michigan, 75, 99, 161, 163, 164, 252,
    253–254
Detroit Black Farmer Land Fund, 161, 163
Detroit School Garden Collaborative, 252
developers. See real estate developers
developing nations vs. Global North, 57–58
Devon, United Kingdom, 204
DeYoung, Raymond, 21
diets, 151–152, 156, 165
  foodsheds, explained, 35–36
  veganism/plant-based diets, 25, 151, 166
  See also food and food production
digital devices. See cell phones, computers,
    television screens, and other electronic
    devices
Dinan, Kim, 168
Diridon Station, 120
Discovery Tool phone app, 251
distributed energy systems, 174, 176, 183, 184
Dollar stores, 83, 84, 87, 96
dopamine, 53, 59, 208
downtowns, transforming into mixed-use
    communities, 76–77
Drawdown Marin, 225
drug abuse, 26, 39, 135
dune habitat, 146
Dunham-Jones, Ellen, 44
Durham, North Carolina, 114, 203
Durning, Alan, 192–193, 196

e-bikes and e-scooters, 111, 115, 117, 118
e-commerce. See online shopping

e-vehicles, 21, 102, 103, 105
East Oakland Black Cultural Zone
    Collaborative, 134
Economic Vote Project, 19
EcoVillage concept, 45, 46
Edible Schoolyard Project, 252
education
  on buying local, 98
  culinary training, 166
  experiential learning, 98, 118. See also
    education, place-based
  See also school facilities
education, place-based, 79, 247–262
  applied learning, 248–249
  barriers, 256
  community-based, 249–250
  definition of PBE (place-based education), 248
  education policy, 261–262
  energy-based, 253
  farmer training, 164–165
  food-based, 252–253
  green schoolyards, 259–260
  impacts on student learning, 254, 255
  nature-based, 250–251
  networking and partnerships, 257–258
  real-world pedagogy, 248–254
  regenerative entrepreneurship, 43
  role in catalyzing systems change, 246
  teacher training, 258–259
  vs. traditional education, 254–255
  transportation-based, 251–252
  whole-school reform, 260–261
Education Outside nonprofit, 259
eduucation and training, 99
El Paso, Texas, 185
electric vehicles (EVs), 21, 102, 103, 105
Elkridge Library, 206
Employee Ownership Catalyst fund, 94
employment. See jobs/work
Energize Schools project, 253
energy consumption, 3, 23, 170–190
  Big Utilities, 8, 49, 53, 173–174
  comfort/cultural expectations, 53, 175–176,
    189
  direct and indirect emissions, 36, 37
  energysheds, explained, 35–36
  fairness/underserved communities, 181–
    182, 184
  federal infrastructure investment, 243
  firewood for home heating, 38
  GHGE statistics, 171
  government structures to support (tables),
    234, 240

land use transformation, 174–175
leveraging other systems, 99, 189–190
local systems, 176–178, 180–181
long-distance *vs.* local energy systems, 170–172, 175
in place-based *vs.* corporate systems (table), 35
planning, 184–185
power shifting, 173–174, 178–180
simplified bureaucracies, 232
solar. *See* solar energy
strategies for creating/revitalizing systems, 178–190
strategies for creating/revitalizing systems (table), 173
streets, transformation, 131–133
water use and, 176
well-being factors, 40
Energy Star program, 187
energysheds, 35–36, 184–185
environmental literacy. *See* education, place-based
Environmental Literacy and Sustainability Initiative (ELSI), 260–261
environmental reviews, as delaying tactic, 245
Equitable Development Plans, 128
Everett, Massachusetts, 112
Exelon Corporation, 174

Faire platform, 93
Fairfield County, Connecticut, 68
Falk, Steven, 229–230
farmers' markets/public markets, 97, 134, 135, 158–159, 162, 165
Farmington, Massachusetts, 183
farms and agricultural land, 45, 55, 57
  Big Ag, 49, 154–156
  Black farms, 152
  clothing supply chain, 197
  land use, 162, 243
  urban agriculture, 43, 100, 153, 162–164, 167, 168, 241
  wasted food, 165–167
fashion industry. *See* clothing and textiles
fast fashion, 192, 195
fast food, 52, 156, 165
Feather River Watershed, 257
FedEx, 93
feedlots, 152–154
Ferguson, Gary, 214
Ferguson, Mary Clare, 214
fertilizers, 152–154, 158, 159
fibersheds, explained, 35–36, 203–204
Figueres, Christiana, 23

The Final Mile project, 110
Finney, Carolyn, 140
fire
  firefighting/public safety, 69, 234, 240
  home fire alarms, 67
  home heating, firewood, 38
  wildfires, 9
First Peoples. *See* Indigenous peoples
Five Ways to Well-Being, 27
floods, 9, 148
food and food production, 6, 42, 55, 60, 151–169, 243
  affordable healthy diets, 165
  Big Ag, 23, 35, 37, 49, 152, 154–156
  BIPOC (black, indigenous, and people of color) communities, 158, 161–162
  community-supported agriculture (CSAs), 158–159, 164
  cooking equipment, 83, 170, 171, 186
  cooperatives, 94, 160, 162
  cultural resets, 164–168
  dairy, 25, 42, 153, 155–157, 159, 160, 166, 200
  disease/processed foods, 5, 152, 156, 163
  education and training, 164–166, 252–253
  farmers' markets/public markets, 97, 134, 135, 158–159, 162, 165
  farms. *See* farms and agricultural land
  fast food, 52, 156, 165
  global systems, land use, 155–156
  government structures to support, 232, 236
  government structures to support (tables), 234, 240
  hubs, explained, 160
  labels, 154, 167, 200
  land trusts, 158, 160
  leveraging other systems, 168–169
  local *vs.* corporate systems, 37
  local *vs.* corporate systems (table), 35
  meat. *See* meat
  organic food, 151, 167
  perfect *vs.* imperfect food, 156
  planning, 128
  plant-based diets, 25, 151, 166
  power shifting, 158–162
  strategies for creating/revitalizing, 158–169
  strategies for creating/revitalizing (table), 153
  urban agriculture, 43, 100, 153, 162–164, 167, 168, 241
  vision, 156–158
  wasted food, 156, 165–167
  well-being factors, 40
  workers, 45, 152, 164, 269
  See also grocery stories/markets

food deserts, 152
Food Project, 164
Food Runners, 166
Food Shift, 166
Food Solutions New England, 162
foodscapes, explained, 163
foodsheds, explained, 35–36
Fort Collins, Colorado, 253
Fossil Free Advertising group, 199
fossil fuels. *See* oil and gas companies
Francis, Lydia, 269
Friends of Duboce Park, 206
From What Is to What If (Hopkins), 92
Fruitvale Transit Village, 116
"fulfillment centers", 87
Full Ecology (Ferguson), 214
Fullilove, Mindi, 264
The Future We Choose: Surviving the Climate Crisis (Figueres and Rivett-Carnac), 23

Gallup-Sharecare Well-Being Index, 26, 27, 38
garage businesses, 97–98
garages, 80, 106, 115, 191, 206
Garden for the Environment, 168
gardens, 167–168. *See also* community gardens
Gather (documentary), 161
Gehl, Jan, 50
General Motors, 104–105
genetically modified organisms (GMOs), 152, 158
"gentle density", 78
gentrification, 74, 77, 139, 140, 143
Georgia Institute of Technology, 184
geothermal power, 177, 183, 184, 187
Get Down Farm, 99
GHGE. *See* carbon/greenhouse gas emissions
Ginsburg, Phil, 129
Global South, 103, 196–197
vs. Global North, 57–58
Going Beyond Land Acknowledgement workshops, 145
Golden Gate Park, 124, 129, 220–221
golf courses, 147
Good Food Economy initiative, 225
Good Kitchens initiative, 225
The Good Place television series, 32
Google
    Alphabet/Google, corporate influence, 50, 93
    American Innovation and Choice Online Act, 93
    Project Sunroof, 176–177
government, 39, 54, 227–246

barriers, removal, 245–246
bureaucratic specialization, 231–232, 237, 238
campaign financing, 50–51, 56, 229
climate action planning, 239
combined city and county governments, 232
connectors, 239
consolidation of departments, process for, 235–236
core departments, 233, 240
food and agriculture support, 236
funding, 241–243
general plan elements (table), 240
general plans, 239–241
paradigm shift, 235
planning, 238–241
reducing demands on, 237–238
regulations, enforcement, and taxation, 245–245
state and federal level support, 243–246
systems-oriented government, 227–246
taxation. *See* taxation
visionary leadership, 229–231
grandparents/multigenerational families, 39, 78
The Great Pivot (Burt), 99
Great Recession of 2008, 104
Great Rivers Greenway, 147
Great trails, 147
Green Cost Share program, 179–180
Green Hairstreak Corridor, 149
Green Mondays, 166
"green products", 195–196, 200
Green Schoolyards America, 258–260
greenbelts, 57, 74, 138, 157, 162, 169
greenhouse gas emissions (GHGE). *See* carbon/greenhouse gas emissions
greening projects. *See* nature spaces
Greenlining Institute, 110
Greensburg, Kansas, 183
Greg Segal, 165
grid, electrical, 174, 177, 179. *See also* energy consumption
GRID Alternatives, 100
grocery stores/markets, 82, 151
    co-ops, 94
    farmers' markets, 135, 158–159, 162, 165
    reusable bags, 30
Grove on Main project, 44
Grow Dat, 164, 165
Growing Up Boulder, 249–250
Guadalupe River, 146
Guangzhou, China, 112

Gudynas, Eduardo, 58
gun violence, 4, 142
Gunthorp, Greg, 154

habitat loss, 147, 149, 193
Habits for a Happier, Healthier Life, 29
Hacker, Jacob, 50
Hake, Shannon, 132
Halloween, 127, 267
Haluza-Delay, Randolph, 140
Hamburg, Germany, 113
happiness, 198
    Blue Zones of happiness, 27, 29, 38–40
    and consumerism, 53
    World Happiness Report, 28
Happy City (Montgomery), 230
Harris, Kamala, 244
Harrison, Marie, 140
Hartford, Connecticut, 75
Hawken, Paul, 194
health care
    food purchasing for health care facilities, 159
    government structure, systems-oriented
        (table), 234
    inequities, need for benefits of nature, 137
    mixed-use communities, 78, 79
    universal health care, 91
    worker-owned cooperatives, 94
"heat islands", 123, 137
heat pumps, 170–171, 187
heating. *See* energy consumption
"hedonic treadmill", 53, 192
herbicides, 152, 154, 158
Herriges, Daniel, 46, 66, 72
Hidalgo, Anne, 114, 230
The High Cost of Free Parking (Shoup), 107
High Line, New York City, 139
high-voltage transmission lines, 171–172, 175
Highway 101 Managed Lane Project, 115
highways and streets
    car culture, 104–105, 124
    congestion fees and tolls, 113, 119
    consumer goods supply chain, 197
    converting/transforming, 74–76, 111–112,
        131–133, 243
    destination streets, explained, 132
    foodscapes on, 163
    pedestrian and cyclist accidents, 114, 119
    pedestrian-only streets and plazas, 131–133
    percentage of public space occupied by
        roads, 125
    slow streets programs, 114, 120, 131, 132,
        221, 269

streams buried under, 250
students' safety recommendations, 251
temporary alterations to create community
    spaces, 131–132
traffic, 105, 106, 119, 125
Hill, Tadodaho Sid, 144
Hilson, Shannon, 141
Himmetkas ("in one place, together"), 133
Ho'ahu Energy Cooperative, 182
Hoffman, Hans, 266
Holloway, Marguerite, 38
Holmberg, Susan, 245
Home Depot, 87
homelessness, 77, 135, 146
HomeServicesof America, 66
Honeywell corporation, 144
Honorable Harvest, 267
*Hope in the Dark: Untold Histories, Wild
    Possibilities* (Solnit), 29
hopelessness, 26, 66
Hopkins, Rob, 92
Horton Plaza, 132
hospitals, 79, 159
hotels, 77, 188
housing, 63–81
    Big Real Estate, 7–8, 49, 65–66
    community spaces, distance from
        homes, 129
    cooperative and community housing, 65,
        71–72
    government leadership, 229–230
    government structures to support, 232
    government structures to support (tables),
        233, 240
    incremental *vs.* large-scale development, 72
    interrelated with work and transportation
        systems, 57, 80
    mixed-use communities, 34–36, 43–47,
        69–81
    multifamily residences, 63, 67, 69, 71, 72, 77,
        78, 179, 186, 230
    in place-based *vs.* corporate systems
        (table), 35
    strategies for creating place-based housing
        systems, 71–81
    strategies to make housing available and
        affordable, 65
    transforming land use for, 57, 73–74, 243
    well-being factors, 40
    See also real estate developers; zoning
        regulations
Houston, Texas, 120, 125, 139
Howard County, Maryland, 206

"hunter-gatherer" DNA, 5
Hurley, Amanda Holson, 44
Huron, California, 269
hurricanes, 9, 139, 177
hydroelectric power, 183
hydroponics, 163
hydropower, 171, 177

Illich, Ivan, 24
ILSR (Institute for Local Self-Reliance), 86, 91, 164, 244–245
immigrants and refugees, 168
Incremental Development Alliance (IDA), 72
India
   healthy diet, 165
   production of goods, 192
India Basin Shoreline Park Renovation Project, 128
India Basin Waterfront Park, 129
Indigenous peoples
   energy systems, 172, 184
   food sovereignty, 161
   housing, 77
   mining sites, 22, 103
   restoration of lands and waters, 144
   wisdom, 5, 25, 133, 203–204, 271
   See also marginalized communities
induction cooktops, 186
infill development, 74, 79
Inflation Reduction Act of 2022, 159
Infrastructure Investment and Jobs Act, 243
insurance industry, corporate power, 49
Intergovernmental Panel on Climate Change, 21
International Food Policy Research Institute, 159
International Union for the Conservation of Nature, 149–150
internet
   advertising, 195
   devices. *See* cell phones, computers, television screens, and other electronic devices
   online interactions/virtual relationships, 5
   search technology, 53, 93
   shopping. *See* online shopping
   universal community-based broadband, 91
   See also social media
investment trusts, real estate market dominance, 66
investor-owned utilities (IOUs), 173–174. *See also* energy consumption
Ithaca, New York, 45–46

jails, food purchasing, 159
Japan, 112, 251
JBS meat packer, 154
Jefferson Union High School District, 79
Jersey City, 131
JFK Promenade, 220–221
Jim Crow laws, 140
jobs/work, 82–100
   adding local employers to residential neighborhoods, 97–99
   business/work ecosystems, 88–90
   commute. *See* commuting to work
   corporate power (tables), 35, 49
   employee recruitment, 91
   government structures to support (tables), 233, 240
   remote work, 45, 74
   wage averages, local *vs.* corporate retail, 89
   well-being factors, 40
   worker-owned cooperatives, 93–94
   workforce development, 99, 232
   workforce housing, 57, 64, 78–80
Johannesburg, South Africa., 202
Johnstone, Chris, 29
Jones, Chris, 22
Joseph, Mark, 216
junk food, 52, 156, 165

Kahn, Peter H. Jr., 5
Kammen, Daniel, 22
Karp, Arnold, 68
Kawano, Emily, 213
Keene, New Hampshire, 257
Keep Growing Detroit (KGD), 163–164
Keller Williams Realty, 66
Kenya, 42, 196
Khan, Lina, 244
Kid Safe SF, 221
Kidd, Emma, 207
Kimmerer, Robin Wall, 267
Klamath River, 161
Knight Foundation, 126
Koch brothers, 105
Kondo, Marie, 207
Kraft, Sam, 97

La Cocina nonprofit, 160
Lafayette, California, 68, 229–230
Lakeside Landing, 130
Lamott, Anne, 29
land pollution, 137, 152
land trusts, 71–72
landfills, 198

biogas capture, 177
  food waste, 156, 165–167
  U.S. trash statistics, 193
Last Child in the Woods (Louv), 137, 150
Last Minute Gear, 204
Latin Quarter in Paris, 132
Latino Outdoors, 150
Launch Alaska initiative, 184
laundry products, 53
lawn conversions, 149
Le Chambeaudie Farm, 163
Learning Landscapes, 257, 258
Lechner, Tamar, 267
LED lighting, 187
Leon, Ray, 269
Let Them Eat Tweets (Hacker and Pierson), 50
Liberation Park, 134
libraries, 126, 206, 220, 230, 233–236, 264, 270
light rail/subways, 43, 44, 55, 101, 107, 112,
  116–117, 119, 120, 243, 245
lithium, 21, 22, 103
litter, 146, 193
Little Rock, Arkansas, 105, 125
Liverpool, UK, 199
Living Local 413, 98
Llano Grande region of Texas, 249
lobbying, 50–51, 56, 173, 196, 229
local, co-opting of term, 87
local business and work, 82–100
  anchor institutions, 92
  "Buy local" campaigns, 99
  employee recruitment, 91
  mixed-income communities, access to
    decent-paying jobs and financial security,
    69–70
  shifting economic power to small
    businesses, 91
  small business networks, explained, 95
  worker-owned cooperatives, 94
Local Business Enterprise program, 92
local economies
  virtuous cycle of regeneration, 6–7, 11, 14
  See also buying local; local business and
    work
local government's role in creating place-based
  systems. *See* government
local resilience, explained, 37
logos, branding of products, 195
London, 75, 132, 145
Los Angeles, 56, 112, 116, 131, 133, 139, 143,
  155, 202
Los Angeles Department of Water and
  Power, 180

Los Angeles Regional Open Space and
  Affordable Housing Collaborative, 143
Los Angeles River Master Plan, 143
Los Angeles River Path, 114
L.O.T.U.S Urban Farm and Garden Supply, 168
Louv, Richard, 137, 150
Love Letters, 134
Loyal to the Soil farm, 163
Lyft, 105, 115

MacGuineas, Maya, 9, 53
Macy, Joanna, 29
Madrid, Spain, 113
mail delivery, 93
Main Street: How a City's Heart Connects Us All
  (Fullilove), 264
Main Street Alliance, 95
Make It In LA, 202
Makers Valley Partnership, 202, 203
makerspaces/making sheds, 35–36,
  202–204, 206
Mandela Worker-Owned Cooperative, 94
manufacturing, 192
  local, 35–36, 202–204, 206
  See also consumer goods
manure, 152, 177
marginalized communities, 5, 6, 25, 34, 94
  "Black Wall Street", 89
  community spaces, 122–123, 128, 129,
    133, 134
  consumer goods, 203, 204
  energy consumption, 181–182, 184
  energy systems, 172, 178–180
  environmental justice education, 259
  food, 152, 158, 160–163
  health inequities, 137
  heat/temperatures in redlined
    neighborhoods, 123
  homelessness, 77, 135, 146
  Latinos, 71
  nature spaces, 137, 139, 140, 143–148, 150
  redlining, 3, 67, 89, 123, 139
  transportation, 107–110
Marin Agricultural Land Trust (MALT), 160
Marin Biomass Project, 225
Marin Carbon Farming Initiative, 225
Market Cities Initiative, 97
markets. *See* grocery stories/markets
Mastercard, 86
Matthaei, Julie, 213
McCarter, Ezekiel, 142
McCormick, Eileen, 88
Meadows, Donella, 10

meat, 3, 30, 151–156, 160, 166
  dairy products, 25, 42, 153, 155–157, 159,
    160, 166, 200
  feedlots, 152–153
Meatless Mondays, 166
Melbourne, Australia, 147
Memphis Tennessee, 87
mental health, 141–142
  depression, 5, 26, 141, 142
  and nature, 5
  well-being factors, table, 28
  See also happiness
mergers, antimerger and antitrust laws, 55,
    90–91, 95, 244, 245
Merwede, Netherlands, 46
Mesa, Arizona, 44
methane, 171, 177
Metropolitan Area Projects (MAPS), 129–130
Meyers, Andrew, 248, 249, 254
Miami, Florida, 168
Microsoft corporation, 50
milk. See dairy products
Millburn, Joshua Fields, 207
Milwaukee, Wisconsin, 125
Miner County, South Dakota, 99
mining operations, 22, 58, 103, 144, 171–172
Minneapolis, Minnesota, 113, 115, 116,
    179–180, 203
"missing middle" housing, 69, 78
Mission Economic Development Agency, 71
Mission Rock in San Francisco, 120
Mitchell, Stacy, 89, 245
mixed-income communities, 69–81, 246
mixed-race communities, 67, 68, 70
mixed-use communities, 34–36, 43–47, 57, 67,
    68, 70–81, 96–97
Mobility Equity Frameworks, 110
Moloka'i, Hawai'i, 182
Mono County, California, 177
monopolies, antimerger and antitrust laws, 55,
    90–91, 95, 244
Monsanto, 154
Montgomery, Charles, 230
Montreal, Canada, 115
Moon Valley Farm, 164
Morris, Minnesota, 185
Motherload (Canning), 58
MountainView, California, 70
multifamily housing, 63, 67, 69, 71, 72, 77, 78,
    179, 186, 230
multigenerational families, 39, 78
multinational corporations, 7–10
  Big Ag. See food and food production

Big Auto. See cars/automobile industry
Big Oil and Gas. See oil and gas companies
Big Plastic. See plastics industry
Big Real Estate. See real estate developers
Big Retail. See consumer goods
Big Tech. See technology companies
Big Utilities. See energy consumption
municipal vehicle fleets, 105
municipally owned utilities (MOUs), 180–181
Munoz, Desiree, 144
murals and public art, 116, 129, 130, 132, 134
Musk, Elon, 231
"My Healthy Plate, Our Healthy Plane", 166

Nairobi, Kenya, 116
Nashville, Tennessee, 105, 205
National Beef Packing Company, 154
National Geographic, 189
National League of Cities, 150
National Main Street Center, 96
native plants and trees, 144–146, 149, 257
natural gas, 8, 170, 171, 186, 187
Nature Climate Change (journal), 192
nature-deficit disorder, 137
Nature in the City, 149
The Nature of Americans National Report, 137
nature spaces, 2, 35, 36, 136–150
  Big Auto and Big Tech, effect of, 138–139
  Big Auto and Big Tech, effect of (table), 49
  cultural issues, 3, 140, 142, 148–150
  health and well-being benefits, 141–142
  human right, nature access as, 149–150
  indigenous groups and nature-based
    coalitions, 144–145
  land use transformation, 147–148
  leveraging other systems, 80–81, 150
  neighborhood nature restoration projects,
    148–149
  pavement, 139–140
  planning, 143
  power shifting, 143–145
  regeneration, virtuous cycle, 6–7, 11, 14
  strategies for creating/revitalizing, 142–150
  strategies for creating/revitalizing
    (table), 138
  transforming land use for, 56–57, 77
  vision, 141–142
  well-being factors, 40
Nature Urbaine farm, 163
Navajo Nation, 172
needs vs. wants, 194–199
neighborhood systems. See place-based
    systems

Neinas Dual Language Learning Academy, 253–254
net metering rates, 170, 179
net-zero energy buildings, 178, 185–186
Netherlands, 31, 46, 199, 201, 206
New Breed Logistics, 87
New Canaan, Connecticut, 68
New Economic Foundation's Five Ways to Well-Being, 27
New England Feeding New England, 162
New Orleans, 98, 110, 139, 164, 177
New York City, 76, 86, 89, 111, 112, 129, 134, 139, 140, 143, 163, 206
Newman, Daniel, 124
Next Generation Science Standards (NGSS), 261
nickel, 103
Nicodemus, Ryan, 207
Nicoya, Costa Rica, 157
NIMBY ("not in my backyard") attitude, 58, 65, 68, 229, 245–246
NoiseCat, Julian Brave, 271
Norman, Oklahoma, 76
North Somerset, UK, 199
Northern Manitoba Food, Culture, and Community Collaborative, 224
Northhampton, Massachusetts, 116
Norway, 250
Norwich, UK, 199
"Nothing Here to Care About" (Haluza-Delay), 140
nuclear energy consumption, 171
Nvidia, corporate influence, 50

Oak Park, Illinois, 70
Oakland, California, 80, 94, 116, 131, 134, 181
obsolescence
    planned obsolescence, 197–198
    repairing *vs.* replacing, 198, 201, 204, 207
Oceanside, California, 96
office real estate, 74, 76
Ohlone people, 144, 146
oil and gas companies, 7, 8, 31, 49–51, 53
    car culture, 104–105, 124
    corporate power (table), 49
    GHGE statistics, 171
    global footprint, 192, 197
    natural gas, 8, 170, 171, 186, 187
    See also plastics industry
Oklahoma City, 129–130, 215–216
on-site parking, 100
online shopping, 7, 53–54, 74, 83, 85–87, 95
    fair online marketplaces, 93–94

one-click shopping, 197–198
    search technology, 53, 93
    tax advantages, online retailers, 245
    See also Amazon
Onondaga Nation, 144
open-pit mining, 22, 58, 103
Orland, Maine, 38
Osaka, Japan, 112
Oslo, Norway, 119
"otherness", 3
Outdoor Afro, 150
Outdoor Core, 257
Outer Spatial app, 150
oxytocin, 59

Pacific Gas and Electric, 174
packaging materials, 193, 200–201
Paiute people, 22, 103
palm oil plantations, 155
Palo Alto, California, 118, 140, 206
Paris, 1, 2, 11, 75, 99, 114, 115, 132, 163, 164, 230
parking space, 46, 87, 106, 107, 138, 139
    minimums, 65, 67, 72, 75, 100, 104
    percentage of land used for, 80
    repurposing, 1, 44, 74–76, 114, 115, 119
parks, 121–122
    parklets, 43, 123, 126, 128, 130, 134, 270
    See also community spaces; nature spaces
Pattern Energy Group LP, 175
Paycheck Protection Program, 86
PBE. *See* education, place-based
Peart, Monica, 195
pedestrians. *See* walking
Peñalosa, Enrique, 230
Peninsula Clean Energy (PCE), 184
People Power Solar Cooperative, 181
People's Restaurants, 236
People's Slow Streets campaign, 221
personal change, 263–272
    indigenous wisdom, 264, 267, 271
    participation with others, 268–271
    place-based identities, 265–266
    simplicity and gratitude, 266–267
pesticides, 152
Philadelphia, Pennsylvania, 76
Phoenix, Arizona, 44
Phoenix Day, 134
physical context
    and human behavior, explained, 31
physical health
    and nature, 5
    well-being factors, table, 28

Pico-Union, Los Angeles, 139
Picuris Pueblo, 182
Piedmont Fibershed, 203
Pierson, Paul, 50
pilates studio, 82
pipelines
   clothing supply chain, 197
Pittsburgh, 97, 110, 116
place-based systems, 34–36
   explained, 10
   self-reliance, 41–43
   transforming land use for, 56–57
   See also connectedness
plastic bags, 196, 200–201
plastics industry, 3, 53, 191, 193, 194, 196
   banning single-use plastics, 200–201
   corporate power (table), 49
   microplastics, 193
playgrounds, 109, 121. *See also* community
   spaces
politics
   campaign financing, 50–51, 56, 229
   fear as political strategy, 125–126
   tribalism/polarization, 156, 265
   voter participation, 74, 79, 113, 129–130,
      220–221, 229, 238, 241
Pollan, Michael, 151
pollinator gardens, 130, 136, 146, 149, 164
pop-up events, 96, 130, 134, 206, 224
Porterville Unified School District, 253
Portland, Oregon, 114, 205, 249
Postma, Martine, 206
poultry. *See* meat
prairie restoration, 147
predatory buying, 85, 86
Preston, England, 92
Prevost, Lisa, 68
Princen, Thomas, 21
Project Equity nonprofit, 94
Project for Public Spaces, 116, 130, 132
Providence, Rhode Island, 110
public markets/farmers' markets, 97, 134, 135,
      158–159, 162, 165
public transit. *See* transportation/transit
PUSH (People United for Sustainable
      Housing) Buffalo, 43
Putnam, Robert, 122

Queensland, Australia, 149

race/racism, 34, 67–69, 89
   food systems, 152, 158, 162
   in nature spaces, 140

residential segregation, 4, 26, 57, 67, 68, 89,
      123, 139
   See also marginalized communities
Rachel Marshall Outdoor Learning
      Laboratory, 257
Radical Suburbs (Hurley), 44
rail travel, 55
   car crashes *vs.* train crashes, 107
   Infrastructure Investment and Jobs Act, 243
   light rail/subways, 43, 44, 55, 101, 107, 112,
      116–117, 119, 120, 243, 245
rain gardens, 148
Rainbow Grocery, 94, 191
Rainier Beach Urban Farm, 163, 165
Raleigh, North Carolina, 114
Razorback Greenway, 147
RE/MAX, 66
real estate developers, 7, 63, 65, 77–78
   Big Real Estate, 49, 51, 65–66
   campaign financing, 50, 56
   corporate power (table), 49
   local developer networks, 72–73
   regenerative projects, 43
Real Food Challenge, 159
Real Food Farm, 159, 162, 165
Realogy Holdings, 66
Reconnecting Communities Initiative, 75, 243
recycling, 30, 99
   Big Plastic, 196
   circular economy policies, 201–202
   makingsheds and fibersheds, explained,
      203–204
   See also secondhand consumer goods
redlining, 3, 67, 89, 123, 139
refrigerators, 162, 187, 193
regeneration of nature, community, and local
      economies, virtuous cycle, 6–7, 11, 14
Regenerative Communities Network, 42
regional government, 242
   metropolitan planning organizations
      (MPOs), 242
   role in creating place-based systems. *See*
      government
regional systems. *See* place-based systems
remote work, 45, 74
renewable energy, 21, 170–171, 175
   and Big Utilities, 173
   See also solar energy
rental property
   corporate control of, 66
   prices, 63, 64, 79, 80, 92
repairing *vs.* replacing, 198, 201, 204, 207
reparations for past harms, 75, 243

repurposing, 44–45
resilience hubs, 133
resilience to threats, 37–38
restaurants, 60, 82, 83, 90, 132, 160, 163, 164,
  166, 236, 265
  food rescue, 166
  food waste, 156, 157
retail
  adding local stores to residential
    neighborhoods, 97–99
  anchor institutions, 92
  Big Retail, 7, 49–50, 53, 83–88, 194–196,
    199, 266
  co-opting of term *local,* 87
  community spaces, proximity to, 133
  corporate power (table), 49
  default transportation to and from, 87
  effect on property values, 86
  government policies to reduce power of,
    90–91
  land use, 86–87
  local retailers, 84–100
  malls, repurposing, 44–45
  mixed-income communities, 78
  mixed-use communities, 80–81
  rebuilding place-based systems, 90–91
  table of strategies for revitalizing local
    business and work, 84
  as third-party sellers on Amazon, 86
  See also Amazon; buying local; consumer
    goods; online shopping
Reteti Elephant Sanctuary, 42
Rethink Outdoors, 150
RetrofitNY, 186
Retrofitting Suburbia (Dunham-Jones and
  Williamson), 44
ReUse Corridor, 201
"rewilding" of cities, 145
Riaz Capital, 67, 79
Richmond, California, 110, 118
ridesharing, 51, 104, 105, 113, 115
Right Relations program, 145
"right to repair" laws, 207
river cleanups, 249
Rivett-Carnac, Tom, 23
Rochester, New York, 75
Rockefeller Foundation, 237
Rocky Mountain High, 253
Rolo, 83
rooftops, 145
  energy. *See* solar energy
  gardens, 2, 23, 163
Roosevelt Institute, 245

Roundup, 154
Royte, Elizabeth, 189
rural areas
  energy cooperatives, 181
  loss of small farms, 155
  regional energyshed planning and
    funding, 184
  wind energy, 183
  See also farms and agricultural land
Russian invasion of Ukraine, 9, 21, 187
Rust Belt, 37
Ryan, John C., 192–193, 196

Sacramento, California, 160
Safe Routes to School (SRTS), 118, 220,
  251–252
Sahu, Roshni, 107, 112
Salinas, California, 71
Salisbury, North Carolina, 96
salmon, 146, 161
salmonella, 153
San Diego, California, 132, 174
San Francisco, 31, 51, 269, 270
  building energy, 184–185
  bureaucratic specialization, 231–232
  Castro area, 63, 83, 95, 122
  community spaces, 122, 124, 128–135
  education, place based, 250, 258–260
  food, 159, 160, 163, 165
  government, 232–236, 241, 242
  housing, 63, 67, 71, 75, 79, 229
  jails and public hospitals, food
    purchasing, 159
  local business and work, 63, 94, 95, 98, 99
  Local Business Enterprise program, 92
  Mission Rock area, 120
  nature spaces, 63, 140, 144–147
  SF Bike, 221
  Small Business Week, 87
  strategic collaboration, 213–214, 218,
    221, 222
  transportation, 63, 112, 114, 242
  UC, San Francisco, 100
San Francisco Bay Area counties, 144–146
San Francisco Bay Area Local Food
    Purchasing Collaborative, 159
San Francisco Bicycle Coalition, 269
San Francisco Recreation and Parks, 129
San Franciscoo, 22, 44
San Francisco's Small Business Week, 87
San Jerardo Cooperative, 71
San Jose, California, 120, 146, 167
San Luis Obispo, California, 56

San Mateo County, California, 102, 227, 260
Santa Barbara, California, 147
Santa Monica, California, 132
São Paulo, Brazil, 75, 117
Saratoga, California, 78
Save JFK Promenade, 221
Save Lafayette nonprofit, 68
school facilities
  asphalt on school grounds, 256, 259–260
  dining services, 159
  green schoolyards, 259–260
  school gardens, 252–253
  schools' role in catalyzing systems change.
    See education, place-based
  student housing, 79
  walking and biking to school, 1, 118, 220,
    251–252
Schwartz, Ken, 56
scooters, 111, 113–118
SCRAP nonprofit, 205
search technology, 53, 93
Seattle, Washington, 69, 97, 113, 130, 150, 163,
  224, 225
secondhand goods, 191, 201–207
local rental businesses and lending
    libraries, 204
  "right to repair" laws, 207
sedentary lifestyle, 52
seed library, 133
Seeding the City, 162
Seine River, 230
self-reliant regions, 34–36, 41–43
"sell by" date on food, 166
Seven Coffee Roasters Market and Café, 97
sewers, 139, 148
Share Shed, 204
sharing
  bike shares, 56, 111, 115–116
  consumer goods, 45, 198, 201, 204
  ridesharing, 51, 104, 105, 113, 115
Shill, Greg, 104
shopping. See retail
Shoshone people, 22, 103
Shoup, Donald, 107
Shove, Elizabeth, 52–53
sidewalks, 1, 95, 97, 114, 116, 117, 119, 122,
  126, 243, 251
Simons, Eric, 146
Singapore, 38, 39, 145
single-family/single-use properties, 60, 67, 68,
  77, 78, 97, 104, 106, 125
single-use plastics, 191, 193, 200–201
slavery, 140

slow consumerism movement, 207–208
slow streets programs, 114, 120, 131, 132,
  221, 269
Small Business Rising, 95
Small Business Saturdays, 88
Small Business Week, 87
small businesses
  consolidation of American economy, 86
  networks of small businesses and
    independent stores, 95
  virtuous cycle of regeneration, 6–7, 11, 14
  See also buying local
"smart cities", 50, 104
Smart Growth American, 100
Smith, Gregory, 249
Sobel, David, 249
social alienation, 26, 123. See also
    connectedness
social media, 166
  Facebook, 53, 124
  influencers, 195
  online interactions/virtual relationships, 5
societal transformation and regeneration,
  41–47
Sogorea Te' Land Trust, 133
soil depletion/soil restoration, 42, 152, 164
solar energy, 21, 45, 56, 100, 162, 170, 174, 182
  batteries, 183–184
  energyshed planning and funding,
    184–185
  Google's Project Sunroof, 176–177
  incentives, 174, 179–180
  K-12 curriculum, 253
  microgrids, 184, 269
  net metering rates, 170, 179
  time-of-use or time-varying-rate energy
    prices, 188
Solnit, Rebecca, 29, 31
South Bend, Indiana, 72, 148
South California Edison, 174
Southeast Michigan Stewardship Coalition,
  258–259
Sow True Seeds, 168
soybean industry, 155
Speck, Jeff, 114
speed bumps, 119
Spike's Coffees and Teas, 83
Springfield, Massachusetts, 95
Squamish people, 77
St. Louis region of Missouri, 147
Stanford University, 255
StayLocal, 98
Stockholm, 200

Stop'N' Swap events, 206
storage containers, 191
Strategic Energy Innovations (SEI), 253
"A Street Tree Revolution in Silicon Valley" (Simons), 146
streetcars
    purchase by General Motors, 104
    streetcar-dependency, 43–44
    See also busing/bus systems
Streetman, Dan, 98
streetscape, 95
streetscaping, 44
stress and anxiety, 26, 141, 142
strip malls, 74, 86
Strong Towns, 46, 66, 72
Students and Teachers Restoring a Watershed (STRAW), 250–251
Stuff: The Secret Life of Everyday Things (Ryan and Durning), 192–193, 196
suburbia, 79, 106, 122
    postwar suburban boom, 72
    urban growth boundaries, 74
    urbanization of suburbs, 44
subways/light rail, 43, 44, 55, 101, 107, 112, 116–117, 119, 120, 243, 245
suicide, 26
Sundays, car-free streets on, 131
SunZia Wind, 175, 185
superblocks, 132, 135
supply chains, 8, 37, 198, 201, 245
Sustainable Neighborhood Action Program (SNAP), 225–226
Swedish Consumer Agency, 200
Syracuse, New York, 144
systems-change framework, illustration, 14

Tabuchi, Hiroko, 22
Tahtinen, Roy, 98
Target, 86
Tax Dodging Is a Monopoly Tactic (Mitchell), 245
taxation, 86, 89, 96, 113, 244–245
    airport taxes, 244
    benefits and incentives, 76, 96, 107, 166, 170, 175, 178–179, 186, 245
    carbon tax, 159
    sales tax to finance parks, 129–130
teacher housing, 79
teacher training, 258–259
technology companies
    American Innovation and Choice Online Act, 93
    and automobile industry, 104, 105
    corporate power (table), 49

education, technology-based instruction, 256
Magnificent Seven, market value, 49–50
techno-salvation, 21–24
television. See cell phones, computers, television screens, and other electronic devices
Tesla, 50
Thacker Pass, 22
Third Street Promenade, 132
Thomure, Lisa, 82
Three Rivers Fibershed, 203
thrift stores. See secondhand goods
Tibbets Brook, 148
tidal energy, 177
tidal marshes, 146, 148
tiered pricing, energy consumption, 188
time-of-use or time-varying-rate energy prices, 188
tipping point for making societal change, 214
tires, 102, 104
Tool Shed Ted, 205
tools, lending and renting, 204
Toronto, Canada, 43–44, 97, 112, 159, 168, 225–226
tourism industry/travel, 49, 55, 77
townhomes, 69, 77
toxic cleanups, 140
toys, planned obsolescence, 197
Transport for London, 100
Transportation Alternatives, 111
transportation/transit, 1, 36, 37, 52, 54, 101–120, 228
    Big Retail, default transportation to and from, 87
    car-centric urban design, 124
    car culture, 106–107
    community spaces, access to, 130
    corporate power, 7–8
    corporate power (table), 49
    fares, 116–117
    government structures to support (tables), 233, 240
    highway construction vs. transit construction, 106
    housing, interrelationship with transportation systems, 57, 80
    incentives for active, community-oriented transportation behavior, 117–118
    Infrastructure Investment and Jobs Act, 243
    light rail/subways, 43, 44, 55, 101, 107, 112, 116–117, 119, 120, 243, 245
    mixed-use communities, 80–81

transportation/transit *(continued)*
  mobility hubs, 116
  opposition to ballot initiatives, 105
  in place-based *vs.* corporate systems (table),
    35
  real-time transit information, 118
  resetting culture, 116–118
  simplified government structure to support,
    232
  space and cost comparisons (table), 108
  strategies for reducing car dependence
    (table), 103
  synergies, 119–120
  trails, trip planning to, 150
  transforming land use for, 57, 111–112
  transit stops, 96
  transportation-disadvantaged communities,
    102, 110–111
  vision of active, community-oriented
    transportation, 107–109
  well-being factors, 40
  See also busing/bus systems; cars/
    automobile industry; commuting to work
trash
  litter, 146, 193
  See also landfills
trees, 95, 130
  nature-based climate adaptation, 143,
    148, 178
  tree canopy inequities, 139
Trump, Donald, 231
Trust for Public Land, 129
Tsq'escen First Nation, 271
Tulsa, Oklahoma, 89–90
turkeys, 154
typhoons, 9
Tyson Foods, 154

Uber, 105, 115
Ukraine, 9, 103
underserved communities. *See* marginalized
  communities
University of California, Berkeley, 101, 269
University of California, San Francisco, 79, 100
University of California, Santa Barbara, 147
University of Kentucky, 159
University of New Hampshire, 162
University of Oxford, 159
University of Toronto, 159
University of Vermont, 184
UPS, 93
urban agriculture, 9, 43, 100, 153, 162–164,
  167, 168, 241, 252

urban growth boundaries, 57, 65, 74, 169
Urban Institute, 126
US Department of Housing and Urban
  Development initiatives, 78
US Department of Transportation's
  Reconnecting Communities Initiative, 75
US Farm Bill, 155
US Solidarity Economy Network, 213
used goods. *See* secondhand goods
Utrecht, Netherlands, 46

Valco Mall, 74
Vancouver, British Columbia, 77
Vander Ark, Tom, 248, 249, 254
Vanderbilt University, 205
veganism/plant-based diets, 25, 151, 166
Vergara, Angela, 258
vertical mergers, 245
victory gardens, 167
video conferencing, 8
Vietnamese Americans, 167
virtuous cycles of improvement, 6–7, 11, 14,
  37, 59, 115, 127, 268
Visa credit card, 86
Vision Zero, 119
voter participation, 74, 79, 113, 129–130,
  220–221, 229, 238, 241

Walgreens, 89
Walk SF, 221
walking, 1, 80, 96, 97, 100, 116, 119, 221
  accidents involving pedestrians and cyclists,
    114, 119
  crosswalks, 95, 119
  fatalities, 125
  health/well-being/connectedness, 20, 40,
    127, 227–228
  networked infrastructures for, 113–115
  pedestrian-only streets and plazas, 123,
    131–133
  to school, 1, 118, 220, 251–252
  sidewalks, 1, 95, 97, 114, 116, 117, 119, 122,
    126, 243, 251
  space and cost comparisons (table), 108
  strategies for reducing car dependence
    (table), 103
  superblocks, 132, 135
  vision of community-oriented
    transportation, 107–111
Wallich, Paul, 154
Walmart, 50, 83, 84, 86, 87, 263
warehouses, 44, 85–87, 96, 120, 197, 200,
  202, 245

washing machines, 187
Washington D.C., 111, 115, 125
wasted energy, 175–176
wasted food, 165–167
water-based nature connections, 145
water supply
    agricultural use, 152, 153
    energy-water nexus, 176
    home use, 170–171
    pollution, 137, 152, 172, 193
    runoff, 102, 139, 146, 148, 152, 260
    wastewater, 57, 176, 177
Waters, Alice, 167, 252
watersheds
    model for regional sheds, 35–36
    student learning, 250–251
Watts, Jonathan, 139
weather
    air-conditioning, 53, 87, 133, 142, 176, 189
    extreme weather events, 9, 133, 139, 148
well-being, 1, 4–7, 25–29, 123
    anxiety and stress, 26, 141, 142
    systems-change framework, 14
    tables of well-being factors, 28, 40
    See also happiness
Wells Fargo, 87
Wellspring Cooperative, 95, 213
West Oakland, California, 142
West Virginia, 91
wetlands, 146, 147
wheat industry, 155

White, Byron, 216
wilderness-based learning experiences, 140
wildflower meadows, 145
wildlife, 141, 145, 146, 149
Williams, Star, 90
Williamson, June, 44
wind-generated electricity, 21, 174, 177, 183,
    184, 188
work. See jobs/work
Working for Northeast Trees, 143
World Happiness Report, 28
Wu, Tim, 52, 86, 89, 197

Yekutiel, Manny, 124
YIMBY ("yes in my backyard") attitude, 58, 65,
    71, 74, 79–80
Yosemite Valley, 141
young people, 43, 44, 129, 133, 161, 250
    farmer training, 164–165
    youth workforce, 43, 99–100
    See also education, place-based
Yurok Nation, 161

Zero Emissions Vehicles project, 225
zero-net energy buildings, 178, 185–186
zero-waste, 166, 201
zoning regulations, 44, 57, 65, 72, 74, 96, 97,
    106
    mixed-income communities, 77–78
    single-use/single-use, 67, 104, 125
    YIMBYism, 79–80

www.ingramcontent.com/pod-product-compliance
Lightning Source LLC
Chambersburg PA
CBHW020456270326
41926CB00008B/628